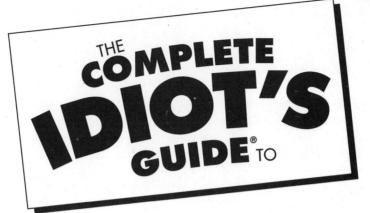

THE COMPLETE IDIOT'S GUIDE® TO

Computer Basics

Fifth Edition

by Joe Kraynak

ALPHA

A member of Penguin Group (USA) Inc.

To my "kids," Nick and Ali, who constantly inspire me to keep up with the latest technology.

ALPHA BOOKS

Published by the Penguin Group

Penguin Group (USA) Inc., 375 Hudson Street, New York, New York 10014, USA

Penguin Group (Canada), 90 Eglinton Avenue East, Suite 700, Toronto, Ontario M4P 2Y3, Canada (a division of Pearson Penguin Canada Inc.)

Penguin Books Ltd., 80 Strand, London WC2R 0RL, England

Penguin Ireland, 25 St. Stephen's Green, Dublin 2, Ireland (a division of Penguin Books Ltd.)

Penguin Group (Australia), 250 Camberwell Road, Camberwell, Victoria 3124, Australia (a division of Pearson Australia Group Pty. Ltd.)

Penguin Books India Pvt. Ltd., 11 Community Centre, Panchsheel Park, New Delhi—110 017, India

Penguin Group (NZ), 67 Apollo Drive, Rosedale, North Shore, Auckland 1311, New Zealand (a division of Pearson New Zealand Ltd.)

Penguin Books (South Africa) (Pty.) Ltd., 24 Sturdee Avenue, Rosebank, Johannesburg 2196, South Africa

Penguin Books Ltd., Registered Offices: 80 Strand, London WC2R 0RL, England

International Standard Book Number: 978-1-59257-859-7
Library of Congress Catalog Card Number: 2008933153

11   10   09   8   7   6   5   4   3   2   1

Interpretation of the printing code: The rightmost number of the first series of numbers is the year of the book's printing; the rightmost number of the second series of numbers is the number of the book's printing. For example, a printing code of 09-1 shows that the first printing occurred in 2009.

Printed in the United States of America

Note: This publication contains the opinions and ideas of its author. It is intended to provide helpful and informative material on the subject matter covered. It is sold with the understanding that the author and publisher are not engaged in rendering professional services in the book. If the reader requires personal assistance or advice, a competent professional should be consulted.

The author and publisher specifically disclaim any responsibility for any liability, loss, or risk, personal or otherwise, which is incurred as a consequence, directly or indirectly, of the use and application of any of the contents of this book.

Most Alpha books are available at special quantity discounts for bulk purchases for sales promotions, premiums, fundraising, or educational use. Special books, or book excerpts, can also be created to fit specific needs.

For details, write: Special Markets, Alpha Books, 375 Hudson Street, New York, NY 10014.

Publisher: *Marie Butler-Knight*
Editorial Director: *Mike Sanders*
Senior Managing Editor: *Billy Fields*
Acquisitions Editor: *Tom Stevens*
Senior Development Editor: *Christy Wagner*
Production Editor: *Megan Douglass*
Copy Editor: *Michael Dietsch*

Cartoonist: *Richard King*
Cover Designer: *William Thomas*
Book Designer: *Trina Wurst*
Indexer: *Brad Herriman*
Layout: *Chad Dressler*
Proofreader: *Mary Hunt*

Contents at a Glance

Part 1:	Firing Up Your Computer: Bare-Bones Basics	1

1 Kick-Starting Your Computer   3
Plug it in, turn it on, and tune it in.

2 Taking the Wheel, er, Keyboard and Mouse   13
Driver's Ed for your keyboard, mouse, and other input devices.

3 Green Computing   21
Reduce, reuse, and recycle your way to environmentally friendly computing.

Part 2:	Navigating Microsoft Windows	29

4 Mastering Windows Basics (Vista and XP)   31
Check which version of Windows you have and discover basic maneuvers.

5 Navigating Windows Vista   43
Take the latest, greatest version of Windows for a test drive.

6 Windows XP, Up Close and Personal   57
Learn your way around your new onscreen desktop.

7 Managing Disks, Folders, and Files   65
Tour your computer's disk drives, folders, and files; copy files; and trash files in the Recycle Bin.

8 Installing, Running, and Uninstalling Programs   79
Kick programs into gear, and evict the ones you never use.

9 Customizing Windows   89
Show your Windows desktop who's boss, and personalize it to suit your tastes.

10 Creating and Managing User Accounts   107
Peacefully share your computer with other users ... if you really want to.

11 Finding Lost or Misplaced Items   117
Rummaging through your files and folders to locate the lost and misplaced orphans.

12 Networking Windows to Other Computers   123
    Connect all your computers so they can share files, folders,
    and expensive equipment.

Part 3:   Getting Down to Business with Office Programs   139

13 Typing and Other Word Processing Chores   141
    Typing 101.

14 Crunching Numbers with Spreadsheets   159
    Number crunching and graphs made (almost) easy.

15 Creating a PowerPoint Presentation   173
    Slapping together a professional-looking digital slideshow,
    complete with audio and special effects.

16 Working With Graphics   185
    Hang pictures and other works of art on your documents to
    make them look pretty.

17 Managing Your Finances   199
    Making a program reconcile your checkbook register and
    perform other personal finance tricks.

18 Printing Documents and Other Creations   209
    Print your documents right the first time.

Part 4:   Tapping the Power of the Internet   221

19 Getting Wired to the Internet   223
    Get your computer its own phone.

20 Poking Around on the World Wide Web   235
    Use your computer and modem to connect to the web and
    experience multimedia sites online.

21 Sending and Receiving E-Mail   245
    Send your first e-mail message in less than 5 minutes.

22 Chatting Online   259
    Find friends, relatives, and perfect strangers online, and
    type messages back and forth.

23 Touring Newsgroups, Message Boards, and More   271
    Hook up with hordes of other people online to get help and
    share your knowledge and interests.

24 Publishing Your Own Web Page or Blog   283
*Establish your presence on the web by building your own
web page or web log online!*

25 Buying and Selling Stuff Online   295
*Comparison shopping, eBay auctions, and travel planning,
all from the comfort of your home.*

26 Internet Safety   307
*Fend off viruses and keep your children from the racier side
of the Internet.*

Part 5:   Going Digital with Music, Photos, and Video   321

27 Playing CDs, DVDs, MP3s, and More   323
*Transform your computer into a jukebox, burn your own
CDs, download audio clips off the web, and watch DVD
movies.*

28 Snapping, Enhancing, and Sharing Digital Photos   337
*Snap, print, and e-mail photos, and order high-quality
prints online.*

29 Editing Digital Video   347
*Edit your home videos, enhance your recordings with
background music, and copy your production to a disc.*

Part 6:   Maintaining and Troubleshooting Your Computer   363

30 Keeping Your Computer Clean   365
*Prolong the life of your computer with some good
housekeeping tips.*

31 Giving Your Computer a Tune-Up   373
*Inexpensive maintenance utilities that can keep your
computer running like new.*

32 Troubleshooting Common Computer Problems   383
Home remedies that work for common computer ills.

33 Help! Finding Technical Support   397
*Where to find valuable assistance when a problem has
you stumped.*

Index   405

Contents

Part 1:   Firing Up Your Computer: Bare-Bones Basics   1

1   Kick-Starting Your Computer   3

Finding a Comfortable Home for Your Computer......................4
Unpacking Your New Toys...5
Identifying Your Computer's Parts and Appendages 6
Making the Right Connections 7
Bringing the Beast to Life...9
Installing the Software That Runs Your Hardware 10
Now What? 11

2   Taking the Wheel, er, Keyboard and Mouse   13

Pecking Away at the Keyboard 14
Cutting Corners with the Windows Key 15
Dual-Function Keys on Notebook PCs 16
Mastering Basic Mouse Moves 16
Customizing Your Mouse..18
Pointing Devices for the Alternative Crowd........................19

3   Green Computing   21

Your PC May Not Be PC (Politically Correct) 22
Estimating Your Computer's Energy Consumption...............22
Wasting Paper and Ink 23
Posing an Environmental Hazard...............................23
Buying Green 23
Cranking Down Your Energy Consumption 24
Turn It Off..25
Saving Energy 25
Reduce, Reuse, and Recycle..26
Conserving Paper 27
Conserving Ink 27
Reusing Paper..27
Recycling Paper, Ink, and Other Stuff 28

Part 2:   Navigating Microsoft Windows   **29**

   4   Mastering Windows Basics (Vista and XP)   **31**

     Checking Out the Windows Desktop 32
       Which Version of Windows Do You Have? 33
       Single-Click or Double-Click? 33
     Ordering from Menus and Dialog Boxes 34
       Clicking Menu Options 35
       Talking With a Dialog Box 36
     Bypassing Menus by Using Toolbar Buttons 37
     Checking Out Some Windows Programs 38
     Rearranging the Windows Inside Windows 39
     Seeing More with Scrollbars 40

   5   Navigating Windows Vista   **43**

     What's New in Vista? 44
       Renovated Desktop 44
       Powerful Tools for Finding Stuff 45
       Beefed-Up Media Features 46
       Improved Digital Photo Management 47
       Tightened Security 47
       New Internet Explorer Web Browser 47
       New Sidebar and Gadgets 48
       New Backup Utility 49
       More Robust Speech-Recognition Capabilities 49
       Windows SideShow 50
       Tightened Parental Controls 50
       Mobility Center 50
       Added Support for Tablet PCs 51
       Improved Synchronization of Devices 52
       Networking Improvements 52
     Exploring Your Computer 53
     Getting Help 54
     Shutting Down 54

   6   Windows XP, Up Close and Personal   **57**

     Touring XP's Desktop 58
     Exploring the Start Menu 58
     Flipping from One Program to Another 59
     Exploring Your Computer 60
       Disk Drives, Folders, and Files 60

Accessing the Windows Control Panel *61*
Getting Help in Windows XP 62
Shutting Down 62

7   Managing Disks, Folders, and Files   65

Disk Drives: Easy as A-B-C 66
The Floppy Drives: A (and Sometimes B) *66*
The Hard Disk Drive: C *67*
The CD-ROM, CD-RW, or DVD Drive: D *67*
Using Floppy Disks 68
Loading and Unloading CDs and DVDs 68
The Hard Disk 69
External Drives and Other Anomalies 70
What's on a Disk? Files and Folders 71
Exploring Your Disks and Folders 72
Copying, Moving, and Dumping Files and Folders 73
Selecting Folders and Files *73*
Making Your Own Folders *74*
Dumping Files in the Recycle Bin *75*
Renaming Folders and Files *76*
Moving and Copying Folders and Files *77*

8   Installing, Running, and Uninstalling Programs   79

Buying Software Your Hardware Can Run 80
Installing Your New Program 83
Running Your Programs 84
Picking a Program from the Start Menu *84*
Making Your Own Program Shortcut *85*
Running Programs When Windows Starts *86*
Running Programs with a Single Click *86*
Removing a Program You Never Use 87

9   Customizing Windows   89

Personalizing Windows Vista 90
Customizing Vista's Desktop *90*
Tweaking the Audio Portion of Your Broadcast *97*
Saving Your Desktop Settings as a Theme *99*
Personalizing Windows XP 100
Maximizing Your Desktop Space *100*
Rearranging Items on the Start Menu *102*
Tweaking the Screen Colors *102*
Hanging Wallpaper in the Background *102*

Controlling the Desktop Icons and Visual Effects *103*
Turning on an Animated Screen Saver *103*
Assigning Sounds to Windows Events *104*
Adjusting the Date and Time 104

10 Creating and Managing User Accounts   107

Adding a New User to Your Computer 108
Establishing Log-On Passwords 109
Giving Your Account Icon a Makeover 111
Wiping Out a User Account 112
Letting Guest Users Log On 113
Logging On and Logging Off Windows....................................114
Logging On at Start-Up *114*
Logging Off Windows *115*
Sharing Files with Other Users 115

11 Finding Lost or Misplaced Items   117

Searching for Missing Files and Folders 118
Tagging Items in Windows Vista..120
Hunting for Your Printer 121

12 Networking Windows to Other Computers   123

The Two Main Network Types 124
Exploring Your Networking Options 125
Installing Your Networking Hardware 126
Running the Network Setup Wizard 128
Enabling or Disabling File and Printer Sharing 130
Sharing Resources Across the Network 131
Checking Out the Network Neighborhood..............................133
Mapping a Network Drive to Your Computer 133
Installing a Network Printer...134
Sharing a Broadband Internet Connection 135
Securing Your Network...136
Activating the Windows Firewall *136*
Limiting Access to Your Network..*136*
Securing Your Notebook PC in Hot Spots 137

Part 3:   Getting Down to Business with Office Programs   139

13 Typing and Other Word Processing Chores   141

Making the Transition to the Electronic Page..........................142
Keyboarding Tips *143*

Getting a Better View 144
Creating New Documents 144
What's with the Squiggly Red and Green Lines? 145
Inserting Today's Date..146
Making the Text Larger or Smaller..147
Shoving Text Left, Right, or Center 148
Changing the Line Spacing 149
Inserting Space Between Paragraphs..150
Save It or Lose It..151
Editing Your Letters and Other Documents 153
Selecting Text 153
Cutting and Pasting Without Scissors....................................154
Oops! Undoing Changes...155
Checking Your Spelling and Grammar 155

14 Crunching Numbers with Spreadsheets **159**
A Computerized Ledger Sheet...160
Building a Spreadsheet from the Ground Up...........................161
Designing the Spreadsheet...162
Labeling Columns and Rows..162
Editing Your Entries 163
Entering Values and Dates..163
Calculating with Formulas and Functions 165
Using Ready-Made Functions for Fancy Calculations.................166
Making the Cells Look Pretty..167
Instant Graphs (Just Add Data) 169
Special Spreadsheet Printing Considerations............................169

15 Creating a PowerPoint Presentation **173**
Touring the PowerPoint Workspace 174
Creating a New Presentation..175
Selecting a Theme..176
Customizing the Slide Master 177
Building a Slide from the Ground Up 177
Inserting a Slide 177
Adding Text to a Slide 178
Formatting Your Text 179
Adding Graphics..180
Rearranging Slides..181
Animating Your Slide Show with Special Effects.....................181
Previewing Your Slide Show and Adding Narration 182
Let the Show Begin!...182

16 Working With Graphics   **185**

Laying Out Pages in a Desktop Publishing Program...............186
Inserting Ready-Made Clip Art Images 187
  Get It Where You Can: Clip Art Sources.................................*187*
  Pasting Clip Art on a Page *188*
  Hey, This Picture's Blocking My Text!.................................*189*
  Resizing and Reshaping Images.......................................*189*
Inserting Other Pictures 191
Scanning Photos, Drawings, and Illustrations 191
Drawing and Painting Your Own Illustrations 192
  Drawing Lines, Squares, Circles, and Other Shapes *193*
  Painting the Screen with Tiny Colored Dots...........................*194*
Adding Text in a Box..195
Manipulating Overlapping Objects 196

17 Managing Your Finances   **199**

Banking Online (Without a Personal Finance Program) 200
Setting Up a Personal Finance Program..............................201
Automating the Check-Writing Process 202
Reconciling an Account with a Statement............................203
Banking Online (with a Personal Finance Program) 204
Setting Up Recurring Entries...204
Tracking Your Budget 205
Tapping the Power of Financial Calculators 206
Preparing Your Annual Tax Return 206

18 Printing Documents and Other Creations   **209**

Setting Up Your Printer in Windows...............................210
Preprint Checklist 212
Setting Your Margins and Page Layout 212
Adding a Header or Footer...214
Sending Documents to the Printer.................................215
Managing Background Printing 217
Hey, It's Not Printing! 218

Part 4: Tapping the Power of the Internet   **221**

19 Getting Wired to the Internet   **223**

Understanding How This Internet Thing Works 224
Picking a Connection Type...224
  Chugging Along with Standard Modems.............................*226*

Avoiding Speed Bumps with ISDN 227
Speeding Up Your Connection with DSL 227
Turbo-Charging Your Connection with a Cable Modem 228
Zipping Along with a Satellite Connection 229
Plugging in Wirelessly with Wi-Fi 229
Installing a Modem 229
Shopping for an Online Service 230
Connecting to Your ISP 232
Testing Your Connection Speed 232

20 Poking Around on the World Wide Web   235

Browsing for a Web Browser 236
Steering Your Browser in the Right Direction 236
A Word About Web Page Addresses 237
Finding Stuff with Google and Other Search Tools 238
Locating People Online 239
Navigating Multiple Pages with Tabs 239
Going Back in Time with History Lists 241
Marking Your Favorite Web Pages 242
Changing the Starting Web Page 242

21 Sending and Receiving E-Mail   245

Using an E-Mail Program 246
Setting Up Your Account 246
Addressing an Outgoing Message 248
Checking Your E-Mail 249
Sending Replies 250
Adding Photos and Other Cool Stuff 250
Attaching Documents to Your Messages 251
What About Free, Web-Based E-Mail? 253
E-Mail Shorthand and Emoticons 254
E-Mail No-No's 255

22 Chatting Online   259

Instant Messaging with AIM 260
Getting Started with AIM 260
Text Messaging with AIM 262
Building a Buddy List 262
Voice-Messaging with AIM 263
Videoconferencing with AIM 264
Exploring Online Chat Rooms 265
Getting Started with Yahoo! Messenger 266

Entering Chat Rooms...*266*
Keeping in Touch with Friends and Family............................268
Living It Up in Second Life 269

23 Touring Newsgroups, Message Boards, and More   **271**

Reading and Posting Newsgroup Messages..............................272
Getting Started with Your Newsreader.....................................*272*
Subscribing to Newsgroups *274*
Reading and Responding to Posted Messages.............................*276*
Starting Your Own Discussions *277*
Pulling Up Message Boards on the Web 278
Registering for E-Mail Mailing Lists 279
Getting Up-to-the-Minute RSS News Feeds 280

24 Publishing Your Own Web Page or Blog   **283**

Behind the Scenes with a Web Page 284
Forget About HTML..285
 Making a Web Page Right on the Web 285
Blogging Your Way to Internet Fame 288
Launching Your Blog *289*
Making Your Blog Your Own...*291*
Becoming a Social Butterfly..292

25 Buying and Selling Stuff Online   **295**

Is It Safe? 296
Comparison-Shopping for the Real Deals 297
Buying Online 298
Booking Travel Reservations Online 300
Buying and Selling on eBay 301
Buying Stuff on eBay...*301*
Selling Stuff on eBay *304*
Checking Out Craigslist..305

26 Internet Safety   **307**

Protecting Children on the Internet 308
Explaining the Rules of the Road...*308*
A Little Personal Supervision Goes a Long Way 309
Censoring the Internet...310
Censoring the Web with Internet Explorer.................................*310*
Using Censoring Software..*313*

Adjusting Your Browser's Security Settings.............................314
Keeping Out Viruses 316
Keeping Hackers at Bay with a Firewall 317
  Configuring Your Router's Firewall.................................... *317*
  Turning the Windows Firewall On or Off............................ *318*

Part 5:   Going Digital with Music, Photos, and Video   321

27   Playing CDs, DVDs, MP3s, and More   323

CD and MP3 Audio Basics 324
Using Your Computer as a Jukebox..325
  Creating Playlists with Windows Media Player *326*
  Changing Media Player's Skin.. *329*
Downloading Music from the Web...329
  Finding and Downloading Music *330*
  Copying Music to a Portable Music Player........................ *331*
Burning Audio CDs 332
  Duplicating CDs.. *332*
  Recording a Custom Mix to a CD *333*
Playing DVDs on Your Computer 334

28   Snapping, Enhancing, and Sharing Digital Photos   337

Learning the Lingo 338
Taking Digital Snapshots 339
Copying Photographs to Your PC..340
Adding Digital Photos to E-Mail and Web Pages.................342
Ordering Photo Prints Online..343
More Ways to Display and Share Photos..................................344

29   Editing Digital Video   347

Getting Started with Digital Video 348
Setting Up Your A/V Equipment 349
Capturing and Saving Video Clips 350
Splicing Your Clips into a Full-Length Movie..........................354
Adding an Audio Background..355
Smoothing Out Your Transitions 357
Saving Your Project..357
Copying Your Movie to a VHS Tape 359

Part 6: Maintaining and Troubleshooting Your Computer   363

30 Keeping Your Computer Clean   365

Tools of the Computer-Cleaning Trade....................366
Vacuuming and Dusting Your Computer.....................366
Cleaning Your Monitor.......................................367
Shaking the Crumbs Out of Your Keyboard.............368
Making Your Mouse Cough Up Hairballs..............369
When Your Printer Needs Cleaning.......................369
What About the Disk Drives?...............................370

31 Giving Your Computer a Tune-Up   373

Eliminating Useless Files...................................374
Checking for and Repairing Damaged Files............376
Defragmenting Files..377
Performing a Diagnostic Start-Up.........................379
Scanning for Performance Glitches.......................380

32 Troubleshooting Common Computer Problems   383

Troubleshooting Tactics....................................384
Thank Goodness for System Restore!....................385
Identifying Troublesome Background Programs.........386
"My Computer Won't Start!"..............................387
"My Computer Locked Up!".............................388
It Could Be a Program 389
Check Your Mouse Driver...............................389
Check the Windows Graphics Acceleration Setting.....390
Get an Updated Video Driver..........................391
Dealing With Windows in Safe Mode...................391
"I Can't Get the Program to Run!".......................392
"I Have a Mouse, but I Can't Find the Pointer!" 393
"I Can't Hear My Speakers!".............................393
"My Printer Won't Print!"................................394
Updating the Software for Your Hardware..............395

33 Help! Finding Technical Support   397

Phone Support (Are You Feeling Lucky?)................398
Finding Tech Support Online.............................399
Troubleshooting with Diagnostic Software..............402

Index   405

Introduction

A funny thing happened on the way to the twenty-first century. Computers became more human. By "human," I don't mean "humanoid." I only mean that the computer has evolved from being a stodgy office tool to a revolutionary home appliance and entertainment system, a device designed to help us manage and enjoy our lives more fully.

Sure, you can still use a computer to type and print a letter, but the latest computer technology can completely revolutionize your professional and personal life. Here's just a glimpse of what you can do with a computer, an Internet connection, and some additional equipment:

- Compose letters and create custom publications.
- Decorate your documents with professional clip art and other graphics.
- Shop at mega-malls and specialty shops without leaving your home—and save money, too!
- Send and receive mail electronically—no postage, and same-day delivery.
- Carry on conversations with friends, relatives, and complete strangers anywhere in the world—without paying long-distance charges.
- Plan your vacation, get medical advice, and find maps to nearly any location.
- Copy music clips from the Internet and from your CD collection and burn your own custom CDs.
- Take photos with a digital camera, transfer them to your computer, make prints, or e-mail photos to your friends and family.
- Create your own websites or blogs (web logs) to express your views, communicate with family and friends, or market your products and services.
- Edit your home videos and copy your video clips to CDs, DVDs, or VHS tapes.
- Find a mate. (I do recommend meeting in person before you make any commitments.)

Sounds pretty cool, huh? Well, it is—assuming, of course, that you know what you're doing. To master the high-tech world of computers and electronic gadgets, you must first master the basics. You need to know your way around a computer, how to point and click with a mouse, how to run programs in Windows, and how to enter commands. After you've mastered a few basics, as explained in the first few chapters of this book, you'll be well prepared to explore and exploit the full power of your computer and the Internet as you proceed through later chapters.

What You Learn in This Book

You don't have to read this book from cover to cover (although you might miss some savvy tidbits if you skip around). If you just purchased a computer, start with Chapter 1 to learn how to get your computer up and running. If you need a quick lesson on using Windows, skip ahead to Chapter 4. If you need to get wired to the Internet, check out Chapter 19. To provide some structure for this hodgepodge of computer skills and techniques, I've divided this book into the following six parts:

Part 1, "Firing Up Your Computer: Bare-Bones Basics," covers the bare minimum: setting up and turning on your computer and using your mouse and keyboard to make it respond to your every command. In this edition, I added a chapter on green computing to help you remain environmentally friendly.

Part 2, "Navigating Microsoft Windows," shows you how to take control of the Windows desktop (a virtual desktop on which you create documents and play games), install and run programs, share your computer peacefully with others, manage and secure your documents, and network your computers so they can share valuable and often expensive resources. In this part, I cover both Windows Vista and Windows XP.

Part 3, "Getting Down to Business with Office Programs," teaches you everything you need to know to type a letter and other documents, add clip art and other graphics, and print your letter. You also learn your way around spreadsheet programs, presentation programs (for creating and presenting slide shows), and personal finance programs.

Part 4, "Tapping the Power of the Internet," launches you into the world of telecommunications. In this part, you find out how to install a modem, connect to an online service, surf the Internet, send and receive electronic mail, wander the World Wide Web, shop online, chat and videoconference with others, and much more.

Part 5, "Going Digital with Music, Photos, and Video," takes you on a tour of the wonderful world of digital audio, imaging, and video. Here you learn how to copy music clips from CDs and from the Internet to burn your own custom CDs and transfer music clips to a portable music player; buy a digital camera and use it to snap and print photos and e-mail them to your friends and family; and use video-editing software to splice your home movie clips into a full-length motion picture.

Part 6, "Maintaining and Troubleshooting Your Computer," acts as your computer maintenance guide. Here, you learn how and when to clean your computer, give it regular tune-ups to keep it running like new, troubleshoot common problems, and find additional technical support when all else fails.

Conventions Used in This Book

I use several conventions in this book to make it easier to understand. For example, when you need to type something, it appears in **bold**.

Likewise, if I tell you to select or click a command, the command also appears in **bold**. This enables you to quickly scan a series of steps without having to reread all the text.

Extras

A plethora of margin notes and sidebars offer additional information about what you've just read. Here's what to look for:

def•i•ni•tion

In the computer industry, jargon and cryptic acronyms rule. When a computer term baffles you or an acronym annoys you, look here for a plain-English definition.

Whoa!

Before you press that button, check out these boxes for precautionary notes. Chances are, I've made the same mistake myself, so let me tell you how to avoid the same blunder.

Inside Tip

When you've been in the computer business for as long as I have, you learn better ways to perform the same tasks and pick up information that helps you avoid common pitfalls. To share in my wealth of knowledge, check out my Inside Tips.

Computer Cheat	Panic Attack
Do the steps required to perform a simple computer task seem convoluted? Then they probably are. Software programs commonly have hidden shortcuts that help you perform a task more efficiently. Check out these boxes for tips from the masters.	You did everything right, but the same error message keeps popping up on your screen—or worse yet, nothing happens. When your computer or program does the unexpected, look to these boxes for an explanation and a fix.

Acknowledgments

Several people had to don hard hats and get their hands dirty to build a better book. I owe special thanks to Tom Stevens for choosing me to author this book and for handling the assorted details to get this book in gear. Thanks to Christy Wagner and Michael Dietsch for guiding the content of this book, keeping it focused on new users, ferreting out all my typos, and fine-tuning my sentences. Megan Douglass deserves a free trip to Aruba for shepherding the manuscript (and art) through production. The Alpha Books production team merits a round of applause for transforming a collection of electronic files into such an attractive book. I also owe special thanks to my agent, Neil Salkind, and the rest of the staff at Studio B for expertly managing the minor details (like paying me).

Special Thanks to the Technical Reviewer

The Complete Idiot's Guide to Computer Basics, Fifth Edition, was reviewed by an expert who double-checked the accuracy of what you'll learn here, to help us ensure that this book gives you everything you need to know about understanding and using your computer. Special thanks are extended to Valerie L. Bird.

Valerie earned her B.S. in math with a secondary education certificate in 1972 from Western Michigan University and her M.A. in liberal studies (concentration in computer education) in 1997 from Empire State College. She has used computers since 1983, taught computers for Long Island Electric Company from 1988 to 1999, and has been teaching computers and math at Wytheville Community College since 1999. She has IC3 Certification; MOS (Microsoft Office Specialist) Master Instructor Certification in Word, Excel, PowerPoint, Access, Advanced Word, and Advanced Excel; Master CIW (Certified International Web Professional) Web Designer Certification; CIW JavaScript and PERL Certificate; CIW Database Specialist

Certificate; and Adobe Dreamweaver CS3 Certification. She enjoys helping people learn about computers and how to use them.

Trademarks

All terms mentioned in this book that are known to be or are suspected of being trademarks or service marks have been appropriately capitalized. Alpha Books and Penguin Group (USA) Inc. cannot attest to the accuracy of this information. Use of a term in this book should not be regarded as affecting the validity of any trademark or service mark.

Part 1

Firing Up Your Computer: Bare-Bones Basics

When you purchase a car, the salesperson sits you down behind the wheel and shows you how to work the controls. You learn how to tune the radio, activate cruise control, adjust the seat, and work the headlights and windshield wipers. When you purchase a computer—a much more complicated piece of machinery—you're on your own. You get several boxes containing various gadgets and cables, and it's up to you to figure out how to connect everything, turn it on, and start using it.

To make up for this lack of guidance, Part 1 acts as your personal driving instructor, leading you step-by-step through the process of setting up and starting your computer and using the controls (the keyboard and mouse) to run programs and enter commands.

Part 1 also introduces you to the concept of green computing, showing you how to be an environmentally friendly computer user.

"Right. Okay. Mr. Van Winkle—this would be the back of the computer."

Kick-Starting Your Computer

In This Chapter

- ◆ Preparing a home for your computer
- ◆ Unpacking the fragile components
- ◆ Connecting your equipment
- ◆ Turning on and starting up

Bringing home your first computer is nearly as exhilarating and worrisome as adopting a new puppy. You're excited, but you really don't know what to expect or how to get started. Where should you set up your computer? How do you connect everything? What's the proper sequence for turning on the parts? How do you respond to your computer the first time you start it?

This chapter shows you what to expect. Here you learn how to prepare a space for your computer, set it up, and turn on everything in the correct sequence. This chapter also provides plenty of tips and tricks to deal with the unexpected the first time you start your computer.

Finding a Comfortable Home for Your Computer

Your home seems spacious until you take delivery of a new sofa or entertainment center. Then you just can't figure out how you'll wedge that new piece of furniture into your existing collection. Likewise, few people spend much time considering where they're going to place their computer until they bring it into their home or office. In their haste to get the computer up and running, they might place the computer on a rickety card table in a dank room, where it teeters precariously until they get the time and money to set it up properly.

This is a risky strategy. Perching your computer on unstable furniture in a damp or dusty room can significantly reduce its life expectancy—not to mention your enjoyment of your computer.

Think ahead and prepare your computer area *before* you start connecting components. Consider how you'll use your computer. If you intend to use it as a tool for the family, don't stick it in the basement next to that treadmill you never use. Place it in a room that's convenient for everyone and where you can supervise your kids without making them feel "supervised."

Be sure to set up the computer next to a grounded outlet that's *not* on the same circuit as a clothes dryer, air conditioner, or other power-hungry appliance. Power fluctuations can damage your computer and destroy files.

Inside Tip _____

If you're in an old house and you're not sure if the outlet is grounded, go to the hardware store and buy an outlet tester. It has indicator lights that show whether the outlet is properly wired.

Also keep the computer away from magnetic fields created by fans, radios, large speakers, air conditioners, microwave ovens, and other appliances, and don't even think about sticking refrigerator magnets your computer or monitor. Magnetic fields can mess up the display and erase data from your disks.

Choose an area near a phone jack, or install an additional jack for your modem. (If you purchased the computer mainly for working on the Internet with a dial-up connection, consider installing a separate phone line for your modem.) If you plan to connect to the Internet through your cable or satellite company, contact the company to install a cable connection near the computer.

Place your computer in an environment that is clean, dry, cool, and out of direct sunlight. If you have no choice, cover the computer after turning it off to keep it clean.

Don't cover it when the power's on; it needs room to breathe. It has fans and vents to keep it cool. If you block the vents, the computer might overheat.

To reduce glare on the monitor, be sure it doesn't directly face a window or other source of bright light. Otherwise, the glare will make it difficult for you to see the screen.

> ### Whoa!
>
> Many experts recommend plugging everything into a high-quality surge suppressor to prevent lightning damage to your computer. I prefer using a UPS (uninterruptible power supply), because it feeds the computer a steady stream of electricity and gives you some time to shut down properly if you experience a blackout. If possible, plug your UPS into an outlet located on an inside wall to further reduce the likelihood that lightning will strike your computer.

Unpacking Your New Toys

When you bring your computer home (or when it's delivered), you will be tempted to tear open the boxes and unpack everything. Wait. You have to be careful unpacking and connecting your equipment.

First of all, take your time. It's easy to get flustered and make mistakes when you're in a hurry. Just as important, clear all drinks from the work area. You don't want to spill anything on your new computer.

If your computer arrives on a cold day, give the components 2 or 3 hours to adjust to the temperature and humidity in the room. Any condensation needs to dissipate before you turn on the power.

When unpacking your equipment, keep the boxes on the floor to avoid dropping any equipment from up high. And don't cut the boxes. Carefully peel off the packing tape. This serves two purposes: it reduces the risk of your hacking through a cable or scratching a device, and it keeps the boxes in good condition in case you need to return a device to the manufacturer. Save all the packing material, including the Styrofoam and bubble wrap. Many manufacturers accept returns only in the original packing. The packing material is also useful if you ever need to move.

If you have trouble pulling a device, such as a monitor, out of the box, turn the box on its side and slide the device out onto the floor. Don't flip the box over and try to pull the box off the device.

Read the packing list(s) thoroughly to be sure you received everything you ordered. If something is missing, contact the manufacturer or dealer *immediately*.

Find all the cables. The cables are often stored in a separate compartment at the bottom of the box. They're easy to overlook. (Some cables, including the all-important printer cable, might not be included.) Inspect the cables. Look for cuts in the cables, and check for bent pins on the connectors. Although you can straighten the pins using tweezers or needle-nose pliers, you can easily snap off a pin, voiding the warranty. If you find a bent or damaged pin, call the manufacturer. The manufacturer probably will instruct you to straighten the pin; but then if it breaks, it's the manufacturer's fault.

Remove any spacers or packing materials from the disk drives and printer. Cardboard or plastic spacers are commonly used to keep parts from shifting during shipping. To avoid damaging your new equipment, remove these spacers before you turn on your computer.

Inside Tip

As you dig through the boxes, find the warranty forms, fill them out, and mail them in. Taking time now to complete the forms could save you hundreds of dollars down the road. Stuff your computer instructions, warranty, and other paperwork in a folder (I use an oversize, sealable plastic bag), and store it in a safe place for future reference. ·

Unlock any devices that might have been locked for shipping. Some scanners, for instance, have a switch that locks the scanner's carriage in place. That switch might be at the back or bottom of the scanner.

When you're making connections, don't force anything. Plugs should slide easily into outlets. If you have to force something, the prongs are probably not aligned with the holes they're supposed to go in. Forcing the plug will break the prongs.

Finally, don't turn on *anything* until *everything* is connected. On some computers, you can safely plug in devices when the power is on, but check the manual to be sure.

Identifying Your Computer's Parts and Appendages

A computer is not a single entity, like a refrigerator or a TV set. A typical computer consists of several components that contribute to its operation and performance. As you work through this chapter to connect the components, you must be able to identify each component and know its common name. Figure 1.1 points out the key parts.

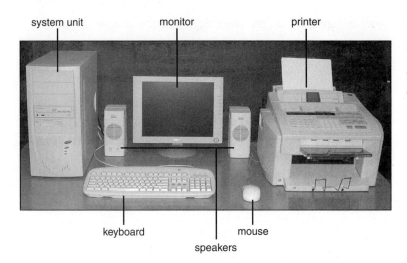

system unit   monitor   printer

keyboard   mouse

speakers

Figure 1.1

A computer consists of several parts.

The central component of all computers is the *system unit*, which contains the brains and memory of the computer and the disk drives where data is stored. All other components are considered *peripheral devices*, and they plug directly or indirectly into the system unit. Peripheral devices include the keyboard and mouse you use to enter commands and data; the monitor, which enables you to see what you're doing; the speakers that provide audio feedback; the printer, which enables you to make paper copies of the documents you create; and the modem, which connects the computer to the Internet. (The modem may be built right in to the system unit.) Peripheral devices also include joysticks for playing games, digital cameras, scanners, and a host of other electronic gadgets.

Making the Right Connections

When everything is unpacked, arrange all the devices on your desk. If you connect the devices before arranging them, the cables get all twisted up when you begin moving things around. If you have a mini-tower or full-tower system unit, you can set it on the floor to conserve desk space. (If the floor is carpeted, set the unit on an antistatic pad to prevent static buildup that could damage the sensitive components inside the system unit.)

After everything is properly positioned, you can connect the devices. This is where life gets a bit complicated. Connections differ depending on the computer's design and the types of components you're connecting. For example, although most computers include a central system unit into which you plug the monitor, keyboard, mouse, and printer, some newer computers combine the system unit, monitor, and speakers as a single device into which you plug other devices. In addition, newer computers make greater use of USB (Universal Serial Bus) ports, special receptacles that allow you to connect a string of up to 127 devices to a single receptacle.

To figure out where to plug in what, look for words or pictures on the back (and front) of the central unit (the system unit or combination system unit/ monitor). Most receptacles (ports) are marked, and some newer systems even have color-coded cables. If you don't see any pictures next to the receptacles, try to match the plugs with their outlets, as shown in Figure 1.2. Look at the overall shape of the outlet to see whether it has pins or holes. Count the pins and holes, and be sure there are at least as many holes as there are pins. As a last resort, look for the documentation that came with your computer.

Figure 1.2

Look for clues on the system unit to figure out where to plug in devices.

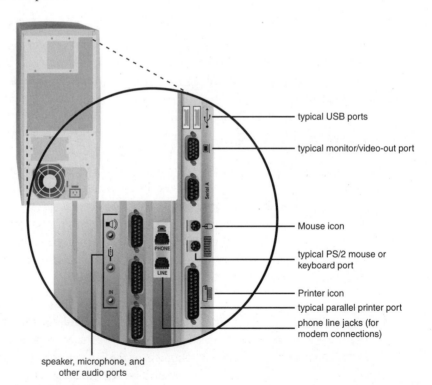

typical USB ports

typical monitor/video-out port

Mouse icon

typical PS/2 mouse or keyboard port

Printer icon

typical parallel printer port

phone line jacks (for modem connections)

speaker, microphone, and other audio ports

Bringing the Beast to Life

Dr. Frankenstein must have had a real rush just before he flipped the switch and sent that mega-volts jolt through his monster's patchworked body. You might get a similar thrill just before you turn on your new computer. What will the screen look like? What sounds will it make? How fast will things pop up on the monitor?

Well, you're about to have all your questions answered as you perform the following steps to start your computer:

1. Press the button on the monitor or flip its switch to turn it on. Computer manufacturers recommend that you turn on the monitor first. This allows you to see the startup messages, and it prevents the monitor's power surge from passing through the system unit's components. (On many newer computers, the monitor turns on automatically when you turn on the system unit.)

2. Turn on the printer if it has a power button or switch. Be sure the online light is lit (not blinking). If the light is blinking, be sure the printer has paper and then press the online or power button (if the printer has an online button).

3. If you have speakers or other devices connected to your computer, turn them on.

4. Press the power button or flip the switch on the system unit. (On notebooks and some newer desktop models, you must hold the button for 1 or 2 seconds before releasing it.)

Inside Tip _____

If this is the first time you're turning on your printer, you must install the ink or toner cartridge. Check the printer manual for instructions.

What happens next varies from one computer to another. Most computers perform a series of startup tests, load a set of basic instructions, and display text messages (white text on a black background) on the monitor. These messages typically disappear before you have time to read them, so don't worry if things seem to rush by too quickly. Your computer then runs its operating system—Windows, on most PCs, although some PCs run Linux and Macintosh computers run Mac OS. The operating system provides the basic instructions your computer needs to function.

Windows prompts you to log on by clicking your user name. If a log-on screen does not appear, your computer is set up for a single user and does not require a password to log on. If a log-on screen does appear, click your user name and then, if requested, enter the password that has been assigned to this user account. (For more about user accounts and logging on and off in Windows, see Chapter 10.)

def•i•ni•tion

A **user account** is an identification badge that enables each user to log on to Windows and set it up to suit his or her own tastes. It also provides some low-level security by requiring each user to sign on using a unique password (if a user chooses to do so).

After you log on, your monitor should display the Windows desktop. Figure 1.3 shows the Windows Vista desktop. If you have a different version of Windows, such as Windows XP, 2000, or Me (Millennium edition), the log-on screens and desktop might look different but function in much the same way. You might also encounter different displays on start-up if your copy of Windows is set up to run additional software when it starts.

Figure 1.3

When your computer finally settles down, it should display the Windows desktop.

Installing the Software That Runs Your Hardware

You're not the first person to have turned on your computer. The manufacturer or dealer turned it on right after it came off the assembly line to test the computer before shipping it. However, the manufacturer typically tests the computer without the printer and other accessories connected, so the first time you run your computer with everything connected, Windows runs the Add New Hardware Wizard. (A *wizard* is a series of screens that lead you step-by-step through the process of performing a task.)

The Add New Hardware Wizard steps you through the process of installing the software (called a *device driver*) that tells Windows how to communicate with a particular device. If a device came with its own device driver (on a CD), use that driver instead of the driver included with Windows. The Add New Hardware dialog box displays a **Have Disk** button, which you can click to install a driver from a CD. Otherwise, you must install the driver from the Windows CD, which may be included with your system. Follow the onscreen instructions, as shown in Figure 1.4, and use your mouse as described in Chapter 2.

> **Panic Attack**
>
> If you have trouble installing a device, see Chapter 32 for some helpful guidance.

Figure 1.4

The Add New Hardware Wizard or Add Printer Wizard leads you through the process of installing a device driver.

Now What?

You've arranged everything to your liking, turned on everything, and responded to any start-up messages. Now what?

At this point, you're ready to start working (or playing). If the Windows desktop is displayed, as shown in Figure 1.3, you can click the **Start** button in the lower-left corner and point to **All Programs** to check out which games and programs are installed on your computer. The chapters in Part 2 show you how to move around in Windows and navigate the Windows desktop.

The Least You Need to Know

- Place your computer in an environment that is clean, dry, and cool.

- Plug all your computer components into a high-quality surge suppressor or uninterruptible power supply to prevent damage from lightning and power fluctuations.

- When inserting a connector into a port, be sure the pins align with the holes, and never force the connection.

- Turn on all the components that are connected to the central unit before you turn on the central unit so your computer can identify the components during start-up and you can view the start-up messages.

- The first time you run your computer, you might need to install hardware drivers (software that tells Windows how to use specific devices).

Chapter 2

Taking the Wheel, er, Keyboard and Mouse

In This Chapter

- Ctrl, Alt, F1, and other bizarre keys
- Fun with a programmable keyboard
- Pointing, clicking, dragging, and other mouse moves
- Alternative pointing devices

If you're brave (and extremely patient), you can strap on a headset and microphone and train your computer to interpret commands and take dictation. However, most people still prefer using the more traditional, low-tech input devices—the mouse and keyboard. But even these tools require a little bit of technological know-how and manual dexterity to master.

In this chapter, you learn how to use these standard input devices along with a few other technologies to "talk" to your computer and enter text and other data.

Pecking Away at the Keyboard

The old, manual typewriter keyboard was fairly basic. It had letter keys, number keys, a Shift key, a backspace key, and a spacebar. When you needed to start a new paragraph, you reached up and took a swipe at the carriage return. Newfangled computer keyboards are much more complex, as you can see in Figure 2.1. They still have the letter and number keys, but they also have several keys you might not recognize.

Figure 2.1

Logitech's Wave keyboard.

(Photo courtesy of Logitech, Inc.)

The *function keys,* or the 10 or 12 F keys at the top or left side of the keyboard (F1, F2, F3, and so on) were frequently used in older programs to quickly enter commands. F1 is still used to display help in Windows and most Windows programs, and you can assign function keys to perform specialized tasks in most programs.

The *arrow keys, Page Up, Page Down, Home, and End keys,* also known as cursor-movement keys, move the cursor (the blinking line or box) around onscreen. Wherever the cursor (also known as the insertion point) ends up is where your text appears as you type.

The *numeric keypad* are the group of number keys positioned like the keys on an adding machine. You use these keys to type numbers or to move around onscreen. Press the NumLock key to use the keys for entering numbers. With NumLock off, the keys act as arrow or cursor-movement keys. Most computers turn on NumLock on start-up.

The *Ctrl* (Control) and *Alt* (Alternate) keys make the other keys on the keyboard act differently from the way they normally act. For example, in Windows you can press

Ctrl+A (hold down the Ctrl key while pressing A) to select all the text or objects displayed in the current document. Some programs enable you to assign commonly used commands to shortcut keystrokes consisting of Ctrl, Alt, and Shift in combination with other keys.

You can use the *Esc* (Escape) key in most programs to back out of or quit whatever you're currently doing.

The *Print Screen/SysRq* or *PrtSc* key sends the screen image to the Windows Clipboard, a temporary storage area for data. (To learn more about the Clipboard, see Chapter 13.)

Another fairly useless key, in some programs, *Scroll Lock* or *ScrLk* makes the arrow keys push text up and down on the screen one line at a time instead of moving the insertion point.

The king of all useless keys, *Pause/Break* is used to stop your computer from performing the same task over and over again—something that old programs seemed to enjoy doing. I have pressed this key only a few times, usually by mistake.

Many newer keyboards try to place everything you need to control your computer—including *volume controls*—right at your fingertips and may offer controls to adjust speaker and microphone volume and other common computer settings.

Most keyboards include special *programmable buttons* that enable you to quickly open your Internet home page, navigate the Internet, check e-mail, and put your computer in sleep mode. In addition, if you don't use one of the buttons for its designated function, you can reprogram it to perform some other time-saving shortcut.

Cutting Corners with the Windows Key

Inspect your keyboard carefully to see whether it has a *Windows* key—a key printed with the Windows logo, a four-paned window that looks as though it's flying through the sky. The key is typically located near the lower-left corner of the keyboard, to the left of the spacebar. If your keyboard has this key, you have a "Windows keyboard," which was probably manufactured after 1995. Besides acting as a decorative addition to your keyboard, the Windows key provides quick access to commonly entered Windows commands, as presented in Table 2.1.

Table 2.1   Windows Key Shortcuts

Press ...	To ...
Windows	Open the Start menu.
Windows+Tab	Cycle through running programs in the taskbar.
Windows+F	Find a file.
Ctrl+Windows+F	Find a computer on a network.
Windows+F1	Display the Windows Help window.
Windows+R	Display the Run dialog box (for running programs).
Windows+Pause/Break	Display the System Properties dialog box.
Windows+E	Run Windows Explorer for managing folders and files.
Windows+D or Windows+M	Minimize or restore all program windows.
Shift+Windows+M	Undo minimize all program windows.

Dual-Function Keys on Notebook PCs

Portable computers, including notebooks, laptops, and tablet PCs, typically lack the space for a full set of keys plus buttons to turn on the computer, adjust the display, and move the mouse pointer. To fit all the keys and buttons in this limited amount of space, many keys are assigned double-duty. For example, some of the keys can be used to adjust the brightness and contrast of the display.

In most cases, the keyboard includes a key labeled Fn that is a different color (typically blue). Keys that perform double-duty have their primary functions displayed in black or white, and their secondary functions displayed in the same color used for the Fn key. To take advantage of the secondary function of the key, hold down the Fn key while pressing the key labeled with the desired secondary function.

Mastering Basic Mouse Moves

If you're the type of person who orders from the menu by pointing at the item of your choice rather than speaking to the waiter, you're going to love your computer's mouse. The mouse provides a more intuitive way for you to enter commands—you simply slide the mouse across your desk until the mouse pointer (on the monitor) is over the desired menu or object and then you click (press and release) the left mouse button. Figure 2.2 shows a typical mouse.

Figure 2.2

Logitech's MX610 Laser cordless mouse.

(Photo courtesy of Logitech, Inc.)

To use a mouse, you must master a few basic moves. First up is the *point*. Simply slide the mouse around until the tip of the onscreen arrow is over the item you want. Easy stuff.

Next up is *click*. Point to something (usually an icon or menu command), and press and release the left mouse button. You can also click in a document to move the insertion point to where you want to type. When you click, be careful not to move the mouse when you click, or you might click the wrong thing or move an object unintentionally.

Getting a little more advanced is the *right-click*. This is the same as click, but you use the right mouse button. The right mouse button is used mainly to display context menus, which contain commands that apply only to the currently selected object.

Inside Tip

A traditional mouse has a rubber ball inside it that turns rollers inside the mouse to move the mouse pointer on-screen. The ball tends to pick up a lot of dust and hair, which eventually makes the mouse pointer move erratically. The newer, optical mouse uses laser technology to sense the mouse movement, making the mouse much more reliable. (To clean a standard mouse, see Chapter 30.)

Double-click is the same as click, but you press and release the mouse button twice really fast without moving the mouse. Mastering this move takes some practice.

Finally, *drag*. To drag something, point to it and hold down the left mouse button while moving the mouse. You typically drag to move an object, select text (in a word processing program), or draw (in a drawing or paint program). In some cases, you can drag with the right mouse button; when you release the mouse button, a context menu typically appears asking what you want to do.

If your mouse has a wheel between the two buttons, you can use the wheel to perform some additional maneuvers. You can rotate the wheel away from yourself to scroll text down and rotate toward yourself to scroll up.

To pan up or down, click and hold the wheel while moving the mouse pointer in the direction of the text you want to bring into view. (Panning is sort of like scrolling, but it's smoother.)

To autoscroll up or down, click the wheel and move the mouse pointer up (to scroll up) or down (to scroll down). Autoscrolling remains on until you click the wheel again.

To zoom in or out, hold down the **Ctrl** key and rotate the wheel. Rotate away from yourself to zoom in or toward yourself to zoom out.

Customizing Your Mouse

If you're a lefty or if you have trouble clicking fast enough to execute a double-click, you can customize your mouse to accommodate the way you work. In Windows, click the **Start** button (in the lower-left corner of the screen) and click **Control Panel.** In Vista, click **Mouse** (under Hardware and Sound). In XP, click or double-click **Printers and Other Hardware** and then click or double-click **Mouse.** This opens the Mouse Properties dialog box, shown in Figure 2.3. You can use this dialog box to specify the function of each mouse button and the appearance of the mouse pointers.

Panic Attack

Click or double-click? Your version of Windows may enable you to click the Mouse icon once to open the Mouse Properties dialog box, or it may require you to double-click the icon. In Chapter 9, you learn how to adjust the setting in Windows that controls this option. For now, know that if the icon's name appears underlined when the mouse pointer is resting on it, you can single-click; otherwise, you must double-click.

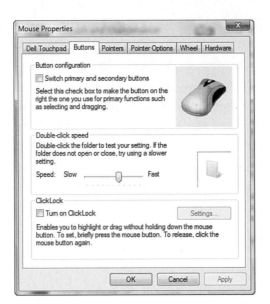

Pointing Devices for the Alternative Crowd

In search of the perfect pointing device, computer manufacturers have toyed with other ideas: trackballs, joysticks, touchpads, light-sensitive pens, and little gear shifts stuck in the middle of keyboards. I've even seen two-foot pedals set up to act like a mouse! The following paragraphs describe the more standard fare:

A *trackball* is an upside-down mouse (sort of). Instead of sliding the mouse to roll the ball inside the mouse, you roll the ball itself. Trackballs typically require less space to operate but can be a little difficult to master.

A *touchpad* is a pressure-sensitive square that you slide your finger across to move the pointer. A typical touchpad has two buttons next to it that act like mouse buttons. With most touchpads you can also tap the touchpad itself to click or double-click.

You've probably seen portable computers with a little red lever smack dab in the middle of the keyboard; these are *TrackPoint* or *AccuPoint pointers.* The lever acts sort of like a joystick; you push the lever in the direction you want to move the mouse pointer. You use buttons next to the keyboard to click and drag.

Inside Tip

Laptops typically come equipped with a touchpad or a pointer (for tablet PCs) or both. Try out the different controls before purchasing a laptop computer to see which you prefer. You can always add an external mouse to the laptop.

A *joystick* is a must-have for most computer games. It has a base with a lever sticking out of it, which you push or pull in the direction you want to move. The lever usually has a few buttons for blasting away at opponents and making a speedy getaway.

For no-hands control over your computer, you can purchase *voice activation* software and bark commands into a microphone. Microsoft Office XP and later versions include voice activation features that enable you to enter commands and text in the Office applications: Microsoft Word, Excel, Access, Outlook, and PowerPoint.

The Least You Need to Know

- The 12 function keys on your keyboard enable you to perform a variety of commands all from one convenient location.

- The Ctrl and Alt keys augment the standard keyboard keys to provide extra functions.

- The cursor keys move the cursor or insertion point around on-screen.

- The five basic mouse moves are point, click, right-click, double-click, and drag.

- The center wheel on most newer mice can be used to make scrolling through documents and web pages easier.

- Other devices for poking around on your computer include a trackball, touchpad, TrackPoint or AccuPoint pointer, joystick, and voice-recognition software.

Green Computing

In This Chapter

- ◆ The environmental impact of personal computing
- ◆ Conserving energy with automated tools
- ◆ Reducing, reusing, and recycling supplies
- ◆ Upgrading to reduce hazardous wastes

Whether or not you're a certified tree hugger, reducing any negative impact you may have on the environment is always a good thing, especially if it can save you some money.

Actually, when you think about it, computers may already play a role in reducing a person's carbon footprint, especially for those who work from home. Instead of driving everywhere, wasting gas and clouding the air with your car exhaust, you simply sit at home, tap away on the keyboard, and suck down a little electricity.

However, you can do better, and in this chapter, I show you how.

Your PC May Not Be PC (Politically Correct)

Just looking at your computer, you'd never think it was actually harming the environment. It's not spewing out exhaust, it's pretty quiet, and it doesn't litter. At least it doesn't appear to be doing any of those things.

However, as I reveal in the following sections, it's not as squeaky clean as you might think.

Estimating Your Computer's Energy Consumption

Most people have no idea how much energy their computers are sucking down. Of course, they also probably have no idea how much electricity it takes to wash and dry a load of laundry. If you want an exact figure, plug all your computer equipment into a single power strip (or a UPS—uninterruptible power supply) and then plug that into a Kill-A-Watt meter, which you can pick up at Radio Shack for about $40.

The Kill-A-Watt meter measures the cumulative kilowatt hours flowing through it, so you can then calculate how much electricity your computer uses per hour, day, week, month, or year. You can then grab your electric bill and divide the total dollar amount you paid by the number of kilowatt hours you used to determine how much you pay per kilowatt hour. Using that number, you can calculate how much it costs to run your computer per hour, day, week, month, or year.

Inside Tip

According to estimates from the Environmental Protection Agency, an average (200-watt) PC running day and night for a year burns through about 1,666 kilowatt hours and costs about $125 to operate per year. Running that same PC only during business hours cuts its energy consumption to 25 percent of those amounts. $125 per year in electricity may not sound like much, but when you consider the fact that most electricity is produced by fossil fuels and that your computer is only one of hundreds of millions of computers in the world, the collective energy wasted and pollution produced by computers that are running when not in use is enormous.

In addition to your computer's direct energy consumption, you also have to calculate the amount of energy needed to cool it. Computers tend to generate a lot of heat, and if you're using it in an air-conditioned facility, the air conditioner has to work harder to make up for that heat. (Of course, your computer might help you save a little on your heating bill during the winter.)

Wasting Paper and Ink

Your computer isn't exactly a litter bug, but it can be a source of wasted paper and ink. When personal computers first arrived on the scene, everyone predicted that we would soon have a paperless society. That never happened. In fact, computers increased paper use.

Not only do paper and ink contribute to trashing our planet, but they also consume energy—the energy used to manufacture the paper and ink, ship the products, and print documents. Later in this chapter, I offer suggestions on how to conserve paper and ink.

Posing an Environmental Hazard

Some pretty nasty stuff goes into the making of computers and peripheral devices, including mercury, phosphor coatings of cathode ray tubes (CRTs), batteries, polychlorinated biphenyl capacitors, liquid crystal displays, high-lead content CRT funnel glass, and plastic containing flame-retardant bromine. Toner and inkjet cartridges that aren't recycled also contribute to polluting the environment.

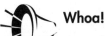

Whoa!

According to a National Safety Council study, only 11 percent of the 20 million computers that went out of service in 1998 were recycled. In 2004, more than 300 million PCs ended up being junked.

Some manufacturers and organizations are working to reduce this e-waste through recycling programs. Later in this chapter, I show you how you can pitch in to help.

Buying Green

The first step in conserving energy and reducing potentially harmful wastes is to "buy green."

Perhaps the easiest thing to do is look for the Energy Star seal when buying your computer or equipment. These devices comply with the Environmental Protection Agency's Energy Star requirements for using less power. They typically have features that automatically power down the devices down not in use.

Some manufacturers are developing computers that not only use less power but also are manufactured in an environmentally less hostile manner. During the writing of this book, these green PCs were not readily available, but they should be soon.

You can also buy an inkjet printer rather than a laser printer because inkjet printers use about 80 to 90 percent less electricity. Also consider networking your computers and sharing a printer rather than having a separate printer for each computer. (See Chapter 12 for more about networking.)

Size the monitor to your needs. If a 15-inch monitor is big enough for your use, don't buy a 17-inch monitor. This can trim your monitor's energy consumption by as much as 30 percent. Also, buy a flat-panel monitor rather than a CRT (cathode ray tube). CRT monitors require about twice as much power.

Buy recycled paper and ink cartridges. Somebody has to buy these recycled goods, or manufacturers will stop making them. (You can even buy recycled or "refurbished" computers, printers, and monitors.)

Upgrade rather than buying new (when it makes sense). Replacing an old energy hog with a new Energy Star–compliant PC may make sense, but if you already have a PC that's compliant and it needs more memory or a larger hard drive, upgrade rather than replacing the entire unit. This will help reduce hazardous wastes.

Or lease equipment. Rather than buying a new PC or printer, consider leasing one. Leased products are usually recycled or refurbished and usually don't require all the fancy packaging that new computers need.

Finally, look for software solutions. Rather than replacing a slow computer, try speeding it up by running Windows utilities designed to optimize its performance. (In Chapter 31, I show you how to give your computer a tune-up.)

Cranking Down Your Energy Consumption

Your computer is not a refrigerator. If you power it down properly, nothing you have stored on it is going to spoil or get lost. You're not going to wear out the power button by turning your computer off at the end of your workday and turning it on the next morning. Nor are you going to harm the electrical components inside the computer by turning it off and on—in fact, keeping your computer running when it's not in use subjects the components to more heat, which can lessen their useful lives.

You can significantly reduce the amount of energy your computer uses by taking two simple steps: turn it off when you're not using it, and make the most of your computer's built-in power-saving features.

Turn It Off

To conserve the most energy, turn your computer off when you're not going to be using it for an extended period of time, such as overnight. (I don't recommend turning it off if you're not going to be using it for an hour or so. Most new computers have power-saving features that can handle this for you.) If you're done at the end of the day, save any documents you've been working on and then use the **Start, Shut Down** or **Turn Off Computer** command to power down properly. In Windows Vista, you click the **Start** button, point to the arrow in the lower-right corner of the **Start** menu and click **Shut Down.**

If you decide to leave your computer on, be sure you save any documents you're working on before you step away from your computer. (You learn how to save documents in Chapter 13.) Saving a document records the document to a permanent storage medium, such as a hard drive, recordable CD, or flash drive, so that if the power goes out, you don't lose your work.

> **Inside Tip**
>
> If you have a laser printer, consider keeping it turned off until you need to print something. You may want to make a list of documents you need to print and print them all at once at the end of the day or at certain times of the day.

Saving Energy

If you have an Energy Star–compliant computer, Windows provides the controls you need to adjust the computer's power saving settings. Windows can power down the monitor, hard drives, and other components when they haven't been used for a certain period of time and then automatically power them up when you return to your computer.

The most recent versions of Windows, including XP and Vista, offer customizable power-saving features. Windows Vista calls them *power plans*, whereas XP refers to them as *power schemes*, but they're essentially the same thing.

By default, the power plan or scheme is set to provide a balance between power savings and performance—it's set up to save as much power as possible without inconveniencing you too much. To find out which power plan or scheme is in effect on your computer or to change to a different plan, take the following steps:

1. Open the Windows Control Panel by clicking the **Start** button and then **Control Panel.** (For more about navigating Windows, see Chapters 4, 5, and 6.)

2. Click **System and Maintenance** (in Vista) or **Performance and Maintenance** (in XP).

3. Click **Power Options.** In Vista, you see the screen shown in Figure 3.1, where you can choose the desired power plan.

Figure 3.1

Windows Vista offers three power plans from which to choose.

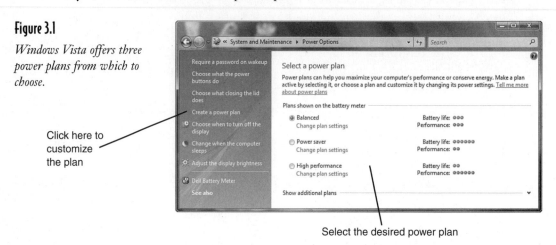

Click here to customize the plan

Select the desired power plan

4. *Optional:* To customize the plan, click the link called **Change plan settings** that's below the plan you selected.

Whoa!

Simply enabling the Windows screen saver to black out the screen after so many minutes does not save a lot of energy. You really need to use a power plan or scheme that powers down your computer's components.

The Power Schemes screen in Windows XP looks quite a bit different, offering a drop-down menu of power schemes from which to choose.

When your computer goes into power-saving mode, the screen might go blank. Don't panic. Your computer is just taking a snooze. The best way to wake it up is to press and release the **Shift** key. If that doesn't work, you may need to press and release your computer's power button. (Just don't hold down the power button too long, because that could turn off the computer entirely.)

Reduce, Reuse, and Recycle

The three R's to being green are almost cliché—reduce, reuse, and recycle—and they apply equally to computer use. I've already discussed reducing energy consumption, but you can reduce your use of other supplies, reuse some items, and recycle others to become even more environmentally friendly.

Conserving Paper

Even though a computer is often the biggest paper wasters on the planet, they have the *potential* of saving a great deal of paper. Following are some suggestions on how you can tap the full potential of your computer's paper-saving capabilities:

- Print as little as possible. Do most of your editing on the computer, read web pages online instead of printing them out, and don't print e-mail messages. Just before printing something, ask yourself, *Do I really need a hardcopy?*

- Use smaller fonts and wider margins on long documents.

- Print or copy on both sides of a page if your printer supports this.

- Sign up to receive as many of your bills as possible online instead of via mail delivery.

- Pay your bills online, as explained in Chapter 17. This can save you a lot on postage, too!

- Download and read e-books instead of ordering paper copies. Amazon.com has a Kindle device specifically designed for e-books.

- Rather than fax documents, scan them and e-mail them as attachments, as explained in Chapter 21. You can also use a special service, such as eFax (www.efax.com) to send faxes to standard fax machines over the Internet or receive faxes from a standard fax machine electronically rather than having to print them.

Conserving Ink

Many of the suggestions offered in the previous section for saving paper will also result in saving a lot of ink, but here are a couple additional ways to trim your printer's ink consumption:

- Print in draft mode if possible. Draft mode is still legible, although it may not be appropriate for documents you need to present to others. (For more about adjusting your printer's settings, see Chapter 18.)

- Print color in grayscale when appropriate. This really won't do much good for the environment, but it will help you save money on that costlier colored ink.

Reusing Paper

If you normally print on only one side of a page, you probably throw away or recycle paper that's perfectly good for printing drafts. Load that same paper into your printer the opposite way (printed side up if your printer normally flips the paper over to print on it), and print on the other side.

If that's not an option, at least use your used paper for taking notes or jotting down your weekly grocery lists.

Recycling Paper, Ink, and Other Stuff

Reducing and reusing are the two best ways to reduce the impact of your computer use on the environment, but most people can't completely eliminate their need to print. So the next best option is to recycle as much of the waste products as possible.

Buy recycled paper and ink or toner cartridges. Take used paper to your neighborhood recycling center or hire a recycling company to pick it up. Take used inkjet and toner cartridges back to the store where you purchased them to drop them off for recycling. Staples has an excellent program in which it gives you in store credit for returning used cartridges; other office supply stores may offer the similar perks.

Recycle any old computer equipment you no longer need or want. You may be able to hand it down to friends or relatives. If that's not an option, call around to computer and office supply stores to determine whether anyone has a recycling program. Most major manufacturers have programs that allow you to ship old equipment back to them for free if you buy a new computer from them. Some local nonprofit organizations may also be interested in your old gear. You may have to pay a few bucks for someone to take it off your hands, but it's a lot better than simply setting your e-waste out on the curb and having it contaminate the environment.

The Least You Need to Know

- When shopping for a computer, printer, or monitor, make sure it is Energy Star compliant.

- To save energy, turn off your computer when you're not planning to use it for an extended period of time.

- Make the most of your computer's built-in power saving features by selecting a power scheme or plan in Windows that automatically powers down components when not in use.

- Opt for an inkjet printer over a laser model to trim both your electric bill and your carbon footprint.

- Cut down on printing as much as possible to save paper, ink, electricity, and wear and tear on your printer.

Part 2

Navigating Microsoft Windows

A computer is like a newborn baby. It's packed with potential, but until it has operating system software that provides it with the instructions it needs to function, it's relatively unproductive. Fortunately, your computer comes equipped with an operating system called *Windows* that enables the computer to communicate with its various components and run application software you can use to perform specific tasks and play games.

The chapters in Part 2 show you how to use Windows (Vista or XP), customize it to look and behave the way you want it to, and manage other computer resources (including the files you create) through Windows. By mastering the Windows basics, you're well on your way to mastering your computer as well as all your applications.

"Now let's get everybody their own desktop image of where they'd prefer to be."

Chapter 4

Mastering Windows Basics (Vista and XP)

In This Chapter

- ◆ Your new electronic desktop
- ◆ Conversing with menus and dialog boxes
- ◆ A few choice Windows programs
- ◆ Moving, resizing, and hiding windows on your desktop

When you start a PC-compatible computer, it automatically runs some version of the *operating system* called Windows: Windows Vista, XP, Me (Millennium edition), 98, 95, 2000, or NT (for networked computers). But what is Windows?

If you pry off the top of your desk and hang it on the wall, you have Windows … well, sort of. Although its initial appearance might be deceiving, Windows is little more than an electronic desktop that's displayed on a two-dimensional vertical surface—your computer's monitor. It even comes complete with its own desktop utilities, including a calculator, a notepad, and a blank canvas that you can doodle on during your breaks. This chapter teaches you the basics of how to work on your new computerized desktop.

Checking Out the Windows Desktop

When you first start your computer, your new desktop appears, very neat and tidy. Several *icons* (small pictures) dot the surface of the Windows desktop, and a strip called the *taskbar* appears at the bottom of the screen (unless you or someone else moved it), as shown in Figure 4.1. On the left end of the taskbar is the all-important **Start** button, which opens a menu containing the names of all the programs installed on your computer.

def•i•ni•tion

Windows is an **operating system,** acting as the puppet master that manages communications between you, the programs you run, and the various components that make up the computer. Windows is, by no means, the only operating system on the planet. Macintosh computers, for example, run Mac OS. PCs not running Windows might run Linux. In this book, I focus exclusively on Windows and primarily on Windows Vista and XP—the most popular operating systems for the PC.

Windows desktop

Figure 4.1

Initially, the Windows desktop is sparsely populated.

recycle bin

start button

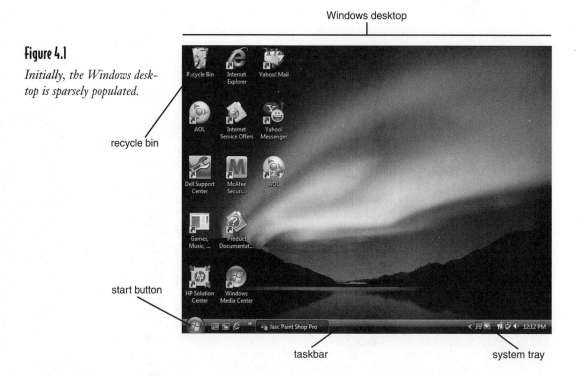

taskbar

system tray

Your Windows desktop is likely to look different from the desktop displayed in Figure 4.1. The appearance depends on which version of Windows you have installed, how it's customized, and whether other programs are installed on your computer. (See Chapter 9 for over a dozen options for personalizing the Windows desktop.)

Which Version of Windows Do You Have?

Before we start exploring the Windows desktop, find out which version of Windows you have. This book assumes you're using a relatively new computer that's running Windows Vista or XP. To find out which version of Windows you're running.

In Windows Vista: Click **Start, All Programs, Accessories, Welcome Center.** At the top of the screen, Windows displays the version along with the processor type and amount of RAM installed.

In Windows XP: Click the **Start** button, right-click **My Computer,** and click **Properties.** The System Properties dialog box appears, displaying the version of Windows along with some additional interesting tidbits.

Windows version

Figure 4.2

In Vista, the Welcome Center tells you which version you're running.

Single-Click or Double-Click?

If the icon names on your desktop and in your folders are underlined, you click an icon once to run its corresponding program. If the icon names are not underlined, you must double-click the icon to run the program. Which is better? That's for you to decide, but here are instructions on how to enable the single-click option if you'd like to try it:

In Windows Vista: Click **Start, Control Panel, Appearance and Personalization, Folder Options.** Click **Single Click to Open an Item (Point to Select),** and click **OK.**

In Windows XP: Click **Start, My Computer.** Open the **Tools** or **View** menu, and click **Folder Options.** Click **Single-click to open an item (point to select),** and click **OK.**

Figure 4.3

In Windows Vista, turn on the Single-click to open an item option.

Ordering from Menus and Dialog Boxes

Computer technology hasn't quite reached the point of *2001: A Space Odyssey* (you know, that 1968 Stanley Kubrick flick in which the astronauts actually converse with Hal, the computer that runs the spaceship). However, Windows provides several ways for you to "talk" to your computer by clicking buttons, selecting menu commands, and responding to *dialog boxes* (on-screen fill-in-the-blank forms).

Inside Tip

Windows Vista is getting pretty close to achieving voice-activated computing. To try it for yourself, click **Start, Control Panel, Ease of Access, Speech Recognition Options,** and follow the on-screen instructions to set up speech recognition. You'll need a microphone, but many newer computers, especially notebook PCs, come with built-in microphones.

Clicking Menu Options

The Windows interactive tool of preference is the *menu*. You'll find menus everywhere: on the left end of the taskbar (the **Start** menu), in menu bars near the top of most program windows, in toolbars, and even hidden inside objects. Then you click the desired menu option. (To display a hidden—*context*—menu, right-click the desired object or the selected text or image.)

Computer Cheat

To quickly open a menu without lifting your fingers from the keyboard, hold down the **Alt** key and press the key that corresponds to the underlined letter in the menu's name. For example, press **Alt+F** to open the **File** menu. Press **Shift+F10** to display a context menu for the currently selected text or object. To open the **Start** menu, press **Ctrl+Esc** or the **Windows** key (if your keyboard has one). Use the arrow keys to highlight the desired command and then press **Enter.**

As you flip through any menu system, you might notice that some of the menu options look a little strange. One option might appear pale. Another might be followed by a series of dots. And still others have arrows next to them. Their appearances tell you how these options behave:

- Light gray options are unavailable for what you're currently doing. For example, if you want to copy a chunk of text but you haven't yet selected the text, the **Copy** command is not available; it appears light gray.

- An option with an arrow next to it opens a submenu that requires you to select another option. Point to the option to open the submenu and then slide over and click the desired option.

- An option with a check mark indicates that an option is currently active. To turn the option off, click it.

- An option followed by a series of dots (...) opens a dialog box that requests additional information. You learn how to talk to dialog boxes in the next section.

> ## Whoa!
>
> To further confuse new users, Microsoft has come up with something called the "smart" menu, featured in its Office applications, which lists only the most commonly selected options. To view additional options, you must point to a double-headed arrow at the bottom of the menu. In addition, the menu is designed to customize itself, so options automatically move up on the menu the more often you use them. In other words, you never know where they'll be. In case you can't tell, I think smart menus are pretty dumb.

Talking With a Dialog Box

If you choose a menu command that's followed by a series of dots (...), the program displays a *dialog box* requesting additional information, as shown in Figure 4.4. You must then navigate the dialog box, select the desired options, type any required text entries, and give your okay.

Figure 4.4

A dialog box asks you to enter additional information and settings.

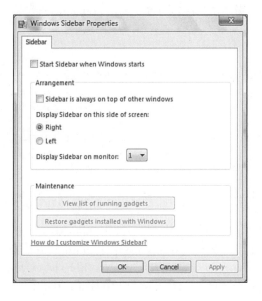

Use the following controls to navigate dialog boxes:

Tabs. If a dialog box has two or more "pages" of options, tabs appear near the top of the pages. Click the tab for the desired page.

Text boxes. A text box is a "fill in the blank"; it enables you to type text, such as the name of a file.

Option buttons. Also known as *radio buttons,* option buttons enable you to select only one option in a group. Click the desired option to turn it on and to turn any other selected option in the group off.

Check boxes. Check boxes enable you to turn an option on or off. Click in a check box to turn it on if it's off or off if it's on. You can select more than one check box in a group.

List box. A list box presents two or more options. Click the desired option. If the list is long, you'll see a scrollbar. Click the scrollbar arrows to move up or down in the list.

Drop-down list box. You'll see only one item when you first view this kind of list box. The rest of the items are hidden initially. Click the arrow to the right of the box to display the rest of the list and then click the desired item.

Spin box. A spin box is a text box with controls. You can usually type a setting in the text box or click the up or down arrow to change the setting in predetermined increments. For example, you might click the up arrow to increase a margin setting by .1 inch.

Slider. A slider is a control you can drag up, down, or from side to side to increase or decrease a setting. Sliders are commonly used to adjust speaker volume, hardware performance, and similar settings.

Command buttons. Most dialog boxes have at least three command buttons: **OK** to confirm your selections, **Cancel** to quit, and **Help** to get help.

Bypassing Menus by Using Toolbar Buttons

Although menus contain a comprehensive list of available options, they can be a bit clunky. To perform a task using a menu, you must click the menu name, hunt for the desired command, and select it. To help you bypass the menu system, most programs include *toolbars* that contain buttons for the most frequently used commands. To perform a task, you simply click the desired button, as shown in Figure 4.5.

Figure 4.5

Toolbars provide quick access to commonly used commands.

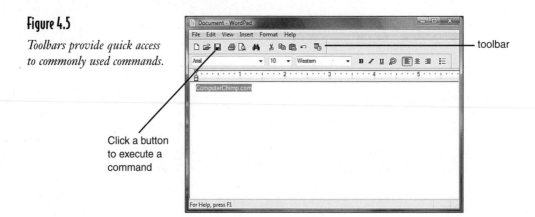

toolbar

Click a button
to execute a
command

Checking Out Some Windows Programs

Chances are good that your computer came loaded with all sorts of software. If you purchased a home PC, it probably came with Microsoft Works or some other program suite (package) and a couple computer games. But even if your computer wasn't garnished with additional programs, Windows has several programs you can use to write letters, draw pictures, play games, and perform other tasks.

To run any of these programs, click **Start, Programs** or **All Programs, Accessories,** and click the program you want to run (some programs are located on the All Programs menu, while others are located on the Accessories submenu or one of its submenus):

- **Games** is a group of simple computer games, including Solitaire. (You might find the Games submenu on the Programs or All Programs menu, rather than on the Accessories submenu.)

- **Windows Media Player** is basically an entertainment center that enables you to play audio and video clips, copy tracks off CDs, and burn your own custom CDs.

- **System Tools** is a collection of programs that help you maintain your system. These tools include a backup program, a program for fixing your hard disk, and a hard disk *defragmenter,* which can increase the speed of your disk. (See Chapter 31 for details.)

- **Calculator** displays an on-screen calculator to perform addition, subtraction, division, and multiplication.

♦ **Notepad** is a text editing program useful for typing notes and other brief documents.

♦ **Paint** is a graphics program for creating, editing, and printing pictures.

♦ **WordPad** is a more advanced word processing program that enables you to create fancier, longer documents.

Rearranging the Windows Inside Windows

Each time you run a program or open a document in Windows, a new window opens on your desktop. After several hours of work, your desktop can become as cluttered as a real desktop, making it difficult to find what you need. To switch to a window or reorganize the windows on the desktop, use any of the following tricks:

To quickly change to a window, click its button in the taskbar. If you can see any part of a window, click it to move it to the front of the stack. To quickly arrange the windows, right-click a blank area of the taskbar and, from the shortcut menu that appears, choose the desired arrangement.

To close a window (and exit the program), click the **Close** button (the one with the *X* on it) that's located in the upper-right corner of the window, as shown in Figure 4.6.

To increase the size of a window so it takes up the whole screen, click the **Maximize** button (just to the left of the **Close** button). The **Maximize** button then turns into a **Restore** button, which you can click to return the window to its previous size.

To shrink a window, click the **Minimize** button (two buttons to the left of the **Close** button). The minimized window appears as a button on the taskbar. Click the button on the taskbar to reopen the window.

To resize or reshape a window that's not at its maximum size, place your mouse pointer in the lower-right corner of the window and, when the pointer turns to a double-headed arrow, drag the corner of the window. (You can't resize a maximized window.)

> **Inside Tip** _____
>
> You can also double-click a window's title bar to maximize the window or restore it to its previous size.

To move a window, drag its title bar. (You can't move a maximized window because it takes up the whole screen.)

Figure 4.6

You can close, maximize, and resize windows.

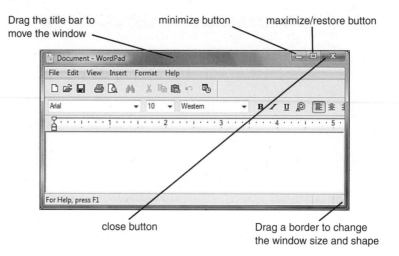

Drag the title bar to move the window

minimize button

maximize/restore button

close button

Drag a border to change the window size and shape

You can also control your windows from the taskbar. Whenever you run a program, a button for it appears in the taskbar. The button acts like a toggle switch; click the program's button to open the program's window, and click it again to hide the program's window. Right-click a program's button to display options for minimizing, maximizing, restoring, moving, resizing, or closing the program's window.

Computer Cheat

To minimize all open windows and return to the desktop in a hurry, click the **Show Desktop** button (in the taskbar to the right of the Start button). Click the button again to bring all those windows back into view. To do the same thing with your keyboard, press **Windows+D**.

Seeing More with Scrollbars

If a window cannot display everything it contains, a scrollbar appears along the right side or bottom of the window. The scrollbar on the right enables you to scroll up and down; the scrollbar at the bottom lets you scroll left and right. You can use the scrollbar to bring the hidden contents of the window into view, as follows (see Figure 4.7).

Click once inside the scrollbar, on either side of the scroll box, to move the view one windowful at a time. For example, if you click once below the scroll box, you'll see the next windowful of information.

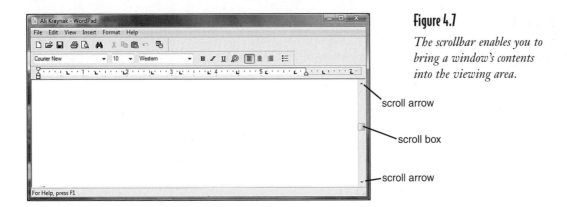

scroll arrow

scroll box

scroll arrow

Move the mouse pointer over the scroll box, hold down the mouse button, and drag the box to the area of the window you want to view. For example, to move to the middle of the window's contents, drag the scroll box to the middle of the bar.

With the mouse pointer over the up or down scroll arrow, hold down the mouse button to scroll continuously in that direction. The insertion point remains in place when you scroll, so you can press the right or left arrow key to return to where you were.

The Least You Need to Know

♦ When you start your computer, Windows presents you with an electronic desktop on which you do all your work.

♦ The Start button gives you access to everything you need on your computer.

♦ When you choose an option that's followed by three dots, Windows displays a dialog box asking for additional information.

♦ Three buttons appear in the upper-right corner of every window. Use these buttons to open, close, or quickly hide (minimize) or restore the window.

♦ To move a window that's not maximized, drag its title bar. To manually resize a window, drag its lower-right corner.

♦ To scroll up or down in a window, click the scroll arrows at the top or bottom of the scrollbar, drag the scroll box, or click inside the scrollbar above or below the scroll box.

Chapter 5

Navigating Windows Vista

In This Chapter

♦ Vista's cool new features

♦ A tour of Vista's new desktop

♦ What's already on your computer?

♦ Shutting down Windows and your PC the right way

Windows Vista is different enough from its predecessors (Windows XP, NT, 2000, and Me) to earn it a chapter of its very own. The good news is that it's more intuitive to use, especially if you're not already accustomed to using an earlier version of Windows. The other good news is that Vista is packed with a host of new features designed to enhance your computing experience, including speech recognition, media tools, a sidebar with gadgets, and so on.

This chapter introduces you to the latest, greatest features and shows you how to make the most of them while highlighting differences in how you perform more traditional tasks in Vista.

What's New in Vista?

Most new computers are being shipped with Windows Vista already installed on them, and Microsoft is working hard to convince users of older versions of Windows to upgrade. In addition to all the new bells and whistles, Windows Vista is designed to make optimum use of the latest technology to make computers, especially new computers, run faster and more reliably.

Whether you're already running Vista or are considering upgrading to it, the following sections get you up to speed on Vista's most attractive new features.

> ### Whoa!
>
> Before you run out and purchase the Windows Vista upgrade, be sure your computer is properly equipped to run it. Check the box for minimum hardware requirements or visit **www.microsoft.com/windowsxp/pro/upgrading/checkcompat.mspx** to download the Windows Vista Upgrade Advisor to determine whether your computer is Vista-ready.

Renovated Desktop

You'll recognize most of the items on the desktop, including the **Start** button, taskbar, and Recycle Bin, but the overall appearance of Windows Vista is slicker, more transparent, and more three-dimensional. If you have multiple windows open, for example, you can click the **Switch between Windows** button in the taskbar to display the windows in 3D, as shown in Figure 5.1. You can then click the window you want to go to.

You may also notice that the application windows (or at least their title bars) are somewhat transparent, so you can see what's behind them. If you have a mouse with a mouse wheel between the buttons, you can rotate the wheel to scroll through the stack of windows.

When you rest the mouse pointer on a taskbar button in Vista, a thumbnail view of the application's window pops up so you can preview the window's contents before switching to it.

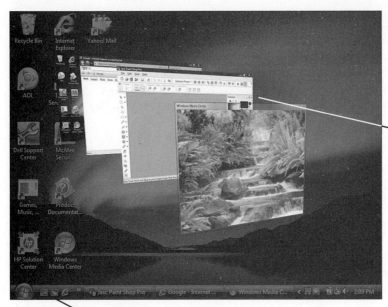

Figure 5.1

In Vista, your desktop is three dimensional.

Click the desired Window

Click Switch between Windows

Powerful Tools for Finding Stuff

Vista makes browsing and finding your files, folders, and programs much easier. If you know what you're looking for but don't know where it is on your computer, click the **Start** button, click in the **Start Search** box, and type a unique word or phrase contained in the item you're looking for. For example, you might type "paint" to find programs that have the word *paint* in their title. The items that match your search appear on the Start menu, as shown in Figure 5.2, from which you can select them.

When you open a disk or folder, the window that appears provides a Search option (in the upper-right corner of the window) you can use to have Vista help you track down a misplaced file or folder. If you perform a search and Vista doesn't locate what you're looking for, click **Advanced Search** to display additional controls for broadening and clarifying your search. (For more about using Vista's search tools, see Chapter 11.)

Figure 5.2

Vista can help you locate mis-placed items.

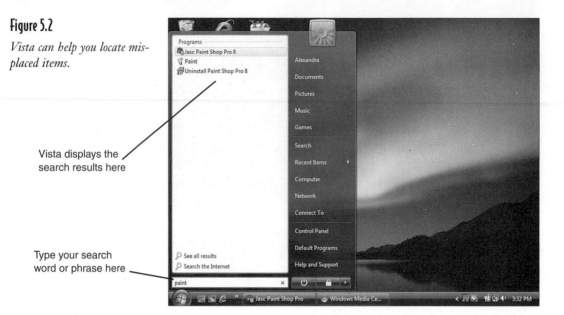

Vista displays the
search results here

Type your search
word or phrase here

Beefed-Up Media Features

Windows Vista supports the latest trends in media, enabling you to use your PC as a media center as well as a computer. With Windows Vista and the necessary hardware, you can watch TV on your computer (assuming the video card is equipped with a TV tuner), and record your favorite shows, download and edit digital photos, and store and play all your favorite tunes.

Check it out by running the Windows Media Center. Click **Start, All Programs, Windows Media Center.** The Media Center appears, as shown in Figure 5.3. Click the desired media type and then the option for playing it. You can scroll through the media types by resting the mouse pointer above or below the list of media types: Pictures + Videos, Music, TV + Movies, and Online Media.

After you've highlighted the type of media you want to play, you can move the mouse pointer to the right side of the window to scroll your play options. (To scroll back, move the mouse pointer to the left side of the window.) You can then click the desired option. (For more about working with digital media, check out the chapters in Part 5.)

Click here to return to the opening screen

Point here to scroll media types up

Click the desired option

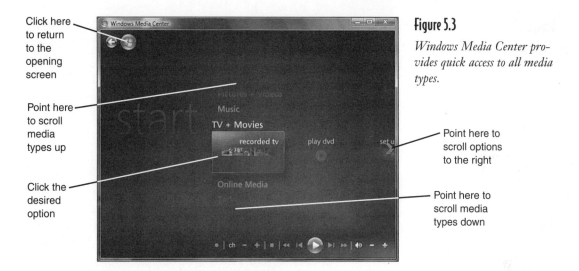

Point here to scroll options to the right

Point here to scroll media types down

Figure 5.3

Windows Media Center provides quick access to all media types.

Improved Digital Photo Management

Managing digital photos in older versions of Windows was anything but a pleasant experience. In Vista, all that has changed. Simply plug your digital camera into your computer, and Vista prompts you to download your photos to your Picture folder. From there, you can use the Windows Photo Gallery to view photos, crop, apply red-eye correction, correct the brightness and contrast, print, and share your photos. (For more about working with digital photos, see Chapter 28.)

Tightened Security

Vista has several built-in security features designed to automatically block unauthorized access to your computer over the Internet, prevent infection from computer viruses, and block Internet adware and spyware. You can check out Vista's beefed-up security features by visiting the Security Center; click **Start, Control Panel, Security.** (Chapter 26 shows you how to make the most of the security features in Windows.)

New Internet Explorer Web Browser

In Chapter 20, you learn how to use a web browser to explore interactive, multimedia "pages" on the Internet. Vista features a new Internet Explorer window that enables you to explore the Internet more securely and flip through several open pages by clicking tabs. I don't want to spoil the mystery, so I'll hold off on revealing the new Internet Explorer until Chapter 20.

New Sidebar and Gadgets

The new sidebar in Windows Vista provides quick access to customizable mini-applications (called *gadgets*), which include weather updates, news headlines, late-breaking sports scores, your personal calendar, a calculator, and other often-used features and tools.

Inside Tip

The new Internet Explorer isn't all that special. If you're using Windows XP, and you upgraded to the latest Internet Explorer, you'll see that your browser looks and functions almost identically.

By default, the sidebar is off. To turn it on, choose **Start, Control Panel, Appearance and Personalization, Windows Sidebar Properties.** Be sure Start Sidebar When Windows Starts is checked. You can also specify the desired location of the sidebar. Click **OK.** After returning to the Control Panel, click **Add Gadgets to Sidebar.** Your Windows desktop should now look something like Figure 5.4.

Figure 5.4

Vista's sidebar provides quick access to information.

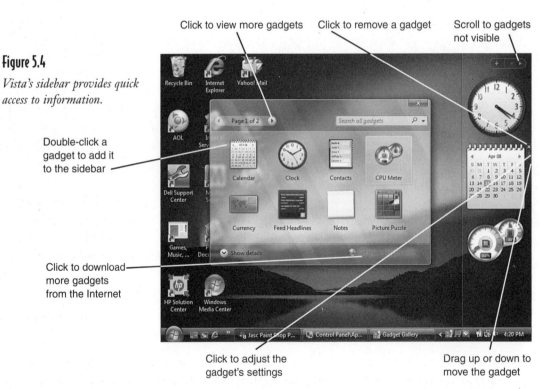

Click to view more gadgets   Click to remove a gadget   Scroll to gadgets not visible

Double-click a gadget to add it to the sidebar

Click to download more gadgets from the Internet

Click to adjust the gadget's settings

Drag up or down to move the gadget

You can now double-click a gadget to add it to the sidebar, point to a gadget and click the X button to remove it, point to a gadget and drag its handle up or down to move it, or point to a gadget and click the wrench button to adjust its settings. To hide the sidebar, right-click a blank area inside the sidebar and click **Close Sidebar;** you can right-click the **Windows Sidebar** button in the system tray (at the right end of the taskbar) and click **Open** to bring the sidebar back into view.

New Backup Utility

Everyone tells you to back up the files on your computer, but Windows XP offers a shoddy backup utility. Vista improves the backup capabilities of Windows, enabling you to back up your files to recordable CDs or DVDs, external hard drives, and other backup media.

To back up or restore files on your computer, click **Start, All Programs, Maintenance, Backup and Restore Center.** Follow the Vista's on-screen instructions to complete the backup.

Whoa!

If you think a file has been lost or damaged, don't panic and immediately restore all files from your backups. You could lose a lot of data that way, replacing new files with older versions. Instead, follow the techniques in Chapter 11 to try to locate any lost files. If your computer isn't working right, you might be able to use the System Restore utility discussed in Chapter 32 to get it back up and running without having to restore backups.

More Robust Speech-Recognition Capabilities

If you'd rather bark out commands than point and click with a mouse, Windows Vista can accommodate your preference. Equip your computer with a microphone, train Vista to tune its ear to your voice, and you're ready to enter commands and type without touching your keyboard or mouse. The more you use the feature, the better it works!

To turn on Vista's speech-recognition feature and start training Vista to recognize your voice, click **Start, Control Panel, Ease of Access, Start Speech Recognition,** and follow Vista's lead.

Training Vista to recognize your speech can be very time-consuming and somewhat frustrating. If Vista suggests taking the training tutorial, take it. Otherwise, you're likely to be completely lost.

Windows SideShow

Windows SideShow enables a computer to display critical information on a secondary or auxiliary screen, whether the computer is on, off, or in sleep mode. In other words, you don't have to power up your computer to view meeting schedules, phone numbers, addresses, or recent e-mail messages or catch up on the latest news. This saves you gobs of time and conserves battery power (on notebook PCs) at the same time. Of course, you need a device that supports Windows SideShow—look for the Windows SideShow logo on the device.

Inside Tip _____

Some devices such as keyboards and computer cases have mini-displays built right into them that support SideShow. This enables the user to quickly check for incoming e-mail, pull up a list of contacts, or check a schedule without having to switch to a different program on the main display.

For more about SideShow, search the Windows Help System for SideShow.

Tightened Parental Controls

Previous versions of Windows came equipped with Parental Controls to help parents prevent their children from accessing inappropriate material online or having such content pushed to their children. The new and improved Parental Controls in Vista enable parents to control their children's access to video games, as well … at least the video games they play on the computer. (For more about setting up Parental Controls, visit Chapter 26.)

Mobility Center

If you have Vista installed on a portable PC (notebook or tablet PC), you can access the Mobility Center as a one-stop location for all the settings you may need to change, depending on your location. From the Mobility Center, shown in Figure 5.5, you can change the screen brightness, volume, power plan, wireless network connection, external display settings (if you have another monitor connected), and sync settings.

Figure 5.5

The Mobility Center provides access to the notebook settings you may need to change most often.

To access the Mobility Center, do one of the following:

◆ Click **Start, Control Panel, Mobile PC, Windows Mobility Center.**

◆ Click the battery icon on the right end of the taskbar and click **Windows Mobility Center.**

◆ Hold down the Windows key while pressing **X.**

Added Support for Tablet PCs

Tablet PCs are pretty nifty devices. They're sort of like notebook PCs, but the screen pivots 180 degrees and allows you to fold it back on the unit, so you can use your PC as a notepad. In addition, most tablet PCs have a touch-screen monitor, so you can select commands by touching them on the screen. With Vista's handwriting recognition capabilities, you can also handwrite notes on the screen and Vista will convert it into typed text.

Vista comes equipped with much greater support for tablet PCs, including improved handwriting recognition, the ability to navigate and perform shortcuts with your pen, and an on-screen keyboard you can use to "type" using your pen (instead of your tablet PC's keyboard).

Inside Tip _____

Tablet PCs are excellent tools for real estate professionals, attorneys, and others who need clients to sign contracts and other documents. You can have the client sign right on the screen and immediately e-mail or fax the documents to the desired destination. Graphic artists may also find them useful because you can draw right on the screen.

For more tablet-PC-specific tools, including Sticky Notes, a Tablet PC Input Panel, and Windows Journal, click **Start, All Programs, Accessories, Tablet PC.**

Improved Synchronization of Devices

Whenever you need to share stuff that's on your computer with other computers, devices, or people, you always run the risk of overwriting newer files with older ones, which is never a good thing. Vista features improved sync and sharing tools to prevent accidental overwrites from occurring. With Vista, you can quickly sync the data between two devices quickly, easily, and securely.

To check out the Vista's new Sync Center, click **Start, All Programs, Accessories, Sync Center.** Press F1 to explore the Windows Help System for instructions on how to set up devices you want to sync with your PC. (In Chapter 27, I show you how to sync the media files on your computer with a portable media player.)

> ### Whoa!
>
> Windows Vista uses the sync capabilities of the device to coordinate the sync operation, so it's impossible to predict exactly how a sync session will take place. Your best option is to run the Sync Center and follow the on-screen clues to figure it out for yourself. Chapter 27 demonstrates one example, but it may not match what you experience. In any event, don't go in expecting it to be easy.

Networking Improvements

Networking and sharing printers, broadband Internet, files, and other resources between two or more computers have become a whole lot easier and more secure with Windows Vista. Vista can detect and automatically set up networking connections for just about any wireless network, including those at public hotspots, with very little input from you.

> ### Inside Tip
>
> Windows Vista is *scalable;* that is, it automatically takes an inventory of your system hardware and scales its fancy graphics features and other advanced features to the capabilities of the available hardware.

To check out Vista's networking tools, click **Start, Control Panel, Network and Internet.** (For details about networking, check out Chapter 12.)

Exploring Your Computer

Vista provides access to everything stored on your computer—disks, programs, documents, music, photos, games, and so on—through Windows Explorer. To start exploring your computer, click the **Start** button. On the right side of the Start menu are the items you can explore: Documents, Pictures, Music, Games, Computer, Network, Control Panel, Default Programs, and so on.

At the very top of the list, you should see your name (or the name of whoever's currently logged in to Windows); Windows stores all the files you save in this folder or one of its subfolders, unless you tell it to save the file somewhere else. See Figure 5.6.

Click the Back button to back up to the previous screen

Click a button to perform the desired task on the selected item

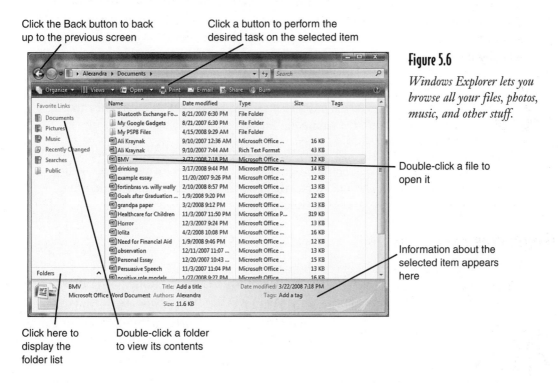

Figure 5.6

Windows Explorer lets you browse all your files, photos, music, and other stuff.

Double-click a file to open it

Information about the selected item appears here

Click here to display the folder list

Double-click a folder to view its contents

In the lower left of the Explorer window is a Folders button with an upward pointing arrow on it. Click the button to display a folder list. You can then choose folders and subfolders in the folder list to have the contents of the selected folder displayed in the pane on the right.

Getting Help

In this chapter, and throughout this book, I show you how to access features and tools in Windows Vista and perform specific tasks, but I can't possibly show you everything there is to know about Vista. I can, however, show you how to get that information for yourself—via the Windows Help System.

You can access help in any number of ways. My favorite is to get to the point at which I'm completely clueless and then press the F1 key. This displays *context-sensitive help*—information about what you're currently in the middle of doing.

Inside Tip _____

To browse Help rather than search for a specific topic, display the Windows Help and Support window and click the Browse Help button—it's the button that has the blue book icon on it.

If you don't know where to begin, click **Start, Help and Support.** This opens an Explorer window that provides several help options, including Windows Basics, Table of Contents, Troubleshooting, and What's New? A search box near the top of the window allows you to look for specific information. You'll also see an Ask button you can click to ask someone for help.

To learn how to perform a common task for the first time, visit the Windows Welcome Center—click **Start, All Programs, Accessories, Welcome Center.**

Shutting Down

As discussed in Chapter 3, you can set up Windows to automatically power down your computer after a certain amount of time passes when it hasn't been used. However, you may want to manually power down your computer if you're sure you won't be using it for a while.

The easiest way to power down your PC with Windows Vista is to click **Start** and then **Power,** as shown in Figure 5.7. Vista saves all your work and puts your system in Sleep mode (assuming your computer supports Sleep mode), so it uses very little power. To turn it back on and return to where you were before shutting down, press and release your computer's power button.

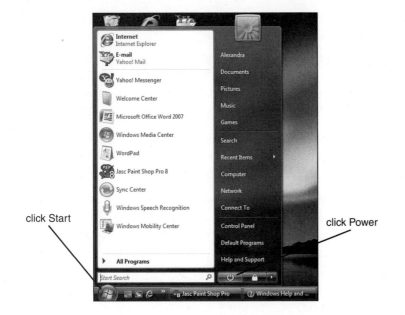

click Start

click Power

Figure 5.7

Windows Vista can power down your PC safely for you.

If you have a notebook PC, you can usually power down simply by closing its lid.

In most cases, using the Windows Power button is the fastest, easiest way to shut down your PC and restart quickly. Don't worry about the possibility that not shutting down the power completely will drain your notebook's battery; if the power does drop below a certain level, Vista will save everything to the hard drive and power down.

If you're installing hardware inside the PC or connect a device that does not support hot plug and play (safely connecting a device when the power is on), shut down completely. To do this, click **Start,** point to the arrow in the lower-right corner of the Start menu, and click **Shut Down.**

> **Whoa!**
>
> If you're plugging something into a USB port, you usually don't have to shut down the computer first, but you should shut it down if you're connecting a non-USB printer, monitor, or other device.

The Least You Need to Know

◆ Windows Vista has plenty of cool new features, so explore your system to take full advantage of them.

♦ To locate anything on your computer, click **Start,** click in the **Start Search** box, type your search word or phrase, and press Enter.

♦ To browse your files, click **Start** and then click your name in the upper right corner of the **Start** menu.

♦ To access the contents of one of your disks, click **Start, Computer,** and double-click the disk icon.

♦ You can get context-sensitive help at any time by pressing the F1 button. To get more help, click **Start, Help and Support.**

♦ To properly power down your computer, click **Start** and **Power.**

Chapter 6

Windows XP, Up Close and Personal

In This Chapter

- ◆ The Windows XP desktop
- ◆ What's available on the Start menu
- ◆ Poking around on your computer
- ◆ Shutting down at the end of the day

Although Windows Vista is the latest, greatest version of Windows, its predecessor, Windows XP, still runs on plenty of computers. Many people are perfectly happy with it and see no need to spend over a hundred bucks to bump up to a newer version that might not be able to run on or work with their older computer and peripheral devices. I can't say I blame them. If you're one of the holdouts, this chapter is for you.

This chapter brings you up to speed on Windows XP basics. Later chapters show you how to perform specific tasks in Windows (both XP and Vista), so you can expect to learn much more as you proceed.

Touring XP's Desktop

When you first start your computer, Windows may prompt you to sign in using your user name and password. (For more about user names, refer to Chapter 10.) After you sign in, the Windows XP *desktop* greets you—a wide open landscape dotted with several *icons* (small pictures), as shown in Figure 6.1. Along the bottom of the screen is a blue strip called the *taskbar*.

Figure 6.1

Initially, the Windows desktop is sparsely populated.

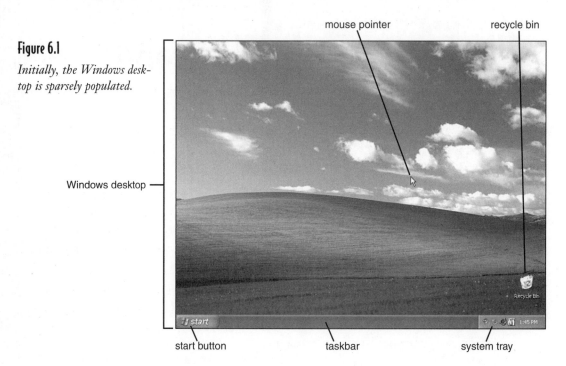

mouse pointer   recycle bin

Windows desktop

start button   taskbar   system tray

On the left end of the taskbar is the all-important **Start** button, which opens a menu containing the names of all the programs installed on your computer.

The icons you see on your desktop might differ, depending on how you or the manufacturer installed Windows and on whether you have additional programs.

Exploring the Start Menu

The Start button is your key to just about everything on your computer, as shown in Figure 6.2.

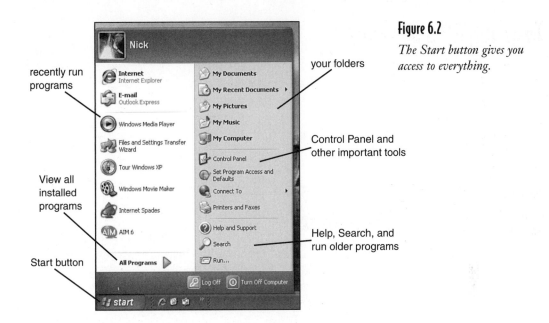

Figure 6.2
The Start button gives you access to everything.

To introduce yourself to your Start button, click **Start,** point to **All Programs,** and view the commands for running all the programs installed on your computer. (For more about installing and running programs, visit Chapter 8.) As you run programs, Windows adds their names to the left side of the Start menu to give you quick access to them later.

In the upper-right section of the Start menu are icons you can click to gain access to your documents, pictures, music, computer, and network places. When you click one of these icons, Windows opens the folder associated with the icon. (You'll find out more about folders in Chapter 7.)

In the middle-right section of the Start menu are icons for checking and configuring your computer. The Control Panel, for example, enables you to change hardware and printer settings, configure security settings, and access performance-boosting tools.

In the lower-right section of the Start menu are options for obtaining help, searching your computer for files or folders, and running older programs via typed commands (something you probably won't do very often).

Flipping from One Program to Another

Whenever you run a program, a button for that program appears in the taskbar. These buttons help you keep multiple programs running and quickly switch from one program to another.

If you prefer to use the keyboard to switch programs, hold down the **Alt** key while pressing the **Tab** key repeatedly to highlight the icon for the desire program and then release both keys.

Inside Tip _____

For quick access to commands that enable you to control a program's window, right-click its button in the taskbar. This displays a pop-up menu with several options, including options to close the window.

Exploring Your Computer

Your computer has a lot of stuff on it, and the more you use it, the more stuff it'll accumulate—programs you install, music you record, documents you create, photos you upload, and so on. Fortunately, Windows provides the navigational tools you need to access all these items.

You've already met the Start menu, which provides access to all of your programs. In the following section, you discover how to access disk drives, folders, and files using Windows Explorer and how to access system settings and utilities using the Control Panel.

Disk Drives, Folders, and Files

In Windows, you can access your disk drives, folders, and files, using either of two tools:

My tool of choice is *My Computer.* To open it, double-click the **My Computer** icon on the Windows desktop or click **Start, My Computer,** or you can just press **Windows+E.** This displays a window containing icons for all the disks installed on your computer and several important folders. You can double-click a disk or folder icon to display the contents of the selected disk or folder.

Windows Explorer is a two-paned window that displays a directory tree (list of disks and folders on the left) and a file list (the contents of the selected disk or folder) on the right, as shown in Figure 6.3. To display Windows Explorer, right-click the My Computer icon (on the desktop or Start menu) and click Explore.

Select a disk or folder here

View the contents of the
selected disk or folder here

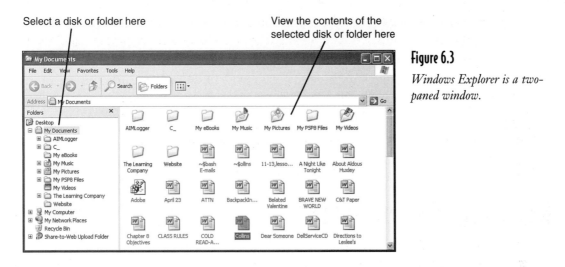

Figure 6.3

Windows Explorer is a two-paned window.

You can explore other objects. For example, click the **Start** button and click **Explore** to see what happens.

Accessing the Windows Control Panel

The Windows Control Panel is packed with tools to customize, optimize, and configure your computer. Using the tools in the Control Panel, you can install and remove programs, install new hardware, give your display a whole new look, configure your mouse and keyboard to suit your tastes, network with other computers, and much more.

To display the Control Panel, click **Start, Control Panel.** The Control Panel appears, as shown in Figure 6.4.

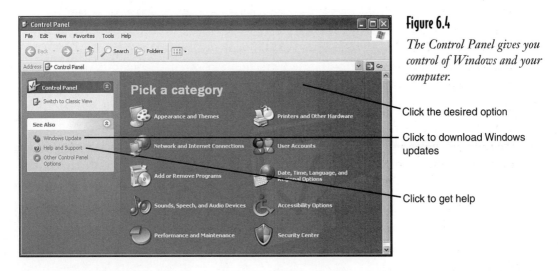

Figure 6.4

The Control Panel gives you control of Windows and your computer.

Click the desired option

Click to download Windows updates

Click to get help

Getting Help in Windows XP

Throughout this book, I show you how to perform specific computer-related tasks in both Windows Vista and XP, so you'll receive plenty of step-by-step instructions for the most common Windows-related tasks. Because of the limited amount of space in this book, however, I can't show you everything. For more coverage, I can only recommend *The Complete Idiot's Guide to Microsoft Windows Vista* by Paul McFedries (an excellent writer, by the way).

Another option is to rely on the Windows help system for more detailed instruction. You can access Windows help in any number of ways, including the following:

◆ For context-sensitive help (assistance for the task you're currently performing), press the **F1** key.

> **Inside Tip**
>
> Near the top of the Help and Support window is a Search box. Click in the box, type one or more words that best describe the help you need, and press Enter. This displays a list of topics that match your search; hopefully, one of the items contains the information you need.

◆ If you don't know where to begin, click **Start, Help and Support.** This opens an Explorer window that provides several help options. On the left is a list of Help topics. On the right are options that enable you to ask for specific help, get help performing common tasks, and Did You Know? which provides some additional tips.

◆ Take a tour. One of the best ways to discover what Windows has to offer is to take the Windows Tour. Click **Start, All Programs, Applications, Tour Windows XP,** and follow the on-screen instructions to start the tour.

Shutting Down

In Chapter 3, I showed you how to select a Windows power scheme to have Windows power down and perhaps even automatically shut down your computer after several minutes (or hours) of inactivity. You may need to (or want to) shut down your computer yourself, however—for example, if you're done using the computer or need to install new hardware that requires your computer to be off.

To shut down your computer or put it in Stand By mode (a low-power state), save any files you've been working on in other programs (using the program's **File, Save** command), click the **Start** button, and choose one of the following options:

- **Stand By** to put Windows and your computer in a low-power state.

- **Shift+Stand By** to place Windows in Hibernation mode.

- **Shut Down** or **Turn Off Computer** to safely power down Windows, so you can turn your computer off. (Your computer may turn itself off after you choose this option.)

Inside Tip

What's the difference between Stand By and Hibernate modes? In Stand By, your computer remains on, for the most part, although some components, such as the hard drive, may be turned off. Your computer is ready to jump into action at a moment's notice. In Hibernate mode, Windows saves everything to the hard drive first and then shuts down the computer. Restarting from Hibernate mode takes more time.

The Least You Need to Know

- The Windows Start button gives you access to everything on your computer.

- To run a program, click **Start, All Programs,** and click the program you want to run (it may be on a submenu).

- When multiple programs are running, you can switch to a program by clicking its button in the taskbar.

- To browse for a file, click **Start** and then one of the folder icons in the upper-right quadrant of the Start menu.

- To get context-sensitive help, press the **F1** key.

- To shut down Windows, click **Start, Shut Down** or **Turn Off Computer.**

Chapter 7

Managing Disks, Folders, and Files

In This Chapter

- ◆ Drives A, C, D, and sometimes B
- ◆ Feed your disk drive
- ◆ Explore disks, folders, and files in Windows
- ◆ Cut, copy, move, and dump files and folders

Your computer comes complete with a well-stocked library of instructions and data that it uses to function, to help you do your job, to keep you entertained, and to play games. This library is stored on various disks inside the computer. The hard disk (or *fixed disk*), which you never see, is built into the system unit. Other disks, called *removable disks*, reside outside the computer; these consist of CDs (compact discs), DVDs (digital video discs), flash drives, and other disks (and discs) you insert into your computer to transfer data to or from your computer.

In this chapter, you learn everything you need to know about disks and drives, including how to insert and remove disks; recognize a drive by its letter; keep your disks, CDs, and DVDs in good condition; and explore and manipulate the files and folders stored on your disks.

Disk Drives: Easy as A-B-C

Your computer assigns a letter to each drive to identify it. The computer shown in Figure 7.1 has three drives: A, C, and D. Newer computers generally don't come with a floppy drive A, but they often include *flash drives*, which you'll learn about later. These drives might show up as E, F, G, or some other letter, depending on the number of drives your computer has.

Figure 7.1

Your computer uses letters from the alphabet to name its disk drives.

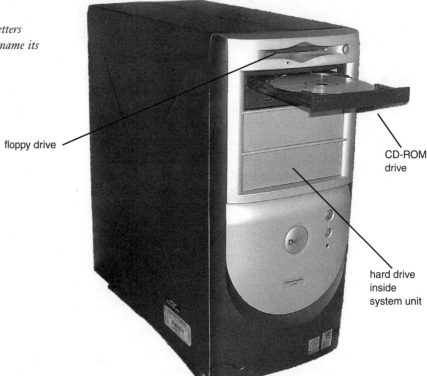

floppy drive

CD-ROM drive

hard drive inside system unit

The Floppy Drives: A (and Sometimes B)

Your computer's system unit may have one or more slits or openings on the front, into which you can insert a disk. The slit may be horizontal or vertical, depending on how your system is set up. This is your computer's floppy disk drive. Your computer typically refers to this drive as drive A. If your computer has two floppy drives, one is drive A and the other is B.

If your computer has no floppy drive, don't panic—you might not need it. Many manufacturers exclude floppy drives from their PCs, because most programs are now distributed on CDs or DVDs or by download from the Internet.

The Hard Disk Drive: C

The drive inside the computer is the internal hard disk drive, usually called drive C. With hard drives you don't handle the disk; it's hermetically sealed inside the drive.

> **Inside Tip**
>
> A hard disk drive can be partitioned (or divided) into one or more drives, which the computer refers to as drive C, drive D, drive E, and so on. The actual hard disk drive is called the physical drive; each partition is called a logical drive. If you encounter a computer that displays letters for more than one hard drive, the computer could have multiple hard drives or a single drive partitioned into several logical drives. In some cases, the manufacturer places a copy of all the original software, including Windows, on a small partition as a backup instead of supplying the software on discs.

The CD-ROM, CD-RW, or DVD Drive: D

A CD-ROM (Compact Disc-Read Only Memory) is standard equipment on every new computer. It typically is located on the front of the system unit above or below the floppy drive, and the computer usually refers to it as drive D. A standard CD-ROM drive can only read data from discs—it cannot write data to discs. However, most computers feature disc drives with more advanced functions.

The CD or DVD drive should be clearly labeled as CD or DVD. Additional designations, such as CD-RW (CD-ReWritable) and DVD-R (DVD-Recordable) are used if the disc drive supports more advanced functions. *Recordable* means you can record to the disc once. *ReWritable* means the drive can record over data, erase data, and write data to the disc many times, making it a better choice for backups. Most DVD drives can handle CDs, too, but CD drives can't handle DVDs.

> **Whoa!**
>
> Be sure you purchase the right discs. If you have a ReWritable drive, for example, you need to purchase ReWritable discs to be able to store data on the discs, erase it, and store new data on it.

Using Floppy Disks

Floppy disks are nearly obsolete, because their storage capacity maxes out at about 1.5 megabytes. That's like having a car with a gas tank that can hold 1 quart of gas. If your computer has a floppy drive, you're more than likely to never use it. I only mention them here in case you're wondering what that small, dusty slit on the front of your computer is for.

One thing you should know is that it's best to have all floppy drives empty before starting your computer, so your computer doesn't get caught up trying to find its start-up instructions on the floppy disk. Before you fire up your computer, press the eject button on the floppy drive to eject any disk it may have in it.

Loading and Unloading CDs and DVDs

If you've ever loaded a compact disc into your audio CD player or a DVD into your DVD player, you have all the technical expertise required to load discs into your computer's CD or DVD drive. Just be sure to handle the disc only by its edges so you don't scratch the surface or get any dirt or fingerprints on it. The technique for loading a disc in a CD or DVD drive differs depending on the drive:

◆ If the drive has an open slot on the front, slide the disk, shiny side down, into the slot, just as you would insert a coin in a pop machine.

◆ If the drive has a drive tray, press the load/eject button on the front of the drive to open it, and then lay the disc in the tray and press the load/eject button to load the disc. (Don't push the tray in to close it, as this may damage the loading mechanism.)

Inside Tip _____

If you ever have trouble playing a CD or DVD, the disc might be dirty. To clean the disc, wipe it off with a soft, lint-free cloth from the center of the disc out to its edges, never in a circular motion. (Wipe the side without the picture or printing on it, because this is the side that the drive reads; some discs are two-sided.) If something sticky gets on the disc, dampen the cloth with a little distilled water and wipe it dry. Let the disc dry thoroughly before inserting it into the drive.

Windows starts to play the disc as soon as you insert it, but how it plays the disk may not match how you want Windows to play the disc. If Windows doesn't "know" what to do, it displays a dialog box asking you to specify what you want to do and providing a list of actions from which to choose. Below the list is an checkbox option **Always Do the Selected Action;** click this before selecting an action if you want Windows to perform this same action without asking for your confirmation later.

If Windows automatically performs the wrong action on this type of disc, you can specify a different action to take by adjusting the AutoPlay settings. To access the AutoPlay settings, take one of the following steps, depending on the version of Windows you're running.

In Windows Vista: Click **Start, Control Panel, Hardware and Sound, AutoPlay.** Next to the type of disc whose AutoPlay settings you want to change, open the drop-down list and click the action you want Windows to perform whenever a disc of this type is inserted, as shown in Figure 7.2.

In Windows XP: Insert the type of disc for which you want to change the AutoPlay settings. Click **Start, My Computer,** and right-click your CD or DVD drive icon and click **AutoPlay.**

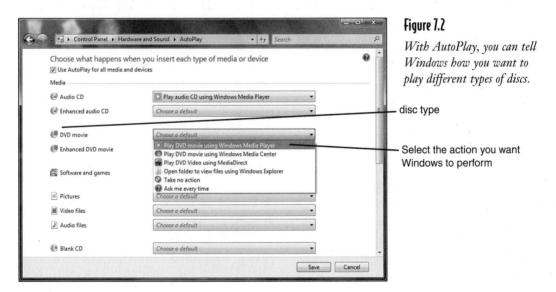

Figure 7.2

With AutoPlay, you can tell Windows how you want to play different types of discs.

— disc type

— Select the action you want
Windows to perform

The Hard Disk

The hard disk drive is like a big floppy drive complete with a nonfloppy disk. (You don't take the disk out; it stays in the drive forever.) A small hard disk drive can store more than 20 gigabytes (GB), the equivalent of about 15,000 3$\frac{1}{2}$-inch, high-density floppy disks. Many new computers come with hard drives that can store more than

100 gigabytes! Sound excessive? Well, 100 gigabytes is excessive if you plan on using your computer to play games and do a little work; if you plan on editing video and storing photo albums on your computer, however, your computer can gobble up a gigabyte in a hurry.

To get information to the hard disk, you copy information to it from floppy disks, CDs, DVDs, or Internet sites, or you save the files you create directly to the hard disk. The information stays on the hard disk until you erase the information. When the computer needs information, it goes directly to the hard disk, reads the information into memory, and continues working.

External Drives and Other Anomalies

Although the hard disk, CD-ROM, and floppy disk drives round out the team lineup for standard drives, other types of disk drives have been and continue to be popular additions to computer systems. Some of these drives are installed in the *drive bays* inside the system unit and appear alongside the floppy and CD-ROM drives, whereas others sit outside the system unit, like your printer, and connect to the system unit with a USB cable or other type of cable (or a wireless connection).

Iomega Zip drives store data on 100 MB, 250 MB, or 750 MB removable disks. These drives are excellent for doing small backups and for storing presentations that you need to take on the road. (Keep in mind that to use Zip disks, your computer must be equipped with a Zip drive.)

External hard drives sit outside the computer and connect to the system unit by a data cable. The extra drive typically is assigned a letter that comes later in the alphabet, such as E or F.

USB flash drives are small enough to fit on a keychain and plug right into your computer's USB port. They typically store 1 GB or more each and are great for carrying around audio clips, digital images, and other files. Before removing a flash drive from a USB port, click the **Safely remove hardware** icon in the lower-right corner of the screen and then click the device you want to remove so you won't lose information stored on the flash drive.

Compact flash drives are used primarily in digital cameras and printers designed to print digital photos. The cards are smaller but a little fatter than a credit card and generally store anywhere from 512 MB to several gigabytes of data.

Tape drives are more similar to audio-cassette players than they are to disk drives. Tape drives are primarily used to back up data. They're too slow for most other purposes.

What's on a Disk? Files and Folders

Your computer uses four types of files: *data files*, *media files*, *program files*, and *system files*. Data files are the files you create and save—your business letters, reports, the pictures you draw, the results of any games you save. Media files can be anything from digital photos to audio recordings, including music, to video clips. Program files are the files you get when you purchase a program. These files contain the instructions that tell your computer how to run the program. A program can consist of hundreds of interrelated files. System files contain the instructions that your computer and operating system need to function. In most cases, you don't want to mess with system files, so by default Windows usually keeps them hidden.

To manage all these files, your computer stores the files in separate folders (also called *directories*). Whenever you install a program, the installation utility (which places the program on your hard disk) automatically creates a folder for the program.

Before you lay your fingers on any folders or files, you should understand how the folders are structured. Think of your disk as an oversize filing cabinet stuffed with manila folders. Each folder represents a directory that stores files or additional folders. The structure of the folders comprises what's called a *directory tree*, which looks a little like a family tree, as shown in Figure 7.3. The drive letter always sits atop the directory tree; the drive letter is considered the *root directory*. Folders then branch off from the root directory. Programs often display the location of a file as a *path* to the directory or folder in which the file is saved.

For example, if Tom's My Documents folder contains a file named taxes.doc, the path to the file would be as follows:

```
c:\documents and settings\tom\my documents\taxes.doc
```

The path begins at the root (drive C), proceeds through the first folder to the second folder, through the third folder, and specifies the file name. Paths can be shorter or much longer, of course.

Figure 7.3

Directory tree.

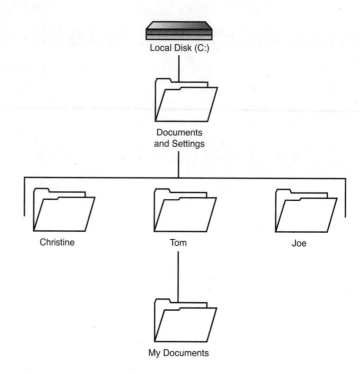

Exploring Your Disks and Folders

As you saw in Chapters 5 and 6, Windows provides you with a tool that enables you to browse and manage the disks, folders, and files on your computer—Windows Explorer. You simply click the **Start** button and then click or double-click the folder where you want to begin your exploration: Documents, Pictures, Music, or Computer. (In Windows XP, these are labeled My Documents, My Pictures, and so on.)

To obtain more information about how to explore your disks, folders, and files, see Chapter 5 (for Vista) or Chapter 6 (for XP). In the following sections, you learn how to manage folders and files by copying, moving, or deleting them.

> **Computer Cheat**
>
> You can make a folder, file, or program more accessible by placing an icon for it on the Windows desktop. In Windows Vista, right-click the object's icon and click **Show on Desktop**. In Windows XP, right-click the object's icon, point to **Send To**, and click **Desktop (Create Shortcut)**.

Copying, Moving, and Dumping Files and Folders

Using Windows Explorer, you can copy files from any disk. On hard disk drives, floppy disks, and other rewritable storage media, you have complete control over the folders and files. You can copy files, move files from one disk or folder to another, or even delete files or folders to completely remove them from a disk.

Selecting Folders and Files

If you're copying, deleting, or moving a single file or folder, selecting it is about as easy as picking a lemon off a used car lot. If you have Windows set up for single-click access to files (point to select), simply rest the tip of the mouse pointer on the icon for the file or folder you want to select. If you have Windows set up for double-click access to files (click to select), click the file or folder to select it.

> **Inside Tip**
>
> Techniques for selecting files and folders vary a great deal, depending on whether Windows is set up to activate icons on a single-click or double-click. By default, you have to double-click a folder or file to open it or a program icon to run the program. Single-clicking selects the icon but does not activate it. To learn how to change your folder settings to have Windows activate an icon on a single click, see the "Single-Click or Double-Click?" section in Chapter 4.

You'd think that if you pointed to or clicked another file or folder you'd select that one, too, but it doesn't work that way. Selecting another file deselects the first one. This can be maddening to anyone who doesn't know the tricks for selecting multiple files or folders; here's how you do it:

- To select neighboring (*contiguous*) files and folders, select the first file or folder and hold down the **Shift** key while pointing to or clicking the last one in the group (see Figure 7.4).

- To select non-neighboring (*noncontiguous*) items, select one item and then hold down the **Ctrl** key while pointing to or clicking the name of each additional item.

- To deselect an item, hold down the **Ctrl** key while pointing to or clicking its name.

- You also can select a group of items by dragging a box around them. When you release the mouse button, all the items within the box's borders are highlighted.

Figure 7.4

You can use the Shift and Ctrl keys to select neighboring or non-neighboring files.

To select neighboring files, select the first file and hold the Shift key while selecting the last file

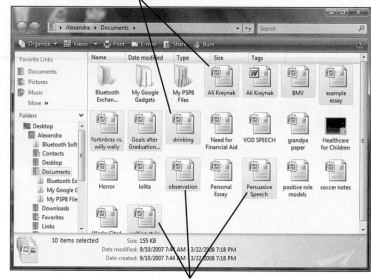

Ctrl+click or Ctrl+point to select non-neighboring files

When you're selecting groups of files, it often helps to change the way the files are sorted or arranged:

In Windows Vista: You can rearrange the order of the items by clicking the desired sort category just above the list of folders and files: **Name, Date Modified, Type, Size,** or **Tags.** (Clicking the category again sorts the items by the same category in reverse order; for example, Z to A instead of A to Z.) To change the size or layout of the icons, click the **Views** menu and click the desired option; you can drag the slider on the left to make the icons a custom size.

In Windows XP: To change the order in which the objects are listed, click the **View** menu, point to **Arrange Icons by,** and click the desired arrangement: **Name, Size, Type,** or **Modified.** (Clicking the same option again sorts the items by the same category in reverse order; for example, 10 to 1 instead of 1 to 10.) To change the appearance or size of the icons, click the **View** menu and select the desired option: **Thumbnails, Tiles, Icons, List,** or **Details.**

Making Your Own Folders

When you install a program, it usually makes the folders it requires or uses existing folders. In addition, Windows creates a folder for you called Documents or My Documents (and several subfolders), in which you can save all the files you create.

However, if you want to store your files in a different folder or you want to store files in a different subfolder inside the Documents folder, you need to know how to create a folder. Give it a shot; create a new folder on drive C. You can always delete the folder later if you don't need it. Follow these steps:

1. Click **Start, Computer** or **My Computer.**

2. Double-click the icon for drive **C.** (If you set Windows up for single-click access, one click does the trick.) A window opens showing all the folders on drive C.

3. Right-click a blank area inside the window to display a shortcut menu.

4. Rest the mouse pointer on **New** and then click **Folder.** Windows creates a folder on drive C, cleverly called New Folder.

5. Type a name for the folder (255 characters or fewer). As you start typing, the **New Folder** name is deleted and is replaced by what you type. You can use any character or number, but you cannot use any of the following characters: \ / : * ? " < > |.

6. Press **Enter.**

Dumping Files in the Recycle Bin

Windows comes complete with its own trash compactor. Whenever a file or icon has outlived its usefulness, either drag it over the trash can icon (the **Recycle Bin**) and release the mouse button, or click the file in My Computer or Windows Explorer to select it and then click the **Delete** button (the button with the *X* on it just below the menu bar) or press the **Del** key. (Another way is to right-click the object and click **Delete.**)

Unfortunately, the Recycle Bin is reserved only for drive C. If you delete files from a Rewritable CD or a flash drive, they're gone, so be careful.

Windows displays a dialog box asking you to confirm the deletion or cancel it; respond accordingly. If you confirm the deletion, Windows moves the file to the Recycle Bin without permanently deleting it so you can recover it later should the need arise.

 Whoa!

Never delete program files, because doing so may incapacitate your program. If you want to remove a program, use the Windows utility for installing and removing programs, which is explained in Chapter 8.

Pulling things out of the Recycle Bin is as easy as dragging them into it. Double-click the **Recycle Bin** icon to display its contents. Select the item you want to restore. **Ctrl+point** or **Ctrl+click** to select any additional items. In Windows Vista, you can now simply click the **Restore the Selected Items** option in the toolbar above the file/folder list. In Windows XP, open the **File** menu and click **Restore.**

To change the properties of the Recycle Bin, including the maximum amount of disk space it can use, right-click the **Recycle Bin** icon and click **Properties.**

To empty the Recycle Bin, first be sure it contains only those files and folders you will never ever need. Then right-click the **Recycle Bin** icon and click **Empty Recycle Bin.**

Renaming Folders and Files

Managing your folders and files is an exercise in on-the-job training. As you create and use folders, you find yourself slapping any old name on them. Later you find that the name doesn't accurately describe the folder's contents, or is too long, or you're just plain sick of seeing it snake across your screen. Fortunately, renaming a folder or file is easy:

♦ If you click files and folders to select them, click the icon for the file or folder you want to rename. The name appears highlighted, as shown in Figure 7.5. Click the name of the file or folder and type the new name. Click a blank area of the screen to make the name change official.

> **Whoa!**
>
> Windows uses the names of program folders to find the program files it needs to run the programs. If you rename a program folder or file, Windows usually throws a fit and won't run the program for you.

♦ If you point to files and folders to select them, right-click the file or folder you want to rename and click **Rename.** Type the new name and press **Enter** or click a blank area in the window.

♦ Whether you point to or click files or folders to select them, highlight the file or folder name by pointing at it or clicking it, press the **F2** key, and type the new name. Press **Enter.**

Figure 7.5

You can easily rename files and folders.

 ——————— Type a new name

Moving and Copying Folders and Files

You can quickly move files and folders to reorganize them. To move an item, simply point to one of the selected objects, hold down the mouse button, drag it over the folder or disk icon to which you want to move it, and release the mouse button. This is particularly easy if you have a two-paned Explorer window with the folder list displayed on the left with the icon for the destination disk or folder displayed.

When moving or copying files and folders, keep in mind that to copy or move multiple files or folders, select the items as explained earlier in this chapter. When you copy or move one of the selected items, a plus sign appears next to the mouse pointer and all the other items follow it.

If you drag a folder or file to a *different disk* (or a folder on a different disk), Windows assumes that you want to *copy* the item to that disk. To move the item, hold down the **Shift** key while dragging.

If you drag a folder or file to a different folder on the *same disk*, Windows assumes that you want to *move* the item to the new destination. To copy the item, hold down the **Ctrl** key while dragging.

To move a file or folder to the Windows desktop, drag it from the Explorer window onto a blank area on the desktop and release the mouse button.

If you're not sure what you want to do, drag the folder or file with the right mouse button. When you release the button a context menu appears, presenting options for moving or copying the item.

Sometimes the easiest way to move a file or folder is to cut and paste it (especially if you don't have the benefit of a two-paned Explorer window). Right-click the icon for the item you want to move and click **Cut.** (To copy the objects, instead, right-click an object and click **Copy.**) Now change to the disk or folder in which you want the cut item placed. Right-click the disk or folder icon (or right-click a blank area in its contents window), and click **Paste.** You also can drag items from one Explorer window to another.

The Least You Need to Know

- ◆ Your computer identifies your disk drives using letters: A and B are for floppy disk drives; typically C is for your hard drive; and D, E, F, and so on are for additional drives, such as CD-ROM and USB flash drives.

◆ When inserting floppy disks, CDs, and DVDs, be gentle, and never force the disk or disc into the drive. This can damage the disks and the drive's read/write head.

◆ When you create and save a document, it is stored as a named file on your computer's hard disk.

◆ Folders hold a group of related files on a disk.

◆ Use My Computer or Windows Explorer to see what's on your disks and to move, copy, rename, or delete files and folders.

Chapter 8

Installing, Running, and Uninstalling Programs

In This Chapter

- ◆ Picking programs your computer can run
- ◆ Installing a program in 10 minutes or less
- ◆ Running programs from the Start menu
- ◆ Making your favorite programs more accessible
- ◆ Getting rid of the programs you don't use

Without programs, a computer is just a fancy box packed with electronic circuitry. Programs enable you to harness the power of that circuitry and use it to perform specific tasks such as typing a letter, keeping your checkbook balanced, surfing the Internet, playing video games, and so much more.

This chapter shows you how to take control of programs. Here you learn how to buy and install programs, run programs installed on your computer, and uninstall programs you no longer use.

A note before we begin: throughout this book, I use the terms *program* and *software* interchangeably. These terms refer to the instructions that control the operation of the computer. Your computer uses two types of software: *system* software (Windows), which controls the overall operation of the computer; and *application* software, which enables you to perform specific tasks, such as typing a letter.

Buying Software Your Hardware Can Run

Even the most experienced computer user occasionally slips up and buys a program that his or her computer can't run. The person might own a PC running Windows and pick up the Macintosh version of the program by mistake. Or maybe the program requires special audio or video equipment the person doesn't have.

Before you purchase any program, read the minimum hardware requirements printed on the outside of the package to determine if your computer has what it takes to run the program. Be sure to note the following information:

Computer type. Typically, you can't run a Macintosh program on an IBM-compatible computer (a PC or personal computer that runs Windows). If you have a PC, be sure the program is for an IBM PC or compatible computer. (Some programs include both the Macintosh and Windows PC versions.)

Operating system. Try to find programs designed specifically for the operating system you use. If your computer is running Windows Vista, don't buy a program developed exclusively for Windows XP. (Although Windows Vista can run most applications designed for Windows XP, Windows XP might have problems running some Windows Vista programs.)

Free hard disk space. When you install a program, the installation routine copies files from the installation floppy disks or CDs to the hard disk. Be sure your hard disk has enough free disk space, as explained in the next section.

CPU requirements. CPU stands for *central processing unit*, and it's the brain of your computer. If the program requires at least a 1 GHz 32-bit (x86) or 64-bit (x64) processor, and you have an 800 MHz, your computer won't be able to run the application effectively, if at all.

Type of monitor. All newer monitors are SVGA (Super Video Graphics Array) or better, and most programs don't require anything better than SVGA.

Graphics card. Some games and graphics programs require a specific type of graphics card (display adapter), such as a 3D card or an advanced video card.

Mouse. If you use Windows, you need a mouse (or some other pointing device). A standard two-button Microsoft mouse is sufficient. Some programs have special features you can use only with an IntelliMouse—a mouse with a wheel between the left and right buttons.

Joystick. Although most computer games allow you to use your keyboard, games are usually more fun if you have a joystick or something else that's a little more versatile than a mouse.

CD-ROM or DVD-ROM drive. Because of their size, many newer software packages (including Windows Vista) come on DVDs. Check for the required speed of the drive, too.

Sound card. Most new applications require sound cards. If you plan on running any cool games, using a multimedia encyclopedia, or even exploring the Internet, you need a sound card. Some applications can use an old 8-bit sound card, but newer applications require a 16-bit or better sound card, which enables stereo output.

Amount of memory. If your computer does not have the required memory (also known as *RAM*, short for *random access memory*), it might not be able to run the program, or the program might cause the computer to crash (freeze up).

def•i•ni•tion

> Your computer has two types of storage—disk storage (permanent) and **RAM,** or **random access memory** (temporary). Memory provides the computer with fast access to data and instructions, but when you turn off your computer, whatever is stored in memory is erased. Disk storage, on the other hand, stores data and instructions permanently or until you choose to delete them. When your computer needs data or instructions, it reads from the disk and stores the information in memory, where it can process it.

You can find out most of what you need to know about your computer from the System Information utility. Click **Start, All Programs, Accessories, System Tools, System Information.** The System Information window appears, as shown in Figure 8.1. Here you can see the operating system name and version number, the type and speed of your processor, and the amount of RAM—physical (actual RAM) and virtual (hard drive space used as RAM).

Figure 8.1

The System Information utility can tell you just about everything you need to know about your computer.

Click to find information about other hardware

operating system and version number

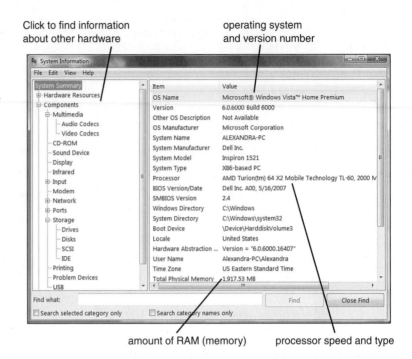

amount of RAM (memory)   processor speed and type

Click the plus sign next to **Components** to explore information about other components of your computer, including the CD-ROM drive, sound device, display, hard drives (under Storage), and so on.

Although the System Information tool can display information about your computer's hard drives, here's a better, quicker way to check your hard drive:

1. Click **Start, Computer.**

2. Right-click the icon for the drive you want to check.

3. Click **Properties.** The Properties dialog box displays the total disk space, the amount in use, and the amount that's free, as shown in Figure 8.2.

If your hard disk does not have sufficient free space for installing the program, you can free up some disk space using the Disk Cleanup tool, as described in Chapter 31.

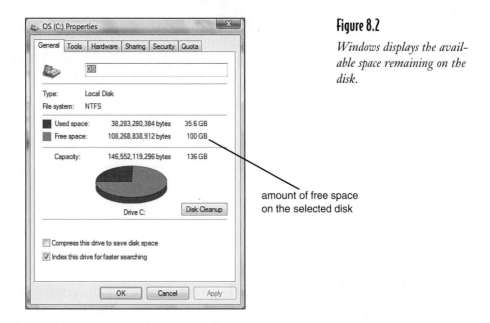

Figure 8.2
Windows displays the available space remaining on the disk.

amount of free space
on the selected disk

Installing Your New Program

Nearly every program on the market comes with an installation component (called Setup or Install) that does everything for you. If the program is on CD or DVD, you can usually pop the disc into the appropriate drive, click a few options to tell the installation utility that it can install the program according to the default settings, and then kick back and watch the installation routine do its thing.

If the program the installation doesn't start automatically when you insert the disc, take the following steps to kick-start the setup routine:

1. If you haven't inserted the program disc into the drive, insert it now.

2. Click **Start, Computer** or **My Computer.**

3. Double-click the icon for the drive you inserted the disc into. This displays a list of files and folders on the disc.

4. Double-click the file named **Setup, Install,** or its equivalent (refer to the program's installation instructions if necessary). This starts the installation utility.

5. Follow the on-screen instructions to complete the installation.

Panic Attack

As a security features, Windows Vista will not install certain programs that may affect the way Windows functions, such as antivirus programs, unless you are acting as administrator. To install these programs, right-click the Install or Setup file and click **Run as Administrator.** The installation instructions that accompany the program should tell you whether you need to run the installation as administrator.

More and more companies are distributing their programs via the Internet. To install a program from the Internet, click the link for downloading the installation file. A dialog box will pop up asking whether you want to Run the installation or Save it to disk to run later. Click the desired option. If you choose to run the installation, Windows downloads the file and then proceeds to install the program. If you choose Save, you need to specify a folder in which to save the file; after downloading the file, double-click it to launch the installation utility.

Whoa! _____

Download and install program files only from websites you trust. Well-established companies regularly scan their systems for viruses, but little-known companies may intentionally or unintentionally offer software that includes viruses, spyware, or other malicious software.

If the file is zipped or compressed, it comes in a folder. Save the folder to your hard drive, double-click the folder to open it, and double-click the Install or Setup file.

Running Your Programs

An empty desktop might be a rare and beautiful sight, but it's useless. To get something done, have some fun, or at least make your boss think you're productive, you need a little clutter. You need to run a program or two.

The standard (albeit slow) method of running a program is to open the **Start** menu, poke around on the submenus until you find the program you want to run, and click the name of the desired program. But Windows provides several more creative and much faster ways to run programs with a single mouse click.

Picking a Program from the Start Menu

Whenever you install a program, the installation utility places the program's name on the Start, All Programs menu or one of its submenus. To run the program, you simply click **Start, All Programs,** click the desired program group (if necessary), and click the program's name, as shown in Figure 8.3.

Figure 8.3

You can find all installed programs on the Start, All Programs menu.

Click the program's name

Click the Start button

As you run programs, Windows automatically adds them to the left side of the Start menu, so you can find them more easily next time. Programs you use often stay put, while those you use less often may get bumped off the menu, but you can still always find them on the All Programs menu or one of its submenus.

To stick a program at the top of the Start menu, where it will stay until you remove it, right-click the program's icon and click **Pin to Start Menu.** You can always remove it by clicking **Start,** right-clicking the icon, and clicking **Remove from This List.**

Making Your Own Program Shortcut

For some programs, the installation utility places an icon, called a *shortcut,* on the Windows desktop so you don't have to poke around on the Start menu to find the program. Unlike bona fide icons that represent files, these clones merely point to the original files. Windows displays a small arrow in the lower-left corner of each shortcut icon to indicate that the icon doesn't represent an actual file.

If you frequently run a program, you can create your own shortcut for that program and place it on the Windows desktop. Here's how:

1. Open the **Start** menu, point to **All Programs,** and point to the submenu that contains the desired program.

Whoa! _____

Deleting a shortcut does not delete the original file it points to. However, deleting an actual file or program icon does delete the corresponding document or program file. Be careful whenever you choose to delete any icon.

2. Right-click the name of the program you want to add to the desktop.

3. Point to **Send To** and then click **Desktop (Create Shortcut).**

You can create desktop shortcuts for just about any object in Windows: a disk, folder, file, or program. Simply right-click the icon and choose **Create Shortcut.** This places the shortcut inside the same window or on the same menu as the original. You can then drag the icon to a blank area of the desktop.

Running Programs When Windows Starts

Here's another trick for running programs: if you always run a particular program right after starting your computer, you can make Windows run the program for you on startup.

Simply drag the icon for the desired program over the Start button, over All Programs, and over the Startup folder icon and drop it in place. The next time Windows starts, it automatically runs all programs in the Startup menu.

Running Programs with a Single Click

Windows includes a nifty little program launch pad called the Quick Launch toolbar. This toolbar roosts just to the right of the Start button and provides single-click access to commonly used programs. If the Quick Launch toolbar is not displayed, right-click the taskbar, point to **Toolbars,** and click **Quick Launch.**

Initially, the Quick Launch toolbar contains several buttons, including the following:

 Show Desktop minimizes all open program windows to take you immediately to the Windows desktop.

 Switch between Windows (Vista only) displays all open windows in 3D on the desktop, so you can easily switch between windows, as shown in Chapter 5.

Internet Explorer Browser runs Microsoft's Internet Explorer, a program for navigating the World Wide Web.

Windows Mail or **Outlook Express** runs Microsoft's e-mail program to allow you to send and receive electronic mail over an Internet connection.

To add more buttons to the bar, simply drag a program's icon over the Quick Launch toolbar and release the mouse button.

If the taskbar is locked, the area assigned to the Quick Launch toolbar may show only a few buttons. To unlock the taskbar, right-click a blank area of the taskbar and click **Lock the Taskbar** to remove the check mark next to it. You should now see a pad to the right of the Quick Launch toolbar that you can drag to change its size.

Computer Cheat

Here are some more tricks you can try: drag the top edge of the taskbar up to make the taskbar taller. Drag the taskbar to the top, left, or right side of the desktop and see what happens. Right-click a blank area of the taskbar and click **Properties** to view additional options. Right-click a blank area of the taskbar, point to **Toolbars,** and click another toolbar to display its buttons.

Removing a Program You Never Use

Your hard disk isn't an ever-expanding universe on which you can install an unlimited number of programs. As you install programs, create documents, send and receive e-mail messages, and view web pages, your disk can quickly become overpopulated.

One of the best ways to reclaim a hefty chunk of disk space is to remove (uninstall) programs you don't use. Unfortunately, you can't just nuke the program's main folder to purge it from your system. When you install a Windows program, it commonly installs files not only to the program's folder but also to the \Windows, Windows\ System, and other folders. It also edits a complicated system file called the Windows Registry. If you remove files without removing the lines in the Registry that refer to those files, you might encounter some serious problems. In short, you can't remove a program from your computer simply by deleting the program's files.

To remove a program safely and completely, you should use the Windows Add/ Remove Programs utility:

In Windows Vista: Click **Start, Control Panel,** and (under Programs), click **Uninstall a Program.** Click the program you want to remove, as shown in Figure 8.4, and click **Uninstall.** Follow the on-screen cues to complete the process.

In Windows XP: Click **Start, Control Panel, Add or Remove Programs.** This displays the Add or Remove Programs window. Click the name of the program you want to remove, and click the **Change/Remove** button. In most cases, a dialog box pops up asking whether you want to completely remove the program from your computer. To confirm the removal, click **Yes.** In other cases, the program runs a custom setup routine, which provides instructions on removing the program entirely or removing only certain components. Follow the on-screen instructions.

Figure 8.4

Let Windows Vista remove the program for you.

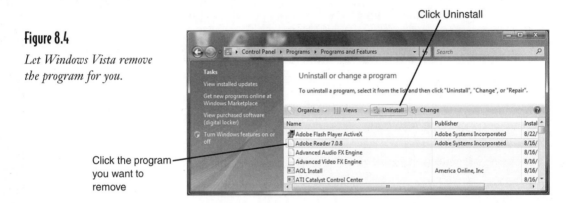

If the name of the program you want to remove does not appear in the Add/Remove Programs list, use the program's own setup utility to remove the program. Search the program's submenu on the **Start, All Programs** menu or in the program's folder for a Setup or Install option.

The Least You Need to Know

◆ Not all programs run on all computers. Before buying a program, be sure your computer meets the requirements printed on the program's box.

◆ To access details about the components that comprise your computer, click **Start, All Programs, Accessories, System Tools, System Information.**

◆ To install a program, you can usually just insert its installation CD or DVD and then follow the on-screen instructions. If the installation doesn't start automatically, change to the drive in which the disc is loaded (using **Start, Computer** or **My Computer**), and double-click the **Setup** or **Install** icon.

◆ To run a program, click **Start,** point to **All Programs,** point to the desired program group, and click the program's icon.

◆ To remove a program you no longer use, open the Windows **Control Panel** and click **Uninstall a Program** (Vista) or **Add or Remove Programs** (XP).

Chapter 9

Customizing Windows

In This Chapter

♦ Fitting more stuff on your desktop

♦ Decorating the Windows desktop with themes and wallpaper

♦ Animating your screen and protecting your privacy with a screen saver

♦ Tweaking the Windows sound system

♦ Adjusting the date and time

If you're like most people, you enjoy decorating your home or office to add your own personal touch. You might paint the walls a different color, hang a few photos of friends or family members, or populate your shelves with knickknacks and family photos. In similar ways, you can customize and decorate the Windows desktop. Windows provides the tools you need to change the color of your desktop, pick a theme for icons and mouse pointers, turn on an animated screen saver, build your own icons and menus, and reset the date and time. This chapter shows you how to completely renovate your computerized desktop.

This chapter is divided into three parts. If your computer is running Windows Vista, the first section shows you how to customize the Vista desktop. If you're still running XP, skip to the second section, where the focus is exclusively on personalizing XP. Near the end of the chapter, I show you how to set the date and time in both versions of Windows.

Personalizing Windows Vista

Windows Vista provides easy access to options for personalizing Windows—changing its appearance and the sounds associated with certain events. To access almost all these options, right-click a blank area of the desktop and click **Personalize.**

Feel free to explore these options yourself or proceed through the following sections, where I provide a guided tour on how to make the most common (and interesting) adjustments.

Customizing Vista's Desktop

Microsoft ships Windows Vista with default settings that control its appearance, but eventually, every user's desktop starts to look a little different as the person customizes it so suit his or her tastes. In the following sections, you discover several adjustments you can make to personalize your copy of Windows Vista.

Maximizing Your Desktop Space

Wouldn't it be great if you could grab the edges of your monitor and stretch it? Maybe turn your 17-inch monitor into a big-screen, 21-inch version? Well, you can't, but you can do the next best thing—shrink everything on the desktop to give yourself a little more real estate. Here's what you do:

1. Right-click a blank area of the desktop and click **Personalize.**

2. Click **Display Settings.** The Display Settings dialog box appears, as shown in Figure 9.1.

3. Drag the **Resolution** slider to the right to fit more on the desktop or to the left to make everything appear larger on the desktop.

4. You can also use the **Colors** drop-down list to display more or fewer colors. (The more colors, the better everything looks, but selecting fewer colors may speed up the display a little.)

5. Click **OK.**

Preview area shows the new desktop appearance (you may see only one monitor here)

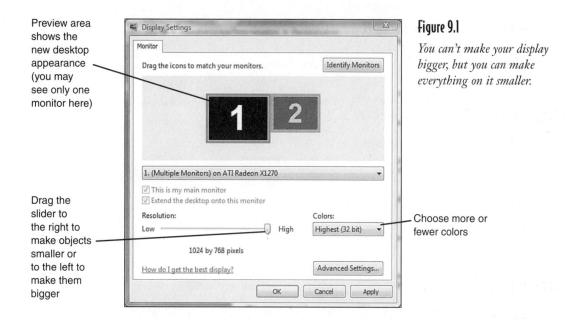

Figure 9.1

You can't make your display bigger, but you can make everything on it smaller.

Drag the slider to the right to make objects smaller or to the left to make them bigger

Choose more or fewer colors

Panic Attack

If the icons have become too small to see, don't worry. You can make some adjustments. Right-click the desktop, point to **View,** and click **Large Icons.** Most programs also have a Zoom option you can use to make text appear larger, too.

If you're wondering about the two-monitor thing, some video cards allow you to connect two monitors and extend the display into the second monitor. This allows you to run two different programs in separate monitors, which is pretty cool, because you can browse the web, check e-mail, or watch YouTube videos on one monitor while working on the other. Many notebook computers have a video connector in addition to the built-in screen, so adding a second monitor is usually pretty easy.

Most video cards come with their own software that provides more advanced controls for setting display options. Right-click a blank area of the Windows desktop and see whether the menu contains an option for running the video card's control panel.

Choosing a Different Background

Windows comes with numerous backgrounds you can use to decorate your desktop. Here's how to check out the selection or choose a different background:

1. Right-click the desktop and click **Personalize.**

2. Click **Desktop Background.** The Desktop Background dialog box appears, as shown in Figure 9.2.

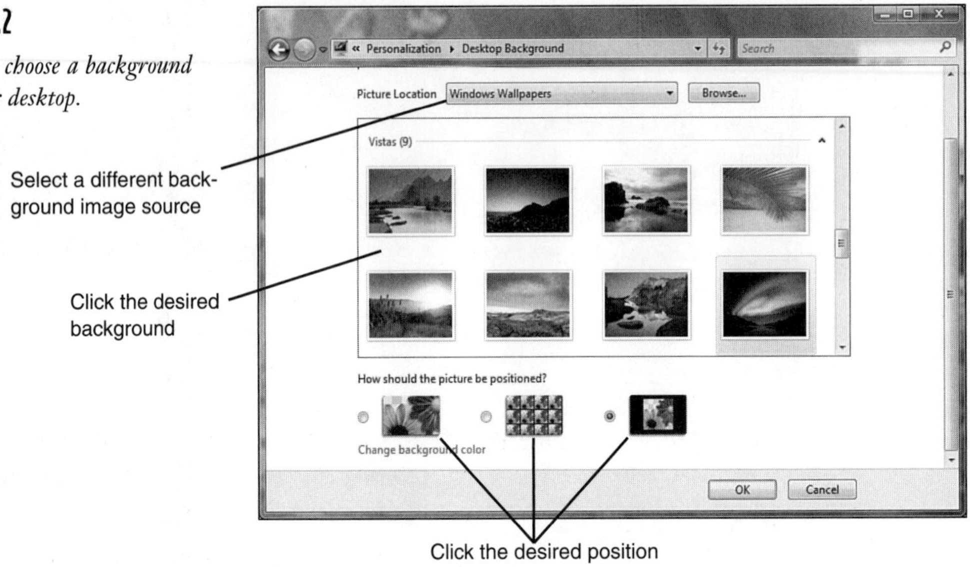

Figure 9.2

You can choose a background for your desktop.

Select a different background image source

Click the desired background

Click the desired position

3. Scroll through the backgrounds, and click the one you want to use. (You can select an option from the **Picture Location** drop-down list above the background list to use a different picture, such as a photo you have stored in your Pictures folder.)

4. Click the desired positioning option for the background.

5. Click **OK.**

Choosing a Different Color Scheme

Windows Vista initially uses a color scheme with a bluish hue for window borders and the Start menu. To pick a different color or adjust the transparency of Windows, take the following steps:

1. Right-click the desktop and click **Personalize.**

2. Click **Windows Color and Appearance.** The Windows Color and Appearance dialog box appears, as shown in Figure 9.3. (Figure 9.3 shows the screen that appears in Vista Home Premium. If you're running a different version of Vista, you may have different options.)

Select a color

Turn transparency on or off

Mix your own custom color

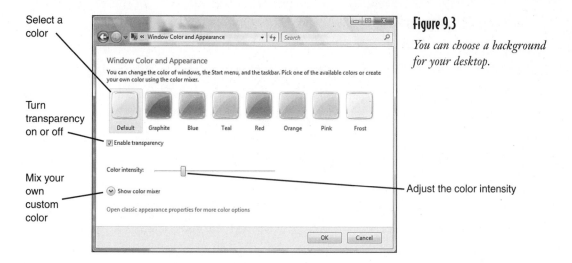

Figure 9.3

You can choose a background for your desktop.

Adjust the color intensity

3. Click the desired color. When you click a color, Windows automatically applies it to the window, so you can see the new effect. (For more options, click **Show Color Mixer** and use the controls to mix your own custom color.)

4. Drag the **Color intensity** slider to the left to darken your color selection or to the left to brighten it.

5. You can remove the see-through effect Vista applies to Windows by clicking **Enable transparency** to remove the check mark next to it (if desired).

6. Click **OK.**

Rearranging Your Desktop Icons

If your desktop gets too cluttered or unmanageable, Windows has several tools to help you reorganize the icons. Try the following techniques:

♦ To move an icon, drag it to the desired location.

♦ To remove an icon, right-click it and click **Delete.**

♦ To have Windows rearrange the icons for you, right-click the desktop, point to **Sort By,** and click **Name, Size, Type,** or **Date Modified.**

♦ To have Windows line up the icons without rearranging them by name, size, type, or date, right-click the desktop, point to **View,** and click **Align to Grid.**

♦ To have Windows automatically line up icons when you move them, right-click the desktop, point to **View,** and click **Auto Arrange.**

Hiding the Taskbar

The taskbar is a great tool to have around, but when you're working on a document, playing a game, or viewing a web page, you might need that extra $1/_2$-inch of screen space where the taskbar resides. To reclaim the space, make the taskbar hide itself when you're doing other stuff:

1. Right-click a blank area of the taskbar and click **Properties.**

2. Click **Auto-hide the taskbar.**

3. Click **OK.**

As you work, the taskbar hides below the bottom of the screen (unless you moved the taskbar to a different edge of the screen, which you can do by dragging it). To bring the taskbar back into view, simply move the mouse pointer to the edge of the screen where the taskbar normally appears. It should pop right up.

Panic Attack

You can make your taskbar larger or smaller by dragging an edge of it. If you make it too small, however, it can virtually disappear. If that happens, roll your mouse pointer around the edge of the screen to see if the taskbar pops up. Position the mouse pointer near the edge of the screen where you usually see the taskbar, until the mouse pointer turns into a two-headed arrow. You should then be able to drag the edge toward the center of the screen to make the taskbar larger (and visible).

Rearranging Items on the Start Menu

If Windows buries your favorite program five levels down on the Start menu, you don't have to live with it. You can move programs to place them right at your fingertips:

1. Click **Start,** open the menu the program appears on, and then, using the right mouse button, drag the program to the desired location.

2. As you drag the item, a horizontal bar appears, showing where it will be placed. When you're in the right spot, release the mouse button.

3. A menu pops up, and you can click **Copy Here** or **Move Here.**

Adding Icons to the Desktop

You can quickly add some standard icons to your desktop so you don't have to go hunting for them on the Start menu:

1. Right-click the desktop, click **Personalize,** and under **Tasks** on the left side of the window that appears, click **Change Desktop Icons.** The Desktop Icon Settings dialog box appears, as shown in Figure 9.4.

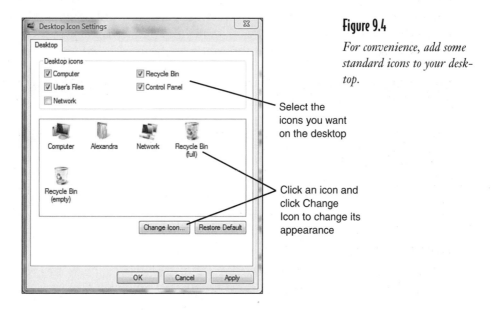

Figure 9.4

For convenience, add some standard icons to your desktop.

Select the icons you want on the desktop

Click an icon and click Change Icon to change its appearance

2. Click the check box next to each icon you want placed on the desktop: Computer, User's Files, Network, Recycle Bin, and Control Panel.

You can also click an icon and click Change icon to choose an icon with a different look. (If you mess up, you can always click the icon and click the Restore Default button to go back to the original icon.)

Securing Some Privacy with a Screen Saver

Have you ever seen a school of fish swimming across a computer screen? How about a flock of flying toasters? A shower of meteors? A pack of creepy crawling cockroaches?

If you've seen any of these animated patterns scurrying about a monitor, you have already witnessed screen savers in action.

Screen savers traditionally serve three primary purposes:

♦ They're pretty or cool.

♦ They prevent burn-in. On older monitors, an image could get burned into the monitor permanently if left on too long.

♦ They provide some level of security—to keep passersby from seeing what you were working on if you step away from your computer for a short time.

A common misconception is that screen savers reduce a monitor's power consumption. As explained in Chapter 3, this is a myth. It's also not true that screen savers are good at preventing unauthorized users from logging into your computer; they do provide some level of protection against unauthorized access, but not much.

To turn on a screen saver in Windows Vista, take the following steps:

1. Right-click the desktop and click **Personalize.**

2. Click **Screen Saver.** The Screen Saver dialog box appears, as shown in Figure 9.5.

Figure 9.5

Animate your desktop while you're away from it.

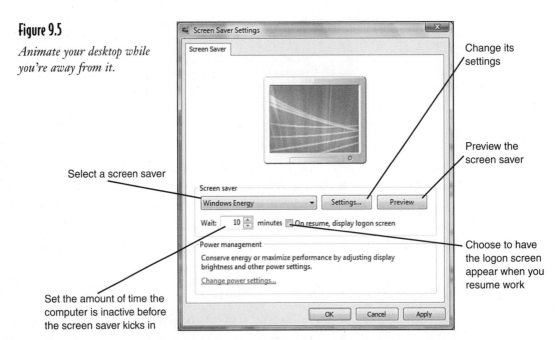

Change its settings

Preview the screen saver

Select a screen saver

Choose to have the logon screen appear when you resume work

Set the amount of time the computer is inactive before the screen saver kicks in

3. Open the **Screen Saver** drop-down list, and click the name of the desired screen saver. (You can see the screen saver in action by clicking the **Preview** button. When you're done previewing, roll the mouse or press the Shift key.)

4. *Optional:* Click the **Settings** button to adjust the screen saver settings.

5. Use the **Wait** spin box (the up and down arrow buttons) to set the number of minutes of inactivity that should pass before the screen saver kicks in.

6. If you want the Windows logon screen to appear when activity resumes, click the checkbox next to **On resume, display logon screen.** This gives you some security to prevent most people from logging on in your place.

7. Click **OK.**

Tweaking the Audio Portion of Your Broadcast

In addition to the beeps and grunts your computer emits at start-up, it can produce more refined tones. When you start Windows, for instance, it ushers itself in with heavenly harp music or some other short audio clip. When you open a menu, close a window, or exit a program, Windows plays a unique audio clip for each of these actions or *events*. If you listen closely as you work in Windows, you'll be able to link each sound with its event.

If you keep listening closely (over several weeks), these sounds might start to annoy you and inspire an overwhelming desire to smash your speakers. Before you take such drastic action, read through the following sections. Here you learn how to pick a different sound scheme, assign different sounds to various Windows events, and even mute your system altogether.

Testing Your Audio Equipment

If you've ever prepared for a speech or presentation, you know how important it is to test your equipment before showtime. After setting up and turning on the microphone, you hold it a few inches from your mouth and do the standard "Testing … one … two … testing …" thing.

Before you start messing with Windows audio, you should test your sound card and speakers. Here's how:

1. Right-click the desktop and click **Personalize.**

2. Click **Sounds.** The Sound dialog box appears, as shown in Figure 9.6.

Figure 9.6

Test your audio output.

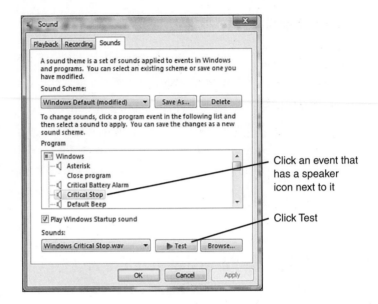

Click an event that
has a speaker
icon next to it

Click Test

3. Click an event that has a speaker next to it (under Program).

4. Click **Test.**

At this point, Vista should play the audio clip that's assigned to the event. If you can't hear the clip, try adjusting the volume (as explained in the following section) or skip to Chapter 32 to troubleshoot.

Adjusting the Volume

The trick to adjusting the volume on a computer is to start with the obvious controls first: the volume dials on the sound card and speakers. Set these controls to the desired level. If you're not sure which way to turn them, set them at the halfway point, so when your computer does start to play audio, it won't burst your eardrums.

Next, check the volume control in Windows. Click **Start, Control Panel, Hardware and Sound, Adjust System Volume.** Windows displays a Volume Mixer with several sliders that control volume for different components. Drag the Device slider to the approximate volume you want, and test the volume as explained in the previous section.

If you're working on a notebook computer or have a newfangled keyboard, you may have volume controls for both the speaker and microphone within easy reach of the keys. Look around the periphery of the keyboard area for volume controls.

Assigning Specific Sounds to Events

Windows comes complete with a default sound scheme that assigns certain audio clips to specific events that occur in Windows. To assign a different audio clip to a particular event, take the following steps:

1. Right-click the desktop and click **Personalize.**

2. Click **Sounds.** The Sound dialog box appears, as shown in Figure 9.6.

3. Click an event whose sound you want to change.

4. Open the **Sounds** drop-down list (below the Program list) and click the sound you want to use. (Click the Test button to play the sound.)

5. Repeat steps 3 and 4 to assign different sounds to other events.

6. To save your new assignments as a scheme, click **Save As,** type a name for your sound scheme, and click **OK.**

> **Inside Tip** _____
>
> Windows comes with a sound recorder you can use to create your own digital recordings. To run the recorder, click **Start, All Programs, Accessories, Sound Recorder.** After recording an audio clip, you can save it as a WAV file and then assign it to a Windows event.

You can choose a different sound scheme at any time. Just right-click the desktop, click **Personalize, Sounds,** open the **Sound Scheme** drop-down list, click the desired sound scheme, and click **OK.**

Saving Your Desktop Settings as a Theme

You can spend a great deal of time personalizing Windows and then lose those settings later if you make additional adjustments. To prevent your settings from being changed, save them as a theme. You can create as many themes as you like and then simply select a theme for the day that best matches your mood.

To save a theme, take the following steps:

1. Right-click the desktop and click **Personalize.**

2. Click **Theme.**

3. Click **Save As.**

4. Type a name for your theme and click **Save.**

You can switch themes at any time. Right-click the desktop, click **Personalize,** **Theme,** open the **Theme** drop-down list, select the desired theme, and click **OK.**

Personalizing Windows XP

Compared to Vista, Windows XP has a little less flash, but it still provides plenty of options for customizing its desktop and sounds. In most cases, it offers the same options, but you access those options in a different way. In the following sections, I show you how to take control of Windows XP and give it a makeover more suitable to your tastes.

Maximizing Your Desktop Space

You can't make your monitor any bigger, but you can make everything on your desktop a little smaller, so it feels like you have more space. Take the following steps to give yourself more room by increasing your screen resolution:

1. Right-click a blank area of the desktop and click **Properties.**

2. Click the **Settings** tab, as shown in Figure 9.7.

Figure 9.7

You can't make your display bigger, but you can make everything on it smaller.

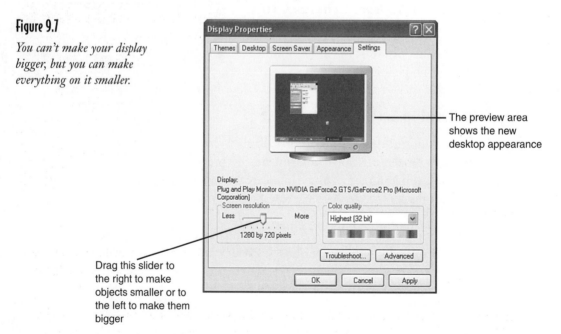

The preview area shows the new desktop appearance

Drag this slider to the right to make objects smaller or to the left to make them bigger

3. Drag the **Screen resolution** slider to the right to fit more on the desktop or to the left to make everything appear larger on the desktop.

4. Click **OK.**

Most video cards come with their own software that provides more advanced controls for setting display options. Right-click a blank area of the Windows desktop and see whether the menu contains an option for running the video cards control panel.

> **Panic Attack**
>
> If the icons have become too small to see, right-click the desktop, click **Properties**, click the **Appearance** tab, click **Effects**, click **Large Icons**, and click **OK.**

Rearranging Your Desktop Icons

You can rearrange the icons on the Windows XP desktop by doing any of the following:

♦ To move an icon, drag it to the desired location.

♦ To have Windows rearrange the icons for you, right-click the desktop, point to **Arrange Icons By,** and click **Name, Size, Type,** or **Modified.**

♦ To have Windows line up the icons without rearranging them by name, size, type, or date, right-click the desktop, point to **Arrange Icons By,** and click **Align to Grid.**

♦ To have Windows automatically line up icons when you move them, right-click the desktop, point to **Arrange Icons By,** and click **Auto Arrange.**

> **Computer Cheat**
>
> Windows XP can automatically remove unused shortcut icons from your desktop. Right-click the desktop, point to **Arrange Icons By,** click **Run Desktop Cleanup Wizard,** and follow the on-screen instructions to move unused shortcut icons to the Unused Desktop Shortcuts folder.

Hiding the Taskbar

You can make the taskbar go into hiding when you're working on other projects. Right-click a blank area of the taskbar, click **Properties,** click **Auto-hide the taskbar,** and click **OK.** To bring the taskbar into view, move the mouse pointer to the edge of the screen where the taskbar usually hangs out.

You also can make the taskbar larger by dragging the edge of the taskbar toward the middle of the screen. To move the taskbar, drag a blank area of it to the left, top, or right edge of the desktop and drop it in place.

Rearranging Items on the Start Menu

Few users realize that the Start menu is completely customizable. To move an item on the Start menu, just drag it to the position where you want it placed and release the mouse button.

To further customize the Start menu, right-click the **Start** button, click **Properties,** and use the options in the Taskbar and Start Menu Properties dialog box to enter your preferences.

Tweaking the Screen Colors

To try out various color combinations in XP, right-click a blank area of the desktop and click **Properties.** The Display Properties dialog box appears. Click the **Appearance** tab to access the color schemes. In Windows XP, you can use the options on the Appearance tab to choose a prefab design, color scheme, and font size that control all your windows.

To make more specific adjustments, click the **Advanced** button and enter your preferences.

Hanging Wallpaper in the Background

Have you ever decorated your desk with wallpaper? Of course not! Maybe a new coat of varnish, some paint, or even contact paper, but never wallpaper. Well that's about to change. In Windows, you can use wallpaper to add a more graphic background to your desktop.

Inside Tip

To use an image from the web as your desktop background, right-click the image and choose **Set as Background.**

To hang wallpaper in Windows, right-click a blank area of the desktop and click **Properties.** Click the **Desktop** tab to bring it to the front. In the list of backgrounds, near the bottom of the dialog box, click the name of the desired wallpaper. If the preview area shows a dinky icon in the middle of the screen, open the **Display** drop-down list and click **Tile** (to use the image as a pattern to fill the screen) or **Stretch** (to make the image cover the desktop). Click **OK.**

Controlling the Desktop Icons and Visual Effects

A quick glance at the desktop icons might give you the impression that they're immutable. However, Windows provides a set of options for controlling the appearance and behavior of these icons and other visual elements that make up the desktop.

To take control of your desktop icons in Windows XP, right-click a blank area of the Windows desktop and click **Properties.** Click the **Desktop** tab and click the **Customize Desktop** button. Using the Desktop Items dialog box, you can customize the desktop icons in any of the following ways:

◆ To display additional system icons on the desktop, including icons for My Computer, Internet Explorer, My Network Places, and My Documents, click the check box next to each icon you want placed on the desktop.

◆ To change the appearance of one of the desktop icons, click the icon and then click the **Change Icon** button. Click the desired icon and click **OK.** You can return to the original icon by clicking it and clicking the **Restore Default** button.

◆ To have Windows automatically remove unused shortcut icons from the desktop after 60 days, click **Run Desktop Cleanup Wizard Every 60 Days** to place a check mark next to the option.

Click **OK** to save your settings and return to the Display Properties dialog box. To access additional preferences that control the overall appearance of the icons, click the **Appearance** tab, click the **Effects** button, and enter your preferences. When you're done, click **OK** to return to the Display Properties dialog box, and click **OK** to save your settings and return to the Windows desktop.

Turning on an Animated Screen Saver

Screen savers have long been the computer toy of choice among Windows and non-Windows users alike. To turn on a screen saver in XP or change the screen saver that's currently turned on, take the following steps:

1. Right-click a blank area of the Windows desktop, click **Properties,** and click the **Screen Saver** tab.

2. Open the **Screen Saver** drop-down list, and click the name of a screen saver that appeals to you. To view the screen saver in action, click the **Preview** button. To deactivate the screen saver and return to the Display Properties dialog box, roll the mouse or press the **Shift** key.

3. *Optional:* Click the **Settings** button to adjust the screen saver settings.

4. Use the **Wait** spin box (the up and down arrow buttons) to set the number of minutes of inactivity that should pass before the screen saver kicks in.

5. If you want the Windows logon screen to appear when activity resumes, click the checkbox next to **On resume, display logon screen.** This gives you some security to prevent most people from logging on in your place.

6. Click **OK.**

Assigning Sounds to Windows Events

Windows is set up to play certain sounds when specific events take place, such as on start-up or shutdown, and when you open or close a file.

To specify which sound is assigned to a particular event, click **Start; Control Panel; Sounds, Speech, and Audio Devices;** and **Change the Sound Scheme.** In the **Program Events** list, click the event whose sound you want to change. Open the **Name** or **Sounds** list, and click the name of the desired audio clip. To preview the sound, click the **Play** button. To save your settings, click **OK.**

You can use the Sounds and Audio Devices Properties dialog box that appears when you select Change the Sound Scheme to adjust the speaker volume, too. Click the Volume tab and use the volume controls to set the desired speaker volume. You may also have volume controls on your sound card, speakers, or even on or near your keyboard. If you're having trouble with audio input or output, visit Chapter 32 for some troubleshooting suggestions.

Adjusting the Date and Time

This works for all versions of Windows: at the right end of the taskbar, Windows displays the current time. Rest the mouse pointer on the time to display the day and date. If the date or time is incorrect, you can adjust either setting:

1. In Windows Vista, click the time display in the taskbar and click **Change date and time settings.** In Windows XP, double-click the time display in the taskbar. The Date and Time dialog box appears.

2. Click the desired date by choosing a month or year from the boxes above the calendar.

3. Click the hour, minute, or second display, and use the spin buttons (the up and down arrow buttons) to adjust the selected setting. You can also double-click the hour, minute, or second and type the desired setting.

4. Click **OK.**

The Least You Need to Know

- To access personalization options in Windows Vista, right-click a blank area of the desktop and click **Personalize.**

- To access desktop and display settings in Windows XP, right-click a blank area of the desktop and click **Properties.**

- To hide the taskbar, right-click it, choose **Properties,** and turn on **Auto hide.**

- To move an item on the Start menu, drag the item to the desired location and drop it in place.

- You can adjust the date and time in Windows by double-clicking the time display in the taskbar (Windows XP) or clicking the time and clicking **Change date and time** settings (Vista) and then changing the settings.

Creating and Managing User Accounts

In This Chapter

- ◆ Creating user accounts
- ◆ Securing your computer with passwords
- ◆ Logging off and back on Windows
- ◆ Playing nice and sharing files

Sharing a computer with other users is like sharing a car with other drivers. When you share a car, each driver adjusts the seat and steering wheel for her own comfort, adjusts the mirrors so she can see out the back, and stores the garage door opener in a unique hiding place. Likewise, some computer users like a plain, uncluttered desktop, while others prefer to populate their desktops with dozens of icons, a sidebar, and other accessories.

Fortunately, Windows enables you to set up a separate user account for each person, so each person can customize Windows without affecting the appearance and function of Windows for other users. In addition, user accounts enable each user to keep a separate e-mail account, which means the messages for all users don't get mixed up in the same mailbox. User account passwords also provide privacy in a shared environment.

This chapter shows you how to create a user account for each person who plans to share the computer, how to log on and log off Windows, how to add a password to the accounts, and how to perform some other tricks with user accounts.

Adding a New User to Your Computer

When you or your computer's manufacturer installed Windows, the setup program automatically created a user account so Windows could greet you on start-up. The user account Windows created is an *administrator account*, which gives you the authority to create additional accounts, assign passwords to users, and limit other users' access to system settings and computer resources.

Whoa!

If you're using a networked computer at your place of business, your business should have a network administrator who is in charge of adding user accounts. The process is much different for setting up user accounts on a corporation's network. Ask the network administrator for help.

To add a user account for another user in Windows Vista, follow these steps:

1. Click **Start, Control Panel.** The Control Panel appears.

2. Click the **Add or remove user accounts** icon (if prompted to confirm, click **Continue**). The Manage Accounts window appears.

3. Click **Create a new account.** Vista prompts you to type a name for the account.

Figure 10.1

You can create a new user account.

Type the new user's name

Select Standard user or Administrator

Click Create Account

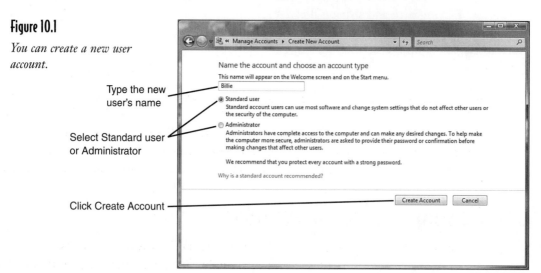

4. Type the user's name as you want it to appear on the Windows Welcome screen and on the Start menu.

5. Click the desired account type:

    ◆ **Standard user** allows the user to change his or her own password, change the picture used to identify the user, change Windows desktop settings, view files that the user created, and view any files in the Shared Documents folder.

    ◆ **Administrator** allows the user to create, edit, and delete accounts; change system settings; install programs; and access all folders and files on the computer.

6. Click the **Create Account** button. Vista returns to the User Accounts window and displays the icon and name of the new user account, as shown in Figure 10.2.

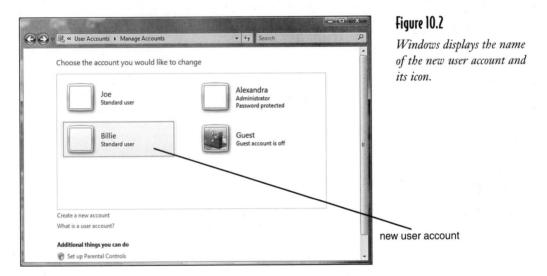

Figure 10.2

Windows displays the name of the new user account and its icon.

new user account

To add an new user account in Windows XP, click **Start, Control Panel, User Accounts.** Under **Pick a task,** click **Create a New Account.** Type the new user's name, click the **Next** button, and follow the on-screen cues to enter your preferences.

Establishing Log-On Passwords

When you first create a user account, the account has no password. When the Windows log-on screen appears, the user can simply click the account icon to freely access that account. If you're looking for privacy, you need to lock the account by adding a password. Windows then requires the password before allowing the user to log on.

To add a password to an account in Windows Vista, take the following steps:

> **Whoa!**
>
> Choose a password that's easy for you to remember but difficult for anyone else to guess. Write down your password and store it in a secure location so if you do forget it, you won't be locked out of your account permanently.

1. Click the **Start, Control Panel.** The Control Panel appears.

2. Click the **User Accounts and Family Safety** icon. (The icon may be called **User Accounts** in different versions of Vista.) The User Accounts and Family Safety window appears.

3. Click **Change your Windows password.** The Make Changes to Your User Account window appears.

4. Click **Create a password for your account.** Vista prompts you to enter your password, as shown in Figure 10.3.

Figure 10.3

A password deters other users from logging on in your name.

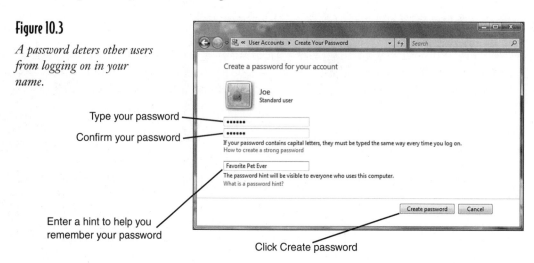

Type your password

Confirm your password

Enter a hint to help you remember your password

Click Create password

5. In the New Password text box, type the desired password.

6. Click in the **Confirm New Password** text box, and type your password again, exactly the same way you typed it in step 5.

7. *Optional:* Click in the **Type a Password Hint** text box and type a hint to help remind you of your password. This hint will appear on the Windows log-on screen, so don't use a hint that can help other users guess your password.

8. Click the **Create password** button.

You can change your password at any time or remove it. To remove a password, log on, repeat steps 1 through 4, and click **Remove the password.** You then have to enter your current password to confirm.

In Windows XP, the steps for adding a password are very similar:

1. Click Start, Control Panel, User Accounts.

2. Choose the account for which you want to add a password, click **Create Password,** and follow the on-screen cues to complete the operation.

Giving Your Account Icon a Makeover

Every account has its own picture to help identify each account and add a little personality to the log-on screen. To personalize your account, consider choosing a picture that represents your personality and interests. Following are the steps for changing your picture in Windows Vista:

1. Click **Start, Control Panel.** The Control Panel appears.

2. Click the **User Accounts and Family Safety** icon. (The icon may be called **User Accounts** in different versions of Vista.) The User Accounts and Family Safety window appears.

3. Click **Change your account picture.** Vista displays a collection of available images, as shown in Figure 10.4.

> **Inside Tip**
>
> You can use nearly any graphic image on your computer as your picture. When selecting a picture, click **Browse** and use the resulting dialog box to locate the desired image. You can navigate drives and folders just as you do in My Computer. When you find the picture you want, click the picture and click the **Open** button.

Figure 10.4

Personalize your account with a unique image.

Click the picture you want to represent you

Click Change Picture

4. Click the desired picture and click the **Change Picture** button.

In Windows XP, the steps for changing a picture are very similar:

1. Click **Start, Control Panel, User Accounts.**

2. Choose the account for whose picture you want to change, click **Change the Picture,** and follow the on-screen cues to complete the operation.

Wiping Out a User Account

When you customize Windows, as discussed in Chapter 9, Windows saves your settings in your user account. In addition, Windows saves all files in your documents folder, your e-mail messages, any websites you add to your Favorites menu (in Internet Explorer), and any passwords to websites you choose to save on the computer. Some of the settings and information Windows saves could be private, so if you stop using the computer, you might want to delete your user account. (Only administrators can delete user accounts.)

Whoa!

Don't delete an account unless you're absolutely sure you won't ever use it again. Deleting an account permanently removes any passwords you've chosen to save and any e-mail messages.

Here's how to delete an account in Windows Vista:

1. Open the **Start** menu and click **Control Panel.**

2. Click the **User Accounts and Family Safety** icon (or simply **User Accounts**), click **Add or remove user accounts,** and then type the administrator password (if prompted to do so), and click **OK.**

3. Click the icon for the account you want to delete and then Click **Delete the Account.**

4. Windows asks whether you want to save the desktop settings and the contents of the various folders associated with this account. To save the desktop settings and the contents of the folders, click the **Keep Files** button. To completely remove the account and any files and settings saved for this account, click the **Delete Files** button.

5. The User Accounts feature asks you to confirm that you want to delete this user account. If you are absolutely sure you want to delete this account, click the **Delete Account** button; otherwise, click the **Cancel** button.

In Windows XP, the steps are nearly identical:

1. Click **Start, Control Panel, User Accounts.**

2. Click the icon for the account you want to delete, click **Delete the Account,** and follow the on-screen cues to complete the process.

Letting Guest Users Log On

If you have guests who occasionally use your computer to check their e-mail, browse the web, or play games, you can enable the Guest Accounts feature to let them log on as guests without having to enter a password. They can run programs and perform other tasks, but they cannot install new software or change any account settings. In short, guest users can use your computer without messing it up.

Here's how to enable the guest account in Windows Vista:

1. Click **Start, Control Panel, Add or remove user accounts.**

2. Click the **Guest** icon.

3. Vista displays a message asking whether you want to turn on the guest account. Click **Turn On.**

You can turn off the Guest Account at any time by following nearly identical steps and then clicking **Turn off the guest account** at the very end.

The steps for turning the guest account on or off in Windows XP are nearly the same:

1. Click **Start, Control Panel, User Accounts.**

2. Click the **Guest** icon.

3. Click **Turn On the Guest Account** or **Turn Off the Guest Account,** depending on whether you want to turn the guest account on or off.

Logging On and Logging Off Windows

On weekends, when my kids and their friends are hanging out, they circle my computer like vultures, just waiting for me to step away from the keyboard. Then they descend to play games, chat with friends, and do other things that don't require them to work or play outside. When I return to the computer, I usually find a couple new programs installed on "my" account and several changes to my desktop.

Inside Tip _____

To find out who's currently logged on to Windows, click the **Start** button and look at the top of the Start menu for the name of the current user.

The moral of the story is: always log off when you step away from the computer. When you log off, Windows shuts down your desktop and user account and displays the log-on screen so another user can log on. This prevents other users from changing your settings, snooping in your e-mail account, and performing other sinister or careless acts.

The following sections show you how to log on, log off, and switch users when sharing your computer.

Logging On at Start-Up

When you turn on your computer, the Windows Welcome screen appears, as mentioned in Chapter 1. To log on, click your user account icon. If your user account is password protected, Windows prompts you to type your password. Type your password and then click the arrow button to log on to Windows. Windows displays the Windows desktop, and you can start working.

Inside Tip _____

To make it more difficult for unauthorized users to log on in Windows XP, disable the Welcome screen. With the Welcome screen disabled, a log-on dialog box appears on start-up, requiring the user to type both a user name and password. Click **Start, Control Panel, User Accounts**. Click **Change the Way Users Log On or Off** and then click **Use the Welcome Screen** to remove the check mark from its check box. Click the **Apply Options** button. (This option is unavailable in Windows Vista.)

Logging Off Windows

You now know you should log off whenever you've finished using your computer to prevent other users from changing your Windows settings. Before logging off, you should save any files you've been working on to avoid losing any of your work.

When you're ready to log off, open the **Start** menu and click **Log Off.** (In Vista, click **Start,** point to the arrow in the lower-right corner of the Start menu, and click **Log Off.**) The Log Off Windows dialog box appears.

At this point, you have two choices. You can click **Log Off** to log off completely, which shuts down any programs that might be running and returns you to the Windows Welcome screen. The other option is to use *fast user switching*, which keeps you logged on to your account but allows another user to log on, too. When the other user is done working, you can then quickly switch back to whatever you were in the process of doing. To remain logged on, click **Switch User** (instead of clicking Log Off). Whichever option you choose, Windows displays its Welcome screen so another user can log on.

def•i•ni•tion

Fast user switching allows a second user to log on without shutting down the first user's programs. For instance, if you're in the middle of writing the great American novel and your son wants to check his e-mail, he can use fast user switching to quickly log on, check his mail, and log off. After he logs off, you can quickly switch back to your account and immediately return to work, because your document remains on-screen.

If you're worried about other users logging on to your account and looking at what you're working on or changing your files, add a password to your account as explained earlier in the section "Establishing Log-On Passwords." If your account is password protected, you'll be prompted to enter your password to log back on.

Sharing Files with Other Users

Each user is provided with his or her own folder where all the documents they create are stored by default. For example, when I log on as Joe, all my documents are stored in My Documents folder, which appears as the Joe's Documents folder to other users when they log on. Normally, each user's folder remains off limits to other users.

To share folders or documents, copy them to the Shared Documents folder or one of its subfolders (in Windows XP) or the Public folder or one of its subfolders (in

Windows Vista). For additional information about sharing files and folders, especially on a network, check out Chapter 12.

The Least You Need to Know

♦ To access most user account settings, display the Control Panel and click the **User Accounts** or **User Accounts and Family Safety** (or simply **User Accounts**) icon.

♦ To prevent others from logging on to your Windows account, add a password to your account.

♦ To enable guest users to log on to Windows and prevent them from making any changes to Windows, enable the Guest Accounts feature.

♦ Fast user switching enables two or more users to remain logged on at the same time and switch accounts without logging off.

Chapter 11

Finding Lost or Misplaced Items

In This Chapter

♦ Finding lost files and folders

♦ Assigning keywords and tags

♦ Tracking down your printer

With all your letters, resumés, photos, records, financial data, and other documents stored on your computer, you might think you'd never lose anything ever again. After all, everything is stored in one place. It's not as though you have stacks of papers scattered in different rooms throughout the house, right?

Wrong. Unfortunately, computer storage is a lot like having stacks of papers scattered in different rooms throughout the house. Although Windows tries to file everything for you in your own personal folder or one of its subfolders whenever you attempt to save or open a document, some applications insist on saving documents elsewhere. Or you may choose to keep your documents organized in special folders you create and then later forget the name and location of the folder where you saved a particular document.

Fortunately, a few tricks can help you harness your computer's innate ability to find stuff. In this chapter, you learn to use various search tools and techniques to track down what you're looking for.

Searching for Missing Files and Folders

I get calls all the time from friends, relatives, and colleagues who claim that a file they were working on mysteriously vanished. In about 1 percent of those cases, they're right—whatever file they were working on did vanish. Perhaps they didn't save it when the program asked them to or a power outage simply wiped the file off the map. In 99 percent of these cases, however, the person simply misplaced the file.

Tracking down misplaced files requires a certain amount of patience and the confidence that the file still exists. It also helps to know some file-hunting tricks:

◆ Click the **Start** button and point to **Recent Items** or **My Recent Documents** to view a list of the last 15 documents or so you opened. Click the name of the desired document.

◆ Run the program you used to create or edit the document and open the **File** menu. Most programs list the last four or five documents you opened at the bottom of the File menu.

◆ Run the program you used to create or edit the document and then click **File, Open.** This usually displays the contents of the folder in which the program normally saves documents.

If you share your computer and are afraid that someone will use the recent items list to find out what you were looking at, you can clear the list. In Windows XP, click **Start, My Recent Documents, Clear List.** In Vista, click **Start,** right-click **Recent Items**, and click **Clear Recent Items List.**)

> **Inside Tip** _____
>
> If Recent Items or My Recent Documents is not on the Start menu, the feature may be turned off. To turn it back on, right-click the **Start** button, click **Properties,** and click the **Start Menu** tab. In Windows Vista, click **Store and display a list of recently opened files** to place a check in its box and click **OK.** In Windows XP, click **Customize,** click the **Advanced** tab, and click **List My Most Recently Opened Documents** to check the box. Click **OK** and then click **OK** again to save your changes.

If none of those quick search tricks turns up the document, you can use the Windows Search utility to hunt for the file by name or by a specific phrase or string of characters included in the document.

Take the following steps to search for a file in Windows Vista:

1. Click the **Start** button.

2. Start typing the name of the file or folder you're looking for. As you type, Windows searches your computer and displays a list of items that match what you typed. The more you type, the narrower the search.

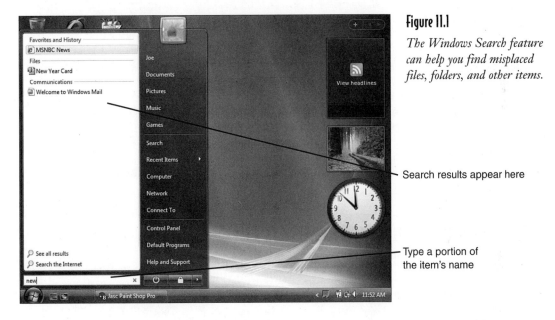

Figure 11.1

The Windows Search feature can help you find misplaced files, folders, and other items.

Search results appear here

Type a portion of the item's name

In Windows XP and Vista, you can perform a more advanced search using the item's name, file name extension (which denotes the file's format), the date on which the file was last modified, the contents of the file, and so on.

1. To begin, click **Start, Search.**

2. *In Windows Vista:* this opens a Search window. Click **Advanced Search** to display additional search criteria, as shown in Figure 11.2. Enter any criteria you want Vista to use to search for items, and click the **Search** button.

   In Windows XP: the Search Results dialog box appears. Click **All Files and Folders** or **Documents** (to limit the search to only the document files on your computer), enter your search criteria, and click the **Search** button.

Figure 11.2

The Windows Search utility can help you find misplaced files and folders.

Type a portion of the file's name

Click Search

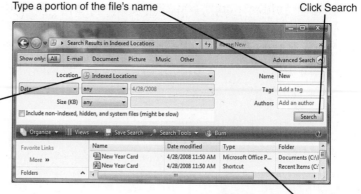

Narrow the search to a folder

Search results appear here

Computer Cheat

Most documents you create in a word processor, such as Microsoft Word, have names that end with the .DOC file name extension. You can type ***.doc** in the **Name** or **All or Part of the Filename** boxes to find all documents that have the .DOC file name extension. The asterisk is a *wildcard character* that stands in for any and all characters that come before the .DOC file name extension. If the program uses a different file name extension, replace the .doc with the extension the program uses.

Tagging Items in Windows Vista

To make your documents even easier to find, Windows Vista allows you to tag them—assign unique keywords to the documents that you can later search for. You can add tags using one of the following methods:

◆ Click **Start, Documents** or open the folder that contains the document you want to tag. Click the name of the document. In the Details pane at the bottom of the window, click **Add a tag,** type one or more unique words to describe the document, and click **Save** (see Figure 11.3).

Whoa!

Vista lets you tag only document files. You can't tag text files, rich text format (RTF) files, program files, folders, or other items Vista doesn't consider bona fide documents.

◆ When saving a document you created for the first time, click **File, Save** (or whatever command the program requires you to enter). The Save As dialog box appears. Type a name for the file, click **Add a tag,** and type one or more unique words to describe the document. You can also choose the folder where you want to save the file and enter an author's name. Click **Save.**

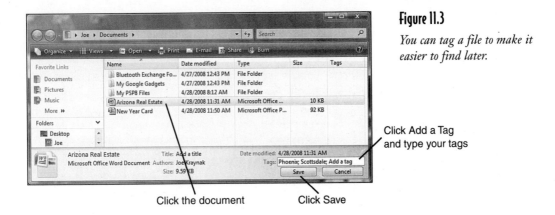

Figure 11.3

You can tag a file to make it easier to find later.

Click Add a Tag
and type your tags

Click the document   Click Save

To add multiple tags, separate the tags with semicolons.

Now, whenever you want to find the file you tagged, simply click **Start** and type one or more of the tags. The file's name should pop up at the top of the Start menu, and you can click the file's name to open it.

Hunting for Your Printer

When you print a document, as explained in Chapter 18, if all goes right and your printer begins printing, you don't need to worry about where your printer happens to be hanging out. If something goes wrong, however, you may need to locate your printer and determine the cause of the problem.

To track down your printer, take one of the following steps:

◆ In Windows Vista, click **Start, Control Panel.** Under Hardware and Sound, click **Printer.** The Printers window appears, as shown in Figure 11.4.

◆ In Windows XP, click **Start, Printers and Faxes.**

The printer with the check mark next to it is the default printer—the printer your computer uses unless you specify otherwise. If you have more than one printer installed, you can make another printer the default printer by right-clicking its icon and clicking **Set As Default Printer.**

Double-click the printer's icon to call up a window that displays any documents currently being printed or waiting to be printed. The list of documents often includes information indicating whether a print job has failed to print or is paused. See Chapter 18 for more information.

Figure 11.4

The Printers and Faxes window displays icons for all installed printers and fax machines.

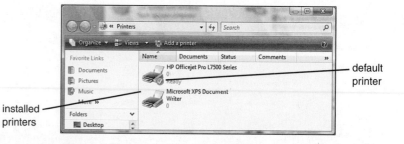

installed printers

default printer

Panic Attack

If no printers are installed and you know your computer is connected to a printer, you can install a printer, as explained in Chapter 18. In the Printers window, you can click **Add a printer** or **Add Printer** to run a wizard that leads you step by step through the process of locating and installing your printer. If your computer is on a network and uses a shared printer that's connected to a different computer on the network, printer setup is a little different; see Chapter 12 for more information.

The Least You Need to Know

◆ To quickly locate a misplaced document you worked on recently, click **Start** and point to **Recent Items** or **My Recent Documents.**

◆ Most programs keep a list of recently opened documents at the bottom of their File menu.

◆ To quickly search for anything in Windows Vista, click **Start** and start typing the name of whatever it is you're looking for.

◆ To perform a more advanced search, click **Start, Search,** (and then **Advanced Search** in Vista), and use the Search Results window to enter your search criteria.

◆ To view all printers installed on your computer, click **Start, Control Panel,** and the Printer option. The printer with the check mark is the one Windows is set up to use.

Networking Windows to Other Computers

In This Chapter

◆ Networking two or more computers

◆ Sharing network folders, files, and more

◆ Printing to network printers

◆ Securing your network

You've mastered the basics of using your computer. You can run programs, create documents, copy and move files, and even dazzle colleagues with the Windows tricks you've learned. Now you need to deal with something more complex—a network. Maybe your boss decided to install a network or you have two or more computers at home and want to connect them to share a printer or an Internet connection or swap files and other resources between the computers. Whatever the case, you're now facing the network challenge.

Perhaps you've heard about networks, and maybe you even have a general understanding of the concept, but you've never actually worked on a network and you don't know what to expect. In this chapter, you learn how to use several Windows features designed especially for networks so you can get up to speed in a hurry.

The Two Main Network Types

The two basic types of networks are *client-server* and *peer-to-peer*.

On a client-server network, all computers (the clients) are wired to a central computer (the network server), as shown in Figure 12.1. Whenever you need to access a network resource, you connect to the server, which then processes your commands and requests, links you to the other computers, and provides access to shared equipment and other resources. Although somewhat expensive and difficult to set up, a client-server network offers two big advantages: it is easy to maintain centrally through the network server, and it ensures reliable data transfers.

Figure 12.1

On a client-server network, clients are connected to a central server.

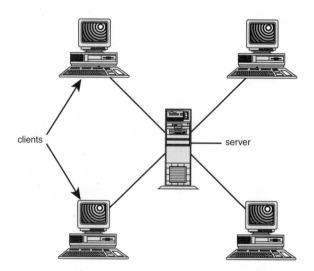

clients

server

Client-server networks typically have a network administrator who is in charge of assigning access privileges to each computer on the network. For example, some users might only be able to open data files on the server and might not be able to run certain programs. The administrator assigns each user a user name and password. You then must enter your user name and password to log on to the network.

On a peer-to-peer network, computers are linked directly to each other without the use of a central computer, as shown in Figure 12.2. Each computer has a network card connected through a network cable (or wireless connection) to another computer or to a central hub (a connection box). Many home users and small businesses use this peer-to-peer configuration because it doesn't require an expensive network server and it's relatively easy to set up.

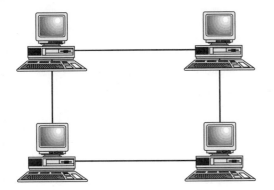

Figure 12.2

On a peer-to-peer network, each computer acts both as a client and a server.

However, a peer-to-peer network does have a few drawbacks: it's more difficult to manage, more susceptible to *packet collisions* (which occur when two computers request the same data at the same time), and not very secure because no central computer is in charge of validating user identities.

Exploring Your Networking Options

If you're looking to set up a large network for a business or school, consult a networking specialist to install, manage, and secure your network. This chapter can help you navigate a large network, but one chapter can't possibly cover the complexities of setting up and maintaining large, corporate networks.

If on the other hand, you need to set up a network for your home or small business, the project is well within the realm of do-it-yourselfers. Your first step is to decide which type of networking hardware you want to use. You have several choices.

Ethernet. Fast, reliable, and secure, Ethernet networks are an excellent choice if you don't mind running network cables throughout your home or business. Building Ethernet capability into a new home or office building is the way to go, but if you have an older home and modest networking needs, consider a less-intensive, less-intrusive approach.

Wi-Fi (Wireless-Fidelity). Relatively fast and reliable, Wi-Fi enables you to set up a network without having to run cables, and you can move the computers anywhere in your home or office without losing your connection. The main drawback is that the radio frequency signals most wireless networking devices use to communicate occasionally run into interference from radios, microwave ovens, and other electronic devices. This can slow or interrupt the connections.

Whoa!

Some Wi-Fi signals can reach pretty far—150 to 350 feet—so be sure to secure your network to keep unauthorized users (such as your neighbors) from accessing your data or using your broadband Internet service (which you're paying for).

Bluetooth or PAN (personal area network). Relatively slow, very secure, and inexpensive (if your computers and devices already are Bluetooth-enabled), this technology lets you connect up to eight devices across short distances (up to 30 feet). Bluetooth is generally used for connecting wireless devices (such as a mouse, keyboard, or headset) to a computer or phone but can also be used to establish a network. Wi-Fi, however, is usually a better option for networking.

Phone line (HPNA or Home Phoneline Networking Alliance network). Phone-line networks enable you to use the phone cables already installed in your home or business to communicate among computers. You can use your phone and network at the same time. HPNA is an affordable option for many home users who would prefer the security of a hard-wired network without having to run networking cables around their home.

Hybrid (mix and match). You can combine the networking technologies discussed here to create a hybrid network. For example, you can build an Ethernet network that connects all the computers in your office and then use a wireless or phone line connection for a computer you generally use in a more remote room of your house.

Inside Tip

I've networked the four computers in my home a couple times. The first time, I bought the standard Ethernet cards and cables and struggled an entire weekend running network cable and getting the darn thing up and running. The second time, I purchased a wireless router for one computer and two wireless networking cards for the other two computers. I connected the wireless devices, installed the software that was included, and spent the weekend with my wife and kids. The installation took about an hour. If you're considering networking the computers in your home, I strongly recommend you go wireless.

Installing Your Networking Hardware

The best way to build your own small network is to visit your local computer store and ask one of the technical wizards there to put together all the hardware you need. Go with one of the top brands, and ask which products seem to be the most trouble-free. Your hardware needs depend on how you want the computers to communicate.

For Ethernet, you need an Ethernet hub with enough ports to connect all the computers on the network. Each computer must have an Ethernet card (often called an *NIC* or *network interface card*), and you need enough Ethernet cable to connect each computer to the hub.

To connect computers in a wireless (Wi-Fi) network, each computer must be equipped with a compatible wireless networking adapter. If you plan to share a high-speed Internet connection, the modem that establishes and maintains the connection to the Internet must be connected to the router so the computers (that also connect to the router) can share the Internet connection (see Figure 12.3). The router controls the data flow between the Internet and your networked computers, and it secures the network from unauthorized access.

Whoa!

Read the hardware installation instructions thoroughly before installing any hardware or networking software. In some cases, you need to install the software *before* installing the hardware or you run into problems.

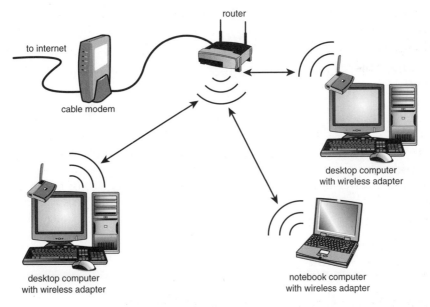

Figure 12.3

A wireless network requires each computer to have a wireless network adapter installed.

If all your devices are Bluetooth-enabled, they already have the hardware required to get connected. All you need to do is run the Windows Network Setup Wizard, as explained in the next section.

For HPNA, each computer you want to network must be equipped with a special HPNA networking card and be located near a phone jack. You can then use standard telephone cords to plug each computer into the nearest phone jack.

When choosing networking hardware, look for networking speeds in the 100Mbps range for Ethernet and 54Mbps for wireless Ethernet connections (the 802.11g standard). You can expect much slower connections over Bluetooth networks. Also if you plan to use *VoIP* (*Voice over Internet Protocol*), which enables you to place phone calls over a high-speed Internet connection such as a cable modem, be sure your networking equipment supports VoIP.

When shopping for a wireless router and adapters, you'll need to know something about the different standards: 802.11 (obsolete), 802.11a (54Mbps, 35 meters), 802.11b (11Mbps, 38 meters), 802.11g (54Mbps, 38 meters), 802.11y (54Mbps, 50 meters), 802.11n (248Mbps, 70 meters). For home use, the 802.11g standard provides sufficient speed and range and is backward-compatible with older standards, including 802.11a and 802.11b.

Running the Network Setup Wizard

Home networking kits and most wireless routers include the software you need to set up and configure the network. If you install an Ethernet network (with Ethernet cards, cables, and a hub), you can use the Windows Network Setup Wizard to get your network up and running.

Inside Tip

Although Windows can lead you through the process of setting up the network, you must first install the drivers for any networking hardware you installed. Refer to the instructions included with your networking hardware for details. In most cases, you turn the computer off, install the hardware, and turn the computer back on. Windows then automatically identifies the new hardware and leads you through the process of installing the drivers for it.

To set up a network in Windows Vista, take the following steps:

1. Click **Start, Control Panel** to display the Control Panel.

2. Click **Network and Internet.**

3. Click **Network and Sharing Center.**

4. Click **Set up a connection or network.** The Set up a connection or network wizard starts, as shown in Figure 12.4, and prompts you to choose the type of connection you want to set up.

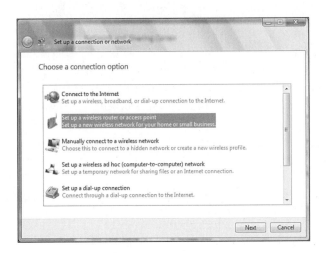

Figure 12.4

The Set up a connection or network setup wizard leads you step by step through the process of getting your network up and running.

5. Follow the wizard's instructions to set up your network.

6. Repeat for each computer you want to include in the network.

To set up a network in Windows XP, take the following steps:

1. Click **Start, Control Panel.**

2. Click **Network and Internet Connections.** The Network and Internet Connections window appears.

3. Click the option for the type of network you want to set up:

   Set up or change your home or small office network runs the

Inside Tip _____

Each computer on the network must have a unique name that identifies it, but you must assign all computers to the same *workgroup.* The workgroup defines which computers can be part of the network. Computers in different workgroups cannot identify one another on the network.

Network Setup Wizard, which enables you to set up, configure, and secure a standard Ethernet network.

Set up a wireless network for your home or small office runs the Wireless Network Setup Wizard, which enables you to set up, configure, and secure a wireless network.

4. Follow the wizard's instructions.

5. Repeat for each computer you want to include in the network.

After a wireless device is installed on your computer, Windows automatically searches for networks that are within range of the device and displays a list of found networks. It then prompts you to choose which network you want to belong to. If you have a close neighbor who has a wireless network, that network may appear on the list. Likewise, if you take your wireless notebook computer into a business that has Wi-Fi, Windows will identify the network and prompt you to connect to it. However, businesses typically set up their Wi-Fi networks to block unauthorized access, so you usually need to enter a special number or password (and pay) to access the wireless Internet.

Enabling or Disabling File and Printer Sharing

Before you can share files and printers over your network connections, Windows file and printer sharing must be enabled. When you set up your network, Windows typically does this for you, but you may want to disable the feature temporarily or permanently on one of your networked computers to prevent unauthorized access to its files. To enable or disable file and printer sharing, take the following steps in Windows Vista:

1. Click **Start.**

2. Right-click **Network** and click **Properties.** The Network and Sharing Center appears.

3. Click the down arrow to the right of File Sharing to view your options.

4. Click **Turn off file sharing.**

5. Click **Apply.**

Inside Tip

If you have a third-party firewall installed, you may need to use it to disable or enable file sharing. Another option is to display the Network and Sharing Center as explained in steps 1 and 2 and then click **Manage network connections.** Right-click the icon for your network connection, click **Properties,** click the check box next to **File and Printer Sharing for Microsoft Networks** (to enable or disable the option), and click **OK.**

To enable or disable file and printer sharing in Windows XP, follow these steps:

1. Click **Start.**

2. Right-click **My Network Places,** and **Properties.**

3. Right-click the icon for your network connection, click **Properties,** click the check box next to **File and Printer Sharing for Microsoft Networks** (to enable or disable the option), and click **OK.**

Sharing Resources Across the Network

Before you can access folders, files, and printers on another networked computer, those resources must be flagged as shared. Here's how to share a folder or file with other users in Windows Vista:

1. Right-click the icon for the disk or folder you want to share and click **Share.** The File Sharing dialog box for the selected item appears, as shown in Figure 12.5.

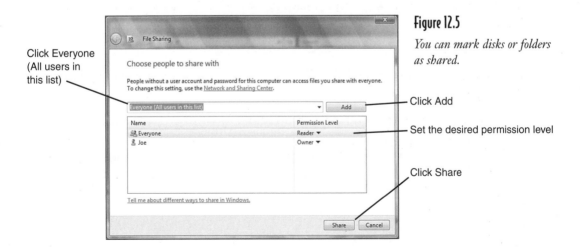

Figure 12.5

You can mark disks or folders as shared.

Click Everyone (All users in this list)

Click Add

Set the desired permission level

Click Share

2. Open the **Choose people to share with** drop-down list, click **Everyone (All users in this list),** and click **Add.**

3. Click the arrow next to **Reader** in the Permission Level list, and click the desired permission level: Reader (can view files without changing them), Contributor (can edit files but not create or delete them), or Co-Owner (has full access to files).

4. Click **Share** and **OK** if prompted to confirm. The File Sharing dialog box appears, indicating that the folder is now shared.

5. Click **Done.** Vista display a special icon for the folder indicating that it is now a shared resource.

Panic Attack

You may have trouble accessing the shared folder over the network unless all the other computers on your network are set up with identical user accounts (Windows logon names and passwords). If they're not, you can remove password protection on the computer that contains the shared folder: Click **Start**, right-click **Network**, click **Properties**, click the arrow to the right of **Password protected sharing**, click **Turn off password protected sharing**, and click **Apply.** You should now be able to access the shared folder over your network.

To share a disk, folder, or file in Windows XP:

1. Right-click the icon for the item you want to share and click **Sharing and Security.**

2. Click **Share This Folder on the Network,** and enter a share name for the item.

3. To give other users on the network permission to edit the files, click the check box next to **Allow network users to change my files,** and click **OK.**

You also can enable other users to share your printer. Use the Control Panel (**Start, Control Panel**) to display the printers installed in Windows, as explained in Chapter 11. Right-click your printer icon and choose **Sharing.** Enter the requested information and click **OK.**

To stop sharing an item, right-click the icon for the item and choose **Share** or **Sharing.** Select the option to stop sharing the item and click **OK.**

Checking Out the Network Neighborhood

When you connect to the network, you can access any shared disks, folders, and printers on other computers connected to the network, assuming you have the right password (if a password is required). However, locating shared resources can be difficult, especially on a large network.

Fortunately, Windows has tools to help you track down network resources and manage them. The most basic tool is My Network Places. When you click **Start, Network** or **My Network Places,** a window appears, displaying icons for all the computers on the network. You can then browse the shared resources on any of these computers, just as if they were on your own computer.

Panic Attack
If the computer you want to access does not appear, try clicking the workgroup icon. Sometimes the icon for a computer doesn't pop up in the first window. If the computer is still unavailable, it might be turned off, or the network settings could be wrong. Open the **Start** menu, click **Help and Support** or **Help** (in XP), click the **Troubleshooting** link, choose the option for troubleshooting network connections, and follow the on-screen instructions.

Mapping a Network Drive to Your Computer

If you frequently access a particular disk or folder on the network, you can *map* the folder to a drive on your computer. If you share your Documents folder on the network, for example, you can map it to a drive letter on one of the network computers. Whenever you want to access the folder, you simply change to that "drive."

To map a shared folder to your computer in Windows Vista, take the following steps:

1. On the network computer from which you want to access the shared folder, display the icon for the folder you want to map to a drive. (This is not the computer where the drive is housed, but one of the other computers on your network.)

2. Right-click the folder icon and click **Map Network Drive.** The Map Network Drive window appears, as shown in Figure 12.6.

Figure 12.6

You can map a disk or folder on another networked computer to the your computer.

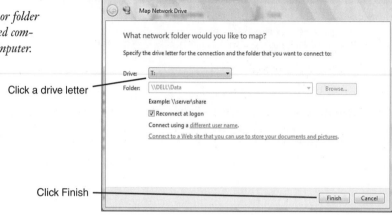

Click a drive letter

Click Finish

3. Open the **Drive** drop-down menu and click the letter you want to map this folder to.

4. Click **Finish.**

The process is a little more complex in Windows XP:

1. Click **Start, My Network Places, Add a Network Place.**

2. The Add a Network Place Wizard appears. Click **Next.**

3. Click **Choose another network location** and click **Next.**

4. Click **Browse,** use the resulting dialog box to select the network folder you want to map to this computer, click **OK,** and click **Next.**

5. Type a name for the network place and click **Next.** Click **Finish.**

Windows creates an icon for the new network place and opens a window displaying its contents.

Installing a Network Printer

Traditionally, you connect a printer to the computer's parallel printer port, but new technologies have provided new methods for connecting printers. Most newer printers connect to the computer's USB port instead of the parallel printer port. Printers designed for networking may plug into the network's router or allow multiple computers to connect to it via a wireless connection.

If the printer is connected to only one of the computers on the network, you have to first mark the printer as a shared resource on that computer. (See "Sharing Resources

Across the Network," earlier in this chapter for details.) You can then install the printer on your other networked computers.

Here's how you install a network, wireless, or Bluetooth printer in Windows Vista:

1. Click **Start, Control Panel.**

2. Click **Printer** (under Hardware and Sound). The Printers window appears, displaying icons for any printers currently installed on this computer.

3. Click **Add a printer.** The Add Printer dialog box appears, asking whether you want to install a local printer (a printer connected directly to this computer) or a network, wireless, or Bluetooth printer.

4. Click **Add a Network, Wireless or Bluetooth Printer,** click **Next,** and follow the on-screen instructions.

To install a printer in Windows XP:

1. Click **Start, Control Panel, Printers and Other Hardware, Add a Printer.**

2. Follow the on-screen instructions.

After the network printer is set up, you can use it to print documents just as if the printer were connected to your computer. However, if you did not set up the network printer as your default printer, you must select the printer when you choose to print your document.

Inside Tip

For more about installing and using a printer in Windows XP or Vista, check out Chapter 18.

Sharing a Broadband Internet Connection

Windows enables networked computers to share a broadband Internet connection, such as a cable modem, DSL (digital subscriber line), or satellite connection. With a shared connection, while you're working on the Internet, your significant other can be surfing the web, chatting online with friends, or checking e-mail on another computer.

To share a connection, your network requires router-managed communications between the modem and the Internet and among all the networked computers. You plug your Internet modem into the router, and your networked computers access the modem through the router. The router typically includes its own security software called a firewall to prevent unauthorized access to your network from the Internet.

Your router should include complete instructions on how to set it up to share a broadband Internet connection. In most cases, after the Internet modem and router are installed, the networked computers identify the connection and display a dialog box asking whether you want to use the connection. You simply confirm that it's okay, and you're connected.

Securing Your Network

A broadband Internet connection is typically an *always-on* connection. That is, as long as you leave your computer on, you're connected to the Internet. This makes your computer and network more vulnerable to attacks from snoopy people and perhaps even vandals on the Internet. With the proper know-how, someone on the Internet can connect to your computer, peek at your documents, and even destroy valuable data.

You can't completely protect your computer or network from such threats, but you can significantly deter potential break-ins by implementing various security measures.

Whoa!

Windows includes a firewall to deter unauthorized access, but it has no antivirus software. I strongly encourage you to install an antivirus program, such as Trend Micro Antivirus (**us.trendmicro.com**), CA Anti-Virus (**shop.ca.com**), Avast (**www.avast. com**), or AVG Anti-Virus (**free.agv.com**).

Activating the Windows Firewall

One of the best ways to protect your computer from break-ins is to install a firewall. A firewall is security software that stands between your computer and the Internet, enabling your computer to freely exchange data with the Internet but blocking access to your computer or network from other users on the Internet.

If you're using a router to connect to the Internet, it probably has its own firewall, which is usually superior to any software firewall, such as the Windows firewall. If it doesn't, you can activate the Windows firewall, as explained in Chapter 26.

Limiting Access to Your Network

A wireless router enables any wireless computer that's in range of the router to connect to it and use it to access the Internet or even break into your network. Your next-door neighbor, for example, can get free Internet service through your router and even poke around on your network!

Most wireless routers have a security protocol called WEP (wired equivalent privacy) that enables you to control which computers can connect to it. This security is typically disabled by default, so you have to enable it. With WEP, you can specify an identification number that each computer must use to access the router. Figure 12.7 shows a router that uses a similar security system based on Mac addresses. You must enter an approved address on each computer you want to be able to access your network.

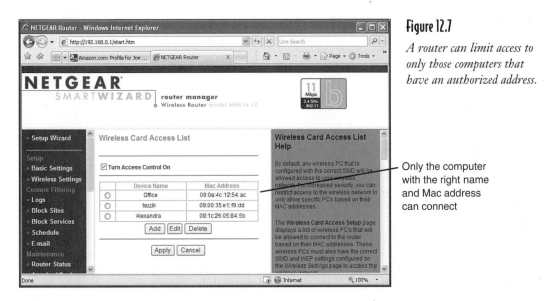

Figure 12.7

A router can limit access to only those computers that have an authorized address.

Only the computer with the right name and Mac address can connect

WEP and similar network security features are not foolproof. A well-trained hacker can get around these features. However, your router's firewall can usually prevent the average neighbor from hacking into your system. Because firewalls can cause problems, I recommend that you enable the firewall on your router and disable any software firewalls on your networked computers. However, if one of your computers is a laptop that you take with you sometimes, be sure to re-enable your laptop's firewall before taking it on the road.

Securing Your Notebook PC in Hot Spots

Wi-Fi is great. You can spend the entire day at Starbucks drinking your caffè latte and playing on your Wi-Fi–enabled laptop. Unfortunately, this makes you vulnerable to anyone else in the near vicinity who may log on to the Wi-Fi network looking to view or steal information stored on your computer or passing between your computer and the network. Here are a few tips to protect yourself:

Be sure you send and receive your e-mail over a secure connection. If you use a web-based e-mail program, you can usually tell whether the connection is secured by looking at the web-based e-mail services address in your web browser. If it starts with "https" instead of "http," you're on a secure site.

If you use a separate e-mail account, check with your e-mail service provider to determine whether it offers a secure connection. This is usually referred to as SSL (secure sockets layer). You'll need to enter special settings in your e-mail program to send and receive e-mail over these secure connections. Your e-mail service provider can give you detailed instructions.

Enable the Windows firewall, as explained earlier in this chapter.

Turn off file and printer sharing, as explained earlier in this chapter.

Be sure any folders that contain sensitive data remain private. In Windows Vista, new folders are automatically made private. In Windows XP, right-click the folder, click **Properties,** click the **Sharing** tab, and click **Do Not Share This Folder.**

Encrypt sensitive files. To encrypt a file, right-click it, choose **Properties,** click **Advanced,** and click **Encrypt contents to secure data.** You can open the file on your computer with no problem, but if you try to open it on another computer, you get an Access Denied message.

Finally, don't lug around sensitive data on your notebook computer. None of the other precautions listed here will protect your data if someone walks off with your computer or steals it out of your car. The only protection is to keep sensitive data at home, although this isn't always practical.

The Least You Need to Know

- A client-server network has a central server to which all computers on the network connect. On a peer-to-peer network, every computer acts as both client and server, depending on whether it's accessing resources on another computer or sharing its resources with another computer.

- Before you can access the contents of a disk or folder, the disk or folder must be marked as shared.

- You can check out what's available on your network by clicking **Start** and then **Network** or **My Network Places.**

- You can map a network folder to your computer to have it appear as a disk or folder on your computer.

- You can use the Add Printer Wizard to set up a network printer on your computer.

- To prevent unauthorized access to your network, learn and implement the security features in both your networking hardware and in Windows.

Part  3

Getting Down to Business with Office Programs

Playing Solitaire and fiddling with the Windows desktop can keep you entertained for hours, but you didn't lay down a few hundred bucks for a computer only to use it as a 99¢ deck of playing cards. You want to type letters, crunch numbers, create dazzling PowerPoint presentations, and take control of your personal finances … you want to use the computer to get more out of life!

In Part 3, you become productive with your computer as you learn how to type and format letters, add images, create automated accounting worksheets, and print your documents. Along the way, you even learn how to perform some basic tasks that apply to most applications, including saving, naming, and opening the files you create.

Typing and Other Word Processing Chores

In This Chapter

- ◆ Typing on an electronic page
- ◆ Adding the date and time
- ◆ Making your text big and pretty
- ◆ Moving your paragraphs around on a page
- ◆ Saving your document

When my wife and I purchased a new computer for our home, I was dazzled by the hardware: the state-of-the-art processor, the all-in-one fax-copier-scanner-printer, the big flat-screen monitor, the surround sound audio system, and the super-speed cable modem. With this bad boy, we'd be cruising rather than just surfing the Internet, building our own websites and blogs, scanning family photos, and editing videos like pros!

As I ran down the list of all the cool things we could do with our new computer, my wife just stared at the screen. When I finished, she looked at me and said, "I just want to type a letter."

With the popularity of the Internet and other computer technologies, it's easy to forget that many people still use a computer primarily to type and print documents. In this chapter, you learn how to type, format (style), edit (cut and paste), and save a document using the most popular word processor on the planet—Microsoft Word.

Making the Transition to the Electronic Page

When you run Word (or whichever word processor is installed on your computer), it displays a blank "sheet of paper." The program also displays a vertical line called the *cursor* or *insertion point* to show you where the characters will appear when you start typing. Just below the insertion point is a horizontal line that marks the end of the document, as shown in Figure 13.1. As you type, this line moves down automatically to make room for your text. (You can't move the cursor or insertion point past this line, no matter how hard you try.)

Figure 13.1

Start typing (Word 2007)!

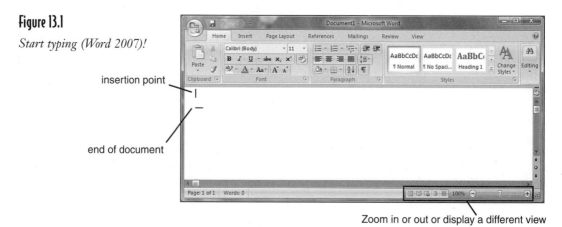

insertion point

end of document

Zoom in or out or display a different view

Figure 13.1 shows you what Word 2007 looks like. If you have an older version, it'll look more like Word 2003, shown in Figure 13.2. In Word 2007, Microsoft completely revamped the user interface to make less use of menus and more use of toolbars and confused the heck out of many old-school Word users like me. Whichever version of Word you're using, you'll catch on to the most common commands pretty quickly.

Word 2007 includes a *ribbon* where it displays commands for doing the most common tasks. Commands are organized in logical groups, such as Font, Paragraph, and Clipboard. To access the commands in a particular group, you click the group's tab.

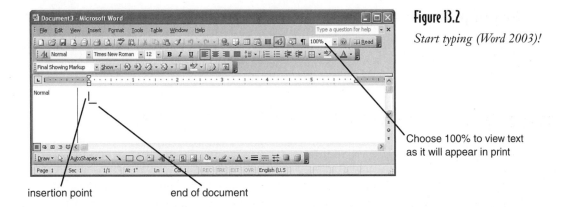

Figure 13.2

Start typing (Word 2003)!

Choose 100% to view text
as it will appear in print

insertion point   end of document

Panic Attack

Although this chapter uses Microsoft Word to show you basic word processing features, don't worry if you're using a different word processor. The basic features and commands covered in this chapter differ only slightly between word processing programs. If you don't have Word or another high-end word processor installed on your computer, run WordPad, which is included with Windows. Open the **Start** menu, point to **All Programs,** point to **Accessories,** and click **WordPad.**

Keyboarding Tips

The best way to learn how to type in a word processor is to start typing. As you type, if the text is too small to read, use the **Zoom** controls, as shown in Figures 13.1 and 13.2, to zoom in. (This simply changes the size of the text as it is displayed on-screen. To change the actual size of the text as it will appear in print, skip ahead to "Making the Text Larger or Smaller" later in this chapter.)

Press the **Enter** key only to end a paragraph and start a new paragraph. Within a paragraph, the program automatically *wraps* the text from one line to the next as you type.

Don't press the **Enter** key to insert a blank line between paragraphs. Later in this chapter, I show you a better way to add space between paragraphs.

Use the mouse or the arrow keys to move the insertion point around in the document. If you're working on a long document, use the scroll bar to move more quickly and then click in the document to move the insertion point where you want it.

Delete to the right; backspace to the left. To delete a character that's to the right of the insertion point, press the **Delete** key. To delete characters to the left of the insertion point, press the **Backspace** key.

Getting a Better View

In addition to allowing you to zoom in and out on a page, most word processing programs offer various views of a page. To change to a view, you typically open the **View** menu and click one of the view options.

Normal or *Draft* shows your document as one continuous document. In this view, the word processor hides complex page formatting, headers, footers, objects with wrapped text, floating graphics, and backgrounds. Scrolling is smooth because this view uses the least amount of memory.

Print or *Page Layout* provides a more realistic view of how your pages will appear in print. Print Layout displays graphics, wrapping text, headers, footers, margins, and drawn objects. This uses a lot of memory, however, and might make scrolling a little jerky.

Web Layout displays a document as it will appear when displayed in a web browser. In Web Layout view, a word processor displays web page backgrounds, wraps the text to fit inside a standard browser window, and positions the graphics as they will appear when viewed online.

Outline allows you to quickly organize and reorganize your document by dragging headings from one location to another in the document.

Creating New Documents

If you're not too keen on starting from scratch, you can begin with one of Word's many templates. In Word 2007, take the following steps:

1. Click the **Office** button and click **New.** The New Document dialog box appears, as shown in Figure 13.3.

2. Click **Installed Templates** to display only the templates currently installed on your computer. If you're connected to the Internet (see Part 4), you can access even more templates by selecting a group under Microsoft Office Online.

3. Click a template in the middle pane to preview it in the pane on the right, and select the template you want to use.

4. Click **Create.** Word copies the template and displays its contents so you can begin editing it.

Click Installed Templates   Preview the template

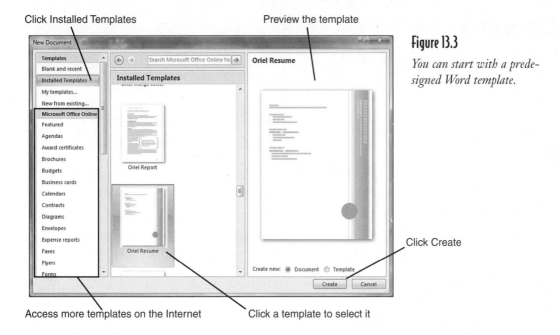

Figure 13.3

You can start with a prede-signed Word template.

Click Create

Access more templates on the Internet   Click a template to select it

In Microsoft Word 2003, use the New Document pane to create a new document from a template:

1. Click File, New.

2. Click one of the options under Templates: **Templates on Office Online** (to download a template from Microsoft's website) or **On My Computer** (to use a template that's already installed).

Computer Cheat

Many of the Word templates use text boxes to control the position of blocks of text on-screen, which can be a little confusing when you first encounter them. To edit the text, click in the text box and make your changes. (For more about moving, resizing, and creating your own text boxes, check out Chapter 16.)

What's with the Squiggly Red and Green Lines?

As you type, you might get a strange feeling that your sixth-grade English teacher is inside your computer, underlining your spelling and grammar mistakes. Whenever you type a string of characters that Word can't find in its dictionary, Word draws a squiggly red line under the word to flag it for you so you can immediately correct it. If the word is misspelled, right-click the word and choose the correct spelling from the context menu. (A squiggly green line marks a questionable grammatical construction.)

If the squiggly lines annoy you, you can turn off automatic spell checking.

In Word 2007: Click the **Office** button, click **Word Options,** click **Proofing,** and turn off both **Check spelling as you type** and **Mark grammar errors as you type.** Click **OK.**

In Word 2003: Open the **Tools** menu and click **Options.** Click the **Spelling & Grammar** tab, and turn off both **Check spelling as you type** and **Check grammar as you type.** Click **OK.**

You can always have Word check your spelling and grammar for you after you've completed the document. See "Checking Your Spelling and Grammar," near the end of this chapter.

Inserting Today's Date

When you're typing a letter, you should include the date as part of the heading, just below your inside address (your address typed at the top of the letter). Of course, you could just type the date, but that's too much like work. Have Word insert the date for you.

To have Word insert the date and time for you, you can either click **Insert** and then in the Text area, click the **Insert Time and Date** button, click the desired format, and click **OK.** Or you can open the **Insert** menu, click **Date and Time,** click the desired format, and click **OK.**

Panic Attack

If the date or time is not current, your computer has the wrong information. In Windows Vista, click the time display on the right end of the Windows taskbar, click **Change Date and Time Settings,** and use the resulting dialog box to reset the date or time. In Windows XP, double-click the time display on the right end of the Windows taskbar, and use the resulting dialog box to reset the date or time.

Making the Text Larger or Smaller

When you first start typing, you might notice that the text looks rather bland. Word processors choose the dullest, dreariest-looking typestyle available as the default text. To give your text a facelift, try choosing a different typestyle (or *font*) and varying the size (measured in *points*) and attributes (such as bold and italic) of the text. Fonts can be serif or sans serif. Serif fonts have short cross lines at the end of the main stroke of each character, which is supposed to make them easier to read. San Serif (without serif) fonts do not have the short cross lines at the end of the main stroke and are used mainly for headings and titles. Arial is an example of San Serif font. Times New Roman is an example of Serif font.

To change the appearance of existing text, drag over the text to *highlight* it. Highlighting displays white text on a black background to indicate that the text is selected. The next step depends on which version of Word you're using.

In Word 2007: After you highlight the text, a small "Mini toolbar" pops up providing you with the most common options for formatting text. You can use these controls or click the **Home** tab to access more controls, as shown in Figure 13.4.

In Word 2003: Choose the desired formatting options from the Formatting toolbar.

def•i•ni•tion

A **font** is a collection of characters that share the same typestyle and size. (Type size is measured in **points**; a point is approximately $1/72$ inch.) Most programs use the terms *font* and *typestyle* interchangeably.

The Home tab offers more formatting options

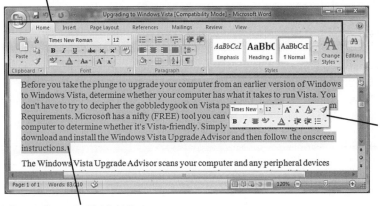

Figure 13.4

Word 2007 presents two ways to apply text formatting.

A Mini toolbar pops up when you highlight text

Drag text over to highlight it

You can apply formatting before you type text, too. Simply enter your formatting preferences and then start typing.

Where do you get fonts? Windows comes with dozens of fonts. Most word processors, desktop publishing programs, and other applications come with additional font sets. You can purchase font collections on CD or download fonts from the Internet, but you probably already have more fonts than you'll ever use.

Shoving Text Left, Right, or Center

As you type a document, you might want to center a heading or push a date or address to the right side of the page to set it apart from surrounding text. To quickly change the text alignment, click anywhere inside the paragraph and then click one of the following buttons on the Formatting toolbar:

 Align Left pushes all lines of the paragraph against the left margin.

 Center positions each line of the paragraph at an equal distance from both the left and right margins.

 Align Right pushes all lines of the paragraph against the right margin. This is a useful option for placing a date in the upper-right corner of a page.

 Justify inserts spaces between the words as needed to make every line of the paragraph the same length, as in newspaper columns.

 The Home tab (Word 2007) and Formatting toolbar (Word 2003) also contain buttons for creating numbered and bulleted lists. Simply highlight the paragraphs you want to transform into a list and click the desired button: **Numbering** or **Bullets.**

To indent the first line of a paragraph, you can press the **Tab** key at the beginning of the paragraph or enter a setting for the first line indent. Most word processors display a ruler, as shown in Figure 13.5, which lets you quickly indent paragraphs and set *tab stops.* (Tab stops determine where the insertion point stops when you press the **Tab** key.) To toggle the ruler on or off in Word 2007, click the Ruler button above the vertical scroll bar on the right.

first line indent marker   hanging indent marker   Click to toggle
                                                                 the ruler on or off

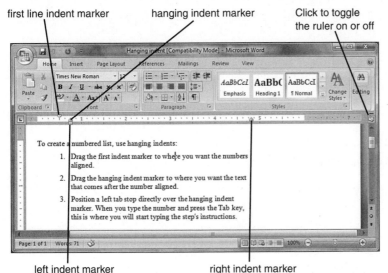

Figure 13.5

Use the ruler to quickly indent paragraphs and set tabs.

left indent marker   right indent marker

To indent text and change margins and tab stop settings, select the paragraph(s) you want the change to affect (to modify a single paragraph, just be sure the insertion point is somewhere inside the paragraph), and take one of the following steps:

♦ To place a tab stop, click the button on the far left end of the ruler to select the desired tab stop type (left, right, center, or decimal). Then click in the lower half of the ruler where you want the tab stop positioned.

♦ To move a tab stop, drag it left or right. To delete it, drag it off the ruler.

♦ To indent the right side of a paragraph, drag the right indent marker to the left.

♦ To indent the left side of a paragraph, drag the left indent marker to the right. (The left indent marker is the rectangle below the upward-pointing triangle.)

♦ To indent only the first line of a paragraph, drag the first line indent marker to the right. (This is the downward-pointing triangle on the left.)

♦ To create a hanging indent, drag the hanging indent marker to the right. (This is the upward-pointing triangle on the left.)

Changing the Line Spacing

Here's a section just for kids. If you're working on a five-page paper for school, and you have only two and a half pages of material, you can stretch it out by double spacing!

Take the following steps to change the line spacing for an entire document in Word 2007:

1. Press **Ctrl+A** to select all the text.

2. Click **Home** to display the Home tab.

3. Click the **Line Spacing** button (in the Paragraph area), and click the desired line spacing.

Here's how it works in Word 2003:

1. Press **Ctrl+A** to select all the text.

2. Click **Format, Paragraph,** and open the **Line Spacing** list.

3. Click the desired line spacing option, and click **OK.**

A quicker way to change line spacing is to select the text and press one of the following keystrokes: **Ctrl+2** for double-spacing, **Ctrl+5** for 1.5 line spacing, and **Ctrl+1** for single spacing.

Computer Cheat

If your teacher wises up and issues formatting restrictions on your next assignment, bump up the text size by 1 or 2 points (barely noticeable); use the **Page Layout** tab (Word 2007) or **File, Page Setup** command (Word 2003) to increase the margins; and increase the line spacing by only a few points instead of double-spacing. An even more subtle technique is to use a larger font. Some fonts, such as Arial and Times New Roman, take up more space at the same point size than other fonts.

Inserting Space Between Paragraphs

Leaving space between paragraphs helps the reader easily see where one paragraph ends and another begins. Of course, you can insert blank lines between paragraphs by pressing the **Enter** key twice at the end of a paragraph, but that's a sloppy technique that limits your control over paragraph spacing later.

By specifying the exact amount of space you want inserted between paragraphs, you ensure that the amount of space between paragraphs is consistent throughout your document.

To change the space between paragraphs, drag over the paragraphs to highlight at least a portion of each paragraph you want the change to affect. (You don't need to highlight all of the first and last paragraphs.) Now, take one of the following steps:

In Word 2007: By default, Word automatically inserts 10 points after each paragraph. To remove this space or add space above the selected paragraphs, click **Home,** click the **Line Spacing** button (in the Paragraph area), and click **Add Space Before Paragraph** (to add 12 points of space before the paragraph) or **Remove Space After Paragraph.** For more control over the space between paragraphs, click the **Line Spacing** button, click **Line Spacing Options,** and use the resulting dialog box to set your preferences.

In Word 2003: Open the **Format** menu and click **Paragraph.** Under **Spacing,** click the arrows to the right of **Before** or **After** to specify the amount of space (measured in points) you want to insert before or after each paragraph. Click **OK.**

Inside Tip

In most cases, 6 points of extra spacing before or after each paragraph does the trick.

Save It or Lose It

Unless you're the type of person who loves the thrill of risking everything for no potential gain, you should save your document soon after you type a paragraph or two. Why? Because right now, your computer is storing everything you type in RAM (random access memory). A little dip in your local electric company's power grid can send your document off to never-never land. To prevent losing your work, save it to a permanent storage area—your computer's hard disk.

The first time you save a document, your program asks for two things: a name for the document, and the name of the drive and folder where you want the document stored. By default, all the documents you create are going to be saved to your Documents folder. Here's the standard operating procedure for saving documents in most Windows programs:

1. 💾 Click the **Save** button on the toolbar, or click **Office** button, **Save** (Word 2007) or click **File, Save** (Word 2003). The Save As dialog box appears, asking you to name the file.

2. Click in the **File name** text box, and type a name for the file, as shown in Figure 13.6. The name can be up to 255 characters long, and you can use spaces, but you cannot use any of the following taboo characters: \ / : * ? " < > |.

Figure 13.6

Use the Save As dialog box to save your document to your computer's hard disk.

Select a drive or folder ⎯

Type a file name ⎯

Click Save ⎯

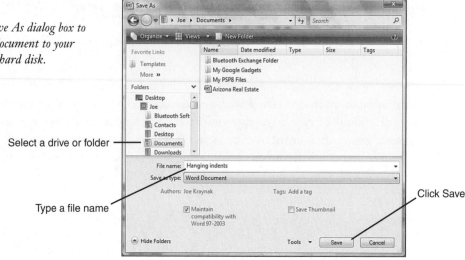

3. *Optional:* Select the disk drive and folder where you want to save the document. In Word 2003, you select the drive and folder using the **Save in** list.

4. Click the **OK** or **Save** button. The file is saved to the disk.

From now on, saving this document is easy; you don't have to name it or tell the program where to store it ever again. The program saves your changes in the document you already created and named. You should save your document every 5 to 10 minutes to avoid losing any work. In most programs, you can quickly save a document by pressing **Ctrl+S** or by clicking the **Save** button on the program's toolbar.

Most new word processors are set up to save files in the Documents (or My Documents) folder. If you create your own folders for storing documents, you might want to set up one of these folders as the one your word processor looks to first.

In Word 2007: Click the **Office** button, click **Word Options,** click **Save,** click the **Browse** button next to Default File Location, and use the resulting dialog box to select the folder where want Word to save your documents.

In Word 2003: Open the **Tools** menu and click **Options.** Click the **File Locations** tab, click **Documents** (under File types), and click the **Modify** button. Use the Modify Location dialog box to pick the desired drive and folder, and click **OK** to return to the Options dialog box. Click **OK** to save your changes.

Now, whenever you choose to open or save a document, Word will display the contents of the folder you selected.

Editing Your Letters and Other Documents

Is your letter perfect? Are you sure? Take a 10-minute break, come back, and read it again with fresh eyes. Chances are good that your letter has at least a couple minor flaws and possibly even some major organizational problems.

To perform the required fixes and purge common errors from your letter, you need to master the tools of the editorial trade. The following sections show you how to use your word processor's editing tools to copy, move, and delete text, and how to check for and correct spelling errors and typos.

Selecting Text

Before you can do anything with the text you just typed, you must select it. You can always just drag over text to select it (as explained earlier in this chapter), but Word offers several quicker ways to select text. The following table describes these techniques.

Quick Text-Selection Techniques

To Select This ...	Do This ...
Single word	Double-click the word.
Sentence	Ctrl+click anywhere in the sentence.
Paragraph	Triple-click anywhere in the paragraph. Alternatively, position the pointer to the left of the paragraph until it changes to a right-pointing arrow and then double-click.
Several paragraphs	Position the pointer to the left of the paragraphs until it changes to a right-pointing arrow. Then double-click and drag up or down.
One line of text	Position the pointer to the left of the line until it changes to a right-pointing arrow and then click. (Click and drag to select additional lines.)
Large block of text	Click at the beginning of the text, scroll down to the end of the text, and Shift+click.
Entire document	Press Ctrl+A. Alternatively, position the pointer to the left of any text until it changes to a right-pointing arrow and then triple-click.
Extend the selection	Hold down the Shift key while using the arrow keys, Page Up, Page Down, Home, or End.
Rectangular block	Hold down the Alt key while dragging over the text.

You can select non-neighboring chunks of text selecting one section and holding down the **Ctrl** key while selecting other sections. If you choose to copy and paste those selections, Word pastes the sections in the order you selected them.

Cutting and Pasting Without Scissors

Every word processor features the electronic equivalent of scissors and glue. With the cut, copy, and paste commands, you can cut or copy selected text and then insert it in a different location in your document. You can even copy or cut text from one document and paste it in another document!

To cut or copy text, first select it, and click either the **Cut** or the **Copy** button on the toolbar (or the Home tab in Word 2007). Move the insertion point to where you want the text inserted, and click the **Paste** button. Note that cutting a selection deletes it, whereas copying it leaves the selection in place and creates a duplicate.

Inside Tip

Master the drag and drop! To quickly move selected text, just drag it to the desired location in the document and release the mouse button. To copy the text instead of moving it, hold down the **Ctrl** key while you drag.

Whenever you cut or copy data in any Windows program, Windows places the data in a temporary storage area called the *Clipboard*. In the old days, the Clipboard could store only one chunk of data. If you cut one selection and then cut another selection, the second selection would bump the first selection off the Clipboard. Since Office 2000, however, Word and other Office programs have been able to store at least a dozen items on the Clipboard (up to 24 in Word 2007).

Pasting items from the clipboard varies depending on which version of Word you're using.

In Word 2007: Click the **Paste** button to paste the most recent item you cut or copied. To paste something you previously cut or copied, click the little button to the lower right of the Clipboard area on the Home tab. This displays the entire contents of the Clipboard, so you can select the item you want to paste.

In Word 2003: When you cut or copy two or more selections, the Clipboard toolbar or task pane appears, displaying an icon for each copied or cut selection. To paste the selection, click its icon. To paste all the cut or copied selections, click the **Paste All** button. If the Clipboard toolbar does not appear in Word 2003, open the **Edit** menu and click **Office Clipboard.**

For quicker copy and paste maneuvers, use the keyboard: **Ctrl+C** to copy, **Ctrl+X** to cut, and **Ctrl+V** to paste.

Oops! Undoing Changes

What if you highlight your entire document, intending to change the font size, and press the **Delete** key by mistake? Is your entire document gone for good?

Nope.

As you cut, paste, delete, and perform similar acts of destruction, your Word processor keeps track of each command and lets you recover from the occasional blunder. To undo the most recent action, take one of the following steps:

In Word 2007: Click the **Undo** button (the button with the counterclockwise arrow on it) at the very top of the window.

In Word 2003: Open the **Edit** menu and choose **Undo,** or click the **Undo** button (the button with the counterclockwise arrow on it) in the Standard toolbar.

Click the **Redo** button (the clockwise arrow) to undo Undo, or again perform the action you just performed. You can also undo and redo with keystrokes: **Ctrl+Z** undoes an action, and **Ctrl+Y** undoes Undo or redoes the action you just performed.

Whoa!

Be sure you use the Undo feature before closing your document. After you save your document and close it, you cannot reopen it and undo actions you performed during a previous work session.

Checking Your Spelling and Grammar

Earlier in this chapter, you learned that Word automatically checks for typos and spelling errors as you type. If you turned off that option, you can initiate a spelling check manually.

In Word 2007: Click the **Review** tab and click **Spelling and Grammar** (in the Proofing area on the left) or simply press **F7**.

In Word 2003: Click **Tools, Spelling and Grammar,** or click the **Spelling and Grammar** button on the Standard toolbar or press **F7**.

Word starts checking your document and stops on the first questionable word (a word not stored in the spelling checker's dictionary or a repeated word, such as *the the*). The Spelling and Grammar dialog box displays the word in red and usually displays a list of suggested corrections, as shown in Figure 13.7. (If the word appears in green, the grammar checker is questioning the word's usage, not its spelling.) You have several options:

◆ If the word is misspelled and the Suggestions list displays the correct spelling, click the correct spelling and then click **Change** to replace only this occurrence of the word.

◆ Double-click the word in the Not in Dictionary text box, type the correction, and click **Change.**

◆ To replace this misspelled word and all other occurrences of the word in this document, click the correct spelling in the Suggestions list and then click **Change All.**

◆ Click **Ignore** or **Ignore Once** if the word is spelled correctly and you want to skip it just this once. Word will stop on the next occurrence of the word.

◆ Click **Ignore All** if the word is spelled correctly but is not in the dictionary and you want Word to skip all other occurrences of this word in the document.

◆ Click **Add** or **Add to Dictionary** to add the word to the dictionary so that the spelling checker never questions it again in any of your Office documents. (The dictionary is shared by all Office applications.)

If you add a word to the Office Dictionary by mistake, you can edit the dictionary. In Office 2007, click the **Office** button, **Word Options, Proofing, Custom Dictionaries, Edit Word List.** In earlier versions, click **Tools, Options, Spelling & Grammar, Custom Dictionaries, Modify.** Then, make and save your changes.

Inside Tip _____

To check the spelling of a single word or paragraph, double-click the word or triple-click the paragraph to select it before you start the spelling checker. When Word is done checking the selection, it displays a dialog box asking if you want to check the rest of the document.

Don't place too much trust in your spell checker. It merely compares the words in your document with the words in its dictionary and highlights any string of text that's not in the dictionary. If you typed "its" when you should have typed "it's," the spelling checker won't flag the error. Likewise, if you type a scientific term correctly that is not in the spelling checker's dictionary, the spelling checker will flag the word, even if it is correct. Proofread your documents carefully before considering them final.

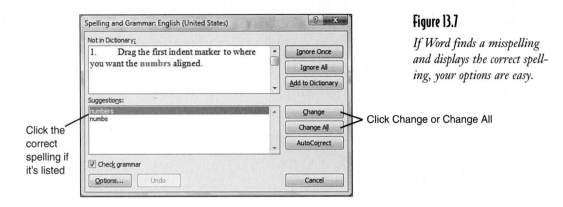

Click the correct spelling if it's listed

Click Change or Change All

Figure 13.7

If Word finds a misspelling and displays the correct spelling, your options are easy.

When Word completes the spelling check, it displays a dialog box telling you so. Click **OK**.

The Least You Need to Know

- Use the Zoom control to zoom in if the text is too small.

- Use the arrow keys or the mouse to move the insertion point.

- Drag the mouse pointer over text to highlight it.

- Use the formatting buttons in the Home tab or on the Formatting toolbar to quickly style and align your text.

- To avoid losing your document, press **Ctrl+S** to save it to your computer's hard disk.

- To undo your most recent action, click the **Undo** button.

14

Crunching Numbers with Spreadsheets

In This Chapter

◆ Comparing your checkbook and a spreadsheet

◆ Typing data into a spreadsheet cell

◆ Adding formulas to a spreadsheet

◆ Graphing values in a spreadsheet

There's no mystery to spreadsheets. A checkbook is a spreadsheet. A calendar is a spreadsheet. Your 1040 tax form is a spreadsheet. Any sheet that has boxes you can fill in is a type of spreadsheet.

So what's so special about computerized spreadsheets? For one thing, they do the math for you. For example, a computerized grade book spreadsheet can add each student's grades, determine the average for each student, and even assign the correct letter grade for each average. And that's not all. The spreadsheet can also display the averages as a graph, showing how each student is doing in relation to the other students or highlighting a student's progress or decline in performance. In this chapter, you learn what it takes to create your own spreadsheets and some of the things you can do with them.

A Computerized Ledger Sheet

A spreadsheet is a grid consisting of a series of columns and rows that intersect to form thousands of small boxes called *cells*, as shown in Figure 14.1. Most spreadsheet applications display a collection of spreadsheets (also called *worksheets*) in a workbook. You can flip the pages in the workbook by clicking the *worksheet tabs* (a.k.a. *spreadsheet tabs*).

Figure 14.1

Here's a popular spreadsheet application, Excel, with a sample file open.

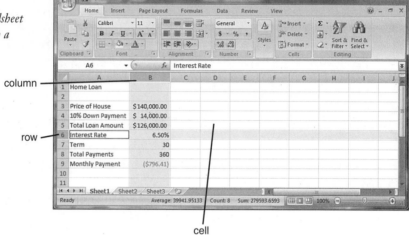

column

row

cell

Look across the top of any computer spreadsheet, and you'll see the alphabet (A, B, C, and so on). Each letter stands at the top of a *column*. Along the left side of the spreadsheet, you'll see numbers representing *rows*. The place where a column and row intersect forms a box, called a *cell*. This is the basic unit of any spreadsheet. You type text, values, and formulas in the cells to make your spreadsheet.

Inside Tip

Some spreadsheet applications let you name individual cells or groups of cells (*ranges*). You can then use the names, instead of the cell addresses, to refer to the cells.

To keep track of where each cell is located and what each cell contains, the spreadsheet uses *cell addresses*. Each cell has an address made up of a column letter and row number. For example, the cell that's formed by the intersection of column B and row 3 has the address B3.

To select a block of cells, drag over the cells to highlight them. To select a row, click the row number that's to the left of the desired row or drag over two or more row numbers to select multiple rows. To select a column, click the letter that's above the desired column or drag over two or more column letters to select multiple columns.

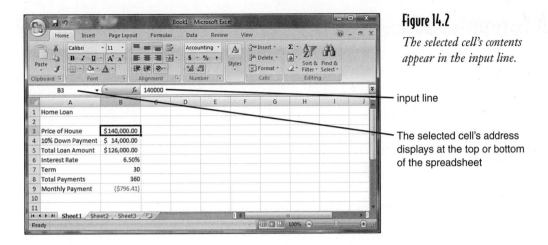

Figure 14.2

The selected cell's contents appear in the input line.

input line

The selected cell's address displays at the top or bottom of the spreadsheet

Building a Spreadsheet from the Ground Up

I bet you're just dying to know how you go about making a spreadsheet. The easiest way is to get a friend to set it up for you—to insert all the formulas and other complicated stuff. Then all you have to do is type in your data and watch the spreadsheet do its thing.

If you're a do-it-yourselfer, however, you need to take the following steps (don't worry, I go into more detail later in this chapter):

1. Design the spreadsheet.

2. Label the columns and rows.

3. Enter your data: labels (text), values (numbers), and dates.

4. Enter the formulas and functions that the spreadsheet will use to perform calculations.

5. Format the cells (to display dollar signs, for instance).

No law says you have to perform the steps in this order. Some users like to enter their formulas before entering their data, so the formulas calculate results as they work. Regardless of how you proceed, you'll probably have to go back to previous steps to fine-tune your spreadsheet.

Computer Cheat

If you need a spreadsheet for a common task, such as determining a loan payment, check to see if your spreadsheet program features a template for the task you want to perform so all you have to do is plug in your data. Click the **Office** button and select **New** (in Excel 2007) or open the **File** menu and select **New** (Excel 2003), and choose the option for creating a spreadsheet from a template. Excel comes with dozens of templates, and later versions of Excel enable you to copy additional templates from Microsoft's "Office on the Web" site.

Designing the Spreadsheet

If you have a form that you want your spreadsheet to look like, use it as a model. For example, if you're going to use the spreadsheet to balance your checkbook (there are better programs for this, as discussed in Chapter 17), use your most recent bank statement or your checkbook register to model the columns and rows.

If you don't have a form, draw your spreadsheet on a piece of paper to determine the columns and rows you need. It doesn't have to be perfect, just something to get you started.

Labeling Columns and Rows

When you have some idea of the basic structure of your spreadsheet, you're ready to enter *labels*. Labels are commonsense names for the columns and rows.

To enter a label, click in the cell where you want it to appear, type the label, and press **Enter.** If your label is a number (for example, 2009), you may have to type something in front of it to tell the spreadsheet to treat it as text rather than as a value. In most applications you type an apostrophe (') or a quotation mark (**Ò**). Usually, whatever you type appears only in the input line until you press Enter. Then the label is inserted into the current cell. (If you type an apostrophe, it remains invisible in the cell, although you can see it when the entry is displayed on the input line.)

If an entry is too wide for a cell, it overlaps cells to the right of it … unless the cell to the right has its own entry. In such a case, the entry on the left appears chopped off (hidden). If you click the cell, you can view the entire entry on the input line. If you want to see the entire entry in the cell, you can widen the column, usually by dragging the right side of the column header, as shown in Figure 14.3.

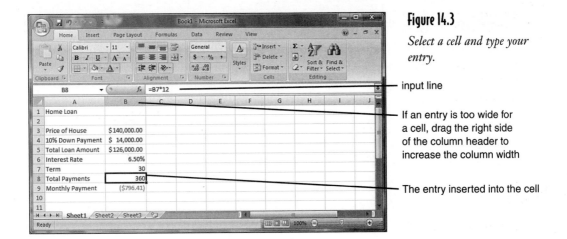

Figure 14.3

Select a cell and type your entry.

input line

If an entry is too wide for a cell, drag the right side of the column header to increase the column width

The entry inserted into the cell

Editing Your Entries

When you make mistakes or change your mind about what you entered, the best way to make corrections usually is to replace the entry. The easiest way to do this is to **Tab** to the cell that contains the entry, type the replacement, and press **Enter.** That's all there is to it.

To edit an entry in most spreadsheet programs, double-click the cell, use the arrow keys or click to position the insertion point, and type your changes. This is called *in-cell editing* and most of the newer spreadsheet programs support this style of making changes. In older programs, you had to click the cell and then edit the entry on the input line, which you can still do.

Entering Values and Dates

After you've labeled your rows and columns, you're ready to enter your raw data: the values or dates that make up your spreadsheet. As you type your entries, keep in mind that values are numbers. So whenever you type a number, the spreadsheet "knows" it's a value. You don't have to do anything special.

Also, you don't need to enter dollar or percent signs or commas, although you do need to type any decimal points. You can

Inside Tip

In some spreadsheets, you must pick a number format before you start typing. For instance, you might type a date and have it appear as a number rather than as a date. (See "Making the Cells Look Pretty," later in this chapter, for more information on how to do this.)

have the spreadsheet add these symbols for you when you format the cells, so just type the number.

Type dates in the proper format for your spreadsheet. In most spreadsheets, you must type the date in the format mm/dd/yy (02/25/09) or dd-mm-yy (02-FEB-09). When you format the cells, you can choose how the spreadsheet displays dates.

Remember that dates are handled as numbers. Although the spreadsheet displays dates in a format people understand, it treats a date as a numeric value (typically the number of days since January 1, 1900). You can then have the spreadsheet use the date in a formula to calculate when a payment or delivery is due.

If a value you type is too wide for a cell, the spreadsheet may display a series of number signs (#) or asterisks (*) instead of the value. Don't worry—your entry is still there. You can click the cell to see the entry in the input line, and if you make the column wider, the spreadsheet will display the entire value.

To enter values or labels quickly, many spreadsheets let you copy entries into one or more cells or *fill* selected cells with a series of entries. For example, in an Excel spreadsheet, you can type **January** in one cell and use the **Fill** command to have Excel insert the remaining 11 months in 11 cells to the right. Fill also enables you to duplicate entries. For example, you can type **250** in one cell and use the **Fill** command (or drag the Fill handle down, as shown in Figure 14.4) to enter 250 into the next 10 cells down.

Figure 14.4

Excel's Fill feature in action.

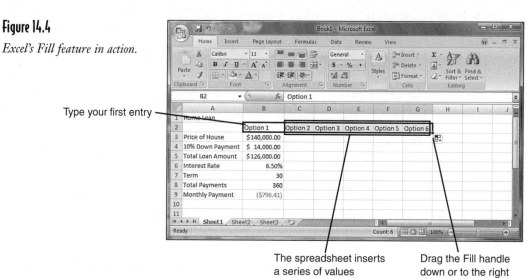

Type your first entry

The spreadsheet inserts a series of values

Drag the Fill handle down or to the right

Calculating with Formulas and Functions

At this point, you should have rows and columns of values. You need some way to total the values, determine an average, or perform other mathematical operations. That's where formulas and functions come in. Spreadsheets use formulas to perform calculations on the data you enter. With formulas, you can perform addition, subtraction, multiplication, or division using the values contained in various cells.

Formulas typically consist of one or more cell addresses and/or values and a mathematical operator, such as + (addition), – (subtraction), * (multiplication), or / (division). For example, if you want to determine the average of the three values contained in cells A1, B1, and C1, you use the following formula:

(A1+B1+C1)/3

To enter a formula, move to the cell where you want the formula to appear, type the formula, and press **Enter.** Some spreadsheets assume you want to type a formula if you start your entry with a column letter. Other spreadsheets require you to start the formula with a mathematical operator, such as an equal sign (=) or plus sign (+). Figure 14.5 shows a basic formula in action.

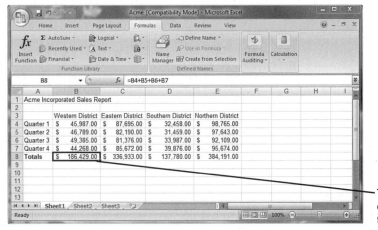

Figure 14.5

A formula at work.

This formula totals the values of cells B4–B7 and displays the total in cell B8

Most spreadsheets let you enter formulas in either of two ways. You can type the formula directly in the cell where you want the result inserted, or you can use the mouse to point and click on the cells whose values you want inserted in the formula. To use the second method, called *pointing*, you use the keyboard and mouse together.

For example, to determine the total of the values in B4, B5, and B6, you perform the following steps:

1. Click the cell where you want to enter the formula. The formula's result will appear in this cell.

2. Type = to mark this as a formula.

3. Click cell **B4** to add the cell's address to your formula.

4. Type + to add the value from a second cell.

5. Click cell **B5.**

6. Type + to add the final value.

7. Click cell **B6.**

8. Press **Enter** to accept the formula.

If any of the cells in the formula (B4, B5, or B6) contains a value, the formula's result appears in the cell where you entered the formula.

Computer Cheat

Σ AutoSum ▾   If your spreadsheet application has a toolbar, it probably has a AutoSum button. (In Excel 2007, click the **Formula** tab to access the AutoSum button.) To quickly determine a total, in the cell where you want the total inserted, click the **AutoSum** button. If neighboring cells contain values, AutoSum highlights the values. If the wrong values are highlighted, drag over the cells that contain the values you want to add. When you release the mouse button and press **Enter,** the spreadsheet performs the required calculations and inserts the result.

Using Ready-Made Functions for Fancy Calculations

Creating simple formulas such as one for adding a column of numbers is a piece of cake, but creating the formulas required for a mortgage refinance spreadsheet can pose quite a challenge. To help you in such cases, many spreadsheet applications offer predefined formulas called *functions.*

Functions are complex ready-made formulas that perform a series of operations on a specified *range* of values. For example, to determine the sum of a series of numbers in cells A1 through H1, you can enter the function **=SUM(A1:H1),** instead of entering =A1+B1+C1+ and so on.

Every function consists of three elements:

♦ The @ or = sign indicates that what follows is a function.

♦ The function name (for example, SUM) indicates the operation to be performed.

♦ The argument (for example, A1:H1) gives the cell addresses of the values the function will act on. For example, =SUM(A1:H1) determines the total of the values in cells A1 through H1.

Inside Tip _____

Use this mnemonic device to remember the order in which a spreadsheet performs mathematical operations: My (multiplication) Dear (division) Aunt (addition) Sally (subtraction). To change the order of operations, use parentheses. Any operation inside parentheses is performed first.

Although functions are fairly complicated and intimidating, many spreadsheets have tools to help. For example, Microsoft Excel offers a tool called the Function Wizard (or Insert Function tool), which leads you through the process of inserting functions. It displays a series of dialog boxes asking you to select the function you want to use and pick the values for the argument. Figure 14.6 shows the Insert Function tool in action.

Tell Insert Function where the values the function needs are stored, and it creates the function for you

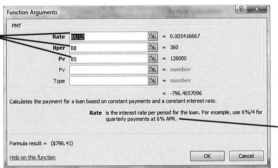

Figure 14.6

The Insert Function tool makes it easier to work with functions.

Click a blank, and Insert Function display a description of the required entry

Making the Cells Look Pretty

When you have the basic layout of your spreadsheet under control, you can _format_ the cells to give the spreadsheet the desired "look." The first thing you might want to do is change the column width and row height to give your entries some breathing room. You may also want to format the values—tell the application to display values as dollar amounts or to use commas to mark the thousand's place.

def•i•ni•tion

Formatting cells means to improve the look of the cells or cell entries without changing their content. Formatting usually includes changing the type style and size of type, adding borders and shading to the cells, and telling the application how to display values (for example, as currency or in scientific notation). Formatting a cell that contains a value or formula may change the appearance of the value in the cell but does not change the actual value stored in the cell.

You also can change the type style and type size for your column or row headings, change the text color, and align the text in the cells. For example, you may want to center the headings or align the values in a column so the decimal points line up. To improve the look of the cells themselves, and to distinguish one set of data from another, you can add borders around the cells and add shading and color to the cells.

To format cells, select the cells you want to format and use the controls on the Home tab (Excel 2007) or the Formatting toolbar or the options on the Format menu to apply the desired formatting.

Many newer spreadsheet applications have an AutoFormat or Format as Table feature that enables you to select the look you want your spreadsheet to have. The application then applies the lines, shading, and fonts to give your spreadsheet a makeover, as shown in Figure 14.7.

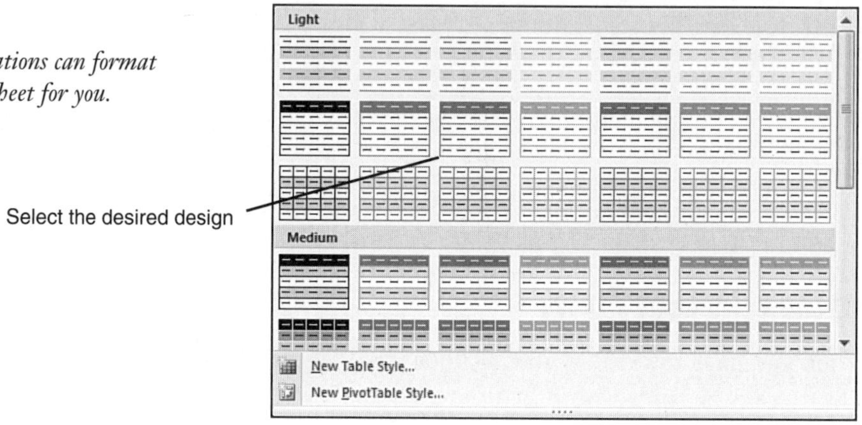

Figure 14.7

Some applications can format your spreadsheet for you.

Select the desired design

After you've formatted your spreadsheet, you can print it. With some spreadsheet applications, such as the latest version of Excel, you can even publish your spreadsheet and graphs electronically on the World Wide Web.

Instant Graphs (Just Add Data)

People, especially management types, like to look at graphs (a.k.a. *charts*). They don't want to have to compare a bunch of numbers. They want the bottom line; they want to see immediately how the numbers stack up. Most spreadsheet applications offer a graphing feature to transform the values you entered into any type of graph you want: bar, line, pie, area, or high-low (to analyze stock trends). The steps for creating a graph are simple:

1. Drag with the mouse over the labels and values you want to include in the graph. (Labels are used for the *axes.*)

2. Enter the **Graph** or **Chart** command. (This command varies from application to application.)

3. Select the type of graph you want to create.

4. Follow the Chart Wizard's instructions to enter your preferences and create the chart. The application transforms your data into a graph and inserts it into the spreadsheet, as shown in Figure 14.8.

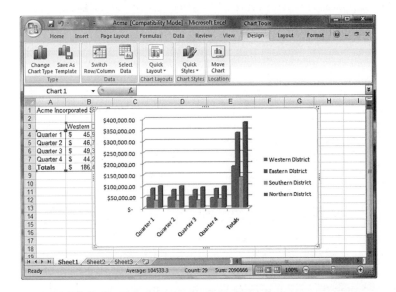

Figure 14.8

Most spreadsheet applications can quickly assemble any type of graph you need.

Special Spreadsheet Printing Considerations

When you print a letter or other document created in a word processing application, you typically don't need to worry that your paragraphs will be too wide for the pages. The word processor automatically wraps the text to make it fit. Spreadsheets, however, can be much wider than a typical 8¹/₂-by-11-inch sheet of paper. To accommodate extra-wide spreadsheets, your spreadsheet application features special print options.

Before you start tweaking the spreadsheet layout and adjusting print settings to make a spreadsheet fit on 8¹/₂-by-11-inch pages, check your page setup to determine how your spreadsheet application is prepared to print your spreadsheet(s). Frequently, the application inserts awkward page breaks, omits titles and column headings from some of the pages, and uses additional settings that result in an unacceptable printout.

To check your spreadsheet before printing, click the **Print Preview** button (or select **File, Print Preview**). In Excel 2007, click the **Office** button, point to **Print,** and click **Print Preview.** This displays your spreadsheet in Print Preview mode, as shown in Figure 14.9.

Figure 14.9

Excel's Print Preview lets you see how a spreadsheet will print before you print it.

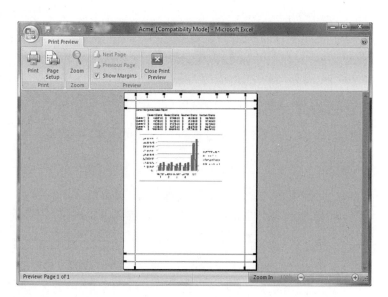

Along the top of the preview area you're likely to see several buttons that enable you to flip pages, zoom in and zoom out on the page, and change some common print settings. If your spreadsheet application displays a **Margins** button, click it to display margin and column markers; you can drag the markers to adjust column widths and page margins right on-screen. If your application displays a **Page Break Preview** button, click the button to see how the application plans on dividing your spreadsheet into pages; you can drag the page break bars to adjust the page breaks before printing.

If your spreadsheet is close to fitting on a single page, you usually can adjust the left and right margins to pull another column or two (or a couple rows) onto the page. If the spreadsheet still doesn't fit, you may need to adjust the page setup. In Excel 2007, you can access most of the page setup options by clicking the **Page Layout** tab. In earlier versions of Excel, select **File, Page Setup.**

The page setup options enable you to adjust the print orientation (portrait or landscape), paper size, margins, and print quality and add a header or footer, which come in handy for automatically numbering your pages.

When you're satisfied with the way your spreadsheet looks in Print Preview, you're ready to send it to your printer. The quickest way to print is to click the tab for the spreadsheet you want to print and click the **Print** button. This sends the spreadsheet off to the printer, no questions asked.

To print more than one spreadsheet or set additional printing preferences, take one of the following steps:

In Excel 2007: Click the **Office** button, point to **Print,** click **Print,** enter your preferences, and click **OK.**

In earlier versions of Excel: Open the **File** menu, click **Print,** enter your preferences, and click **OK.**

> **Computer Cheat**
>
> In Excel 2007, you can add a Quick Print button to the Quick Access toolbar that appears in the upper-left corner of the Excel window. Click the arrow to the right of the toolbar and click **Quick Print.**

The Least You Need to Know

- A cell can contain any of the following entries: a row or column heading, a formula, a function with an argument, or a value.

- Formulas perform calculations on the values in the cells. Each formula consists of one or more cell addresses and a math operator.

- A function is a ready-made complex formula that performs calculations on a range of values.

- You can format the cells in a spreadsheet to control the text size and style, row height, column width, borders, and shading.

- Spreadsheet programs include several special page setup options to cram wide spreadsheets onto narrow sheets of paper.

15

Creating a PowerPoint Presentation

In This Chapter

- ◆ The basics of PowerPoint
- ◆ Creating a PowerPoint presentation from scratch
- ◆ Making your presentation pretty
- ◆ Adding audio and visual effects

One of the most popular programs in the Microsoft Office suite is PowerPoint. Not only is it one of the most common business tools, but it's also embraced by the younger generation for creating presentation slide shows for their classrooms. I estimate that by eighth grade, most kids have at least met PowerPoint, and a good percentage of them have mastered PowerPoint basics.

What exactly is PowerPoint? It's a presentation program that enables you to create slide shows and present those slide shows on a computer screen, a slide-show projector attached to a computer, an overhead projector, or in print. Each slide typically consists of a title, a bulleted or numbered list, and a chart or other graphics. You can even add background music or record narration for your slide show or convert the slide show to a series of web pages visitors can watch over their Internet connections.

In this chapter, I take you on a brief tour of the PowerPoint screen and lead you step by step through the most common tasks.

Touring the PowerPoint Workspace

When you start PowerPoint (**Start, All Programs, Microsoft Office, PowerPoint**), PowerPoint greets you with window that consists primarily of six parts, as shown in Figure 15.1.

Office button: The *Office button* gives you easy access to common commands, including **New** (create a new document), **Open, Save, Save As, Print, Prepare** (review and edit), **Send** (via e-mail), and **Close.**

Title bar: Like all title bars, this one contains the name of the file currently opened; the program's name (Microsoft PowerPoint); and controls on the far right for minimizing, expanding, restoring, or closing the window. Unlike other title bars, however, this one contains a Quick Access toolbar (on the left), which initially contains the Save, Undo, and Redo buttons. To customize the Quick Access toolbar, click the arrow to the right of it.

Ribbon or menus: Below the title bar, you'll see a ribbon with several tabs (PowerPoint 2007) or a series of menu names (earlier versions of PowerPoint). In PowerPoint 2007, you click a tab to view the corresponding collection of related commands. In earlier versions of PowerPoint, you click a menu name to display a list of commands you can enter; below the menu bar are one or more toolbars that contain quick-access buttons almost identical to those on PowerPoint 2007 tabs.

Slide list: The main work is made up of two panes. The left pane contains a list of slides. You can click the Outline tab near the top of the pane to view your presentation's outline rather than viewing small versions of the slides.

Selected slide: The right pane displays a larger version of the selected slide so you can work on it more easily.

Status bar: At the bottom of the window is a status bar that displays the number of the currently selected slide and the name of the design template (on the left). On the right end of the status bar are controls for changing views (Normal, Slide Sorter, or Slide Show) and for zooming in or out on the current slide.

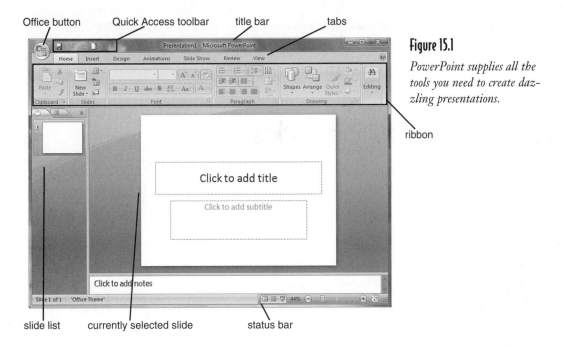

Office button   Quick Access toolbar   title bar   tabs

ribbon

Figure 15.1

PowerPoint supplies all the tools you need to create dazzling presentations.

slide list   currently selected slide   status bar

Creating a New Presentation

When PowerPoint starts, it initially displays a new, blank slideshow so you can immediately create a slide. In the following sections, I show you how to get started by selecting a theme (to give all the slides in a presentation a consistent design) and configure the master slide (so all slides in your show will have a consistent structure or layout).

You can create a new, blank presentation at any time by clicking the New button. Originally, this button is hidden on the Quick Access toolbar. To select it, click the arrow to the right of the Quick Access toolbar and click **New.** After you select this button the first time, it's added to the Quick Access toolbar so you don't have to open a menu to access it. (In earlier versions of PowerPoint, the New button is on the Standard toolbar.)

To create a new presentation that already has a design, click the **Office** button or open the **File** menu and click **New.** This displays the New Presentation dialog box, as shown in Figure 15.2. In the Templates list, click **Installed Templates** or **Installed Themes.** This displays a list of accessible designs in the center panel. Click a template or theme to preview it in the right panel. When you find one you like, click **Create.** PowerPoint creates the first slide in your presentation, which you can then modify.

Figure 15.2

You can save some time by starting with a predesigned template.

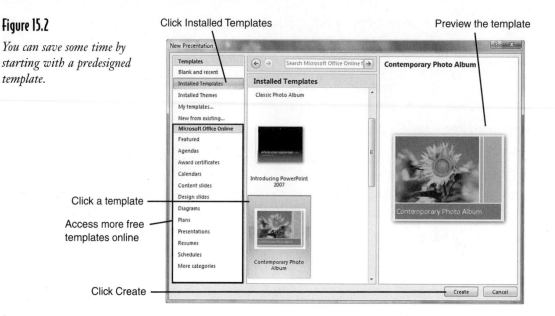

Click Installed Templates

Preview the template

Click a template

Access more free templates online

Click Create

Selecting a Theme

Whether you start with a template or a blank slate, you can always choose a different theme to completely change the appearance of your presentation without affecting its content. To change themes, take one of the following steps:

In PowerPoint 2007: Click the **Design** tab and click the desired theme, as shown in Figure 15.3.

Figure 15.3

You can change the appearance of your slides at any time by selecting a new theme.

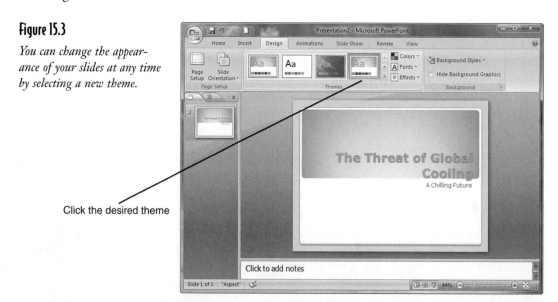

Click the desired theme

In PowerPoint 2003: Click **Format, Slide Design** to display the Slide Design Task Pane on the right. Click the desired template.

Whichever step you take, PowerPoint immediately applies the selected theme to your entire presentation, giving your slides a consistent appearance.

Customizing the Slide Master

Behind every slide show is a Slide Master controlling the puppet strings. The Slide Master controls the overall layout of each slide, unless you choose to override its settings on individual slides. The Slide Master controls the position and appearance of all slide titles, bulleted lists, footers, and any objects you add to the slide. In addition, any graphics you add to the master slide (such as a company logo) appear on all slides in the presentation.

To display the Slide Master, perform the one of the following steps:

In PowerPoint 2007: Click the **View** tab and in the Presentation Views section, click **Slide Master.** The Slide Master looks and acts almost identical to standard slides. The only difference is that it has more power over other slides in your presentation.

In earlier versions of PowerPoint: Click **View, Master, Slide Master.**

Building a Slide from the Ground Up

When you're putting together a slide show presentation, you're likely to spend most of your time creating slides. This process consists of four steps:

1. Insert the slide (probably the easiest step).

2. Add some text (usually a slide title followed by a bulleted list of items).

3. Format the text (if you want the text to appear different from the text on your Slide Master).

4. Add other stuff, like charts, logos, or other graphics.

The following sections lead you through this four-step process.

Inserting a Slide

 Inserting a new slide in a slide show is probably one of the easiest tasks in PowerPoint. Simply select the slide after which you want the new slide inserted, click the **New Slide** button, and select the desired layout. (The New Slide button is on the Home tab in PowerPoint 2007 and on the Standard toolbar in earlier versions.)

If you don't see the New Slide button on the Standard toolbar, click the arrow on the far right of the Standard toolbar and then click the **New Slide** button or simply press **Ctrl+M.** PowerPoint will add the button to the toolbar, for quick access in the future.

Adding Text to a Slide

Whenever you create a new presentation, PowerPoint displays a fill-in-the-blank title slide with instructions to insert a title and subtitle for your presentation. Simply click where instructed and type your title and subtitle.

Unless you chose some other default layout for your slides, each new slide you insert contains two text boxes—one for the slide title and one for a bulleted list, as shown in Figure 15.4. Follow the instructions on the slide itself to add a title and bullet list. In the center of the bullet list text box are several icons you can click to insert a table, chart, small graphic, picture, clip art, or a video clip (see "Adding Graphics" later in this chapter for details).

Figure 15.4

Follow the instructions on the slide to add content to it.

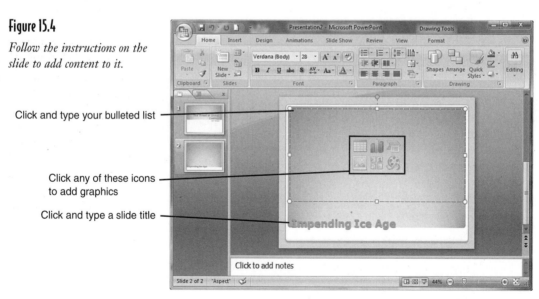

Click and type your bulleted list

Click any of these icons to add graphics

Click and type a slide title

Inside Tip

To make your slides more effective, consider following these good-practice guide-lines: use no more than 6 words per line and no more than 6x lines per slide to keep your slides less busy. Also, use a 20-point or larger font to ensure your audience can read the words. The slide should guide the presentation rather than including detailed information provided in your speech.

Formatting Your Text

Formatting text on slides is very much like formatting text in your word processor (see Chapter 13). You can access most of the formatting options by clicking the Home tab (in PowerPoint 2007) or from the Formatting toolbar (in earlier versions of PowerPoint). Simply highlight the text you want to change, and use the text formatting controls to apply the desired formatting:

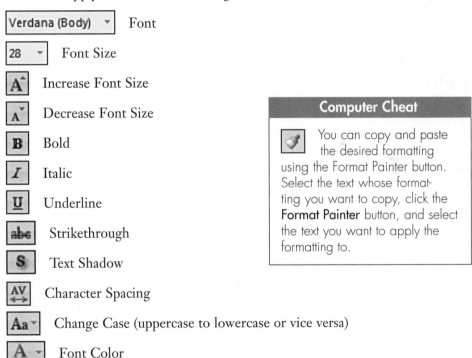

Font

Font Size

Increase Font Size

Decrease Font Size

Bold

Italic

Underline

Strikethrough

Text Shadow

Character Spacing

Change Case (uppercase to lowercase or vice versa)

Font Color

Computer Cheat

You can copy and paste the desired formatting using the Format Painter button. Select the text whose formatting you want to copy, click the **Format Painter** button, and select the text you want to apply the formatting to.

The Home tab or Formatting toolbar contain additional formatting options to convert selected paragraphs into bulleted or numbered lists, center or right-align text, indent text farther to the right, and so on. In PowerPoint 2007, you can click the Format tab to display additional options for controlling the appearance and position of the current object. For example, you can add a border to display a box around the perimeter of a text box.

Adding Graphics

Any new slides you insert contain icons you can click to add graphics to your slides, as shown in Figure 15.4. Click the desired tool, and follow the on-screen cues to complete the operation (options vary depending on the version of PowerPoint you're using):

Insert Table: The Insert Table dialog box appears, prompting you to specify the number of columns and rows. Enter your preferences and click **OK.** PowerPoint inserts the table on the slide, and you can then type entries into the cells that comprise the table.

Insert Chart: This displays the Insert Chart dialog box. Choose the desired chart type (for example, column, line, pie, or bar), and click **OK.** Excel starts and displays a spreadsheet into which you can enter the data that Excel uses to create the chart. (If you already created a chart in Excel, simply select and copy the chart in Excel and switch back to PowerPoint to paste it on your slide.)

Insert SmartArt Graphic: The Choose a SmartArt Graphic dialog box appears, prompting you to choose the type of image you want to insert. SmartArt Graphics are business graphics for presenting lists, illustrating processes or cycles, drawing up the corporate hierarchy, showing relationships, illustrating a pyramid structure, and so on.

Insert Picture from File: If you already have an image or photo you want to use, click this option and select the image or photo file that's stored in a folder on your computer.

> **Inside Tip**
>
> You're not limited to inserting the six types of objects listed here. To insert other objects, click the **Insert** tab (in PowerPoint 2007) or use the **Insert** menu (in earlier versions of PowerPoint).

Clip Art: Microsoft Office comes with a well-stocked Clip Art Gallery from which you can select a suitable image for the slide.

Insert Media Clip: If you have a movie clip stored as a Windows Media file (asf), Windows video file (avi), Microsoft Recorded TV Show (dvr-ms), movie file (mpeg), Ogg file (ogv), or Windows Media Video file (wmv), you can click this option to insert the clip on your slide. When viewing the slide, the video will appear in a small frame on the slide.

Rearranging Slides

PowerPoint offers several methods for rearranging the slides in your presentation:

◆ In the Slides list (on the left), drag a slide to the position where you want it to appear and drop it in place. (If you can't see the destination where you want to drop the slide, you can use the Cut and Paste commands to move the slide.)

◆ Click **View, Slide Sorter** to switch to Slide Sorter view, which displays a miniature version of each slide, as shown in Figure 15.5. Simply drag the slide to where you want it and drop it in place.

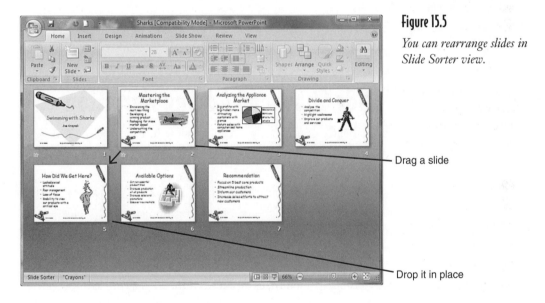

Figure 15.5

You can rearrange slides in Slide Sorter view.

Drag a slide

Drop it in place

◆ Above the Slides list (on the left), click the Outline tab. Drag the slide icon (to the left of the slide's title) up or down to the position where you want it to appear and drop it in place.

Animating Your Slide Show with Special Effects

You can add sound effects to each slide, play background music, add animation to transition smoothly from one slide to the next, or create *builds,* an animation effect that adds items to a slide during your presentation. You simply select the desired effect in PowerPoint and enter a few settings that tell PowerPoint exactly how to execute the special effect. Adding slide transitions and animations is pretty easy:

In PowerPoint 2007: Click the **Animations** tab. To add an animated build, click the text you want to animate, open the **Animate** drop-down list (on the Animations tab), and click the desired animation—Fade, Wipe, Fly In, or Custom. (As you point to the various animation effects on the menu, you can preview them on your slide.) To add a slide transition, select the slide you want to transition to and click the desired slide transition. (Again, as you point to different slide transitions with the mouse, you can preview the transitions on the slide.)

Whoa!

Take it easy on the animated text and slide transitions. They should enhance the presentation, not entertain (or annoy) the audience. Hold your animations to a minimum and stick with the same slide transition for all your slides.

In earlier versions of PowerPoint: Use the options on the Slide Show menu to add transitions and animations to slides.

Previewing Your Slide Show and Adding Narration

When your presentation is nearly complete, you can preview it, rehearse the timings between slide transitions, and record narration to play along with your presentation:

In PowerPoint 2007: Click the **Slide Show** tab. Use the controls in the Start Slide Show group to run your slide show from the beginning or from the current slide. The Custom Slide Show button allows you to create a presentation using only selected slides; this is great if you need to create a 30-minute presentation for one group and a 45-minute presentation for another. The Set Up group provides options for customizing the slide show, recording narration, and setting the timings for automated slide shows (so slides advance without your having to click a button).

In earlier versions of PowerPoint: You access the Slide Show options via the Slide Show menu.

Let the Show Begin!

PowerPoint provides several ways to output your presentation. You can create a standard on-screen presentation to display on your computer screen or with a projector that connects to your computer, save your presentation as a file that you can play on other computers, convert your slide show into web pages for viewing on the Internet, print audience handouts, create your own overhead transparencies, or send the file to a photo shop to have it transformed into 35-millimeter slides!

You can access most of these output options by doing one of the following:

In PowerPoint 2007: Click the **Office** button and select **Print, Print** (to print slides on paper or transparencies or print handouts), **Publish** (to burn the presentation to a CD, prepare custom handouts, share the presentation on a document management server, or create a document workspace so you can access the presentation online), or **Save As** (to save the presentation as a PowerPoint slide show, PDF or XPS file, or other format).

In earlier versions of PowerPoint: Click the **File** menu and select **Print** (to print slides on paper or transparencies or print handouts), **Save As Web Page** (to publish your presentation to a website), **Package for CD** (to burn the presentation to a CD), or **Send To, Microsoft Office Word** (to transform the presentation into an outline you can edit in Word).

Perhaps the coolest and most popular way to present a slide show is to connect a projector to laptop computer and play the slide show on your laptop in *Presenter View*. (Your computer must have dual-display capability to pull this off.) In Presenter View, you control the slide show from your laptop while your audience views it on-screen. This gives you total control of the presentation (along with the ability to black out the audience's screen when you want their attention focused on you). To enable Presenter View, do the following:

In PowerPoint 2007: Click the **Slide Show** tab and click **Use Presenter View.** You can then start the slide show by clicking one of the buttons in the Start Slide Show group on the Slide Show tab. Your audience will see only the slides, while your laptop screen displays the slides along with controls for advancing slides, backing up, darkening the screen, and so on.

In earlier versions of PowerPoint: Click **Slide Show, Set Up Show,** and use the options under **Multiple Monitors** to set up the presentation to run in Presenter View. To start the slide show, click the **Slide Show** button or press **F5.**

The Least You Need to Know

- To create a new presentation, click the **Office** button (PowerPoint 2007) or the **File** menu (earlier versions of PowerPoint), and click **New.**

- Before you add slides to your presentation, change to the Slide Master and customize it.

- You can insert a slide at any time by selecting the slide after which you want the new slide inserted and clicking the **New Slide** button.

- Follow the instructions on the slide to insert text and graphics.

- You can rearrange slides by dragging and dropping their icons in the Slide list, Outline, or Slide Sorter view (**View, Slide Sorter**).

16

Working With Graphics

In This Chapter

◆ Designing greeting cards, newsletters, and more

◆ Decorating your documents with ready-made clip art

◆ Scanning drawings, photos, or illustrations into your computer

◆ Drawing in a paint or draw program

◆ Adding text with text boxes

In this age of information overload, most of us would rather look at a picture than wade through a sea of words. We don't want to read a newspaper column to find out how many trillions of dollars we owe as a nation. We want a graph that shows how much we owed in 1960 and how much we'll owe in 2020, or maybe a map that shows how much of our nation we could have housed with $200,000 homes given the amount of our debt, maybe even a picture of a tax dollar that shows how much of each dollar goes to pay interest on the national debt. We want *USA Today!*

But what about your presentations and the documents you create? Are you as kind to your audience as you expect the media to be to you? Do you use pictures to present information more clearly and succinctly? Do you *show* as well as *tell?* After reading this chapter, you'll know about several types of programs that can help you answer "yes" to all these questions.

Laying Out Pages in a Desktop Publishing Program

You've probably received computer-generated greeting cards or invitations from friends showing off what they can do with their computers. Now that you have a computer (and hopefully a color printer and a desktop publishing program), you, too, can create your own greeting cards, invitations, brochures, flyers, business cards, calendars, newsletters, and any other fancy documents you can imagine.

If you're slapping together a standard publication, few skills are required. The desktop publishing program does most of the heavy lifting. In Microsoft Publisher, for example, a Publishing Wizard leads you step by step through the process of choosing the type of publication you want to create, entering your text, and positioning graphics and other objects on the page.

When you're done, you have a page or several pages, each of which is decorated with several objects—typically *text boxes* and clip art. A text box, as explained later in this chapter, is a box with text in it. You can move the box anywhere on the page and resize and reshape it to fit in the allotted space. You can do the same with the clip art image, as shown in Figure 16.1.

Figure 16.1

In a desktop publishing program, you place and arrange objects on a page to create your publication.

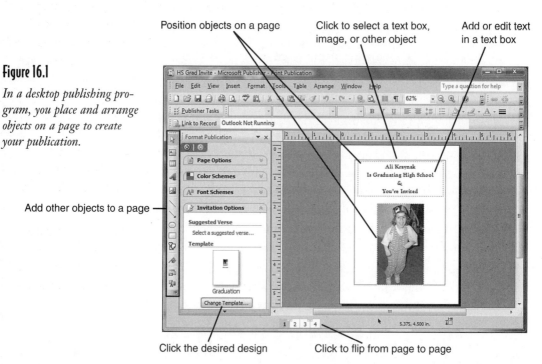

Position objects on a page

Click to select a text box, image, or other object

Add or edit text in a text box

Add other objects to a page

Click the desired design

Click to flip from page to page

Later in this chapter, you discover how to use the various drawing tools available in a desktop publishing program. You find many of these same tools in graphics programs, word processors, and other applications that offer graphics features.

Inside Tip

You can lay text and graphics on a page in a word processor, but a desktop publishing program supports more precise positioning of objects on a page. With a desktop publishing program, for example, you can print objects upside down and right side up on the same page so that when you fold the page, you end up with a greeting card. In a word processor, you might be able to pull off that same feat, but it would take the better part of your day. Word processors are better for creating long documents that don't require intricate formatting and layout.

Inserting Ready-Made Clip Art Images

The easiest way to begin adorning your documents with graphic objects is to insert *clip art images*—small images rendered by professional artists. Suppose you're creating a newsletter and you want to spruce it up with some pictures. Nothing fancy; maybe a picture of a fireworks display for a company newsletter or a drawing of a baseball player to mark upcoming games for your softball league. You create the newsletter and then enter a command telling the program to insert a piece of clip art. You select the piece you want, click **OK,** and voilà, instant illustration, no talent required!

Get It Where You Can: Clip Art Sources

Some programs (desktop publishing, word processing, presentation, and spreadsheet programs) come with a collection of clip art on the installation disks or CDs. Microsoft Office, for example, includes a huge collection of clip art you can use in all programs in the suite.

You also can purchase separate clip art libraries on disc, just as you would purchase a program. These libraries typically include hundreds or even thousands of clip art images divided into several categories: borders and backgrounds, computers, communications, people and places, animals, productivity and performance, time and money, travel and entertainment, words and symbols—you name it.

Whoa! _____

Never use a picture some-
one else created in your
own publication without the
artist's permission. That's stealing.

You can find gobs of graphics on the Internet, as you'll see in Part 4. You can use a web search tool, as explained in Chapter 20, to find clip art libraries and samples. When you see an image you like, just right-click it and choose **Save Picture As.** You can purchase clip art at Clipart.com or subscribe to the site and download a number of clip art images every day for a fixed fee.

Pasting Clip Art on a Page

Now that you have a satchel full of clip art, how do you get it from the satchel into your documents? Well, that depends. Sometimes you have to open the library, copy the picture you want, and paste it onto a page. Other times, you import or insert the image by specifying the name of the file where the image is saved (it's sort of like opening a file). In Microsoft Word and other Office applications, you position the insertion point where you want the image inserted and click **Insert, Clip Art** (in Microsoft Office 2007 applications) or **Insert, Picture, Clip Art** (in earlier versions of Office). This opens the Clip Art task pane, shown in Figure 16.2.

Click in the **Search for** text box, type a brief description of the desired image, and press **Enter.** The Clip Art task pane displays all the images in the collection that match your search term. Scroll down the list to check out the images, and click an image to insert it.

Figure 16.2

You can paste a piece of clip art onto a page.

Type a search word

Images that match your
search instructions

Click an image to insert it

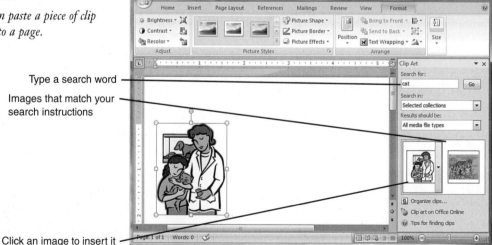

Hey, This Picture's Blocking My Text!

When you lay a picture on top of text, the text typically moves to make room for the picture. In most programs you can set text wrap options to control the way text behaves around the picture. To set the text wrap options, click the picture and enter the command for formatting the picture (for example, enter **Format, Picture**). In many programs, you can right-click the image to find text wrap options or an option for formatting the image, which includes settings that control the way text wraps around the image.

You have a few options when it comes to text wrapping:

◆ *Square* places the picture on an imaginary rectangle and wraps the text around the rectangle. For example, if you have a circular picture, you can set text wrapping to square to make the text wrap in a more regular pattern around the image.

◆ *Tight* makes the text follow the contour of the picture.

◆ *None* places the picture right on top of the text. Choose this only if you have a see-through picture you want to use as a watermark. Otherwise, it obscures your text.

◆ *Top and Bottom* places text above and below the picture but does not wrap it around the sides.

◆ *Distance from Text* specifies how close the text can get to the image.

> **Panic Attack**
>
> Your text wrapping choice seriously affects how the image moves when you drag it. Choosing no text wrapping gives you the most freedom—you can drag the image anywhere, even on top of a chunk of text. If the image refuses to budge when you drag it, the text wrap setting may be restricting its movement.

Resizing and Reshaping Images

When you plop down a picture in a document, it rarely places itself in the perfect position. It's usually too big or too small, too far up or too far down, too far to the left or too far to the right. Fortunately, you have full control over the size and placement of the picture.

Changing the size of an image is a fairly standard operation. When you click the picture, squares or circles (called *handles*) surround it, as shown in Figure 16.3. To move the image, position the mouse pointer over the image itself (not over its handles) and drag the image to the desired location.

To change the size and dimensions of the image, use the following techniques:

- Drag a top or bottom handle (not in the corner) to make the picture taller or shorter.

- Drag a side handle (not in the corner) to make the picture thinner or wider.

- Drag a corner handle to change both the height and width proportionally.

- If the image has a green circle handle floating above it, drag the green handle to spin the image around its center point.

- Hold down the **Ctrl** key while dragging to increase or decrease the size of the image from the center out.

- Hold down the **Shift** key while dragging a corner handle to adjust the figure height and width proportionally.

Figure 16.3

You can quickly resize and reshape an image.

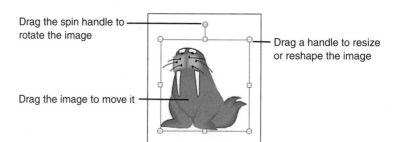

Drag the spin handle to rotate the image

Drag a handle to resize or reshape the image

Drag the image to move it

For more control over the size and dimensions of an image, right-click the image, and click **Size** or click **Format Picture** (or **Format Object,** where *Object* is the name of the selected object), and click the **Size** tab. This page of options enables you to enter specific measurements for your picture. The Size options typically include Lock Aspect Ratio, which is on by default. This ensures that when you change the height or width of a picture, the corresponding dimension is resized proportionally.

Many programs also feature a cropping tool that lets you "trim" the edges off an image. Click the **Crop** button, and drag a handle toward the center of the image to trim an edge off the image. If you crop too much, drag the handle away from the image to uncrop it. In Microsoft Office 2007 applications, when you select an image, the Picture Tools Format Mini toolbar appears; click the **Size** button on the far right to display the Crop button. In earlier versions of Microsoft Office, you can find the Crop button on the Picture toolbar.

Inside Tip _____

To turn on a toolbar, right-click any toolbar or the menu bar and click the name of the desired toolbar.

Inserting Other Pictures

Clip art galleries are not the only source of graphic images. You can obtain digitized photos using a digital camera (as explained in Chapter 28), draw your own images, obtain images someone else has created and sent to you, or copy images from the web.

Digitized images are stored in a variety of *file formats.* The file format is computer code a program uses to render a particular image on-screen and in print. Not all programs can translate all file formats, but most programs support numerous common and uncommon graphic file formats, including WMF (Windows Metafile) , TIFF (Tagged Image File Format) , GIF (Graphics Interchange Format) , JPG or JPEG (Joint Photographic Experts Group) , and BMP (Bitmapped) , to name a few.

Although you can obtain images from numerous sources, the process for inserting an image in most programs is fairly standard:

1. Change to the document you want to add the picture to.

2. Click **Insert, Picture, From File.** An Insert Picture dialog box appears.

3. Select the image file you want to insert and click the **Insert** button.

Inside Tip _____

You can tell a particular file's format by looking at its file name extension—the three characters tacked on to the end of a file name, after the period. Your computer may be set up to hide file name extensions, but if you right-click a file or a thumbnail view of the image and click **Properties** or **Preview, Properties,** you can see the complete file name, including its extension.

Scanning Photos, Drawings, and Illustrations

Another way that we, the artistically challenged, overcome our artistic handicap is to scan photos and other images into the computer using a gadget cleverly called a *scanner.* A scanner is sort of like a copy machine, but instead of creating a paper copy of the original, it creates a digital copy that can be saved as a file. You can then print the image, fax it, or even insert it in a document.

Most scanners on the market are *flatbed* scanners. You lay the picture face down on the scanner's glass and run the scan program by pressing a button on the scanner or selecting the program from the **Start, All Programs** menu. Another popular type of scanner is the *sheet fed.* With a sheet fed scanner, you load the original picture into a slot on the scanner, and the scanner pulls the original past its scanning mechanism to create the copy.

Whichever way you choose to scan, the scanning program typically displays a dialog box, like the one shown in the Figure 16.4, which prompts you to specify the type of document you're scanning and any preferences.

Figure 16.4

Enter your scanning preferences.

If you have an application that features TWAIN (technology without an interesting name) support, you can scan an image directly into a document. For example, in Microsoft Word, you position the insertion point where you want the image inserted and choose **Insert, Picture, From Scanner or Camera.** Word runs your scanning program and scans the image. When you exit your scanner's program, the scanned image appears in your Word document.

Drawing and Painting Your Own Illustrations

Clip art, photos, and scanned images are a great source of ready-made art; but when you need a custom illustration, why not draw it yourself? Most word processors and desktop publishing, spreadsheet, and presentation programs include their own *drawing tools* that enable you to draw lines, arrows, basic shapes, and other objects. Office 2007 includes a feature called SmartArt that provides tools for creating top-notch illustrations complete with text, including organizational charts, flow diagrams, and pyramids. (You can find SmartArt on the Insert tab.)

In addition, Windows includes its own *paint program* that transforms your monitor into a virtual canvas on which you can paint using an on-screen brush, pen, and "can" of spray paint.

Inside Tip

Paint programs and drawing tools differ in how they treat objects. In a paint program, objects consist of thousands of tiny colored dots that comprise the image. Drawing tools treat each shape as a continuous line. Drawn objects are easier to resize and move because you manipulate the shape rather than trying to move a bunch of dots.

Drawing Lines, Squares, Circles, and Other Shapes

Drawing tools consist of on-screen pens, rulers, and templates that enable you to draw lines and basic shapes to create your own custom illustrations. By assembling a collection of these lines and shapes, you can create sophisticated illustrations to adorn your documents.

But first you need to know how to draw a line or shape on-screen. If you're working in a Microsoft Office application, you can access the drawing tools by clicking **Insert, Shapes** (in Office 2007) or right-clicking the menu bar or any toolbar and clicking **Drawing** (in earlier versions of Office).

To draw a line or shape, follow these steps:

1. Click the button or select the command for drawing the desired line, arrow, or shape. When you move the mouse pointer over the page, it changes into a crosshair pointer.

2. Move the crosshair pointer to the position where you want one corner or one end of the object to appear.

3. Hold down the mouse button and drag the pointer away from the starting point in the desired direction until the object is the size and shape you want, as shown in Figure 16.5.

4. Release the mouse button.

Figure 16.5

You can drag a line, arrow, or shape into existence.

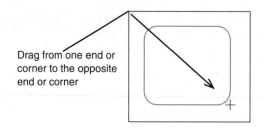

Drag from one end or corner to the opposite end or corner

To save some time and reduce frustration when drawing objects, try some of the following tricks of the trade:

- To draw several objects of the same shape, double-click the desired button and use the mouse to create as many of those shapes as you like.

- To draw a uniform object (a perfect circle or square), hold down the **Shift** key while dragging.

- Hold down the **Ctrl** key while dragging to draw the object out from an imaginary center point. Without the Ctrl key, you drag the object out from its corner or starting point.

- To select an object, click it.

- To delete an object, select it and press the **Del** key.

- To move an object, select it and drag one of its lines.

- To resize or reshape an object, select it and drag one of its handles.

- To copy an object, hold down the **Ctrl** key while dragging it.

- To quickly change the appearance of an object, right-click it and select the desired option from the shortcut menu.

After you have an object on the page, you can use some of the other buttons on the Drawing Tools/Format tab or Drawing toolbar to change qualities of the object, such as its fill color and the color and width of the line that defines it. Select the shape whose qualities you want to change, click the button for the aspect of the object you want to change (line thickness, line color, or fill color), and choose the desired option.

Painting the Screen with Tiny Colored Dots

Have you ever seen a painting by Georges Seurat, the famous pointillist? His magnificent paintings consist of thousands of tiny dots. Paint programs use the same technique to generate an image. Each image you create in a paint program consists of thousands of tiny, on-screen colored dots called *pixels*.

Windows comes with a paint program, called Paint, which you can find on the **Start, All Programs, Accessories** menu. Run Paint to display a screen like the one shown in the Figure 16.6.

When you have the Paint screen up, play around with some of the line, shape, and paint tools. The procedure is pretty basic:

def•i•ni•tion

Your computer screen is essentially a canvas made up of hundreds of thousands of tiny lights called **pixels**. Whenever you type a character in a word processing program or draw a line with a paint or draw program, you activate a series of these pixels so they form a recognizable shape on-screen.

click a line, shape, or paint tool (such as the Airbrush tool), choose a line thickness, and click a color. Then drag the mouse pointer over the "canvas." To create a filled shape, click the desired color for the inside of the shape, right-click the color for the outside of the shape, and drag your shape into existence. To fill a shape with color, click the paint can, click a color, and click anywhere inside the shape.

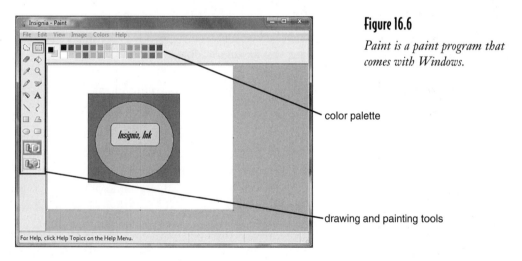

Figure 16.6

Paint is a paint program that comes with Windows.

color palette

drawing and painting tools

Adding Text in a Box

As you saw earlier in this chapter, you can place text and images on the same page and have text wrap around the image. However, in some cases, you might need to add a label to an image or position a block of text in a precise location on a page. In such cases, you should add the text inside a *text box*.

To place text in your publication, you must first draw a text box and type something in that box. As you fine-tune your publication, you can drag and stretch the box as needed to position it on the page and accommodate your text.

Inside Tip

Moving a text box is kind of tricky. You can't just drag the center of the box, as you do when you move a picture. First click the outline of the box so handles appear around it. Then drag the border that defines the box, being careful not to drag a handle, which would resize the box, not move it.

To create a text box, click **Insert, Text Box.** (If you have a pre-2007 version of Office, you can also find the Insert Text Box button on the Drawing toolbar.) The mouse pointer turns into a cross-hair pointer. Position the pointer where you want the upper-left corner of the box to appear, and drag down and to the right to create a box of the desired height and width. When you release the mouse button, your program inserts the text box. Type your text in the box, and use the options on the Format tab (in Office 2007) or on the Formatting toolbar (in earlier versions of Office) to style the text and format the border and shading of the text box.

Manipulating Overlapping Objects

Working with two or more objects on a page is like making your own collage. The trouble with objects is that when you place one object on top of another, the top object blocks the bottom one and prevents you from selecting it. You have to flip through the stack to find the object you want. It's like trying to eat the pancake on the bottom of the stack first.

Most programs that enable you to stack objects on a page offer tools to help you rearrange the objects in a stack. You can send an object that's up front back one layer or all the way to the bottom of the stack, or you can bring an object from the back to the front. First click the object you want to move (if possible). Some objects are buried so deep that you can't get to them. In such a case, you have to move objects from the front to the back to get them out of the way until you find the one you want.

After selecting the object you want to move, do the following:

In Office 2007 applications: Click the **Format** tab and click the button for the desired movement in the Arrange group: **Bring to Front** or **Send to Back.** For more options, click the arrow on the right end of the Bring to Front or Send to Back button. These options let you bring an object forward or send it back one layer or bring it in front of or send it in behind the text layer.

In earlier versions of Office: Open the **Arrange** menu, point to **Order,** and select the desired movement: **Bring to Front, Send to Back, Bring Forward, Send Backward, Bring in Front of Text,** or **Send Behind Text.**

Inside Tip

If you have a half-dozen objects on a page and you want to nudge them all to the right, you don't have to move each object individually. **Shift+click** each object you want to move. (To select all objects, press **Ctrl+A.**) Drag one of the objects, and all the rest follow like little sheep. To group the objects and make them act as a single object, right-click one of the objects and click **Group.** (To ungroup the objects, right-click the grouped object and click **Ungroup.**)

The Least You Need to Know

◆ A desktop publishing program enables you to create your own greeting cards, business cards, flyers, brochures, newsletters, and other publications.

◆ When you need some professionally drawn, ready-made art, check out the clip art collections included with your word processor and other programs and on the Internet.

◆ To move an image, drag any part of it. To resize an image while retaining its relative dimensions, drag a corner handle.

◆ In any of the Office applications, you can insert images from the Internet or from a scanner, digital camera, or graphics program by using the **Insert, Picture, From File** command.

◆ To draw a line, shape, or text box on-screen, click the button for the object you want to draw, position the mouse pointer where you want one end or corner of the object to appear, and drag away from that point.

◆ You can create a free floating text box on a page by clicking **Insert, Text box.**

Chapter 17

Managing Your Finances

In This Chapter

- ◆ Finances, meet computer
- ◆ Draw up a monthly budget
- ◆ Manage your money from home
- ◆ Pay your bills online
- ◆ Using financial calculators

The whole concept of money was supposed to simplify things, to make it easier to exchange goods. Instead of trading a fox pelt for a lobster dinner, you could sell the pelt to someone and then take the money to your local seafood restaurant and pay for your lobster dinner.

Somewhere in history, though, things got all fouled up. We now buy and sell money, store our money in banks and use checks and debit cards to get at it, and even have chunks of our money removed from our paychecks before we've even touched it to cover taxes and pay monthly bills!

But your computer can help you simply all this. In this chapter, I show you some handy things your computer can do to help you manage your finances.

Banking Online (Without a Personal Finance Program)

Most of this chapter is about using a personal finance program (sometimes called a check-writing program) to simplify the process of managing all your personal finances—writing checks, paying bills, tracking income and expenses, reconciling your accounts against your monthly bank statements, and much more.

But you don't need a personal finance program to tap the power of computerized banking. Many banks, credit card companies, and companies that supply goods and services support online banking and online bill pay, so you can perform your banking and pay bills online.

I can't really step you through the process because most online banking/bill-paying sites behave differently depending on how they're set up. In most cases, you use your web browser, as discussed in Chapter 20, to pull up the site's opening page. Then, you click the option to log in to the system and enter your login name and password (you'll have to register first). When you're logged in, the site presents you with a page that allows you to bank online, view your statements, and pay your bills. Figure 17.1 shows a sample online-banking website.

Figure 17.1

With online banking, you can view statements, transfer funds, and pay bills online.

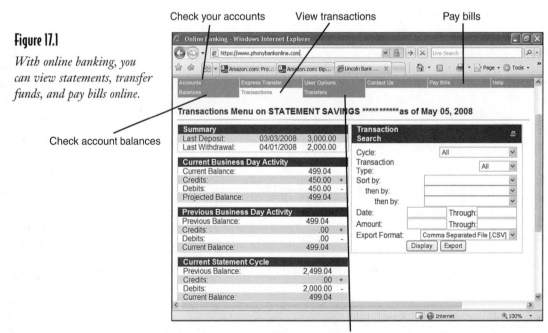

Check your accounts   View transactions   Pay bills

Check account balances

Transfer money from one account to another

On a credit card site, you're likely to see your current balance, credit limit, available credit, payment due, payment due date, and a list of transactions on your current statement. (You can view transactions on past statements, too.) Most credit card companies also provide tools that enable you to download data into a personal finance program, if you have one.

Inside Tip

If your credit card gives you some sort of perk[md]frequent flyer miles, free groceries, in-store credit, whatever—pay everything you can with this credit card and then pay the credit card balance in full when you receive your statement. You may even want to set up automatic credit card payments with your utility companies to pay phone, gas, electric, and water bills. Not only does this allow you to earn money with your credit card, but it also simplifies your accounting; you have only one bill to pay each month—your credit card balance.

Setting Up a Personal Finance Program

To start using a personal finance program, you first need to supply the program with information about your accounts. This typically includes the account name, type of account (savings, checking, cash, and so on), and the current balance or the balance according to your most recent statement.

To set up an account, you enter the command for creating an account and then follow the on-screen instructions, as shown in Figure 17.2, to supply the requested information. (Throughout this chapter, Quicken is used to illustrate common tasks, but other personal finance programs are available, including Microsoft Money and Moneydance.)

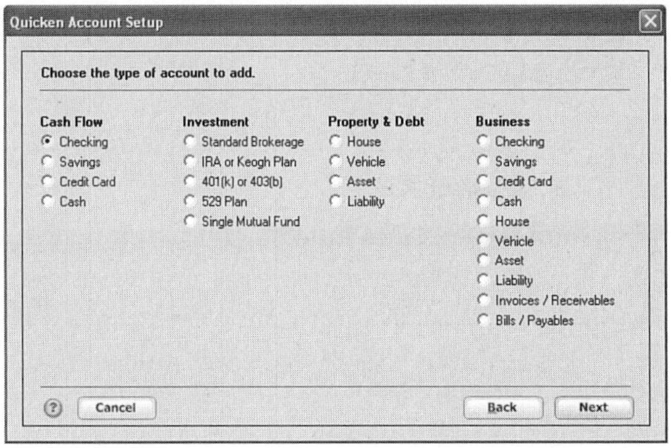

Figure 17.2

Your personal finance program gathers the information it needs to set up and manage your accounts.

Automating the Check-Writing Process

The problem with writing checks by hand is that you have to enter a lot of duplicate information. You write the date, the name of the person or business, the amount of the check (both numerically and spelled out), and a memo reminding you what the check is for. Then, you flip to your check register and enter all the same information again. If you happen to make a mistake copying the information from your check to your register, you'll have loads of fun at the end of the month when you try to reconcile your register with your bank statement.

With a personal finance program, your computer enters the date automatically. You enter the name of the person or business to whom you're writing the check. The program spells out the amount for you, copies the required information into the register, and calculates your new balance, as shown in Figure 17.3. This eliminates any discrepancy between what's written on the check and what's recorded in the register. It also eliminates any errors caused by miscalculations.

Figure 17.3

When you write a check, the personal finance program automatically transfers the information to the register.

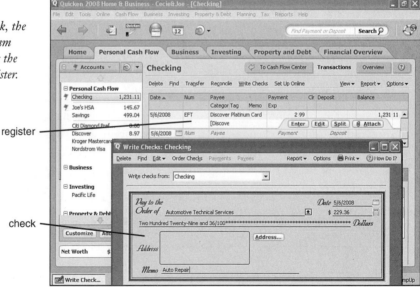

What about printing checks? That sounds like a good idea … until you realize some of what's involved. You have to get special checks designed for a printer, and some printers require that you print a full page of checks (up to three) at a time. If your printer jams, you may need to void the damaged checks and shred them. If you go grocery shopping, you need to fetch checks from the printer. Many users, including me, continue writing checks by hand and use the personal finance program to record the checks, reconcile their balances, and manage their budgets.

Reconciling an Account with a Statement

Back in the old days, reconciling your checking account with the bank statement was an exercise in frustration. You calculated and recalculated until you started seeing double. With a personal finance program, you simply enter the ending balance (from your most recent statement) and then mark the checks that have cleared, mark the deposits, and record any service charges and interest, as shown in Figure 17.4. The program takes care of the rest, determining whether or not your register balance matches the balance on your bank statement.

Mark cleared checks   Mark cleared deposits

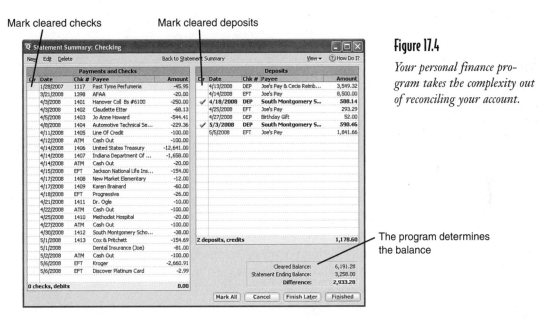

Figure 17.4

Your personal finance program takes the complexity out of reconciling your account.

The program determines the balance

If the total on your register doesn't match the total on your bank statement, the program lets you know. If you have to correct an entry in the register, the program automatically recalculates the total, saving you the time of starting over from scratch.

Banking Online (with a Personal Finance Program)

If your computer has a modem or other connection to the Internet, you may be able to pay your bills without the hassle of writing a check and the expense of mailing it. Your personal finance program may be able to connect to your bank or an online bill-paying service and remit payments electronically. You can often use online bill paying to pay your utility bills and make credit card and loan payments. If you owe money to a person or business that's not connected to the system, the online bill-paying service can print and mail out an old-fashioned paper check for you!

Inside Tip

Check with your bank or credit card company to find out what online bill-paying service they offer for free. No sense paying for a service you already have for free.

Most banks and credit unions that offer online banking don't require you to use a personal finance program to access it. But if you use a personal finance program to manage your finances, it makes sense to do your online banking through the program. The program can automatically retrieve information from your bank, mortgage company, or credit card company and record it so you don't have to manually enter the information. This keeps your account information current and relatively error-free.

Panic Attack

Before you attempt to set up your account online, check with your bank or credit union to determine whether it supports online banking. Tell the bank what program you plan to use, so it can supply you with specific instructions on how to proceed. When you're setting up new accounts, you may be able to automate the account setup by having your personal finance program obtain information directly from the bank. Not only does this save you some time, but it can also prevent costly errors.

Setting Up Recurring Entries

If you get paid the same amount every 2 weeks or you have a bill that's the same amount each month (such as a mortgage payment, rent, or budgeted utility payment), you can set up a recurring entry that automatically records the transaction at the scheduled time or reminds you to enter it. If you're set up to pay bills online, you can even automate the payment.

When you enter the command to create a new recurring entry, the program displays a dialog box, like the one shown in Figure 17.5, requesting details about the transaction. Enter the requested information.

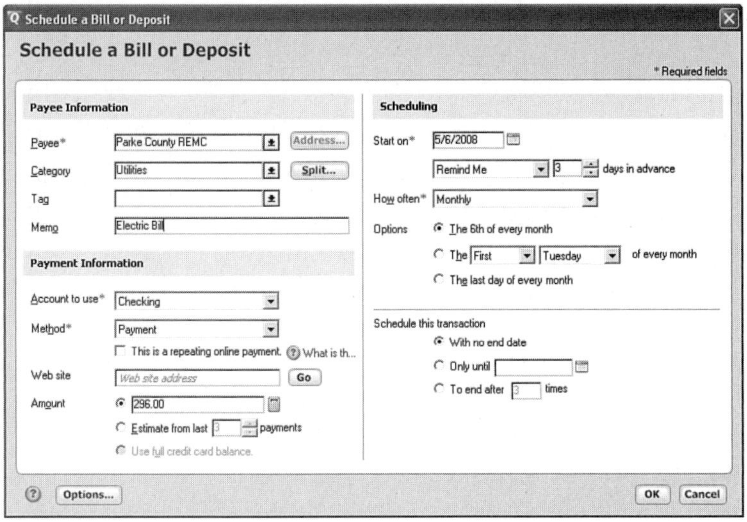

Figure 17.5

With a recurring entry, the personal finance program automatically records the transaction on schedule.

Tracking Your Budget

To take control of your financial destiny, you have to figure out where all your money is going. For instance, you can't decide whether you're spending too much on car repairs unless you know exactly how much you're spending. Would you save money by buying a new car instead? Is there any way you can set aside some money for investments? With accurate budget information, you can make financially sound decisions.

With most personal finance programs, you can establish a budget and have the program keep track of each expense for you. Many programs come with a set of home or business expense categories you can use when recording your transactions. If an expense is not listed, you can create a new category. Whenever you record a transaction (check, cash, credit card, debit), you specify the category. At the end of the month, you tell the program to generate a budget report, as shown in Figure 17.6. The report displays the total for each category and helps you spot the pork in your budget.

Figure 17.6

A personal finance program can generate a budget report that helps you track your income and expenses.

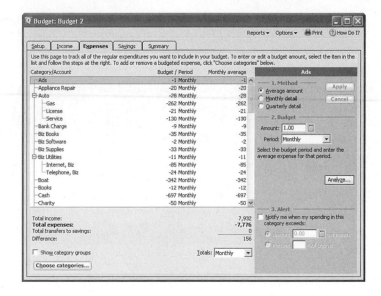

Tapping the Power of Financial Calculators

Personal finance programs typically include several financial calculators that can help you determine the monthly payment on a loan, how much you need to invest to retire comfortably at 65, how much you can save by refinancing your mortgage for a shorter term or a lower interest rate, etc. You simply plug in the numbers you know, and the calculator supplies you with the missing figures.

If you purchase the basic version of a personal finance program, it may not be equipped with calculators. When you're shopping for a program, be sure you get the version that includes the calculators. They're indispensable … I guess that's why the software developers charge extra for them.

Preparing Your Annual Tax Return

About the only thing a personal finance program can't do for you (financially speaking) is your taxes. However, assuming you did a good job of recording all your transactions, accounting for every penny of income and expenses, and assigned a category to each transaction, the program can package up your financial data and ship it off to a tax preparation program, such as TurboTax.

TurboTax and similar tax preparation programs lead you through the process of preparing your taxes by asking you a series of questions, as shown in Figure 17.7. You simply answer the questions and supply the requested data, and the program fills out the tax forms for you. The program can even submit your tax returns online so you get your refund sooner.

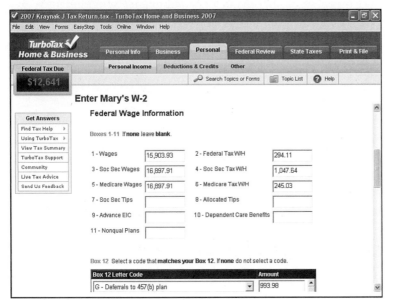

Figure 17.7

TurboTax leads you through an interview to gather the information necessary to complete your tax return.

Inside Tip

In a tax preparation program, all the forms are linked, so you enter a piece of data only one time. For example, you enter your name, address, and Social Security number one time. The tax program transfers that information to every form that requires it. If you fill out the form to itemize your deductions, the tax program automatically transfers the total amount of your deductions to your 1040 form.

The Least You Need to Know

◆ A personal finance program can help you track your income and expenses and manage your bank accounts.

◆ When you write a check in a personal finance program, the program automatically records it in the register.

◆ Check with your bank to determine whether it offers online banking and how to access its features with your personal finance program.

◆ By assigning a category to each transaction, you enable your personal finance program to account for every penny of income and expenses and generate a monthly budget report.

◆ You can set up recurring entries to have your personal finance program automatically enter transactions on schedule.

◆ A personal finance program can help you gather all your financial data for the year, simplifying the task of preparing your taxes.

18

Printing Documents and Other Creations

In This Chapter

- Installing a printer
- What will it look like?
- Tweaking the page margins
- Printing your masterpiece
- Troubleshooting common printer problems

When printing goes as planned, it's a snap. You click the **Print** button and then kick back and play Solitaire while the printer spits out your document. However, not all print jobs proceed without a hitch. You finish your game of Solitaire only to find a stack of papers covered with foreign symbols. Or you get an error message saying the printer's not ready. After hours of fiddling and fumbling, you find and correct the problem only to face a new problem: getting your printer back online.

In this chapter, you learn all you need to know about glitch-free printing and how to recover from the occasional print failure.

Setting Up Your Printer in Windows

You can't just plug your printer into the printer port on your system unit and expect it to work. No, that would be far too easy. You also need to install a printer driver—instructions that tell your programs how to use your printer. (If you have a printer that supports plug-and-play, Windows leads you through the installation at start-up.)

In Windows, you install one printer driver that tells Windows how to communicate with the printer. All your applications then communicate with the printer through Windows. When you set up a printer, Windows asks for the *printer make and model.* Windows comes with printer drivers for most common printers. In addition, your printer might include a CD containing an updated printer driver.

Windows also asks for the *printer port.* This is the connector at the back of the system unit where you plug in the printer. Standard printers connect the LPT1 (*parallel* printer) port, but many newer printers use the *USB* (Universal Serial Bus) port, a network cable that plugs into a router (see Chapter 12 for more about networking), or a wireless connection. A few oddball printers connect to the *serial* port, but those are rare. During the installation, Windows searches for printers connected to your computer and to the network and provides you with a list to choose from.

Inside Tip

All printers are commonly categorized as parallel, serial, USB, network, or wireless (using Bluetooth technology). Parallel printers connect to one of the system unit's parallel printer ports: LPT1 or LPT2. A serial printer connects to the system unit's serial port: COM1, COM2, or COM3. USB printers plug into one of the computer's USB ports. Most people use parallel or USB printers because they're faster; parallel and USB cables can transfer several instructions at once, whereas a serial cable transfers them one at a time. Wireless printers are also available for wireless-enabled computers, while network printers typically plug into a router so all computers that connect to the network via the router can share the printer.

When you installed Windows, the installation program asked you to select your printer from a list. If you did that, Windows is already set up to use your printer. If you're not sure, you can check whether Windows is set up to use a particular printer.

In Windows Vista: Click **Start, Control Panel.** Under Hardware and Sound, click **Printer.**

In Windows XP: Open the **Start** menu and click **Printers and Faxes.**

If there's an icon for your printer and it has a checkmark on it, Windows is set up to use this printer as the default printer, so you're in good shape. If the printer icon doesn't have a checkmark on it, right-click it and click **Set As Default Printer.** If no icon is available for your printer, you must install a printer driver.

If your printer came with its own installation disk or CD, install the printer driver from that disk or CD. Insert the disk or CD, and if Windows doesn't launch the installation program automatically, display the contents of the disc in Explorer or My Computer (as discussed in Chapter 7), double-click the Install or Setup file, and follow the on-screen instructions to complete the installation.

If you don't have a disk or CD for your printer, try installing one of the printer drivers included with Windows. Windows comes with printer drivers for hundreds of printers currently on the market and many older printers, too. To install one of the Windows printer drivers, take the following steps:

1. If the Printers window is not displayed in Windows Vista, click **Start, Control Panel.** Under **Hardware and Sound,** click **Printer.** In Windows XP, open the **Start** menu and click **Printers and Faxes.**

2. Double-click the **Add a Printer** icon. The Add Printer Wizard appears.

3. Follow the Wizard's instructions to install the driver for your printer or one that's similar. One of the first questions the Wizard asks is whether you are installing a *local printer* or *network* or *wireless printer.*

def•i•ni•tion

A **local printer** is one that's connected directly to your computer's printer port. A **network** or **wireless printer** may be connected via a network cable to a central networking hub or via wireless technology.

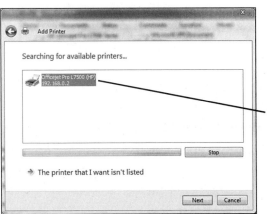

Figure 18.1

Windows displays a list of installed printers.

Select the printer you want to use

When you install your printer, click the option to set it up as the default printer. Otherwise, when you print documents, Windows may assume you want to use a different printer (if other printers have been installed), even if your computer is currently not connected to one of these other installed printers.

Preprint Checklist

Most programs display a print button in the Standard toolbar (or in the Quick Access toolbar in Office 2007 applications) that enables you to quickly send your document to the printer. It's tempting to click the button and see what happens. Resist the temptation. You can avoid 9 out of 10 printing problems by checking your document in Print Preview first.

To view a document in print preview in most applications, open the **File** menu and click **Print Preview** (or its equivalent command), or click the **Print Preview** button in the Standard toolbar. (In Office 2007 programs, click **View, Print Layout.**) Flip through the pages to see how they'll appear in print, and look for the following:

Chopped text. Many printers have a nonprinting region near the margins. If you set your margins so the text falls in these areas, the text will be chopped off and not printed.

Strange page breaks. If you want a paragraph or picture to appear on one page and it appears on the next or previous page, you might need to manually insert a page break. Position the insertion point where you want the page break inserted and press **Ctrl+Enter.**

Overall appearance. Be sure your fonts look good next to one another, that text is aligned properly, and that no pictures are lying on top of text.

If you checked your document in Print Preview and it looks fine, feel free to skip ahead to the "Sending Documents to the Printer" section to start printing your document. If you noticed some problems, proceed to the following section.

Setting Your Margins and Page Layout

You can correct many undesirable page layout issues by checking and adjusting the page margins and layout settings in your program. To display the page setup options:

In most programs: Open the **File** menu and select **Page Setup.** The Page Setup dialog box appears, as shown in Figure 18.2, presenting numerous options for changing the page layout and print settings.

Click the
desired tab

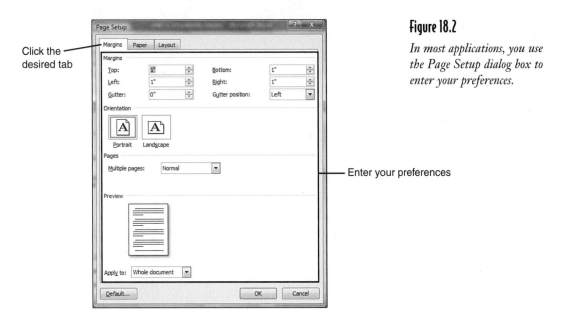

Enter your preferences

Figure 18.2

In most applications, you use the Page Setup dialog box to enter your preferences.

In Office 2007 applications: Click the **Page Layout** tab and use the options in the Page Setup group to enter your preferences, as shown in Figure 18.3.

Click the Page Layout tab

Use these buttons to control your page setup

Figure 18.3

In Office 2007 applications, the Page Layout tab gives you access to your Page Setup options.

Here are some common settings you might want to adjust:

Page margins: You can set the margins for the top, bottom, left, and right sides of the page. The gutter setting lets you add margin space to the inside margin of the pages, in case you plan to insert the pages into a book or binder.

Orientation: You can choose to print in *portrait* mode (right side up) or *landscape* mode (sideways) on a page. In most case, you'll be printing in portrait mode. Landscape mode is useful for printing wide spreadsheets and other items that are wider than they are tall.

Paper size: Most documents are printed on standard $8\frac{1}{2}$ by 11-inch paper, but you may need to print a document on legal-size paper or on envelopes. (If your printer has two paper trays, you may also need to specify the paper source—which tray is loaded with the selected size paper.)

> **Inside Tip** _____
>
> If you don't see an option you need to access on the Page Layout tab in Office 2007 applications, click the **Margins** button and click **Custom Margins.** This displays the Page Setup dialog box, which includes the tabs Margins, Paper (where you can choose a paper source), and Layout (which includes settings for positioning the header and footer). The Layout tab also contains a handy Vertical Alignment option; if you have a short letter, for example, you can choose to center it vertically on the page so you don't end up with too much white space at the bottom.

Adding a Header or Footer

Most applications that allow you to create and print documents include a feature for printing a header (at the top) or a footer (at the bottom) on each page. A typical header or footer contains the title of the document, the date on which it was printed, and the page number (the application can automatically insert the correct page number on each page). Here's how to create a header or footer:

In most applications: Click **View, Header and Footer.**

In Word 2007: Click **Insert, Header** or **Insert, Footer,** or double-click the top or bottom of the page.

In Excel 2007, click **Insert, Header & Footer.** (You'll see the header or footer only in Page Layout or Print Preview mode.)

In earlier versions of Excel: Display the **Page Setup** dialog box, as explained earlier in this chapter.

In most applications, this displays an area on the page reserved for the header or footer and a toolbar or tab with controls for switching between the header and footer; inserting the date, page numbers, number of pages, and so on; and using a different header or footer for even- and odd-numbered pages (see Figure 18.4).

header and footer tools

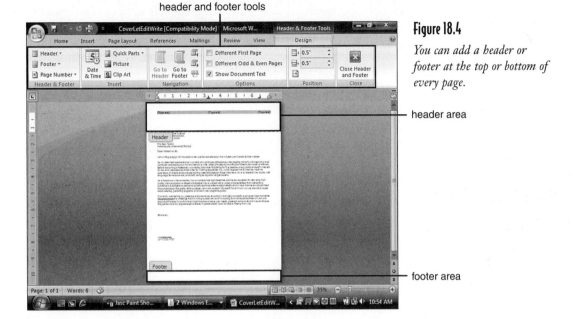

Figure 18.4

You can add a header or footer at the top or bottom of every page.

header area

footer area

Sending Documents to the Printer

After your printer is installed and online, printing is a snap. Although the procedure for printing might vary, the following steps work in most Windows programs. If you just want to print one copy of your document, using the default settings, click the **Print** button on the toolbar. If you need to customize a bit, follow these steps:

1. Open the document you want to print.

2. In Office 2007 applications, click the **Office** button, point to **Print,** and click **Print.** In most other applications, open the **File** menu and click **Print.** The Print dialog box appears, prompting you to enter instructions. Figure 18.5 shows a typical Print dialog box.

3. In the **Print range** section, select one of the following options:

   ♦ **All** prints the entire document.

   ♦ **Selection** prints only the highlighted portion of the document. (This is available only if you highlighted text before choosing the Print command.)

♦ **Pages** prints only the specified pages. If you select this option, type entries in the **From** and **To** boxes to specify which pages you want to print. Some programs display a single text box into which you type the range of pages you want to print—for example, 3-10 or 3,5,7.

Figure 18.5

The Print dialog box lets you enter specific instructions.

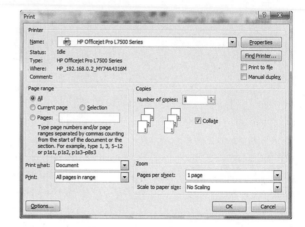

4. Click the arrow to the right of the Print Quality option (or click the **Options** or **Properties** button), and select the desired quality. (If you have a color printer, you might have the option of printing in grayscale or black and white.)

5. To print more than one copy of the document, type the desired number of copies in the **Copies** text box.

6. Click **OK.** The program starts printing the document. This could take a while, depending on the print quality, the document's length and complexity, and the speed of your printer; documents that have lots of pictures can take a long time.

Whoa!

Did your printer spit out an extra blank page at the end of your document? If it did, you might have told it to by pressing the Enter key three or four times at the end of your document. Doing this adds extra blank lines to your document, which can cause the program to insert a page break. If you see an extra page in Print Preview, delete everything after the last line of text in your document. Some programs also offer an option of spitting out a blank page to separate multiple documents. Check your printing options.

To enter default settings for your printer (including the quality settings):

In Windows Vista: Click **Start, Control Panel.** Under **Hardware and Sound,** click **Printer.** Right-click the icon for your printer, and click **Properties.**

In Windows XP: Click **Start, Printers and Faxes.** Right-click the icon for your printer, and click **Properties.**

Enter your preferences and click **OK.** The default settings control the operation of the printer for all applications. You can override the defaults any time you print a document without changing the default settings.

Managing Background Printing

If you ever need to stop, cancel, or resume printing, you must access the *queue* (a waiting line documents line up in to be printed). Whenever you print a document in Windows, a picture of a printer appears in the taskbar (near the lower-right corner of the Windows desktop). Double-click the printer icon to view the print queue, as shown in Figure 18.6. You then can perform the following steps to stop or resume printing:

- To pause all printing, open the **Printer** menu and select **Pause Printing.**

- To pause the printing of one or more documents, **Ctrl+click** each document in the queue, open the **Document** menu, and select **Pause Printing.**

- To resume printing, open the **Printer** or **Document** menu and click **Pause Printing.**

- To cancel all print jobs, open the **Printer** menu and select **Cancel All Print Jobs.**

- To cancel individual print jobs, **Ctrl+click** each print job you want to cancel, open the **Document** menu, and select **Cancel.**

- To move a document in the print queue, drag it up or down.

If you choose to cancel printing, don't expect the printer to immediately cease and desist. Fancy printers have loads of memory and can store enough information to print several pages. If you're serious about canceling all printing, press the Cancel button on your printer.

Figure 18.6

You can supervise and control printing using Print Manager.

Panic Attack

If you chose to print only one copy of a document but your printer spits out several copies, this usually indicates that you printed the document more than once. When the printer doesn't start printing right away, many people lose patience and keep clicking the Print button. Each time you click the Print button, another copy of the document is sent to the queue, and your printer dutifully prints it.

Hey, It's Not Printing!

If your printer refuses to print your document, you must do a little detective work. The following questions can help you track down the cause:

◆ Is your printer plugged in and turned on?

◆ Does the display on the printer indicate a problem, such as a paper jam? Refer to your printer's manual for information on clearing paper jams and solving other common printer-related problems.

◆ Does your printer have paper? Is the paper tray inserted properly?

◆ Is the printer's On Line light on (not blinking)? If the On Line light is off or blinking, press the **On Line** or power button to turn on the light and make the printer print.

◆ Display the Print dialog box again and be sure **Print to file** is not selected. This option sends the document to a file on your disk instead of to the printer.

◆ Is your printer marked as the default printer? Follow the instructions earlier in this chapter to determine whether the printer that's connected to your computer or network is the default printer in Windows.

◆ Is the printer paused? Double-click the printer icon on the right end of the task-bar, open the **Printer** menu, and be sure **Pause Printing** is not checked. If there is a check mark, click **Pause Printing** to turn off this option.

◆ Is the correct printer port selected? Right-click the icon for your printer and choose **Properties.** Click the **Details** tab, and be sure the correct printer port is selected.

Inside Tip

A network printer that's connected to a central router is usually assigned an IP (Internet Protocol) address that looks something like 192.168.0.3. Check your printer setup using the controls on your printer[md]it may have an option that allows you to print a Printer Configuration page that includes the printer's IP address. Open your web browser, as explained in Chapter 20, type your printer's IP address in the address bar at the top, and press **Enter.** This may open a page that enables you to check ink levels and enter default settings for your printer.

The Least You Need to Know

◆ Before you print a document, click the **Print Preview** or **Print Layout** button to see how the finished product will look.

◆ To check the page layout settings, click the **Page Layout** tab (in Office 2007 applications) or open the **File** menu and click **Page Setup** (in most other applications).

◆ To quickly print a document, no questions asked, click the **Print** button. For more control over printing, choose **Office** button, **Print** or **File, Print.**

◆ To pause or cancel printing, double-click the printer icon on the right end of the taskbar to display the Print Manager. Choose the desired option from the **File** menu.

◆ If your document doesn't start printing, double-click the printer icon on the right end of the taskbar to determine what's wrong.

Part 4

Tapping the Power of the Internet

Faster than U.S. Postal Service. More powerful than the Home Shopping Network. Able to leap wide continents in a single click. Look, up on your desktop. It's a phone! It's a network! No, it's the Internet!

With your computer, a modem, and a standard phone line (or better yet, a broadband connection), you have access to the single most powerful communications and information network in the world: the Internet. The chapters in Part 4 show you how to get wired to the Internet and use its features to exchange electronic mail, chat with friends and strangers, shop for deals, manage your investments, plan your next vacation, research interesting topics, and even publish your own creations via the web!

"Just Google it to see. Type: international sherbet delivery."

Chapter 19

Getting Wired to the Internet

In This Chapter

- The Internet 101
- Deciding on the right connection for you
- The hardware you need to establish a connection
- Getting on the information superhighway
- Checking out your connection speed

How would you like to access the latest news, weather, and sports without stepping away from your computer? Track investments without having to call a broker or wait for tomorrow's newspaper? Connect to an online encyclopedia, complete with sounds and pictures? Order items from a computerized catalog? Send a postage-free letter and have it arrive at its destination in a matter of seconds? Mingle with friends and strangers in online chat rooms? Transfer files from your computer to a colleague's computer anywhere in the world?

With your computer, a modem, and a subscription to an Internet service provider, you can do all this and more. This chapter introduces you to the wonderful world of the Internet and shows you how to connect your computer to the outside world.

Understanding How This Internet Thing Works

The Internet is a worldwide network of computers that can communicate with one another and share resources. The computers are all interconnected by a massive collection of fiber-optic cables, phone lines, and wireless signals that enable the Internet to transfer data at lightning-fast speeds. The network of cables, phone lines, and wireless connections that carry the data are known as the Internet's *backbone*.

For your computer to plug into this network and tap its resources, it needs a modem and an Internet service provider (ISP). The modem is the hardware your computer uses to send and receive data on the Internet—it's sort of like a telephone for your computer. The ISP functions as a communications hub between your computer and the Internet. Using the modem, your computer connects to the ISP, and the ISP connects to the Internet, as shown in Figure 19.1.

Figure 19.1

Your computer uses a modem to connect to your ISP, which connects your computer to the Internet.

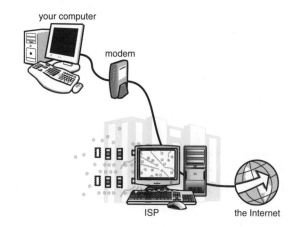

Picking a Connection Type

Although myriad options are available for connecting to the Internet, they boil down to two choices: *dial-up* or *broadband*.

Dial-up is a relatively slow connection, but it's available wherever you have access to a phone line, which is pretty much everywhere. Dial-up stinks, but sometimes it's your only choice.

Broadband is a fast connection, which you can get through some cable companies, digital satellite services, phone companies, and wireless ISPs, but keep in mind that *fast* is a relative term. A dedicated (leased) line (such as a T3 line) is typically the fast-est at data transfer rates (about 45Mbps or megabits per second), followed by fixed wireless (as opposed to mobile wireless), cable, DSL (Digital Subscriber Line), and satellite, but several factors can affect the actual speed at which your computer con-nects. One user's DSL connection may be faster than another user's cable connection.

If you live in a major metropolitan area, you have plenty of Internet connection types from which to choose: dial-up using a standard modem over your existing phone line, DSL modem, cable modem, satellite, and perhaps even some type of wireless connec-tion (fixed or mobile). Your choice hinges on the following three factors:

◆ *Availability.* You might not have cable or DSL service in your area, so that can significantly limit your choices. Dial-up service over an existing phone line and satellite service are almost universally available.

◆ *Speed.* You should choose the fastest connection you can afford. You may think you won't use the Internet that much, but when Windows or your other pro-grams need to download huge software updates, you'll be wishing you had a faster connection.

◆ *Price.* Monthly service charges range from about $10 per month for dial-up ser-vice (plus the cost of local phone service) to more than $60 a month for cable or satellite service. (Satellite also costs about $600 up front for the installation, although satellite Internet companies often offer special deals if you make a long-term commitment.)

The following sections provide a brief overview of your choices, but you need to shop around to find out what's available in your area and compare prices.

Inside Tip

Connection speeds are measured in kilobits per second (Kbps), which is equivalent to 1,000 bits per second, and megabits per second (Mbps), which is roughly equiv-alent to 1 million bits per second. Dial-up connections top out at about 44Kbps. Cable modem speeds range from 512Kbps to 20Mbps, but you're likely to see speeds of about 3 to 6Mbps. DSL ranges from 1.5 to 9Mbps. Fixed wireless is super-fast, at least in theory—about 30Mbps. Satellite service tops out at about 6Mbps, although the connection is typically much slower when you're sending data (uploading) from your computer to the Internet. A newer technology called BPL (Broadband over Power Lines) offers speeds ranging from 500Kbps to 3Mbps over existing electrical lines.

Chugging Along with Standard Modems

Because standard modems are the least expensive of the lot and because they can send and receive signals over existing phone lines, they remain the most popular type of modem. However, not all standard modems are created equal. As you shop for a modem, consider the following features:

Speed. Don't settle for anything slower than 56Kbps.

Internal versus external. Most computers come with an internal modem built in to the computer. All you see of the modem are jacks for connecting the modem to a phone line and (optionally) plugging in a phone so you can use the line for phone calls when you're not connected to the Internet. An external modem sits outside the computer and connects to the computer's serial (COM, or communications) port or a USB (Universal Serial Bus) port using a cable. External modems are typically more expensive.

> **Inside Tip** _____
>
> Your computer has a big circuit board inside it that everything else plugs into. This board is called the motherboard. The motherboard typically has five or more expansion slots that are about $\frac{1}{2}$-inch wide and 4 to 6 inches long, depending on the slot type. On most computers, the expansion slots are located in the back. You can plug smaller circuit boards, called *expansion cards,* into these slots to upgrade your computer and add capabilities. An internal modem is considered an expansion card.

Serial port or USB connection. If you decide to purchase an external modem, and your computer is equipped with one or more USB ports, consider a USB modem. USB allows you to connect up to 127 devices to a single port, giving your computer virtually unlimited expandability. This leaves your sole serial port open for other devices.

ITU or V.90 support. ITU or V.90 is the international standard for 56K modems. You might find modems that advertise the x2 standard. In the past, these modems did not conform to the V.90 standard, but newer x2 modems support V.90.

Fax support. Like fully equipped fax machines, a fax/modem enables you to exchange faxes with a conventional fax machine or another computer that has a fax/modem.

Voice support. If you plan to have your computer answer the phone and take messages, be sure the modem offers voice support. Without voice support, your modem can answer the phone, but it can only emit annoying screeching noises, which is useful for making telemarketers back off.

Videoconferencing support. Some modems are also designed to handle video calls, sort of like on *The Jetsons.* Of course, you'll need a video camera to take advantage of this feature.

Standard modems offer three benefits:

◆ The modem itself is inexpensive and easy to install.

◆ The modem plugs into a standard phone jack.

◆ Online services offer modem connections at bargain rates.

However, for speedy Internet connections, consider the options described in the following sections.

Avoiding Speed Bumps with ISDN

Unlike standard modems that must perform analog-to-digital (voice-to-data) conversions, ISDN (Integrated Services Digital Network) deals only with digital signals, supporting higher data transfer rates: 128Kbps, which is more than twice as fast as 56K modems.

ISDN modems use two separate 64Kbps channels, called *B channels*, that, when used simultaneously, achieve the 128Kbps transfer rates. This two-channel approach also lets you talk on the phone while surfing the web; one channel carries your voice while the other carries computer signals at 64Kbps (half speed). When you hang up, the modem can use both channels for computer communications. The phone company uses a third, slower, channel (channel D) to identify callers and do basic line checking, so you don't really need to think about it.

Shop for the ISDN service before you shop for an IDSN modem or adapter, and ask your phone company for recommendations. The performance of your ISDN connection relies on how well your ISDN adapter works with your phone company's connection.

Speeding Up Your Connection with DSL

DSL can achieve data transfer rates of 1.5 to 9Mbps over standard phone lines by using frequencies not used by voice signals. The only catch is that your computer has to be within about 3 miles of the phone company's switching station.

Several types of DSL are available, including ADSL and SDSL. In North America, ADSL (Asynchronous DSL) is most common. "Asynchronous" indicates that the system uses different data transfer rates for upstream and downstream communications—typically 1 or 2Mbps for downstream traffic and 32Kbps to 1Mbps for upstream traffic. In Europe, SDSL (Symmetric DSL) is most common. SDSL lines use the same data transfer rates for both upstream and downstream traffic (typically about 3Mbps).

Because there's no single DSL standard, don't purchase a modem without first checking with your phone company. Most DSL providers market their service as a package deal and include a DSL modem that works with the service.

Whoa!

Before you jump on the DSL bandwagon, do some research and ask your phone company to provide details on the cost, reliability, and performance boost you can expect from the service. One of the nice things about moving up from dial-up to DSL with your phone company is that you may get to keep your e-mail address. Some companies can also make it more affordable by offering a package deal with unlimited local/long-distance phone and DSL Internet.

Turbo-Charging Your Connection with a Cable Modem

Like cable television connections, a cable Internet connection supports high-speed data transfers to your PC, enabling you to cruise the Internet at the same speed you can flip TV channels. In addition to speed, cable modems are relatively inexpensive (starting at about $100) and are easy to install. You can expect to pay about $40 to $60 per month for cable Internet access, which makes it competitive with DSL service. If your cable company offers broadband Internet service, I strongly recommend you at least try it for a month. (Most cable companies offer package deals with phone, cable TV, and cable Internet.)

The main drawback with cable service is that you share the bandwidth with other users in your area, so the speed of your connection can fluctuate depending on how many users are currently using the service and how much data they're transferring over the connection. Still, in most areas, broadband cable is the fastest and most reliable option available.

Zipping Along with a Satellite Connection

In a major metropolitan area where plenty of broadband options are available, satellite is rarely a rational option. Installation costs are upward of $600, you pay $60 to $100 a month for the service, depending on how much speed and reliability you can afford; you have to hang one of those ugly satellite dishes on your house; and you're likely to lose your signal in heavy storms or cloud cover.

However, if you're living out in the boonies, where cable, DSL, and wireless service are unavailable, satellite might be the only broadband connection option available. It's pretty quick, but it doesn't quite stack up to cable service. I currently use both satellite and dial-up; the dial-up service lets me connect when the satellite signal is down.

Plugging in Wirelessly with Wi-Fi

The latest craze in Internet connectivity is Wi-Fi (wireless fidelity). Many hotels, airports, coffee shops, bookstores, colleges, and other places where people like to tote around their notebook computers and pretend they're working offer Wi-Fi service. Wi-Fi enables computers equipped with wireless modems to connect to the Internet whenever they're in range of the Wi-Fi network.

Supporting connection speeds of up to 30Mbps, Wi-Fi is definitely the way to go, assuming you have ready access to a Wi-Fi *hotspot*. Although Wi-Fi is popular in corporations, university settings, and businesses that cater to the mobile computing crowd, it hasn't become readily available for residential use.

def•i•ni•tion

Many businesses that offer wireless Internet connectivity advertise themselves as hotspots. A **hotspot** is a wireless adapter that's hardwired to the Internet. As many as 100 computers within range of the hotspot can use it to access the Internet at any one time. Most new notebook computers are equipped with a wireless Internet adapter that enables it to connect to a Wi-Fi hotspot.

Installing a Modem

To establish any type of Internet connection, your computer needs a modem. Most computers come equipped with a standard internal modem (the 56Kbps variety). To connect to the Internet, you connect a standard phone cord to the modem and plug it into a phone jack, just as you would plug in a phone. Your computer can then use the modem to dial the ISP and establish a connection to the Internet.

If your computer isn't equipped to use the type of Internet connection you plan on using, you need to install the required modem and perhaps some additional equipment. In most cases, you connect a modem to your computer using one of the following options:

◆ *Install an internal modem.* An internal modem is an expansion card that plugs into one of the expansion slots inside your computer. Installation requires turning off your computer, popping the hood, and properly inserting the card.

◆ *Install an external modem.* Some modems plug into the Ethernet (networking) port. Others connect to the USB port or the serial port on your computer. Connecting an external modem is pretty easy. You plug the modem into the correct port and then plug the modem into the power supply.

◆ *Insert a PC card.* Notebook computers have PC card slots that enable you to easily upgrade the computer and add optional devices. You can purchase a standard modem for dial-up access or a wireless adapter for Wi-Fi connectivity.

Whenever you install a new device, you must install the software that tells Windows how to use that device. In most cases, Windows identifies the new device on start-up and leads you through the process of installing the required software. In other cases, the manufacturer may recommend installing the software before installing the device, so read the instructions beforehand.

Shopping for an Online Service

The best way to shop for an online service is to connect to the Internet and search the web for services in your area. That certainly sounds like a chicken-and-egg scenario, doesn't it? How can you shop online for an Internet service provider if you don't yet have a connection to the Internet? Well, you can use a friend's or relative's computer or head down to the public library and use one of its computers.

If you have no way of shopping for an ISP online, employ one of the following old-fashioned techniques to track down an ISP:

◆ *Call your phone company.* Most phone companies feature an ISP service, and if they don't, they'll have plenty of suggestions on where to go.

◆ *Call your cable or satellite company.* If you have cable or satellite TV service, your cable or satellite company may also be able to provide you with Internet service.

♦ *Look in your yellow phone book under ÒInternet.Ó* Most phone books list the Internet service providers in the area.

♦ *Ask your neighbors.* Neighbors love to swap horror stories and success stories about their Internet service. They've probably tried several local services and can steer you clear of the less-reliable ones.

If you're getting a broadband connection through your ISP (such as cable, satellite, or DSL), your ISP is going to schedule a date and time for installation, and the installer will set up your connection for you. If you choose dial-up service, the ISP may provide you with some Internet connection settings you need to enter to establish a connection—a phone number, login name, and password. You must then enter the connection settings in Windows. Let the New Connection Wizard lead you through the process:

In Windows Vista: Click **Start, Connect To, Set Up a Connection or Network.** Click **Set Up a Dial-Up Connection** and click **Next.** The New Connection Wizard prompts you to enter the connection information you obtained from your ISP, as shown in Figure 19.2.

In Windows XP: Click **Start, All Programs, Accessories, Communications, New Connection Wizard,** and follow the wizard's lead.

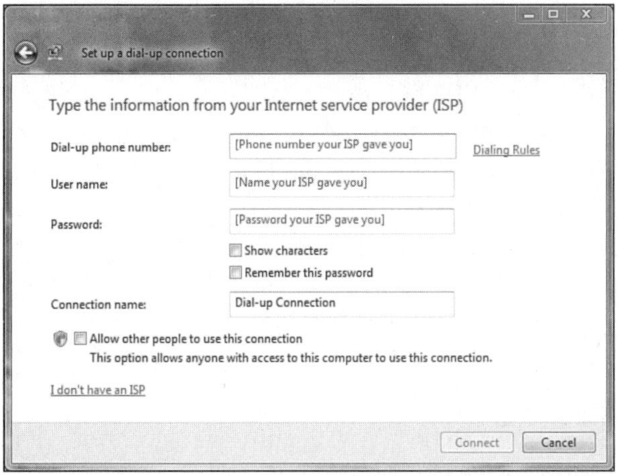

Figure 19.2

The Internet Connection Wizard prompts you for information required to establish a dial-up connection.

Inside Tip

To acquaint yourself with the Internet, sign up for a service that provides you with a free month of Internet service. If you decide you don't like the service, simply call and cancel before your first month is up. Be careful, though. Some services make it very difficult to cancel; when you call to cancel, you have to be assertive.

Connecting to Your ISP

If you set up a broadband connection, your computer remains connected to the Internet as long as the computer and modem remain turned on.

With a dial-up connection, your modem must dial in to the ISP and log on to connect before you can access the Internet. When you install software for most ISPs, the installation places an icon on the desktop that you can click or double-click whenever you want to connect. If you don't see an icon for connecting to the service, take one of the following steps:

In Windows Vista: Click **Start, Connect To,** and double-click the desired connection.

In Windows XP: Click **Start,** right-click **My Network Places,** and click **Properties.** Then double-click the icon for connecting to the service, and click the **Dial** button.

After you've established a connection, a Dial-Up icon typically appears in the system tray (in the lower-right corner of the Windows desktop). It looks like two overlapping computers. Rest the mouse pointer on the icon to check out your connection speed, or click the icon for additional details. You can right-click the icon and click **Disconnect** to hang up.

Inside Tip

Dial-up connections are typically configured to disconnect after a specified period of inactivity. You can disable this feature and change other settings for your dial-up connection:

In Windows Vista: Click **Start, Connect To,** right-click the icon for your connection, and click **Properties.** When the Properties dialog box appears, click the **Options** tab and enter the desired settings.

In Windows XP: Click **Start,** right-click **My Network Places,** and click **Properties.** Right-click the icon for your dial-up connection, and click **Properties.** When the Properties dialog box appears, click the **Options** tab and enter the desired settings.

Testing Your Connection Speed

No matter how your computer connects to the Internet, connection speeds can vary depending on the speed of your modem, the condition of the phone and fiber-optic cables, the amount of traffic on the network, and various other factors outside your control. If your Internet connection seems more sluggish than usual, you can check your connection speed at any of several websites:

1. Click **Start, Internet Explorer.** The Internet Explorer window appears and then downloads and displays the page it's set up to load on start-up.

2. Click in the address bar near the top of the window, type **reviews.cnet.com,** and press **Enter.** This connects you to CNET's review page.

3. Scroll down and click the **Bandwidth Meter** link. The Bandwidth Meter Speed Test page appears, prompting you to enter some details.

4. Enter your area code, select your connection type, and enter any additional details you'd like to submit.

5. Click **Go.** The Bandwidth Meter proceeds to download and upload files to determine your connection speed. This can take some time, depending on your connection.

When the Bandwidth Meter has completed the process, it displays your system's connection speed, as shown in Figure 19.3.

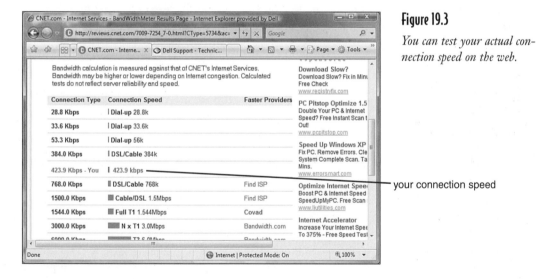

Figure 19.3

You can test your actual connection speed on the web.

The Least You Need to Know

◆ To connect to the Internet, your computer needs a modem to establish a connection and an ISP to open a line of communications between your computer and the Internet.

◆ A dial-up connection is slow, but it enables a computer to connect to the Internet over a standard phone line.

◆ Cable Internet service is typically the fastest and most reliable, but it can be a bit costly.

◆ The process for installing a modem varies on the type: an internal modem requires you to install an expansion card inside the computer, an external modem plugs into one of the computer's ports, a PC card modem slides into the PC card slot on a notebook computer.

◆ To set up an Internet connection, run the Internet Connection Wizard and follow its instructions.

◆ To check the speed of your Internet connection, go to CNET's review page at reviews.cnet.com, click the **Bandwidth Meter** link, and follow instructions.

Chapter 20

Poking Around on the World Wide Web

In This Chapter

- ◆ Launching your web browser
- ◆ Opening specific web pages
- ◆ Skipping from one web page to another with links
- ◆ Finding stuff on the web
- ◆ Bookmarking pages for quick return trips

The single most exciting part of the Internet is the World Wide Web (or web for short)—a loose collection of interconnected documents stored on computers all over the world. What makes these documents unique is that each page contains a link to one or more other documents stored on the same computer or on a different computer down the block, across the country, or overseas. You can hop around from document to document, from continent to continent, simply by clicking these links.

When I say *documents*, I'm not talking about dusty old scrolls or text-heavy pages torn from books. Web documents contain pictures, sounds, video clips, animations, and even interactive programs. When you click a multimedia link, your modem pulls the file into your computer, where the web browser or another program displays or plays the file.

As you'll see in this chapter, the web has plenty to offer, no matter what your interests—music, movies, sports, finance, science, literature, travel, astrology, body piercing, shopping—you name it.

Browsing for a Web Browser

To navigate the web, you need a special program called a *web browser*, which works through your Internet service provider (ISP) to pull up documents on your screen. You can choose from any of several web browsers, including the most popular browser for PCs, Internet Explorer, which is included with Microsoft Windows. In addition to opening web pages, browsers contain advanced tools for navigating the web, finding pages that interest you, and marking the pages you might want to revisit.

To keep things simple, I use Internet Explorer in the examples throughout this chapter. However, if you're using a different browser, don't fret. Most browsers offer the same basic features and similar navigation tools. Be flexible, and you'll be surfing the web in no time.

Steering Your Browser in the Right Direction

To run your web browser, click **Start, Internet Explorer.** (Most computers have the Internet Explorer icon on the desktop and in the Quick Launch toolbar at the bottom of the screen for easy access.)

When your browser starts, it immediately opens a page that's set up as its starting page. (You'll learn how to change your browser's starting page later in this chapter.) You can begin to wander the web simply by clicking links (typically, blue, underlined text; buttons; or graphic *site maps*). You can tell when the mouse pointer is over a link because the pointer changes from an arrow into a pointing hand. Click the **Back** button (the button with the left-pointing arrow on the button bar just above the page display area) to flip to a previous page, or click the **Forward** button (the button with the right-pointing arrow) to skip ahead to a page you've visited but backed up from (see Figure 20.1).

Click Back or Forward to return to pages you previously viewed

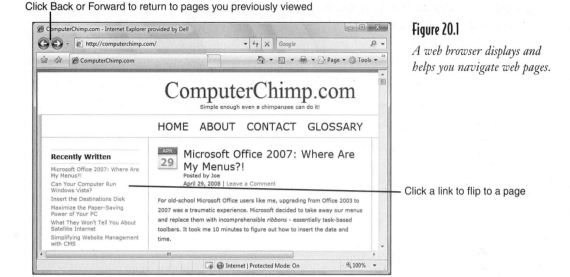

Figure 20.1

A web browser displays and helps you navigate web pages.

Click a link to flip to a page

If you click a link and your browser displays a message that it can't find the page or that access has been denied, don't freak out. Just click the **Back** button and try the link again. If that doesn't open the page, try again later. In some cases, the web page creator (the webmaster) may have mistyped the page address that the link points to or moved or deleted the page. On the ever-changing web, this happens quite often. Be patient, be flexible, and don't be alarmed.

Panic Attack

If you're not connected to the Internet when you start your browser, it might display a message indicating that it cannot find or load the page. If you have a standard modem connection, reestablish your connection as discussed in Chapter 19.

A Word About Web Page Addresses

Every page on the web has an address that defines its location, such as www.si.edu for the Smithsonian Institution or www.walmart.com for Wal-Mart. The next time you watch TV or flip through a magazine, listen and keep your eyes peeled for web page addresses. Not only do these addresses look funny in print, but they sound funny, too; for instance, www.walmart.com is pronounced "dubbayou-dubbayou-dubbayou-dot-walmart-dot-kahm."

Web page addresses are formally called *URLs* (uniform resource locators); when they don't work, you can refer to them as *unreliable resource locators.* URLs allow you to open specific pages. You enter the address in your web browser, usually in a text box near the top of the window, and your web browser pulls up the page.

Every web page **URL** starts with http://. Newsgroup sites start with news://. FTP sites (where you can get or upload files) start with ftp://. You get the idea. HTTP (short for Hypertext Transfer Protocol) is the coding system used to format web pages. The rest of the address reads from right to left (from general to specific). For example, in the URL http://www.mitsubishi.co.jp, *jp* stands for Japan, *co* stands for corporation (a company in Japan), *mitsubishi* stands for Mitsubishi (a specific company), and *www* stands for World Wide Web (or Mitsubishi's web server, as opposed to its FTP server or mail server). Addresses that end in .edu are for pages at educational institutions.

Whoa!

If you make any typos when typing in a URL, your browser either loads the wrong page or displays a message indicating that the page doesn't exist or that the browser cannot locate the specified page.

Addresses that end in .com are for commercial institutions. You can omit the http:// when entering web page addresses, but omitting ftp:// or news:// causes the browser to attempt to connect to a web server rather than the FTP or newsgroup server.

All you really have to know about a URL is that if you want to use one, type it exactly as you see it. Type the periods as shown, use forward slashes, and follow the capitalization.

Finding Stuff with Google and Other Search Tools

The web has loads of information and billions of pages, and this vast amount of information can make it difficult to track down anything specific. The web often seems like a big library that gave up on the Dewey decimal system and piled all its books and magazines in the center of the library. How do you sift through this mass of information to find what you need?

The answer: use an Internet search tool. You simply connect to a site that has a search tool, type a couple words that specify what you're looking for, and click the **Search** button (or its equivalent). The following are the addresses of some popular search sites on the web:

www.google.com   www.yahoo.com

www.ask.com   www.lycos.com

www.go.com   www.altavista.com

www.excite.com

Most web browsers have a Search option that connects you to various Internet search tools. Internet Explorer, for example, displays a Search box near the upper-right corner of the window. Simply click in the Search box, type a couple key words that describe what you're looking for, and click the **Search** button, as shown in Figure 20.2.

Type your search word or phrase in the Search box

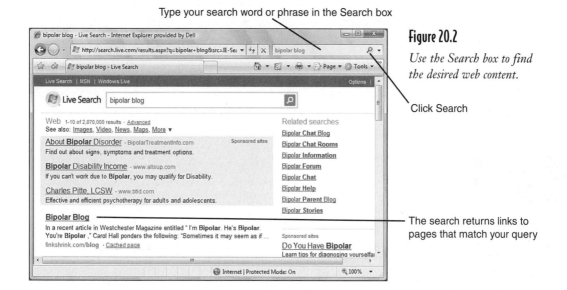

Figure 20.2

Use the Search box to find the desired web content.

Click Search

The search returns links to pages that match your query

Locating People Online

You can also use special search tools to find long-lost relatives and friends on the Internet. These search tools are electronic telephone directories that can help you find mailing addresses, phone numbers, and even e-mail addresses. To search for people, check out the following sites:

www.whitepages.com   www.anywho.com

people.yahoo.com   www.bigfoot.com

www.infospace.com

Navigating Multiple Pages with Tabs

Most web browsers, including the latest versions of Internet Explorer, feature tabs that enable you to keep multiple web pages open in a single window. You can then quickly switch to a page by clicking its tab.

To open a new tab, click the **New Tab** button, as shown in Figure 20.3, or press **Ctrl+T.** By default, Internet Explore opens a blank tab. You can then click in the address box and enter a website address to open the desired page.

Figure 20.3

Tabs enable you to open several web pages in a single window.

Enter the address of the page you want to open   Click New Tab to add a tab

Click a tab to display its contents

Click the tab's Close button to remove it

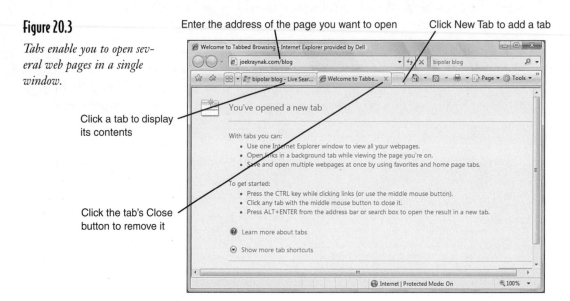

If you'd rather have Internet Explorer display the page it opens on start-up rather than displaying a blank tab, take the following steps:

1. In Internet Explorer, click **Tools, Internet Options.** The Internet Options dialog box appears with the General tab in front.

2. Under Tabs, click the **Settings** button. The Tabbed Browsing Settings dialog box appears.

3. Click the check box next to **Open Home Page for New Tabs Instead of a Blank Page** to place a check in the box.

4. Click **OK.**

To have Internet Explorer display a different page on start-up, refer to "Changing the Starting Web Page," later in this chapter.

> **Computer Cheat**
>
> When clicking links, you can choose to have a link's target open in a new tab or window. Right-click the link and click **Open in New Tab** or **Open in New Window.**

Going Back in Time with History Lists

Although the Back and Forward buttons eventually take you back to where you were, they don't get you there in a hurry or keep track of pages you visited yesterday or last week. For faster return trips and a more comprehensive log of your web journeys, check out the history list.

In Internet Explorer, click the **Favorites Center** button and click **History.** Click the day or week when you visited the website, and click the website's name to see a list of pages you viewed at that site. To open a page, click its name, as shown in Figure 20.4.

Click Favorites Center   Click History   Click the website's name   **Figure 20.4**

Use the history list to retrace your steps.

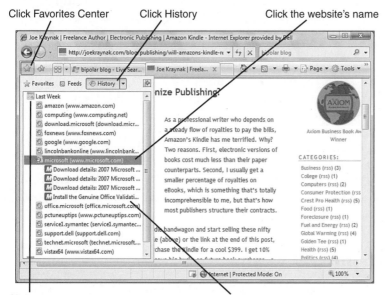

Click the day or week icon   Click the page you want to revisit

---

Whoa!

If you share your computer with someone, you might not want that person to know where you've been on the web. To cover your tracks, clear the History list. In Internet Explorer, click **Tools, Internet Options, Delete, Delete History.** If you'd like to preserve most of your history list, you can remove individual items by right-clicking them in the history list and clicking **Delete.**

Marking Your Favorite Web Pages

As you wander the web, you pull up pages that you know you want to return to in the future. When you happen upon such a page, flag it by bookmarking the page as one of your favorites. This adds the page's name to the Favorites menu. The next time you want to pull up the page, you simply select it from your customized menu.

To mark a page, right-click a blank area of the page and select **Add to Favorites.** You can then add and edit the name of the page as it appears in your favorites list, create a new folder to store related favorites, and choose the folder where you want to insert your new favorite. When you're done entering your preferences, click the **Add** button. (Other browsers have similar features but may refer to favorites as *bookmarks*.)

Computer Cheat
Right-click a blank area of the page and click **Create Shortcut.** This places a shortcut icon for the page on your desktop.

After you've added a page to the Favorites menu or one of its submenus (folders), you can quickly open the page by opening the Favorites menu (and the submenu, if you added it to a submenu) and clicking the name of the page.

You can rearrange items on your Favorites menu by dragging them and dropping them where you want them to appear. If you drag an item over a submenu and wait a moment, Internet Explorer opens the submenu. You can then drag the item to the position where you want it to appear in the submenu and drop it in place.

Changing the Starting Web Page

Whenever you fire up your browser, it opens with the same page every time. If you have a page you'd like your browser to load on start-up, just let your browser know. To change your starting page in Internet Explorer, take the following steps:

1. Open the page you want to view on start-up.

2. Click **Tools, Internet Options.**

3. On the **General** tab, under **Home page,** click **Use Current.**

4. Click **OK.**

The Least You Need to Know

♦ To start Internet Explorer, double-click its icon on the Windows desktop or select it from the **Start, All Programs** menu.

♦ Links typically appear as buttons, icons, or specially highlighted text (typically blue and underlined).

♦ Click a link to open the page that the link points to.

♦ If you know a web page's address, type it in your browser's **Address** or **Go to** text box and press **Enter.**

♦ To search for a topic or site on the web, use a search engine, such as www.google.com, and enter a few words to describe what you're looking for.

♦ To bookmark a page in Internet Explorer, right-click a blank area of the page and select **Add to Favorites.**

Chapter 21

Sending and Receiving E-Mail

In This Chapter

- ◆ Addressing and sending e-mail messages
- ◆ Checking your electronic mailbox
- ◆ Jazzing up your messages with photos and fancy fonts
- ◆ Attaching files to outgoing messages
- ◆ Following proper e-mail etiquette

How would you like to send a message to a friend and have it arrive in a matter of seconds instead of days? Send dozens of messages every day without paying a single cent in postage? Never again stare out your window waiting for the mail carrier?

Well, your dreams are about to come true. When you have a connection to the Internet and an e-mail program, all these benefits are yours. In this chapter, you learn how to start taking advantage of them.

Before you set sail on your maiden voyage, you have a choice to make: do you want to use your own program to access e-mail (such as Outlook Express) or access your e-mail via the web? Using an e-mail program allows you to download all incoming messages to your computer and read them at your leisure—whether you're connected to the Internet or not. These programs also provide enhanced tools for managing your messages. See the "Using an E-Mail Program" section. Web-based e-mail offers the advantage of being able to access your e-mail from any computer. You simply use your web browser to connect to the site, log in, and send and receive your messages. See the "What About Free, Web-Based E-Mail?" section.

Using an E-Mail Program

An e-mail program (or *client*) connects to your Internet mail server to send messages from and receive messages to your computer. You can use any of several programs to access e-mail, including Outlook Express, Outlook, Eudora (**www.eudora.com**), and Thunderbird (**www.mozilla.com/thunderbird**), to name a few.

In the following sections, I show you how to set up your e-mail account in your e-mail program and use the program to send, receive, and read messages.

Setting Up Your Account

The hardest part about e-mail is setting up an e-mail account—getting your e-mail program to connect to your Internet service provider's *mail server* for the first time.

def•i•ni•tion

A **mail server** is an electronic post office that routes your incoming and outgoing messages to their proper destinations.

To send and receive e-mail, you must use an e-mail program such as Outlook Express and enter settings that tell it how to connect to the *mail server*. Before you start your e-mail program, be sure you have the following information from your ISP:

E-mail address. Your e-mail address is usually all lowercase and starts with your first initial and last name (for example, jsmith@iway.com). However, if your name is John Smith (or Jill Smith), you might have to use something more unique, such as JohnHubertSmith@iway.com. (All e-mail addresses must contain the @ sign to separate the recipient's name from the mail server's address.)

Outgoing mail (SMTP). The SMTP (Simple Mail Transfer Protocol) server is the mailbox where you drop your outgoing messages. It's actually your Internet service provider's computer. The address usually starts with mail or smtp, such as mail.iway.com or smtp.iway.com.

Incoming mail (POP3). The POP (Post Office Protocol) server is like your neighborhood post office. It receives incoming messages and places them in your personal mailbox. The address usually starts with pop, such as pop.iway.com.

Account. This one is tricky. It could be your user name, the name you use to log on to your service provider (for example, jsmith), or something entirely different your ISP assigned to your account.

Password. Typically, you use the same password for logging on and for checking e-mail. I can't help you here; you pick the password or have one assigned to you.

When you have the preceding information, you must enter it into your e-mail program. To enter e-mail settings in Windows Mail (which is included in Windows Vista) or Outlook Express (packaged with earlier versions of Windows), take the following steps:

1. Run Windows Mail or Outlook Express. (You can find an icon for it at the top of the **Start** menu; on the **Start, All Programs** menu; on the Windows desktop; or in the Quick Launch toolbar.) When you first run your mail program, it steps you through the process of entering the required information, as shown in Figure 21.1.

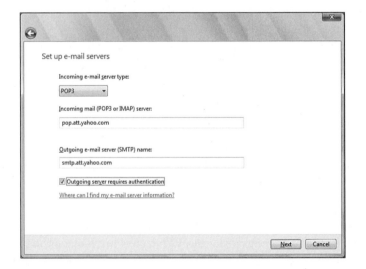

Figure 21.1

Before you can use your e-mail program, you must enter connection settings.

2. Follow the on-screen instructions. If the Internet Connection Wizard does not start, or you need to enter information for a different e-mail account, open the **Tools** menu and click **Accounts.** Click the **Add** button, click **Mail,** and follow the on-screen instructions to enter your settings.

Addressing an Outgoing Message

The procedure for sending messages over the Internet varies, depending on which e-mail program or online service you're using. In most cases, you first click the button for composing a new message. For example, here's how it works in Windows Mail:

1. Click the **Create Mail** button.

2. A window appears, prompting you to compose your message. Click in the **To** box and type the person's e-mail address (see Figure 21.2).

3. Click in the **Subject** box and type a brief description of the message.

4. Click in the large box near the bottom of the window and type your message.

5. When you're ready to "mail" your message, click the **Send** button.

Figure 21.2

Here's how to send mail with a typical Internet e-mail program (Windows Mail).

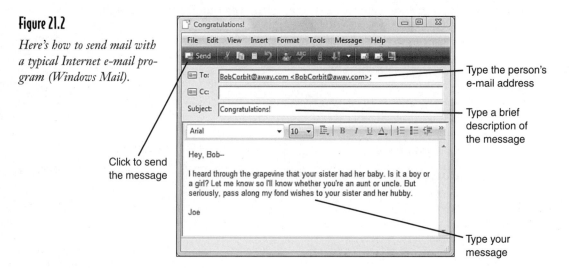

Click to send the message

Type the person's e-mail address

Type a brief description of the message

Type your message

Some e-mail programs send the message immediately. Other programs place the messages you send in a temporary outbox; then, when you're ready to send the messages, you click the button to initiate the send operation. For example, in Windows Mail, you click the **Send/Receive** button. Windows Mail then sends all messages from the outbox and checks for incoming messages.

Computer Cheat

Most e-mail programs, including Windows Mail and Outlook Express, include e-mail address books. (Windows Vista features a Contacts utility you can access from Windows Mail.) Instead of typing the person's e-mail address, you simply select it from a list. To quickly display the address book in Windows Mail, click the **Contacts** button (on the right end of the toolbar). In Outlook Express, click the **Addresses** button. You can then add contacts to your address book and select contacts from the address book rather than typing their e-mail addresses each time.

Checking Your E-Mail

When someone sends you an e-mail message, it doesn't just pop up on your screen. The message sits on your service provider's incoming mail server until you connect and retrieve your messages.

There's no trick to connecting to the mail server—assuming you entered the correct connection settings. Most programs check for messages automatically on start-up or display a button you can click to fetch your mail. The program retrieves your mail and then displays a list of message descriptions. To display a message, click or double-click its description, as shown in Figure 21.3.

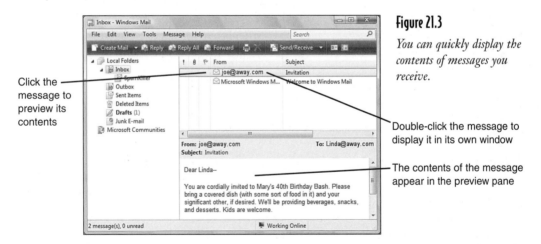

Click the message to preview its contents

Double-click the message to display it in its own window

The contents of the message appear in the preview pane

Figure 21.3

You can quickly display the contents of messages you receive.

Most e-mail programs use several folders to help you keep your messages organized. For example, Windows Mail and Outlook Express store the messages you receive in the Inbox folder, messages that are waiting to be sent in the Outbox folder, messages you sent in the Sent Items folder, messages you deleted in the Deleted Items folder, and messages you composed but chose not to send in the Drafts folder.

To switch from one folder to another, click the desired folder. To display a message you received, for instance, click the Inbox folder and then click the description of the message.

Sending Replies

In most e-mail programs, to reply to a message, you select the message and click the **Reply** or **Respond To** button. This opens a window that automatically inserts the e-mail address of the person who sent the message, along with the sender's description of the message (usually preceded by Re:). (If the original message was addressed to multiple recipients, you can click the **Reply All** button to address your reply to everyone.)

Many e-mail programs also include the contents of the received message so everyone who receives your reply can easily follow the conversation. To differentiate between the sender's original message and your reply, some e-mail programs add a right angle bracket (>) at the beginning of each line of the original message. To respond, type your message in the message area, and click the **Send** button.

Inside Tip

When replying to a long message, delete most of the original material from the message you received, leaving only one or two lines to establish the context. This makes the message travel faster and takes up less disk space on the recipient's computer.

If you received a message that you would like to pass along to other recipients, you can *forward* the message. Click the message you want to forward, and click the **Forward** button. This opens a window that automatically inserts the sender's description of the message (usually preceded by Fwd:).

In the **To** text box, enter the e-mail addresses of the people to whom you want to forward the message. Your e-mail program automatically inserts the original message in the message area. If you'd like to add an introduction to or comment about the original message, type this text in the message area. When you're ready to forward the message, click the **Send** button.

Adding Photos and Other Cool Stuff

How would you like to add a photo to your message or jazz it up with some fancy fonts? Most e-mail programs let you use special type styles and sizes, add backgrounds, insert pictures, and embellish your messages with other formatting options.

Windows Mail and Outlook Express offer a toolbar that contains buttons for the most common enhancements. You can use the toolbar to make text bold or italic; add bulleted and numbered lists; and insert pictures, horizontal lines, links, and other objects. (If the toolbar does not appear, check the **Format** menu for an **HTML** or **Rich Text** option. HTML stands for Hypertext Markup Language, the coding system used to format web pages.)

The buttons for inserting pictures and formatting text work the same way as in your word processing and desktop publishing programs (see Chapter 13). The only new thing here is the button for inserting links. (A *link* is highlighted text that points to another web page.)

To insert a link, first drag over the text you want to appear as the link. Then, click the button for inserting the link, type the address of the web page you want it to point

Whoa!

When you send a message that has pictures, lines, and fancy fonts, the e-mail program sends it as a web page. The recipient's e-mail program must support web page formatting (most do); otherwise, the message will appear to be packed with cryptic codes.

to, and click **OK.** Most e-mail programs automatically convert any web page addresses or e-mail addresses you type in the message area into links. Just type the address and press the **spacebar** or **Enter** key. You can also drag links from a web page into the message area and plop them right down in the message area. (For more about links, see Chapter 20.)

Attaching Documents to Your Messages

You can fit most e-mail messages on a Post-it note. A person typically rifles off a message or reply in less than a minute. However, at times, you might want to send something more substantial—perhaps an outline for a book, a photo of yourself, a copy of an article you found on the web, or a document with its formatting intact.

Whatever the case, you can send files along with your messages by creating *attachments.* For instance, if you have a resumé you created in Word, you can e-mail it as an attachment to a prospective employer. That person could then open the resumé in

def•i•ni•tion

An **attachment** is a file in its original condition and format that you clip to an e-mail message.

Word and view or print it. Without attachments, you would need to copy the text of the resumé and paste it into your e-mail message, losing any formatting you applied to the text and any graphics you inserted.

The process for attaching a file is fairly simple, but the steps vary, depending on the e-mail program you use. In most e-mail programs, you follow the same steps as you do for composing and addressing the message:

1. To attach a file to the message, click the appropriate button (for example, **Attach** or **Insert File**).

2. This displays a dialog box that lets you select the file you want to send. The dialog box looks just like the dialog box you use to open or save files. Go to the folder that contains the file you want to send, and double-click the file's name.

3. When you're ready to send the message, along with the attachment, simply click the **Send** button.

Many word processing and spreadsheet programs have built-in support for e-mail, allowing you to send a document right from the program. In Word, for instance, you can open the document you want to send, open the **File** menu, point to **Send To,** and click **Mail Recipient.** This displays the e-mail program's toolbar with text boxes for typing the recipient's e-mail address and a description of the message.

If you receive a message that contains an attached file, your e-mail program usually displays some indication that a file is attached. For example, Outlook Express displays a paper clip icon. If you double-click the message (to display it in its own window), an icon appears at the bottom of the window or in an attachments text box. You can double-click the icon to open the file or right-click and choose **Save** to save the file to a separate folder on your hard drive.

Panic Attack

When you receive an attachment, use an antivirus program to scan the file before opening it (if it's a document) or running it (if it's a program). Programs are especially notorious for carrying viruses, but documents can contain macro viruses, which can cause as much havoc. (Most antivirus programs are set up to run in the background and automatically scan attachments when you choose to open them or save them to disk.)

In many cases, when someone forwards a message to you, the person's e-mail program sends the forwarded message as an attachment. If the message has been forwarded several times, you might need to meander through a long line of attachments to view the original message.

What About Free, Web-Based E-Mail?

You probably have heard of "free e-mail" services, such as Gmail (Google Mail), Yahoo!, Hotmail, and Juno, and wondered why anyone would need free e-mail. Isn't all e-mail free? Does your ISP charge extra for it? Of course, your e-mail account is included with the service that your ISP provides; your ISP does not charge extra for it. But there are several good reasons to explore these free e-mail services.

Free e-mail is typically web based, allowing you to send messages and check your mail on the web. If you travel, you can manage your e-mail from anywhere in the world using any computer that's connected to the Internet. You don't need a computer that has your e-mail account settings on it.

Free e-mail lets everyone in your home or business have his or her own e-mail account. When Junior starts corresponding with his chat room buddies, he'll want his privacy, and he can have it with his own e-mail program.

Free e-mail is good to use when you register "anonymously" for free stuff. Whenever you register for contests, shareware, and other freebies on the Internet, you must enter your e-mail address. Use your free e-mail account to register so companies will send any junk mail to that address, keeping your real e-mail address private.

Free e-mail also provides you with a stable e-mail address. In the event that you change ISPs, you don't need to notify all your friends, relatives, and colleagues that you changed your e-mail address.

To get a free e-mail account, connect to any of the following sites, click the link for free e-mail, register, and follow the instructions at the site to start using your free e-mail account:

Inside Tip

To find more free e-mail services, use your favorite web search page to search for the phrase "free e-mail."

AOL Mail	mail.AOL.com
Gmail	mail.google.com
MSN Hotmail	www.hotmail.com
ICQ Mail	www.icqmail.com
Yahoo!	mail.yahoo.com

E-Mail Shorthand and Emoticons

If you want to look like an e-mail veteran, you can pepper your messages with *emoticons* (pronounced *ee-mow-tick-ons*). These icons look like facial expressions or act as abbreviations for specific emotions. (You might need to turn your head sideways to see the tiny faces.) You can use these symbols to show your pleasure or displeasure with a particular comment, to take the edge off a comment you think might be misinterpreted, and to express your moods.

Emoticon	Meaning
:) or :-)	I'm happy, or it's good to see you, or I'm smiling as I'm saying this. You can often use this to show you're joking.
:D or :-D	I'm really happy or laughing.
;) or ;-)	Winking.
:(or :-(	Unhappy. You hurt me, you big brute.
;(or ;-(	Crying.
:| or :-|	I don't really care.
:/ or :-/	Skeptical.
:# or :-#	My lips are sealed. I can keep a secret.
:> or :->	Devilish grin.
;^)	Smirking.
%-)	I've been at this too long.
:p or :-p	Sticking my tongue out.
<g>	Grinning. Usually takes the edge off whatever you just said.
<vbg>	Very big grin.
<l>	Laughing.
<lol>	Laughing out loud.
<i>	Ironic.
<s>	Sighing.
<jk>	Just kidding. (These are also my initials.)
<>	No comment.

In addition to the language of emoticons, Internet chat and e-mail messages are commonly seasoned with a fair share of abbreviations. The following table samples of some of the abbreviations you'll encounter and be expected to know.

Abbreviation	Meaning
AFAIK	As far as I know
BRB	Be right back
BTW	By the way
CUL8R	See you later
F2F	Face to face (usually in reference to meeting somebody in person)
FAQ	Frequently asked questions. (Many sites post a list of questions that many users ask, along with the answers. They call this list a FAQ—pronounced like *fact* without the "t.")
FOTCL	Falling off the chair laughing
FTF	Another version of face to face
FYA	For your amusement
FYI	For your information
HHOK	Ha ha; only kidding
IMHO	In my humble opinion
IMO	In my opinion
IOW	In other words
KISS	Keep it simple, stupid
LOL	Laughing out loud
MOTOS	Member of the opposite sex
OIC	Oh, I see
PONA	Person of no account
ROTFL	Rolling on the floor laughing
SO	Significant other
TIC	Tongue in cheek
TTFN	Ta ta for now

E-Mail No-No's

To avoid getting yourself into trouble by unintentionally sending an insulting e-mail message, be sure you use the proper protocol for composing e-mail messages.

The most important rule is to NEVER EVER TYPE IN ALL UPPERCASE CHARACTERS. This is the equivalent of shouting, and people become edgy when they see this text on their screen. Likewise, take it easy on the exclamation points!!!

Avoid sending bitter, sarcastic messages (*flames*) via e-mail. When you disagree with somebody, a personal visit or a phone call is usually more tactful than a long e-mail message that painfully describes how stupid and inconsiderate the other person is. Besides, you never know who might see your message; the recipient could decide to forward your message to a few choice recipients as retribution.

Also in a business or educational email, use correct spelling and grammar. Abbreviations for words or sentences, such as CUL8er (for "see you later") may be acceptable in text messaging and e-mailing friends, but they're taboo in formal circles.

def•i•ni•tion

When you strongly disagree with someone on the Internet, via e-mail or (more commonly) in newsgroups, it's tempting to **flame** the person with a stinging, sarcastic message. It's even more tempting to respond to a flaming message with your own barb. The resulting flame war is usually a waste of time and makes both people look bad.

If you're in marketing or sales, avoid sending unsolicited ads and other missives. Few people appreciate such advertising. In fact, few people appreciate receiving anything that's unsolicited, cute, "funny," or otherwise inapplicable to their business or personal life. In short, don't forward every little cute or funny e-mail message, "true" story, chain letter, joke, phony virus warning, or free offer you receive.

And no matter what business you're in, avoid inserting emoticons in your messages. Some professionals consider this unprofessional.

Finally, avoid forwarding warnings about the latest viruses and other threats to human happiness. Most of these warnings are hoaxes, and when you forward a hoax, you're just playing into the hands of the hoaxers. If you think the warning is serious, check the source to verify the information before you forward the warning to everyone in your address book. Virus hoaxes are posted at www.symantec.com/avcenter/hoax.html and vil.mcafee.com/hoax.asp.

The Least You Need to Know

♦ To set up a new e-mail account in Outlook Express, open the **Tools** menu, click **Accounts,** click the **Add** button, choose **Mail,** and follow the on-screen instructions.

♦ To create a new e-mail message, click the **Create Mail** or **New Message** button or its equivalent in your e-mail program.

- Incoming e-mail messages are often stored in the Inbox. Simply click the **Inbox** folder and click the desired message to display its contents.

- To reply to a message, select the message and click the **Reply** button.

- To attach a document to an outgoing message, click the button for attaching a file and select the desired document file.

- DON'T TYPE IN ALL UPPERCASE ... and follow all the other rules of proper e-mail etiquette.

Chapter **22**

Chatting Online

In This Chapter

- Instant messaging friends and relatives
- Audio and video conferencing
- Chatting in chat rooms
- Setting up a group site
- Exploring Second Life

Instant messaging and online chat rooms provide fun and inexpensive ways to meet people and converse with friends, relatives, colleagues, and even complete strangers.

With an instant messaging (IM) program and an Internet connection, you can exchange text messages with any of your "buddies" who happen to be connected at the time. If you both have a microphone and speakers connected to your computers, you can carry on a voice conversation without the expense of placing a long-distance phone call. With the addition of a digital camera, you can even videoconference like *The Jetsons!*

If you prefer to party online with groups of friends or complete strangers, chat rooms or virtual worlds may be more to your liking. When you're in a chat room, you simply type and send a message, and it immediately pops up on the screen of every person in the room. When anyone else in the chat room sends a message, it pops up on your screen. This makes for a frenetic conversation that can be quite stimulating. In virtual worlds, such as Second Life, you can become a virtual inhabitant of a new world and interact with others sort of like you do in real life.

This chapter shows you how to use IM and chat tools on the Internet. You learn how to use AIM, America Online's Instant Messaging program, to chat privately with friends, relatives, and colleagues and use the audio and video features of your computer to place voice and video "phone calls" across the Internet. This chapter also introduces you to online chat rooms and virtual worlds, where you can engage in a verbal free-for-all, and shows you how to set up a group site to keep in touch with friends, classmates, and your other circles of friends, colleagues, and acquaintances.

Instant Messaging with AIM

America Online's Instant Messaging program AIM is the most popular program of its kind. Millions of people, most likely including some of your friends and relatives, use it daily to keep in touch with one another. In the following sections, you learn how to download a free copy of AIM to your computer, install it, and start using it to communicate with your other computer-savvy pals.

Inside Tip

Most IM programs enable you to exchange messages only with people who are using the same program, so if all your friends are using AIM, you should use AIM, too. If your friends are using another program, download and use that program. Some IM programs, including ICQ and Trillian, do enable users of different IM programs to communicate with one another. Check out some of these IM programs: Google Talk (www.google.com/talk), MSN Messenger (messenger.msn.com), Yahoo! Messenger (messenger.yahoo.com), ICQ (www.icq.com), and Trillian (www.ceruleanstudios.com).

Getting Started with AIM

Most IM programs, including AIM, are free for the taking. To download and install a copy of AIM and create a screen name that identifies you on the IM network, take the following steps:

1. Connect to the Internet and start your web browser.

2. Click in the Address bar, type **www.aim.com,** and press **Enter.** AIM's home page appears.

3. Click **Install Now.**

4. Follow the on-screen instructions to install AIM and set a screen name and password.

AIM starts automatically after you install it and whenever Windows starts. If you exit the program and decide to restart it later, click **Start, All Programs, AIM,** and click the icon for running AIM. When AIM starts, it prompts you to enter your screen name and password, as shown in Figure 22.1.

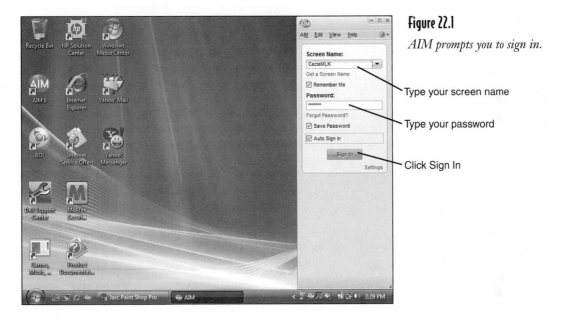

Figure 22.1

AIM prompts you to sign in.

Type your screen name

Type your password

Click Sign In

Click in the **Screen Name** box and type your screen name, and click in the **Password** box and type your password. To have AIM remember your password so you don't have to enter it next time, click **Remember Me** and **Save Password** to place a check in each box. You can also click **Auto Sign In** to have AIM automatically sign you in whenever you start the program. Click the **Sign In** button to go online. At this point, anyone who knows your screen name can contact you by sending you a message.

If you want to be signed in but don't have time or the desire to chat, you can remain signed on but hidden. Click **Available** and click **Invisible.** You'll be able to see your friends, but they won't be able to see that you're signed in. To step away from your computer and notify your friends that you're unavailable, click **Available, Away Messages, I Am Away.**

Text Messaging with AIM

If you know someone's AIM screen name, you can click the **IM** button to text message that person, assuming he or she is online. When you click the IM button, a window appears prompting you to enter the person's screen name. Type the person's screen name and then click **View Status.** If the person is available, you can type a message in the IM box, and click **Send** or press **Enter** to initiate a conversation. Figure 22.2 shows a typical conversation taking place inside the AIM window.

Figure 22.2

Start text messaging!

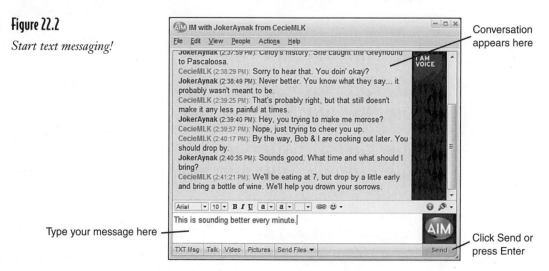

In addition to typing text, you can format the text to use a different type style, shrink or enlarge the text, add enhancements such as bold and italics, apply highlighting, insert a link to a web page, or even insert small icons that represent your emotional reactions. Use the toolbar just above the area where you type your messages to give your message a personal touch.

Building a Buddy List

Although you can click the IM button and type a person's screen name to contact them, it's a whole lot easier if you can select the person's screen name from a list. That's why AIM provides a feature called the buddy list. To add a buddy to your list, follow these steps:

1. Click **Edit, Add Buddy** or press **Ctrl+D.** The New Buddy window appears, as shown in Figure 22.3.

Select the desired group

Type the person's screen name here

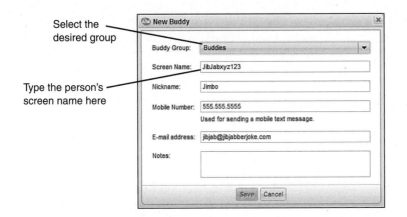

Figure 22.3

Add a buddy to your buddy list.

2. Type your buddy's AIM screen name or ICQ number or screen name in the IM box.

3. You can send text messages to a mobile phone by typing the 10-digit phone number; but your buddy must enter the required settings to receive the message.

4. To assign the person to a specific buddy group, click the arrow to the right of the Buddy Group box and click the desired group.

5. *Optional:* Type the person's first and last name in the boxes at the top of the New Buddy window.

6. Click **Save.**

Whenever you sign on to AIM, AIM checks to see which of the people on your buddy list are currently online and willing to accept messages. When a buddy's online, you simply click that person's screen name in your buddy list and start chatting.

Inside Tip

If you have loads of buddies, create your own buddy groups to make your buddy list less crowded and overwhelming. To create a new group, click **Edit, Add Group** (or press **Ctrl+G**), type a descriptive name for the group, and click **Save.**

Voice-Messaging with AIM

Plug a set of speakers and a microphone into your computer, and AIM can transform your computer into an overpriced phone that you can use to talk to your buddies online. You might even be able to trim that long-distance bill! Depending on the speed of your connection and computer and on the quality of your microphone and speakers (and the speed of your buddy's connection and computer and the quality of your buddy's microphone), it might even sound pretty good. Over slow connections, however, the conversation can get a little choppy.

To engage in a voice chat with a buddy who has the proper equipment, simply click your buddy's name and click the **Start a Talk Session** button. If you're already text messaging, click the **Talk** tab in the message box, as shown in Figure 22.4. Your buddy will then need to click **Accept** to answer the "phone."

Figure 22.4

Assuming you and your buddy have the right equipment, you can carry on a voice conversation through AIM.

Click the Talk tab

Wait for your buddy to accept your invite

Videoconferencing with AIM

If that voice thing didn't impress you, AIM has another trick up its sleeve. By equipping your computer with an affordable webcam, you can videoconference with colleagues and loved ones. Again, you need a fairly speedy Internet connection and excellent equipment for a smooth conference, but when everything works right, you not only hear the person you're talking with, but you see the person, too, and that person gets a peek at you.

To videoconference with AIM, click the **Video** tab and click **Start.** A message pops up on your buddy's screen inviting him or her to a video chat. Assuming your buddy accepts the invitation, his or her image appears on your screen, as shown in Figure 22.5, and your image appears on your buddy's screen.

Figure 22.5

With video chat, you and your buddy can see and hear one another chat.

Your image appears here

Your buddy's image appears here

Click the Video tab

Computer Cheat

Have you ever sent a large file to someone via e-mail and had it rejected because it was too large? With AIM, you can send someone a file, large or small, while conversing with that person. Simply click the **Files** tab, click the **Send File** button, and select the file or folder you want to send. Assuming your friend chooses to accept the file or folder, AIM transfers it over your current connection. You need to be a little careful with this feature, however. Don't accept files or folders from suspicious sources, and always scan an incoming file or folder for viruses before opening it. For details about how to protect yourself on the Internet, see Chapter 26.

Exploring Online Chat Rooms

When America Online first introduced chat rooms, at any time of the day or night you could find hundreds of chat rooms packed with thousands of complete strangers engaged in witty and often witless repartee. Today, anyone with an Internet connection and an AIM user name (which you can obtain for free) can skip from chat room to chat room to party online. You can find plenty of other chat rooms scattered all across the Internet, too, from large communities such as Yahoo! and SpinChat to individual sites where members with similar interests discuss specialized topics.

Web chat tools vary from service to service. To access AIM Chat, point your web browser to **chat.aim.com.** Yahoo! also offers chat rooms you can access using Yahoo! Messenger, covered in the following sections. Some sites have their own built-in chat rooms that use other tools to enable members to chat online.

Getting Started with Yahoo! Messenger

Yahoo! has injected the power and simplicity of its search tools into its Internet chat rooms. The best way to access these chat rooms is to use Yahoo! Messenger, an IM program very similar to AIM. Take the following steps to download and install Yahoo! Messenger for free and register for a user name and password:

1. Connect to the Internet and start your web browser.

2. In the Address box, type **messenger.yahoo.com** and press **Enter.** Internet Explorer opens and displays the Yahoo! Messenger page.

3. Click **Get It Now.**

4. Follow the on-screen instructions to download and install Yahoo! Messenger and register for a user name and password.

> **Panic Attack**
>
> Online services typically limit the capacity of a chat room so the conversation doesn't become too overwhelming. In most cases, if a popular room, such as Romance, is full, the service automatically spins you off into a similar room, where you can immediately begin conversing.

After you've installed it, Yahoo! Messenger runs automatically whenever you log on to Windows. If you exit the program and need to run it later, you can find it at **Start, All Programs, Yahoo! Messenger.** When you run Yahoo! Messenger, it displays a Sign in window. Simply enter your Yahoo! ID and password, and click **Sign In.** You can then exchange instant messages with your friends and acquaintances, make voice calls, and videoconference, just as you can with AIM.

Entering Chat Rooms

With Yahoo! Messenger and Yahoo! Chat, you're never at a loss for someone to talk to. Yahoo! Chat features hundreds of active chat rooms you can prowl at any time of the day or night. To enter a chat room, take the following steps:

1. In Yahoo! Messenger, open the **Messenger** menu, point to **Yahoo! Chat,** and click **Join a Room.** The Join Room window appears, displaying a list of chat room categories.

2. Browse through the list for your desired category. Click the plus sign (**+**) next to a category to view a list of subcategories.

3. Click the desired category. A list of available rooms appears on the right.

4. Double-click the desired room or click the room's name and click **Go to Room.** The chat room's window appears, as shown in Figure 22.6.

Messages from all chat room participants appear here

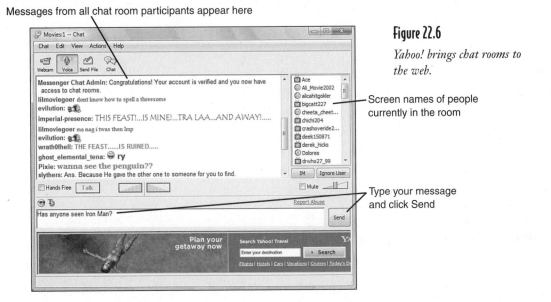

Figure 22.6

Yahoo! brings chat rooms to the web.

Screen names of people currently in the room

Type your message and click Send

When you're in a chat room, you can start chatting. The ongoing discussion is displayed in the large frame in the upper left. To send a message to the other chatters, click in the text box just below the ongoing discussion, type your message, and press **Enter** or click **Send.**

When you tire of this simple banter, you can do other stuff. For example, click the smiley face icon (below the message area) and click the desired smiley face to send it to the room.

You can also right-click the name of someone in the room. This displays a menu with options that let you find out more about the person, send the person a private message or a file, add the person to a list of friends, or ignore the person (prevent the person's messages from appearing on your screen).

Just above the message area are several menus. Use the various options on these menus to display your Friends List (see which of your friends are online), turn voice chat on or off, turn webcam on or off, change the chat room settings, or create a list of your favorite chat rooms.

To move to a different room, open the **Chat** menu and click **Change Chat Room.** This opens the Join Room window, where you can choose the desired chat room category and a specific room. (When I was writing this book, the ability to create your own rooms was unavailable.)

Inside Tip

Although Yahoo! is on the cutting edge of web chat, check out some these other web chat services: www.spinchat.com, www.talkcity.com, www.flirt.com, www.chatting.com, and www.chat-web.com.

To edit your own profile, return to the Yahoo! Messenger window, open the **Messenger** menu, and click **My Profiles.** This displays a link with your user name that you can click to go to Yahoo! Messenger on the web and change your profile.

To learn other maneuvers, ask the people in the chat room. Most of them are happy to answer your questions, and it's definitely more fun than reading about it.

Keeping in Touch with Friends and Family

Developers have come up with an innovative communications feature for the web that enables users to create their own online community centers, family circles, or special-interest groups to keep in touch. For example, if you have a large extended family, you can create a family circle and have all your family members (at least those who have Internet access) join the circle. Members can post messages, digitized photos, announcements, and calendar dates in a special area where everyone in the family can check them out. Many of these "community" centers also enable you to set up a members-only chat room and exchange electronic greeting cards and virtual gifts.

One of the best online community centers I know of is Yahoo! Groups, which you can find at **groups.yahoo.com.** If you already registered for Yahoo! Chat, you are registered for Yahoo! Groups, too. If you didn't register, you must register to obtain a member name and password. Use your member name and password to log in and then create your own group or join existing groups, invite others to join, create your own online photo albums, enter important dates, post messages, and much more.

Inside Tip

Other sites host groups, too. Check out groups.google.com, groups.msn.com, and www.classmates.com.

To create your own group, click the **Start a group now** link, as shown in Figure 22.7, and follow the on-screen instructions.

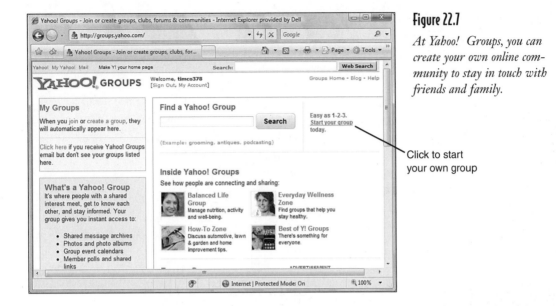

Figure 22.7

At Yahoo! Groups, you can create your own online community to stay in touch with friends and family.

Instead of hosting groups on services such as Yahoo! Groups and MSN Groups, many web users are beginning to use blogs for the same purpose. For details on blogs, skip to Chapter 24.

Living It Up in Second Life

Second Life is a 3D virtual world equipped with all the amenities (good and bad) that you've become accustomed to in the real world. In Second Life, you can walk up to people and introduce yourself rather than just exchanging typed messages. You can invest in real estate, buy and sell virtual goods (for virtual or real money), and become involved in a host of activities.

Second Life is far too robust and complex to cover in one short section in one short chapter. Entire books have been written about it. Getting started, however, requires very little knowledge. Visit **secondlife.com,** click **Get Started,** and follow the on-screen instructions to register, choose a persona (avatar), and download and install the required software.

The installation routine places an icon for running Second Life on your Windows desktop and on the **Start, All Programs** menu. Click or double-click the icon to run Second Life. Figure 22.8 shows what you can expect when you enter the virtual world of Second Life.

Figure 22.8

In Second Life, you embody a character in a virtual world.

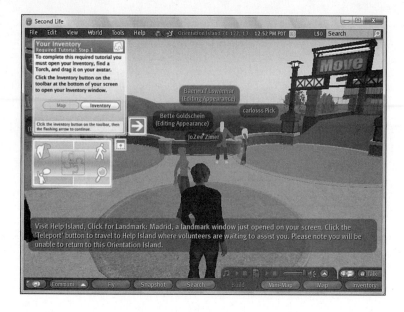

The Least You Need to Know

◆ AIM and other instant messaging programs enable you to chat with others on the Internet using text messages, voice, and video.

◆ After connecting to the Internet and signing on with AIM, you can send a text message to a buddy by double-clicking your buddy's name, typing the message, and clicking **Send.**

◆ Online chat rooms enable groups of people to gather and converse online via text messaging, voice, and webcams.

◆ Yahoo! Groups and similar services provide families and other groups of people who have shared interests with a central meeting place to swap messages, photos, and calendars.

◆ If reality is just too boring for you, visit Second Life (**secondlife.com**).

Chapter 23

Touring Newsgroups, Message Boards, and More

In This Chapter

- ◆ Reading and posting in newsgroups
- ◆ Reading and posting on message boards
- ◆ Signing up for mailing lists or newsletters
- ◆ Staying up-to-date with RSS news feeds

As you've already gleaned from Chapters 21 and 22, the Internet is an incredible communications tool. It enables you to e-mail and chat with your circle of friends, converse with voice and video, and mingle with complete strangers.

But that's not all.

The Internet also enables people to share common interests in slightly less personal ways through newsgroups, message boards, mailing lists, newsletters, and RSS news feeds. With newsgroups and message boards, people post messages where anyone (or members only) can read them. On message boards, you can commonly find answers, solutions, guidance, support, and camaraderie without having to know someone's e-mail address or screen name. With mailing lists and newsletters, organizations can keep members posted of the latest news and information, notify members of upcoming events, and call members to action. And with RSS news feeds, you can create your own custom newspaper that updates itself!

In this chapter, you learn how to stay in the loop with all these powerful communication tools.

Reading and Posting Newsgroup Messages

What's a newsgroup? Think of it like a bulletin board where people can share ideas, post questions and answers, and support one another. The Internet has thousands of newsgroups, covering topics from computer programming to cooking, from horses to cars, from politics to tattoos. With your Internet connection and a newsreader, you have access to newsgroups 24 hours a day, 7 days a week.

In the following sections, you learn how to connect to newsgroups, subscribe to newsgroups that interest you (for free), and read and post newsgroup messages.

Getting Started with Your Newsreader

The best way to access newsgroups is to use a specialized program called a *newsreader*, whose sole purpose is to connect to newsgroups and display messages. This chapter focuses on Windows Mail and Outlook Express, the e-mail/newsreaders included with Windows. (Windows Mail and Outlook Express are nearly identical.) If you're using a different newsreader, the options should be similar enough for you to make the transition.

To run Windows Mail (in Windows Vista), click **Start, All Programs, Windows Mail.** To run Outlook Express (in earlier versions of Windows), click **Start, All Programs, Outlook Express.** Depending on how your version of Windows is set up, you may also have an icon for running Windows Mail or Outlook Express on your desktop, at the top of the Start menu, or in the Quick Launch toolbar at the bottom of your screen.

To access newsgroups, you must set up your newsreader to connect to your service provider's *news server*. This consists of entering the news server's address, for instance, news.internet.net—ask your service provider for the address. Windows Mail is already set up to use Microsoft's news server, but it provides access to a very limited number of specialized Microsoft newsgroups.

The first time you run your newsreader, it should lead you through the process of setting up a news server account. You can check your settings or create a new account in Windows Mail or Outlook Express by performing the following steps:

Computer Cheat

If you don't know your news server's address, stick **news** at the beginning of your service provider's domain name. For example, if your service provider's domain name is internet.com, the news server address likely would be **news.internet.com**.

1. Click **Tools, Accounts.** The Internet Accounts dialog box appears.

2. In Outlook Express, click the **News** tab. If you haven't set up a newsgroup account, the News list should be blank. In Windows Mail, the Accounts window shows all your existing e-mail and newsgroup accounts. Under News, you should see "Microsoft Communities (default)," but you'll still need to add a news server to access a wider selection of newsgroups.

3. Click **Add, Newsgroup Account, Next** (in Windows Vista) or click **Add, News** (in Windows XP). The Internet Connection Wizard appears, prompting you to type your name.

4. Type your name as you want it to appear in messages that you post to newsgroups and click **Next.**

5. Type your e-mail address and click **Next.** Sometimes instead of or in addition to posting a reply in a newsgroup, a person will reply to your post through e-mail.

6. Type your news server's address, as shown in Figure 23.1.

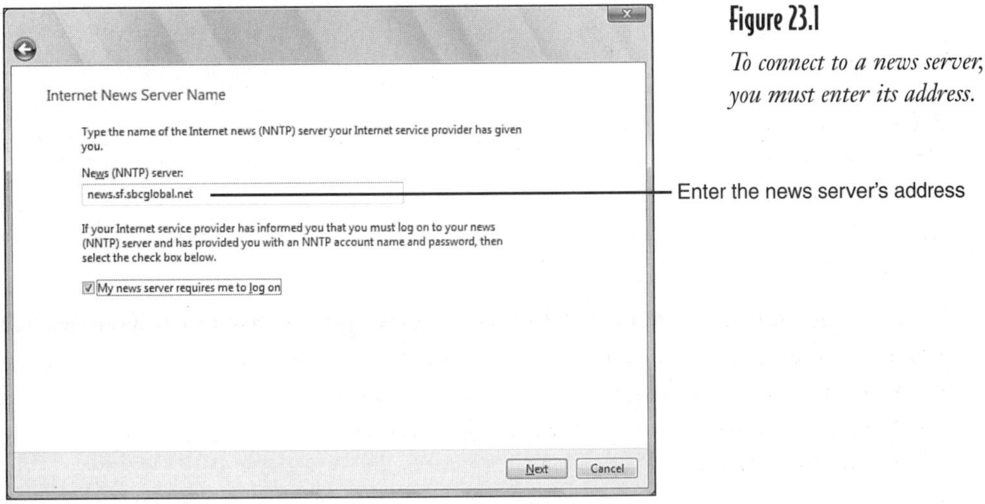

Figure 23.1

To connect to a news server, you must enter its address.

Enter the news server's address

7. If the news server requires you to log on to use it, click the check box next to **My news server requires me to log on,** and click **Next.**

8. If you checked the box in step 7, enter your user name and password in the appropriate text boxes and click **Next.** Otherwise, skip to step 9.

9. Click **Finish.** Outlook Express creates a new newsgroup account for you and displays its name in the News list.

10. Click the **Close** button.

At this point, you might be prompted to download a list of newsgroups. Feel free to either proceed with the on-screen instructions or skip to the next section to download a list of newsgroups later.

Subscribing to Newsgroups

Before you can start reading messages about do-it-yourself body piercing or other topics of interest, you must download a list of the newsgroups available on your news server and subscribe to the newsgroups that interest you. Your newsreader might automatically download the list the first time you connect or after you set up a new newsgroup account. Be patient; even over a fairly quick modem connection, it might take several minutes to download this very long list. You then can subscribe to newsgroups to create a list of newsgroups that interest you.

Inside Tip

You usually can determine a newsgroup's focus by looking at its address. Most addresses are made up of two or three parts. The first part indicates the newsgroup's overall subject area; for example, *rec* is for recreation and *alt* stands for alternative. The second part of the address specifically indicates what the newsgroup offers. For example, rec.arts is about the arts. If the address has a third part (most do), it focuses even further. For example, rec.arts.bodyart discusses the art of tattoos and other body decorations.

Although the steps you take to subscribe to newsgroups vary depending on the newsreader you're using, the procedure is fairly straightforward in any newsreader. Let's take a look at just how easy it is by following the procedure for Outlook Express:

1. Run Windows Mail or Outlook Express, as instructed earlier in this chapter.

2. At the bottom of the folder list (left pane), click the name of your news server.

3. Click the **Newsgroups** button in the toolbar. Your newsreader logs into the news server and downloads a list of newsgroups, which can take several minutes. The Newsgroups dialog box appears, as shown in Figure 23.2, displaying a list of available newsgroups. You can update the list at any time by clicking the **Reset List** button.

Click your news server   Click Newsgroups

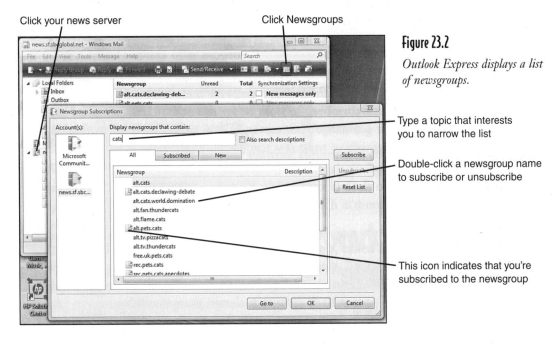

Figure 23.2

Outlook Express displays a list of newsgroups.

Type a topic that interests you to narrow the list

Double-click a newsgroup name to subscribe or unsubscribe

This icon indicates that you're subscribed to the newsgroup

4. In the **Display newsgroups that contain** text box, type a topic. Let's use cats, for example. This filters the list to show only those newsgroups that have "cats" in the name.

5. Double-click the name of the newsgroup to which you want to subscribe. A newspaper icon appears next to the name. You can unsubscribe by double-clicking the newsgroup's name again.

6. Repeat steps 3 and 4 to subscribe to additional newsgroups and click **OK.**

7. In the folder list (left pane), click the plus (**+**) sign next to your news server to display a list of subscribed newsgroups.

8. Click the newsgroup's name to display a list of posted messages in the upper-right pane.

Reading and Responding to Posted Messages

Although the names of newsgroups can provide hours of entertainment by themselves, you didn't connect to a news server just to chuckle at the weirdoes. (Well, maybe you did.) You connected to read what people have to say and to post your own messages. If you used Windows Mail or Outlook Express to read e-mail messages in Chapter 22, you'll notice that the steps for reading newsgroup postings are similar:

1. Click the plus (+) sign next to your news server's name to display a list of subscribed newsgroups.

2. Click or double-click the name of the desired newsgroup. Descriptions of posted messages appear.

3. Click a description to display the message contents in the message pane, as shown in Figure 23.3, or double-click the message to display it in its own window.

Click a message description to view its contents

Figure 23.3

Windows Mail displays a list of messages in the selected newsgroup.

The contents of the message are displayed in a separate pane

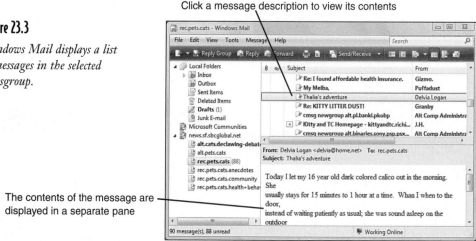

As people post messages and replies, they end up creating *discussions*. Most newsreaders are capable of displaying related messages as *threads*, so you can follow the discussion from its beginning to its end. If you see a message that has a plus sign next to it, click the plus sign to view a list of replies to the original message. Then, click the descriptions of the replies to view their contents.

When you read a message that inspires you to write a reply, you have two choices: you can reply to the group by posting your reply in the newsgroup or reply to the individual through e-mail. Some people request that you reply through e-mail for privacy or just because they're too lazy to check for replies in the newsgroup itself.

In Windows Mail or Outlook Express, you can reply to the group by clicking the **Reply Group** button. This displays a window that addresses the message to the current newsgroup and to any other newsgroups in which the original message was posted. It also quotes the contents of the original message. (If the original message was long, you should delete some of the quoted material to be polite.) Type your reply and click **Send** or **Post Message.**

To reply privately, click the **Reply** button. This displays a message window addressed to the person who posted the original message. Type your reply and click **Send,** as you normally would do to send an e-mail message. The reply is sent directly to the author and is not posted in the newsgroup.

Inside Tip

Before you post a message in a newsgroup, get a feel for its culture and history, as if you were visiting a foreign country. See whether the newsgroup has a FAQ (frequently asked questions list) to determine whether the question you want to ask or the issue you want to address has already been addressed. And don't pick a fight … unless, of course, that's what the newsgroup is all about.

Starting Your Own Discussions

Newsgroups are great for expressing your own ideas and insights, having your questions answered by experts, and finding items that might not be readily available in the mass market (for example, books that are no longer in publication, parts for your 1957 Chevy, and so on). When you need help or you just feel the overwhelming urge to express yourself, you can start your own discussion by posting a message.

Computer Cheat

Most newsreaders enable you to attach files to your messages. Although most messages consist of simple text, people post graphics in some newsgroups such as hk.binaries.portrait.photography. (For details on how to work with file attachments, see Chapter 21.)

Posting a message is fairly easy:

1. Connect to the newsgroup where you want the message posted.

2. Click **Write Message** or **New Post** (or whatever command your newsreader uses for posting the new message). Your newsreader automatically addresses the message to the current newsgroup, as shown in Figure 23.4. You also can add newsgroup addresses to post the message in other newsgroups.

Figure 23.4

You can start a discussion by posting your own message.

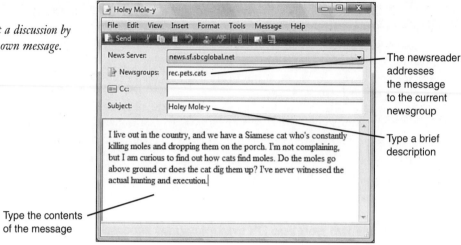

The newsreader addresses the message to the current newsgroup

Type a brief description

Type the contents of the message

3. Type a brief but descriptive title for your message, type the contents of your message, and click **Send** or **Post.**

Your message is posted in the newsgroup, where anyone can read it. It might take a while for people to reply, so check back every day or two for responses. (Sometimes nobody responds, so don't expect too much.)

Pulling Up Message Boards on the Web

Many websites have their own *message boards* (commonly called *discussion groups* or *forums*), which are nearly identical to newsgroups but may not show up in your newsreader. To access a message board, simply click its link and follow the trail of links until you come upon a list of posted messages, as shown in Figure 23.5. (To keep out the riffraff, many sites require you to register to gain access to their message boards, but it's usually free, so go ahead.)

To read a message, click the message description or whatever link the site provides for reading the message. You can then reply to the message by posting a response (in most cases) or reply to the originator of the message via e-mail (in some cases). You can also choose to start a new discussion by posting your own message. The steps vary depending on the message board, but they're usually fairly intuitive.

> **Computer Cheat**
>
> To search web-based message boards for specific topics, point your web browser to www.google.com. Type your search words in the Search box as you usually do, but instead of clicking Google Search, click the **more** link at the top of the page and click **Groups.**

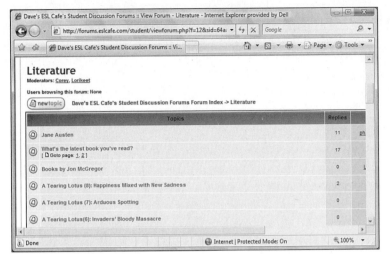

Figure 23.5

A message board is basically a web-based newsgroup.

Registering for E-Mail Mailing Lists

Many websites have a huge following and thousands of members and other interested parties. Rather than communicating with members individually, the site often enables members and sometimes even nonmembers to subscribe to its mailing list or newsletter. You typically click a link to subscribe to the site and then enter your name and e-mail address and perhaps some additional information.

In many cases, clicking the Subscribe link runs your e-mail program and simply addresses a message from you to the site. To subscribe, you just send the message. Your e-mail address is added to the list, and whenever the next scheduled mass mailing occurs, you receive your copy via e-mail.

When you've had enough, you can unsubscribe from the list. Most legitimate companies insert a message, typically near the bottom of the mail message or newsletter, providing instructions about how to unsubscribe and remove yourself from the mailing list.

Panic Attack

If you don't completely trust the website you're visiting, don't subscribe to its newsletter or mailing list. Some sites pass your e-mail address to other sites, in which case, you begin to be inundated with unsolicited messages. Create a separate (free) e-mail account, as discussed in Chapter 21, and use that to register. That will save your primary e-mail account from spam.

Getting Up-to-the-Minute RSS News Feeds

As you're cruising around the web, you might encounter some sites that offer RSS news feeds. RSS stands for Really Simple Syndication. News feeds are typically flagged with an orange icon that has the letters RSS or XML or an icon that looks like radio broadcast waves. With an RSS newsreader or a web browser that supports RSS, you can subscribe to RSS content and have sites deliver late-breaking news directly to you rather than having to visit the site and poke around for what you want. It's sort of like creating your own custom newspaper that's automatically updated 24/7.

In Internet Explorer, you can subscribe to RSS feeds by pulling up the feed (clicking the RSS or XML button on the web page offering the feed) and then clicking on the **Subscribe to This Feed** button and clicking **Subscribe to This Feed,** as shown in Figure 23.6. You can access your feeds at any time by clicking the **Favorites Center** button and clicking **Feeds.**

Subscribe to This Feed button

Figure 23.6

Internet Explorer enables you to subscribe to RSS content on the web.

Favorites Center button

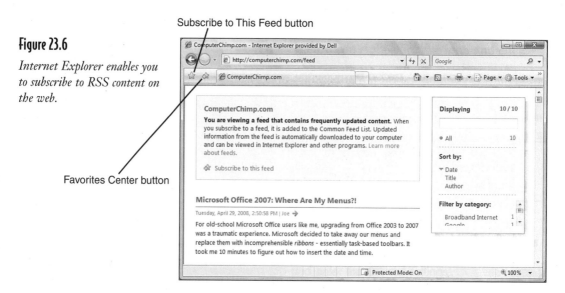

The Least You Need to Know

♦ To connect to your ISP's news server, you must specify the news server's address in your newsreader. In Windows Mail or Outlook Express choose **Tools, Accounts.**

♦ When you first connect to a news server, your newsreader downloads a list of available newsgroups.

- ◆ To display the contents of a newsgroup message, click the description of the message. Double-click the description to display the message in its own window.

- ◆ Web message boards are nearly identical to newsgroups, although they may not show up in your newsreader.

- ◆ You can subscribe to mailing lists and newsletters on the web to have news and notices e-mailed to you.

- ◆ With an RSS-enabled web browser, you can subscribe to content on several websites and have it delivered to a single location.

24

Publishing Your Own Web Page or Blog

In This Chapter

- ◆ Understanding how the web works
- ◆ A sneak peek at the codes behind web pages
- ◆ Creating your own web page
- ◆ Finding free enhancements for your web page
- ◆ Blogging 101

You wandered the web. Perhaps you sent out a few electronic greeting cards, played some audio and video clips, and even ordered products online. You can use search tools to track down information about the most obscure topics, and you can keep up with all your hobbies and other interests with newsgroups.

But now you want more. You want to establish a presence on the web, publish your own stories or poems, place pictures of yourself or your family online, show off your creativity, and communicate your ideas to the world.

Where do you start? How do you create a web page or blog from scratch?

How do you insert photos and links? How do you add a background? And after you've created the page, what steps must you take to place the page on the web for everyone to see?

This chapter shows you how to whip up your first web page or blog right online, without having to learn any special programs or deal with any cryptic web page formatting codes. And because you create the page online, you don't have to worry about publishing your web page when you're done. Quick. Easy.

Behind the Scenes with a Web Page

Behind every web page is a text document that includes codes for formatting the text, inserting pictures and other media files, and displaying links that point to other pages. This system of codes (commonly referred to as *tags*) is called *HTML* (Hypertext Markup Language) .

Most codes are paired. The first code in the pair turns on the formatting, and the second code turns it off. For example, to type a heading such as "Apple Dumplin's Home Page," you would use the heading codes like this:

```
<h1>Apple Dumplin's Home Page</h1>
```

The <h1> code tells the web browser to display any text that follows the code as a level-one heading. The </h1> code tells the web browser to turn off the level-one heading format and return to displaying text as normal. Unpaired codes act as commands; for instance, the <img> code inserts a graphic, so <img src=Òhttp://www.sample.com/horse.jpgÓ> inserts a graphic file named horse.jpg that's stored in the root directory of the website www.sample.com.

Inside Tip

Even if a browser is set up to display all level-one headings in a particular way, HTML codes can override the browser's setting and give the heading a different look. For example, they might make the heading appear in a different color or font.

Web browsers use HTML codes to determine how to display text, graphics, links, and other objects on a page. Because the browser is in charge of interpreting the codes, different browsers might display the same page slightly differently. For example, one browser might display links as blue, underlined text, whereas another browser might display links as green and bold.

Forget About HTML

A basic introduction to HTML is helpful in understanding how the web works, troubleshooting web page formatting problems, and customizing web pages with fancy enhancements, but don't worry—you don't need a certification in HTML to create your first web page. Many companies have developed specialized programs that make the process of creating a web page as easy as designing and printing a greeting card.

You can use programs such as Web Studio, FrontPage, HotDog, or Dreamweaver to create and format web pages on your computer and then upload (copy) the pages from your computer to a web server (typically your ISP's web server). Or you can create and format your web pages right on the web simply by specifying your preferences and using forms to enter your text. The next section shows you just how easy it is to create and publish your own web page online at Yahoo! GeoCities.

Inside Tip

One of the easiest ways to create and manage a website is to use a content management system (CMS). A typical CMS provides a collection of tools that enable you to create and edit web pages right online, inside your browser window, just as if you were editing a document in a word processor.

Yahoo! GeoCities has its own CMS. If you register your own domain name (such as www.yourname.com) and sign up with a web hosting service, the service may have its own CMS. If it doesn't, consider installing a CMS, such as WebYep (www.obdev.at/products/webyep). It's easier if you start with a CMS from the very beginning; adding it later can be a nightmare, if it's even possible.

Making a Web Page Right on the Web

When it comes to publishing your own web page, you have simple needs—a single web page that lets you share your interests with others and express yourself to the world. For someone with such simple needs, the web offers free *hosting* services, such as Yahoo! GeoCities. These services provide tools for building your web page online, along with access to a web server where you can publish your page.

def•i•ni•tion

A web **host** is a server where you can store your web page and all files related to it, such as photos and other graphics. Think of it as a neighborhood where you can build your home. Your ISP might even provide free hosting services.

Here's how to publish a simple web page at Yahoo! GeoCities:

1. Point your web browser to **geocities.yahoo.com.**

2. Unless you registered with Yahoo! earlier (for example, for Yahoo! Chat), follow the series of links required to sign up as a new user. (Websites are notorious for changing steps and commands, so specific instructions would only confuse you. You have to wing it.)

3. Fill out the required form, read the legal agreement(s), and jump through whatever hoops you need to jump through to get your free membership. This gives you an ID (member name) and password so you can sign in.

4. Use your ID and password to sign in to Yahoo! GeoCities. Your browser loads the Yahoo! GeoCities welcome page, asking you for some general information, including the type of page you intend to create and where you heard about Yahoo! GeoCities.

5. Enter the requested information and click **Submit.** Yahoo! displays your user name and the address (URL) of your website.

6. When you click **Build your web site now!** Yahoo! displays several options, including an option to build a website or blog.

7. Click **Create a Web Site.** Yahoo! gives you the option of building your web site by filling out forms on the web or by the Yahoo! PageWizards, as shown in Figure 24.1.

Figure 24.1

Yahoo! GeoCities gives you a choice of tools.

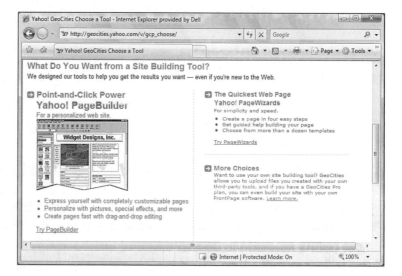

8. Click the **Try PageWizards** link. Yahoo! displays a list of predesigned web page templates you can use to get started.

9. Click one of the PageWizard designs. Yahoo! GeoCities displays a brief introduction to the wizard, as shown in Figure 24.2. (If you change your mind and decide to use a different template, click the **Cancel** button and choose another.)

Figure 24.2

Yahoo! GeoCities provides a brief introduction to the selected wizard.

10. Click **Launch Yahoo! PageWizard** to start the wizard with the selected design, or click one of the alternative color schemes or designs near the bottom of the page. The first PageWizard dialog box appears, welcoming you to the wizard.

11. Click the **Begin** button. The wizard prompts you to select a color scheme.

12. Click the desired color scheme and click **Next.**

13. Follow the wizard's instructions to complete your web page and save it to the Yahoo! GeoCities web server. (The steps vary, depending on which wizard you're running.)

You can change your page at any time. Just go to Yahoo! GeoCities at geocities.yahoo.com, sign in, and run the PageWizard. When the PageWizard appears this time, it displays an option for editing an existing page. Click **Edit Existing Page,** and open the drop-down menu and click the name of the page you want to edit. Click **Next** and follow the on-screen instructions to enter your changes.

> **Computer Cheat**
>
> To delete a web page, log on to **geocities.yahoo.com,** click the **Manage** tab, click **File Manager,** click **Open File Manager,** click the check box next to each file you want to delete, and click **Delete.**

For more options and control over your web page design and layout, use Yahoo! PageBuilder. This is a full-featured web page creation and editing tool. To run PageBuilder, simply open the Yahoo! GeoCities home page and click **Yahoo! PageBuilder.** This displays an introduction to PageBuilder. Click the **Launch PageBuilder** link to run the program.

You can edit the page later using PageWizard:

1. Log on to **geocities.yahoo.com.**

2. Click the **Manage** tab, click **File Manager,** and click **Open File Manager.**

3. Click the check box next to the file you want to edit and click **Edit.** This displays an HTML version of the page. If you originally created the page with Yahoo! Page Builder or PageWizard, a warning appears indicating that you can edit the HTML, but if you choose to edit the file later with PageWizard, you'll lose your changes.

4. Click **Launch PageWizard,** and follow the on-screen instructions to enter your changes.

Blogging Your Way to Internet Fame

In the not-so-distant past, publishing your insights and words of wisdom was nearly impossible. Unless you won a few poetry contests or tirelessly submitted high-quality articles to magazines or manuscripts to book publishers, your hopes of being published were slim to none. With the advent of electronic publishing via the web, anyone with a little technical expertise can publish his or her own writings. But creating and managing a website and keeping it up-to-date is both challenging and time-consuming.

Relatively recently (sometime in the late 1990s), self-publishing on the web became easier with the introduction of *web logs,* or *blogs* for short. These relatively simple web pages are primarily text based, and you can create and update them by filling out a form. You type a message, comment, or other text and then *post it* to the blog. The most recent posting appears at the top of your blog followed by prior postings. As your list of posted messages grows, old messages are pushed off the main blog and archived.

The first blogs focused on news and commentary. Bloggers would read an article online and then post a link to the article along with their comments, insights, questions, and sometimes corrections or additional facts concerning the article. Over the years, the scope of blogs has broadened considerably. Now people commonly use blogs to publish their own poetry and fiction; broadcast news stories that are overlooked by the mainstream media; communicate with family members, friends, and colleagues; promote grassroots movements; keep an online journal; and much more.

def•i•ni•tion

A **blog** (short for **web log**) is a publicly accessible personal journal that enables an individual to voice his or her opinions and insights, keep an online record of experiences, and gather input from others. People also use blogs to share photos with friends and family and set up their own online clubs.

Launching Your Blog

To start blogging, you need a blogging platform, or an application that provides the tools you need to post messages to your blog and maintain it. Several developers offer platforms for free and can even host your blog for you. The following steps show you how to launch your own blog using the popular WordPress blogging platform:

1. Run Internet Explorer and go to **wordpress.com.**

2. Click the link to sign up and follow the on-screen instructions to sign up for a WordPress account. When you log in to WordPress, it displays a page that's packed with information and links to other people's blogs.

3. Click the **Register a Blog** link (near the message that welcomes you to WordPress). The Register a Blog page appears, as shown in Figure 24.3.

4. Click in the **Blog Domain** box, and type a name for your blog. This name will be added to the beginning of wordpress.com to create your blog's domain name. You won't be able to change this later, although you can delete the blog later and create a new one.

5. Click in the **Blog Title** box, and type the title you want to appear at the top of every page of your blog.

6. If you want to prevent search engines from indexing your blog, click the check box next to the Privacy option to remove the check mark.

Figure 24.3

Register a new WordPress blog for free.

7. Click the **Create Blog** button. As long as the domain name you entered is not already in use, WordPress displays a message indicating that the domain name is now yours and showing you the user name to use to log in.

You can now visit your blog by entering its address (for example, **yourblogname. wordpress.com**) into Internet Explorer, but it consists of only an opening page that contains a welcome message.

Inside Tip

To check out blogging in action, visit my blogs at **computerchimp.com** and **joekraynak.com**. I created both of these blogs using WordPress. To check out some other online blogging sites, try www.livejournal.com, www.blogger.com, and www.typepad.com.

To log in to your blog, launch Internet Explorer, type **yourblogname.wordpress.com/wp-admin** in the address box near the top of the window, and press **Enter.** You're already logged in, so this displays the WordPress Dashboard for your blog, as shown in Figure 24.4. However, if you log out and then try to use Internet Explorer to go to **yourblogname.word-press.com/wp-admin** later, WordPress displays a page prompting you to enter your user name and password. When you enter the correct information, WordPress displays the Dashboard.

Figure 24.4

The WordPress Dashboard gives you access to the tools you need to post messages and manage your blog.

Making Your Blog Your Own

The WordPress Dashboard provides all the tools you need to post content to your blog, redesign it, and manage it. For example, you can *write a new post.* Writing a post is as easy as typing in a word processing application, as shown in Figure 24.5. You simply type a title for the post, type and format your content, and click **Publish.** Posts appear on your opening page with the newest post first.

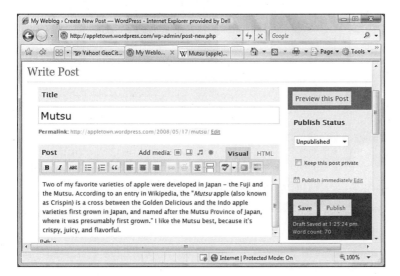

Figure 24.5

*Posting content to your blog is as easy as filling out a form and clicking **Publish.***

Whoa! _____

If you post a blog and regret it later, you can delete it. Simply pull up your blog, scroll down to the end of the entry you want to delete, and click **Remove** or click **Edit** to change your entry.

You can also *write a new page*. Pages are almost identical to posts, but they're used for static content. In other words, they function more like web pages. Links for the pages you create appear under "Pages" in your blog's navigation bar.

Managing your blog is easy with Dashboard. If you click the **Manage** link, you can access tools for editing or deleting posts, pages, comments, and other elements of your blog. (Comments consist of content that visitors post in response to your posts or pages.)

You want things to look nice, and *designing your blog* is easy with Dashboard. You can select a theme to apply to your blog to completely change its appearance and layout without affecting the content. You can even edit the theme to create a customized version.

You'll need to be able to *review comments*. Visitors to your blog may post comments that you don't approve of. From the Dashboard, you can click **Comments** to review comments, edit them, approve or reject them, mark them as spam, or delete them.

Inside Tip _____

I use Bluehost as my web hosting service. Through Bluehost, you can register your own domain name (such as www.yourname.com) for about $10 per year. The hosting itself costs about $80 per year, and if you use Bluehost to host your website and/or blog, it throws in the $10 registration for free. Bluehost also includes several tools to simplify everything, including free CMS for building a website and tools for installing the blogging platform you want to use (installing a blogging platform can be somewhat complicated).

Becoming a Social Butterfly

Blogging allows you to socialize on the web, but you're essentially creating your own community. Some areas of the web, however, already have large, well-established communities you can join to connect with people of similar interests and network either socially or professionally—and most times for free.

For example, with *MySpace* (www.myspace.com), you can enter your profile and create a MySpace blog. After creating a MySpace account, you can invite other MySpace members to be your friends. You can also e-mail people in your address book who may or may not be MySpace members to ask them to join MySpace and be your friends. If they accept your invitation, you can post to one another's pages and comment on each other's pictures. You can also restrict other activities to friends only, including instant messaging, your calendar of events, and the ability to comment on blog posts.

Facebook (www.facebook.com) is another social networking site that enables you to contact and keep in touch with friends, family, colleagues, and acquaintances. You can share photos, links, videos, and other content with people you know and meet others who share your interests. When you register at Facebook, you can join a network based on a company, region, or school to connect with people in that network. Facebook is particularly useful if you're trying to get in touch with old colleagues and classmates.

LinkedIn (www.linkedin.com) is a business networking site. You register and provide a list of all the places you worked and your titles. You can then ask other LinkedIn members to add you as a "connection." If they add you as a connection, you're connected to all that person's other connections. If you're very active, your LinkedIn network begins to grow exponentially. You can also ask people you know to write recommendations for you. This is a great way to network for jobs.

The Least You Need to Know

- ◆ HTML (Hypertext Markup Language) is a system of codes used to format web pages.

- ◆ You don't need to master HTML to create your own attractive web pages.

- ◆ The easiest way to create a page at Yahoo! GeoCities is to use one of the Yahoo! PageWizards. To edit your Yahoo! GeoCities web page, sign in at **geocities. yahoo.com** and click the link for running the PageWizard.

- ◆ An easy way to establish a presence on the Internet is to create and maintain your own blog.

- ◆ Social networking sites such as MySpace, Facebook, and LinkedIn enable you to get connected and remain in touch with old friends, family members, colleagues, and classmates.

Chapter 25

Buying and Selling Stuff Online

In This Chapter

- ◆ Gauging the safety of shopping online
- ◆ Finding great deals on comparison-shopping sites
- ◆ Becoming a savvy Internet shopper
- ◆ Booking travel reservations online
- ◆ Buying and selling stuff on eBay and Craigslist

The World Wide Web is home to one of the largest free-market economies in the world. At any time of the day or night, 7 days a week, 365 (and sometimes 366) days per year, you can find millions of people buying, selling, and giving stuff away online. And because the competition is so stiff among sellers, you can often find better deals online than what local brick-and-mortar discount stores offer.

In this chapter, I introduce you to the wonderful world of online shopping and reveal some of the best places to go and strategies to use to find some great deals online.

Is It Safe?

Generally speaking, shopping online is about as safe as shopping offline. If you head out to your local shopping mall, for example, you take the risk that someone will break into your car, steal your purse or wallet, or even sneak a peak at the name and number on your credit card. Restaurant servers have been known to steal credit card information, too.

You face similar risks online, but you face these risks whether you shop online or not. As you'll discover in Chapter 26, con artists often phish for information by sending e-mails prompting you to log onto phony sites and supply sensitive information about your accounts.

You can reduce the risks by shopping only on sites you trust. Buying merchandise from a reputable online retailer like Amazon.com is generally much safer than placing an order on an individual seller's website. If the site's address is only a number, such as http://169.86.198.0, beware. These cryptic numeric website addresses are often used to hide the company's true identity.

If you're buying from a little-known company, check its background. A site with only a website address and an e-mail address with no phone number is a little suspicious. Try to find a phone number and call it.

Inside Tip _____

Search the web to find out anything you can about a company if you're not sure whether it's legit. If other shoppers have been burned by that company, they usually post something on the web warning others.

Enter your name, credit card number, and other sensitive information only on secure websites. You can tell if a site is secure by looking at the address bar in your browser. The address of a secure site begins with "https" rather than "http." In addition, Internet Explorer displays a lock icon to the right of the address bar if the site is secure. Other browsers also display the lock icon somewhere.

If you receive an e-mail message asking for account information, be highly skeptical. Legitimate companies rarely request account information via e-mail or request that you log in to a website to verify account information.

Also don't place orders on a shared computer. Any information you enter on the shared computer could be stored for future use. If it is, someone else can log into the site where you placed the order and access your account information.

Pay for orders with a credit card rather than a debit card, or with an escrow service such as PayPal, so you have the opportunity to cancel the order or at least file a dispute if you don't receive your order or are dissatisfied with it. Credit card companies are usually pretty cooperative and successful in ensuring customer satisfaction.

Overall, trust your instincts. If a deal sounds too good to be true, it probably is. If a website asks for your Social Security number, birthday, driver's license number, or other information that's rarely needed to process a transaction, it's probably up to no good.

Comparison-Shopping for the Real Deals

Savvy shoppers always compare prices, and you can compare prices online, too. However, several comparison-shopping sites can do all the legwork for you and display a list of merchants who offer the same or similar products.

Check out the following popular comparison-shopping sites; many also offer product reviews to help you make your decision:

Shopzilla (www.shopzilla.com; see Figure 25.1)

Google Product Search (www.google.com/ products)

PriceGrabber (www.pricegrabber.com)

BizRate (www.bizrate.com)

MonsterMarketplace (www.monstermarket-place.com)

mySimon (www.mysimon.com)

CNET Shopper.com (shopper.cnet.com; check it out for computers, cameras, and electronics)

> **Whoa!**
>
> Don't automatically assume that just because you're buying something online, you're getting a better deal than what local stores are offering. You must still perform your due diligence and compare prices. In addition, buying online usually means you pay shipping fees, which can boost the price of goods higher than what you'd pay locally.

Figure 25.1

Shopzilla is one of many comparison-shopping sites you can find online.

Buying Online

The procedure for shopping at most online stores is fairly standard—you find the product you want, check out the product details and what other consumers have to say about it, click a button to order the product or place it in your shopping cart, and check out by entering your payment and shipping information. As an example, here's the step-by-step procedure for ordering a product on Amazon.com:

1. Use your web browser to go to **www.amazon.com.**

2. Open the **Search** list and select the type of product you're looking for. This helps narrow the search.

3. Click in the search box, type one or more words describing the product you're looking for, and click the **Go** button or press **Enter.** Amazon displays a list of available products, as shown in Figure 25.2.

4. When you click the link for the product that interests you, Amazon displays the product's page. You can scroll down the page to view the product description and photos and read reviews from customers who previously ordered the product.

5. If the product does not appeal to you, click your browser's back button to return to the list of products and keep shopping.

Go to Amazon.com   Select a product category   Describe the product

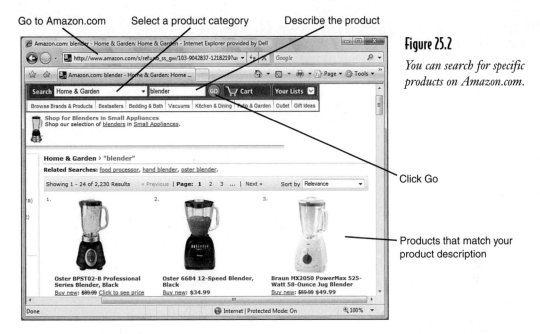

Figure 25.2

You can search for specific products on Amazon.com.

Click Go

Products that match your product description

6. When you find a product you like, choose the quantity of the item you want to order and click the **Add to Shopping Cart** or **Add to Cart** button. Amazon adds the item(s) to your shopping cart and updates the quantity of items in your cart and the total dollar amount of your order.

7. You can continue shopping by repeating steps 2 through 6 to add more items to your shopping cart.

8. When you're done shopping, click **Proceed to Checkout.** Amazon displays a screen prompting you to enter your e-mail address.

9. Follow the on-screen instructions to place your order. The steps vary depending on whether you want to create an account, which makes it easier to place orders later, or simply place a one-time order. You do need to enter your shipping information (the address where you would like the order shipped) and billing information (credit card type, number, expiration date, your name as it appears on the card, and the three-digit security code usually located on the back of the card).

After you've successfully placed your order, Amazon sends you a confirmation e-mail describing what you ordered, the price of each item, the shipping cost, and your grand total.

Booking Travel Reservations Online

If you do any traveling, whether for business or pleasure, you can often save considerable amounts of money by serving as your own travel agent and booking your reservations online. Several companies offer one-stop shopping for airline tickets, hotel and motel accommodations, and car rental. Visit the following sites to see what they have to offer:

Expedia (www.expedia.com)

Orbitz (www.orbitz.com)

Yahoo! Travel (travel.yahoo.com)

Travelocity (www.travelocity.com)

Hotwire (www.hotwire.com)

Priceline (www.priceline.com)

Don't stop at simply making reservations online. Plenty of websites offer free information and resources on just about any destination you can imagine. You can go online and check Eurorail routes and schedules and buy your Eurorail pass online, visit museum websites to plan which exhibits you'd like to see, explore an area's hottest attractions to figure out what you'd like to do, find the best restaurants and entertainment, and much more.

Inside Tip

Some websites specialize in providing information about your preferred mode of travel. For example, Hobo Traveler (www.hobotraveler.com) can show you how to travel around the world even if you have no travel budget to speak of. If you're looking to trim your travel budget by staying in lower-priced accommodations, visit Hostels. com (www.hostels.com), where you can obtain information about hostels located in just about every country. You can also find sites that specialize in timeshare rentals, cruises, and other special travel opportunities.

Buying and Selling on eBay

Even if you've never placed a bid or purchased anything on eBay, you've probably heard about it. eBay bills itself as "The World's Marketplace," where its eager community of online sellers and buyers from all around the world gather to buy, sell, and trade products every day. When most people think of eBay, however, they think "online auction," and even though eBay now has its own eBay Stores, it still serves primarily as an online auction.

In the following sections, I step you through the process of buying and selling stuff on eBay, including how you pay for items you buy and collect money for items you sell.

Buying Stuff on eBay

Most people get their first taste of eBay by bidding on and eventually purchasing an item. The process is very similar to buying a product on Amazon.com or from any online store, except you set the maximum price you're willing to pay for an item. In the following sections, I step you through the process of buying something on eBay.

Inside Tip

eBay also functions as an online mall, where users can set up their own stores. These stores operate like online retail stores where, instead of placing a bid, you simply place an order and pay whatever the proprietor of the store charges for the item. You'll also see that some listings contain a Buy It Now option. Instead of placing a bid, you can simply choose to pay the set price the eBay Seller is charging.

You don't need to be an eBay member to window shop on eBay. Point your web browser to **www.ebay.com.** A Search bar appears at the top of the opening page. Click in the **Search** box and type one or more words to describe what you're looking for. To narrow the search to a specific category of products, open the Categories list and click the desired category. Now, click the **Search** button. eBay displays a list of items that match your description, as shown in Figure 25.3.

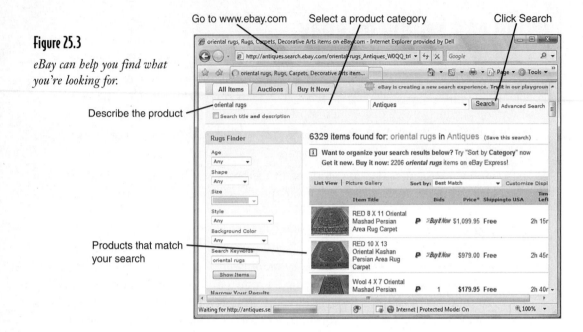

Figure 25.3

eBay can help you find what you're looking for.

Go to www.ebay.com   Select a product category   Click Search

Describe the product

Products that match your search

Before placing a bid on an item, click the item that interests you to display more information about it. Check the product description to determine whether the item looks and sounds like the product you want.

Also check out the Meet the seller area, where you can view information about the person who has listed the product for sale. eBay encourages buyers to rate sellers and provide feedback, so future buyers know how trustworthy or untrustworthy a particular seller may be. The Meet the seller area also contains a link you can click to ask the seller questions about the product or about payment, shipping, or customer service.

Inside Tip

If you're not sure what you're looking for or just want to check out what's for sale on eBay, click a category link on the opening page and follow the trail of links to a subcategory of products that catch your eye.

Placing a bid is very easy. Click in the **Your maximum bid** box, type your bid amount, and click the **Place Bid** button, as shown in Figure 25.4. (Below the Your maximum bid box is the minimum amount you can enter to place a bid. The seller can specify how much each bid must be over the current bid in order to be acceptable.)

product description   information about the seller   **Figure 25.4**

You can learn more about the item and the seller and place a bid.

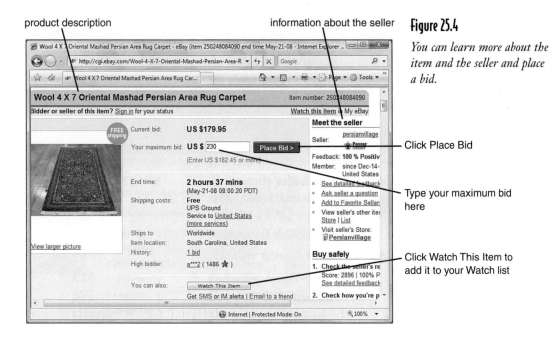

Click Place Bid

Type your maximum bid here

Click Watch This Item to add it to your Watch list

After you place your bid, eBay refreshes the page to show your bid amount as the high bid. However, in a matter of seconds, someone else can enter a higher bid, so if you really want the item, you'll need to keep a careful watch on the bidding activity. You can click the **Watch This Item** button to have eBay add the item to a list of items you're interested in. This makes it easier to keep an eye on what you're bidding on.

After you win an auction or choose to Buy It Now, eBay sends you and the seller an e-mail message confirming the transaction. Your e-mail message contains a Pay Now button. Click the **Pay Now** button and follow the on-screen instructions to submit your payment.

Inside Tip

Most eBay sellers accept PayPal payments, so if you're planning on making regular purchases, I strongly recommend you set up a PayPal account at www.paypal.com. PayPal is an escrow service that protects your primary account information. You fund your PayPal account from your bank or credit card account and use PayPal to buy products, pay vendors, send money to relatives or friends, etc. The person you pay never sees your bank account or credit card information. PayPal also protects against fraud and insures you against unauthorized payments from your account.

After you receive the item(s) you purchase, remember to return to eBay to rate and provide feedback to the Seller. These ratings and feedback not only help other eBay buyers determine whom they can trust, but positive feedback helps Sellers become more successful. Sellers often succeed or fail based on their feedback ratings.

Selling Stuff on eBay

eBay began as an tool to help collectors of Pez dispensers connect with one another and swap dispensers online. From there, it evolved into more of an online flea market, where people would try to sell their collectibles and anything else they no longer wanted to store in their basements or attics. (There's still a lot of that going on.) Now, eBay also provides a forum where professional retailers can sell brand-new products for sale.

Whoa!

Before you list an item for sale, do some research to find out the going price of the item or similar items and see how other sellers are marketing these items online. Using other sellers' marketing materials (photos and product descriptions) is a no-no, but existing product listings can give you some ideas of what works and what doesn't.

When you have something for sale, all you have to do is take a photo of it, write a description of it, log on to eBay, and list the item. Keep in mind, however, that eBay charges listing fees, whether or not your item sells. You pay an *insertion fee* to list an item for sale. This fee varies depending on the type of item and the starting bid or reserve price (the lowest bid you'll accept), but it ranges from $.15 to $4.00. The *final value fee* is the amount the buyer ultimately pays for the item. If nobody buys the item, you pay no final value fee. Otherwise, the fee is calculated as a percentage of the purchase price, starting at 8.75 percent on the first $25 and decreasing for items that sell for more than $25.

The following steps show you just how easy it is to list an item for sale on eBay:

1. Use your web browser to go to **www.ebay.com** and click the link to sign in.

2. Log on by entering your user name and password.

3. Click the **Sell** button in the upper-right corner of the screen.

4. Type a descriptive name for your item.

5. Click the **Start Selling** button. eBay displays a page that steps you through the process of creating and posting your listing, as shown in Figure 25.5. You will choose a product category, add one or more photos, type a product description, set the opening bid amount and duration of the auction, specify shipping charges, and select the desired method of payment.

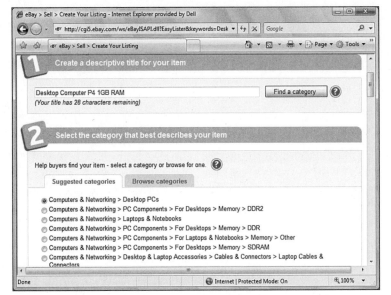

Figure 25.5

eBay makes it easy to list items for sale.

6. Follow the on-screen instructions to create and post your listing.

After you list an item, you can monitor your auctions to observe the bidding process. When the auction is over, you receive an e-mail message informing you of the winning bid. The buyer then submits the payment, and you package and ship the product.

If you don't have anything to sell, you can purchase items on eBay, at garage sales, or at discount stores and try to resell them online. You can also try using a product sourcing company like Doba (www.doba.com) that offers drop-shipping. With drop-shipping, you list the item for sale, but when it sells, the product sourcing company ships the product to your customer, so you don't have to worry about storing the product or packaging it and shipping it. Of course, the convenience is going to cost extra.

Checking Out Craigslist

Another popular (and free) online shopping venue is Craigslist, which is essentially a free online classifieds service. Craigslist members can list products and services for sale (or for free), job openings, positions wanted, rooms for rent, roommates wanted, and so on, just as in a newspaper's classifieds section. Visitors to Craigslist can then e-mail the person who posted the listing to finalize the transactions.

To see what Craigslist has to offer, point your Web browser to www.craigslist.com, and click the link for your city (or the nearest city). You'll see a screen similar to Figure 25.6 that displays the available listings, grouping them by category. Follow the trail of links to find what you're looking for, and use the online help to find out how to post your own listings.

Figure 25.6

Craigslist offers free classifieds for nearly every major city in the world.

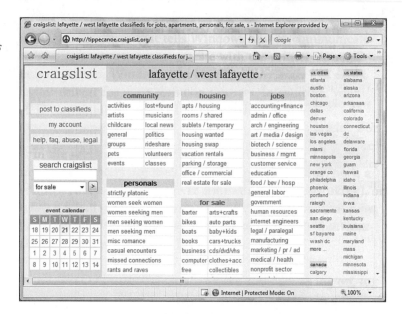

When you join Craigslist, you enter your e-mail address, but this address does not appear on your listings. All correspondence is handled behind the scenes, so you get to choose the people you pass along your contact information to.

The Least You Need to Know

◆ To shop safely online, stick with well-established stores until you gain more experience, and place orders only on secure websites.

◆ Comparison-shopping sites such as Shopzilla and PriceGrabber can help you track down the best deals.

◆ Buying something online usually consists of finding what you want, checking the product details, adding the item to your shopping cart, and checking out.

◆ On eBay you can buy and sell items, through an auction, the Buy It Now option, or an eBay Store.

◆ Craigslist is the world's most popular free classified ad service.

Chapter 26

Internet Safety

In This Chapter

- Keeping your kids safe online
- Spying on … er … supervising your kids
- Blocking undesirable web content
- Safety in chat rooms and via e-mail
- Scanning incoming files for viruses
- Keeping your computer safe

The Internet is a virtual city packed with shopping malls, libraries, community centers, museums, newsstands, meeting rooms, and other valuable offerings. But like any city, the Internet has its dark side—a section of town ruled by pornography, violence, bigotry, vandalism, and theft. You want access to all the positive material the Internet offers, but there's so much offensive and just unsafe material out there, too, you're right to be concerned for your safety, especially if you have children who are online. In addition, you need to protect your computer from viruses and from unauthorized access, to prevent your files from being damaged or stolen.

This chapter shows you how to protect yourself, your children, and your computer from the various threats on the Internet.

Protecting Children on the Internet

As a society, we want our children to have the freedom to explore the Internet, but we have the responsibility of protecting them from media and individuals who threaten their innocence. We want our children to visit online museums, communicate with students in other parts of the world, take classes, visit political institutions, and research topics of interest. We *don't* want our kids or students pulling up pornography pages, reading racist propaganda, hacking the Pentagon's computer system, or sitting in the Hot Tub chat room conversing with a bunch of old guys and gals who should know better. And we sure don't want our 11-year-olds corresponding via e-mail with deviants twice or three times their age.

The following sections serve as a parent/teacher guide to the Internet. These sections show you how to make your kids more street smart so they won't fall prey to con artists, how to supervise their Internet use, and how to block access to offensive material by using various censoring tools. Along the way, you will become a little more savvy yourself and begin to understand the perils of the Internet.

Explaining the Rules of the Road

Most kids aren't rotten. They're confused, frustrated, careless, and selfish, but not intentionally bad. A child usually makes a wrong choice or breaks a rule either because he doesn't understand the rule, he's overly curious, or he faces no consequence for misbehaving. So before you let your child or student fire up the web browser, lay down the rules and explain the consequences. Here are a few rules to pass along to your kids:

Keep passwords secret. Anyone who knows your user name and password can use your account, racking up connect time charges, placing credit card orders, and performing illegal activities in your name.

> **Whoa!**
> Be sure your children understand that they are *never* to tell someone their real name, address, phone number, or the school they attend in a chat room, where anyone can see it.

Don't enter any personal information online without permission from a parent or guardian. Using your real name, address, or phone number in your profile gives stalkers the information they want. Registering for contests and "free" stuff can make your private information public.

Don't use a credit card. Leaving your child alone on the web with your credit card can lead to disaster. The web is the biggest shop-at-home network in the world.

Don't run or install any programs without permission. Downloading and running programs from unreliable sources can introduce computer viruses. You and your kids should also be careful with any program files or iffy attachments you receive via e-mail.

Don't view sites that you wouldn't view with parents or guardians next to you. Later in this chapter, I show you how to block undesirable content, but censoring programs are not foolproof. Be sure your kids know that you expect them to use good judgment.

Don't chat or correspond with creeps. Some creepy adults use the Internet to prey on kids. Have your kids notify you immediately of any suspicious individuals or messages. Tell your kids not to send photos of themselves to strangers or post their photos on their web pages. Let your kids know that people on the Internet can pretend to be anybody; the 14-year-old girl your daughter thinks she is chatting with could be a 35-year-old guy.

Don't meet anyone in person you only know from online contact. If your child wants to meet a friend from the Internet, have your child schedule a meeting in a public place and take you along.

In addition to laying down the rules, specify limits on Internet use, just as you would limit TV viewing. Specify the time of day your child can access the Internet and the amount of time he or she can spend at the keyboard. Although the computer and the Internet can be great tools for education and entertainment, they can also interfere with a child's education and social and physical development.

> **Inside Tip** _____
>
> Use computer time as a reward for proper behavior. If your child fails to follow the rules, reduce or eliminate the time your child spends on the computer. Your kid might claim that the punishment is harming his education, but don't buy it.

A Little Personal Supervision Goes a Long Way

When my kids started watching TV, I was pretty naive. I told them to watch only those shows that they would feel comfortable watching with me or their mom. A couple days later, I walked into the den and caught my 13- and 10-year-old watching MTV's *Celebrity Death Match*. Of course, they saw nothing wrong with it.

Whoa!

To be sure your kids can't surf the Internet without your permission, keep the password you use to connect to your ISP secret. Also remove the check mark from the **Save password** check box in the Connect to dialog box. If you have a cable connection (which is connected all the time), this trick isn't an option.

As a parent, it's your obligation not to be stupid. Don't stick a computer in your kid's bedroom and then celebrate because you now have more quality time to spend with your spouse. The reason your son isn't pestering you or picking on his kid sister is probably because he has found something much more sinister to do on the Internet.

Place the computer in a room that you can enter without looking like a spy. A room that's open to traffic, such as a living room or family room, is a good choice. If you have young children, spend some time exploring the Internet with them and supervising their activities. Your kids might balk and think you're a control freak, but that's your job.

Censoring the Internet

Over the years, people have debated whether the government should censor the Internet. As society wrestles with this issue, offensive material remains readily available. As a parent or teacher, you need to learn what you can do to prevent this material from reaching you and your children.

Computer Cheat
You can check your web browser's history to see where your kids have been. In Internet Explorer, click the **Favorites Center** button and then the **History** button to display the History bar. Click the folder for the week or day you want to check. The History bar displays a list of sites visited during the selected week or day. Click the site folder to view a list of pages that were opened at the site, and click the page name to view the page. If your kids are wise to the history list, they might know how to clear it, so if it's blank, suspect foul play.

Censoring the Web with Internet Explorer

If you use Internet Explorer as your web browser, you can use its built-in Content Advisor to filter undesirable content. However, Content Advisor is a lousy tool for filtering web content. If you don't configure it, it blocks just about every website you can imagine. If you configure it to allow access to unrated sites, it gives you access to just about everything, including playboy.com.

If you're going to use Content Advisor, I strongly recommend that you configure it to allow unrated sites and then manually create your own list of sites you want it to block. As you might imagine, you could spend a month creating a list of sites with objectionable material and still block only a small fraction of them.

If you still want to use Content Advisor after my caveats, take the following steps to enable it:

1. Run Internet Explorer.

2. Open the **Tools** menu and click **Internet Options.** The Internet Options dialog box appears.

3. Click the **Content** tab, as shown in Figure 26.1.

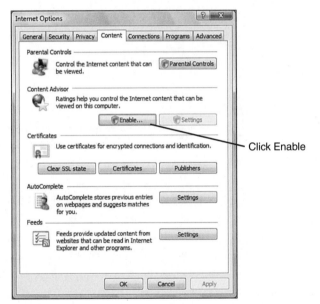

Figure 26.1

Internet Explorer's Content Advisor can block potentially offensive web pages.

4. Under Content Advisor, click the **Enable** button. The Content Advisor dialog box appears.

5. Click the **General** tab and click **Create Password.**

6. Type the desired password, press **Tab,** type the password again to confirm it, and click **OK.** Use a password that's easy for you to remember but impossible for your kids to guess. (Don't forget this password; otherwise, you'll never be able to disable Content Advisor or change your configuration settings.) A dialog box appears informing you that the Content Advisor has been turned on.

7. Click **OK** to return to the Internet Options dialog box.

8. Under Content Advisor, click **Settings.** The Supervisor Password Required dialog box appears.

9. Type your password and click **OK.** The Content Advisor dialog box appears, as shown in Figure 26.2, enabling you to set the desired level of restrictions for several categories of potentially offensive content, including Language, Nudity, Sex, and Violence.

Figure 26.2

The Content Advisor enables you to set the desired level of access for several types of content.

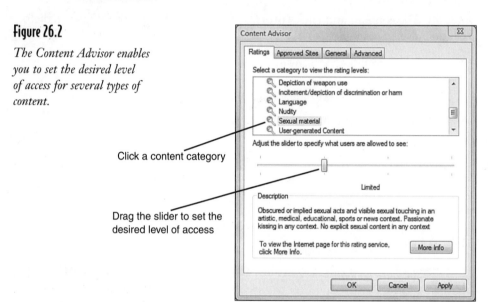

Click a content category

Drag the slider to set the desired level of access

10. To relax the level of censorship for a category, click the category and drag the slider to the desired level.

11. Click the **Approved Sites** tab, type the address of a site you always want Content Advisor to block or always allow access to in the Allow This Site or Allow This Website box, starting with **http://.** To block the site, click **Never.** To allow the site, click **Always.**

12. Click the **General** tab and select **Users Can See Websites That Have No Rating** to place a check in the box; otherwise, Content Advisor will block even the most harmless of sites.

13. Enter any additional preferences as desired, and click the **OK** button as many times as necessary to save your settings and exit out of all open dialog boxes.

Don't set the kiddies in front of the screen just yet. Test your setup first. Try going to one of the sites you added to your list of blocked sites. If you can view the site, there's a problem. Close Internet Explorer, run it again, and try going to the blocked site. You should see the Content Advisor dialog box, shown in Figure 26.3, telling you why you have been denied access to this site (as if you didn't know). Click **OK.**

Figure 26.3

The Content Advisor won't let you view websites on your list of prohibited sites.

Using Censoring Software

If your web browser does not have a built-in censor, or if you want more control over the content and features your children can access, purchase a specialized censoring program. Following is a list of some of the better censoring programs, along with addresses for the web pages where you can find out more about them and download shareware versions:

CyberPatrol (www.cyberpatrol.com) is the most popular censoring program on the market. CyberPatrol uses a list of forbidden words to block access to objectionable material or uses a list of child-friendly words to block access to all web pages except those that contain one of the specified words. Passwords let you set access levels for different Windows User Accounts, and CyberPatrol can keep track of the amount of time each user spends on the Internet and can block or filter chat and instant messaging. It also enables parents to set time periods of when and how long their children can use certain Internet features, and it enables parents to track attempts to access particular sites or features.

Whoa!

No censoring program is perfect. Some objectionable content can slip through the cracks, and the program can block access to unobjectionable sites. Use the censoring program only when you personally are unable to supervise your kids.

CYBERsitter (www.solidoak.com) is another fine censoring program. CYBERsitter is a little less strict than CyberPatrol but is easier to use and configure. CYBERsitter has a unique filtering system that judges words in context, so it doesn't block access to inoffensive sites, such as the Anne Sexton home page. This company also markets a device called the SnoopStick that enables you to monitor and control your computer remotely, so you can monitor your child's computer usage from your office.

KaZipster (www.kazipster.com) is a free, web-based content filtering program. You simply create a KaZipster account and set up your Dashboard. You obtain a themed web browser that provides access only to approved websites. You can disable the filter temporarily or permanently at any time to remove the filter—for example, if your child needs broader Internet access to do research for a report. You can also add your own safe sites.

Computer Cheat

If your computers are networked and they all access the Internet through a network router, you may be able to use your router settings to control access to the Internet. When my kids used to try to sneak onto the Internet after my wife and I headed to bed, I used my router's settings to block access to the router (and hence the Internet) between the hours of 10 P.M. and 7 A.M. My router also enables me to enter keywords or domain names the router should look for to block access to certain sites. Optionally, I can have the router keep a log of every site visited and have it e-mail the log to me whenever someone on the network tries to access a prohibited site.

Adjusting Your Browser's Security Settings

Your web browser has its own security guard on duty that checks incoming files for potential threats. If you try to enter information such as a credit card number on a form that's not secure, the web browser displays a warning message asking if you want to continue. If a site attempts to install a program on your computer, your browser displays a confirmation dialog box asking for permission to download and install the program. At times, these warnings can become more annoying than useful, but they do provide you with some confidence that your browser is on the lookout for security threats.

Internet Explorer sets different security levels for different *zones*, enabling you to relax the security settings for sites that you trust and tighten security settings for untested sites or those you don't trust. Internet Explorer offers the following four security zones:

♦ *Internet* enables you to specify security settings for untested sites. When you wander off to sites that you don't often frequent, you might want to tighten security. All sites that aren't in one of the other zones in this list fall into the Internet zone.

♦ *Local intranet* enables you to relax security for sites on your company's intranet or network so you can freely access those sites without being bombarded with warnings. By default, the security level for local intranet sites is set at low.

♦ *Trusted sites* enables you to deactivate the security warnings for sites you trust. This prevents you from being inundated with warning messages at the sites you visit most frequently and trust completely.

♦ *Restricted sites* enables you to create a list of sites that you don't trust and tighten security for those sites. For example, you might want to prevent a particular site from automatically installing and running programs on your computer.

You can add sites to the Local, Trusted, and Restricted sites lists. Here's how:

1. Open the **Tools** menu, select **Internet Options,** and click the **Security** tab.

2. Click the desired zone at the top of the dialog box, as shown in Figure 26.4, and click the **Sites** button.

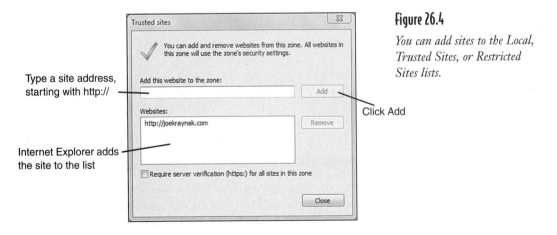

Type a site address, starting with http://

Internet Explorer adds the site to the list

Click Add

Figure 26.4

You can add sites to the Local, Trusted Sites, or Restricted Sites lists.

Inside Tip _____

If you use a browser other than Internet Explorer, the browser has its own security features that may be quite different. Check the browser's help system for information on how to enter your security preferences. All browsers have security features, although they all handle them a little differently.

3. Click in the **Add this website to the zone** box, type the address of the site, starting with **http://,** and click **Add.** If you're adding sites to the Trusted Sites zone, addresses need to start with https:// unless you turn off the option **Require server verification (https://) for all sites in this zone** to remove the check mark.

4. When you're done adding sites, click **OK** as needed to save your changes and close the dialog boxes.

To specify a security level for a zone, open the **Tools** menu, click **Internet Options,** and click the **Security** tab. Click the desired zone at the top of the dialog box and click the zone whose security level you want to change. Click the **Custom Level** button and enter your preferences. You can enter individual settings to specify the type of content you want Internet Explorer to be able to download, or you can open the **Reset To** list and choose the desired security level, **High, Medium, Medium-Low,** or **Low.**

Keeping Out Viruses

Picking up a virus on the Internet is like coming home from vacation with some exotic illness. You were having so much fun; how could this happen? And how can you prevent it from happening again? First, you should follow a few simple rules:

Download programs only from reputable and known sites. If you know the company that created the program, go to its web page or FTP server and download the file from there. Most reputable sites regularly scan their systems to detect and eliminate viruses.

Don't accept copies of a program from another person (for example, by e-mail). Although the program might not have contained a virus when your buddy downloaded it, your buddy's computer could have a virus that infected the program. Ask your friend where he or she got the file and then download the file from its original location yourself.

If your web browser displays a message indicating that a program it's being asked to download is unsigned or from a questionable source, cancel the download.

If you receive a file attachment from someone you don't know or from a questionable source, delete the message along with the attachment. Do *not* `open it`.

Keep an antivirus program running at all times. Antivirus programs scan any incoming program files for viruses and scan your computer on a regular basis to identify viruses before they can damage any files. One of the best antivirus programs around is also free for home users—Avast (www.avast.com).

Whoa! _____

> If you receive e-mail, you'll eventually receive virus warnings indicating that a nasty new virus is infecting thousands of computers all over the world and wiping out hard drives. Most of these warnings are hoaxes, and you should not forward the message as it instructs you to do. Check the source of the hoax first. Virus hoaxes are posted at www.symantec.com/avcenter/hoax.html and vil.mcafee.com/hoax.asp.

Keeping Hackers at Bay with a Firewall

Whenever you're connected to the Internet, you run the risk of having a mischievous hacker break into your system, steal information, and even damage some files. Hackers rarely break into home PCs that are connected to the Internet by a standard modem, because you typically disconnect when you're done working. If you have a DSL or cable modem connection, which keeps your computer connected to the Internet at all times, consider installing a *firewall* to prevent unauthorized access to your system.

If you have two or more computers that are networked and share an Internet connection through a router, the best option is usually to use your router's firewall to limit outside access to your networked computers. If your computer is connecting directly to the Internet through a modem or a Wi-Fi connection, for example, you should turn on the Windows Firewall.

Configuring Your Router's Firewall

If you have several computers sharing an Internet connection, you probably have a modem that connects to the Internet. The modem is connected to a router, and every computer on the network accesses the modem (and hence, the Internet) through the router. Your router should have come with instructions that show you how to configure it or at least access the configuration settings. In most cases, you can access the configuration settings by running your web browser and then entering the IP address of your router, as shown in Figure 26.5.

Figure 26.5

Configure your router's fire-wall and security settings.

router's IP address

computers on network

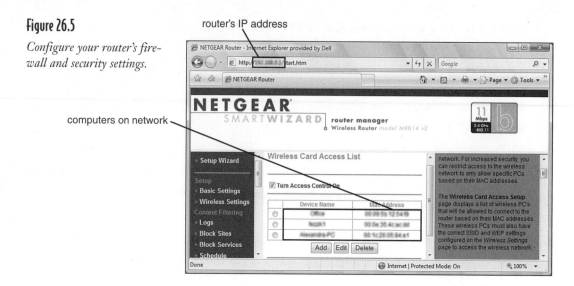

Like most routers, my router enables me to specify which computers are permit-ted to connect to the network (see Figure 26.5). I turn on the Access Control option and then, from a list of computers within range of my wireless router, I choose the computers I want to be able to access my network. You might not see any "Firewall" option, but by controlling access to your network, you are using a firewall, regardless of whatever your router calls it.

If you're controlling network access through your router, you'll probably want to turn off any software firewalls, including the Windows Firewall. Many Internet security programs, such as Norton Internet Security, also contain their own firewalls, which you'll probably want to disable. At most, you should have a hardware firewall (on your router) to block external threats and a software firewall to monitor any programs on your computer that may attempt to establish connections without your approval. Having more firewalls often leads to conflicts that can harm your computer's perfor-mance.

Turning the Windows Firewall On or Off

The Windows Internet Connection Firewall (ICF) keeps track of every request for data your computer makes and then checks incoming traffic to ensure that your computer initiated the transaction. If an outside source attempts to initiate com-munications, ICF drops the connection. Unlike many firewalls that display warnings of potential security breaches, ICF works in the background, automatically blocking unauthorized access.

To turn ICF on or off, do one of the following:

In Windows Vista: Click **Start, Control Panel, Network and Internet.** Under Network and Internet, click **Turn Windows Firewall On or Off.** If a dialog box pops up, indicating that Windows needs permission to continue, click **Continue.** This displays the Windows Firewall Settings dialog box, shown in Figure 26.6. Click **On** or **Off,** and click **OK.**

In Windows XP: Click **Start,** right-click **My Network Places,** and click **Properties.** Right-click the icon for the network card or modem your computer uses to connect to the Internet, and click **Properties.** Click the **Advanced** tab. Under Windows Firewall, click **Settings.** Click **On** or **Off** and click **OK.**

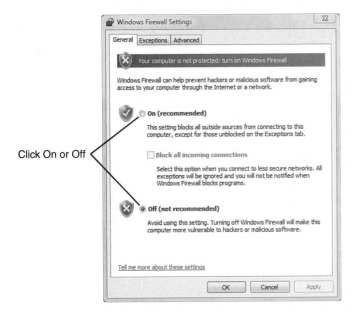

Click On or Off

Figure 26.6

You can easily enable or disable the Windows Internet Connection Firewall.

Panic Attack

A firewall can cause Internet connection problems for some features, including instant messaging, especially when you're trying to share files or videoconference. If you experience a connection problem after enabling the firewall, you may need to set up exceptions to exempt specific programs from firewall protection. In Windows, display the Windows Firewall Settings dialog box again, click the **Exceptions** tab, and use the options you find there to exempt the program that you're having problems with.

The Least You Need to Know

◆ Before you unleash your kids on the Internet, lay down the rules you want them to follow.

◆ The most essential rule kids must follow is to never give out any personal or sensitive information, including passwords, phone numbers, addresses, credit card numbers, or even the name of the school they attend.

◆ No censor program can replace the supervision of a loving, caring parent or teacher.

◆ If you cannot supervise your kids every minute they're on the Internet (what parent can?), install a content filter and learn how to use it.

◆ To protect your computer against viruses, purchase and install a good antivirus program and keep it updated with the latest virus definitions.

◆ To prevent unauthorized access to your computer, enable the Windows firewall or configure your router's firewall settings.

Part 5

Going Digital with Music, Photos, and Video

Although you may think your food processor is the most versatile tool in your home, your computer has it beat. With the right software and accessories, your computer can moonlight as a powerful jukebox, photo lab, and video studio.

The chapters in Part 5 introduce you to the most popular home-based computer gadgets. Here you learn how to download and play music clips from the Internet, burn your own custom music CDs, transfer music to a portable MP3 player, snap and print photos, and edit your home movies. Part 5 takes you from tech weenie to tech wizard in just a few short chapters.

MP3 PLAYERS CONTEMPLATE

"I don't know. I mean—boom boxes, Walkmans, CD players—it all moves so fast. I just feel so transient on this Earth. So mortal."

Chapter 27

Playing CDs, DVDs, MP3s, and More

In This Chapter

◆ Playing music on your computer

◆ Finding and installing a music player

◆ Copying music clips to a portable MP3 player

◆ Burning your own audio CDs

◆ Watching DVD movies on your computer

If you thought the move from LPs to CDs was impressive (if you're old enough to even remember that!), you're going to love the latest in audio and video technology. With your computer, a *CD drive*, a sound card, and a decent set of speakers, you can create your own computerized jukebox that can play hundreds of your favorite songs. Add an Internet connection, and you can download music to add to your collection. With a portable music player, you can take your favorite tunes wherever you go. And if you have a CD-R or CD-RW drive, you can even "burn" your own custom CDs and play them on any CD player! And that's not all. With a DVD drive, you can watch your favorite movies on your computer!

This chapter steps you through the process of building your own "recording studio," points out the best places on the web to get free MP3 players and music, and shows you how to transform your computer into a personal DVD player so you can watch movies while you pretend to work.

CD and MP3 Audio Basics

To understand CD and MP3 audio basics, you must first know that standard audio CD players and computers differ in how they store and play audio files, or clips. On an audio CD, data is stored in a format called Red Book, which has been the standard format for more than 20 years. Computers, on the other hand, store audio data in various formats, the most popular of which is MP3 (short for Moving Picture Experts Group 3, an audio compression format). This format compresses an audio clip to about $\frac{1}{12}$ its size with an imperceptible loss of quality. MP3 and similar technologies enable you to download audio clips more quickly over the Internet and store them in less space on your computer's hard drive.

The only trouble is that a standard audio CD player can't play MP3 files, and a computer can't process audio data stored on an audio CD in the Red Book format. (Although all newer CD-ROM drives can play audio CDs through your computer's sound card and speakers or an earphone jack.) Fortunately, some programs can handle the required format conversions for you.

An *MP3 player* enables your computer to play MP3 audio clips. You can copy MP3 clips from websites or convert audio clips from your CDs into MP3 files with a CD ripper (described next). An MP3 player converts MP3 files into a standard digital audio format (typically a WAV format) that your computer can play through its sound card and speakers.

A *CD ripper* converts audio clips from a CD into the MP3 format or another format that a computer equipped with the required software can play. A CD ripper is commonly called a jukebox, because it stores all the clips you record and lets you play them simply by selecting them from a list or creating your own custom playlists.

A *CD burner* converts MP3 audio clips stored on your computer into the standard Red Book format used to store audio data on CDs and controls the process of recording the audio clips to the recordable CD. You can then play the CD in a standard audio CD player. Some newer audio CD players can play MP3 files stored on CDs, making it unnecessary to convert MP3 clips into the Red Book format before burning them on a CD. This enables you to store more than 10 times as much music per CD.

Before you run out and buy a case of CD-R or *CD-RW discs*, you should understand the difference between the two types of discs. CD-R discs let you write to the disc only once; you can't erase the data on a CD-R disc and then record over it. With a CD-RW disc, you can record data to the disc, erase the data, and write new data to the disc. This makes CD-RW discs an excellent storage medium for backing up files. However, CD-RW discs are typically less reflective than CD-R discs, making them a poor choice for recording audio CDs. Some audio CD players have a tough time reading a CD-RW disc. When you're burning audio CDs, stick with CD-R discs.

Also many new computers are equipped with disc drives that can read and record to both CDs and DVDs, but be sure the discs you buy are compatible with the drive. Most drives have something printed on the outside of the loading tray that indicates whether it is a CD-R, CD-RW, DVD-R, or DVD-RW.

def•i•ni•tion

The surface of a compact disc has smooth, reflective areas and pits or dyed areas that refract rather than reflect light. A **CD drive** or player reads data from a disc by bouncing a laser beam off the disc's surface and interpreting differences in the intensity of the returning beam. On **CD-RW discs,** the contrast between the reflected areas and the non-reflective dyed areas is less than the contrast found on CD-R discs.

Although MP3 gets all the press, you'll encounter many other audio formats on the web. Some are designed specifically for streaming audio; that is, they're designed to start playing an audio clip as soon as your computer begins receiving it. Streaming audio, such as RealAudio, is commonly used for online radio stations and "live" broadcasts.

Using Your Computer as a Jukebox

If you insert an audio CD into your computer's CD-ROM drive, Windows should display the Audio CD dialog box, prompting you to specify which action you want Windows to perform: **Play Audio CD** (with Windows Media Player), **Rip Music from CD** (with Windows Media Player), **Open Folder to View Files** (in Windows Explorer), or perform another action with some other audio program that's installed on your computer. To start listening to the CD, click one of the options for playing it and then click **OK.** Or the audio CD might begin to play automatically when you insert the CD, depending on how your system is configured.

Playing an audio CD makes your computer little more than an overpriced CD player. To make your computer a *superior* overpriced CD player, record your favorite audio clips to your computer's hard drive as files. This provides you with a virtual jukebox, which you can program to play only the songs you want to hear in the order you want to hear them.

Windows Media Player, included as part of Windows XP and Vista, not only plays audio CDs but also can copy entire CDs or selected tracks to your computer's hard drive to create custom *playlists*. To see whether Windows Media Player is installed on your computer, check the Windows **Start, All Programs** menu. Depending on your version of Media Player, it may appear on the Start, All Programs, Accessories, Entertainment menu. If Media Player is not installed, you can install it from the Windows installation CD or download and install the latest version from www. microsoft.com/windows/windowsmedia.

> **Inside Tip** _____
>
> Windows Vista is much more media savvy than earlier versions of Windows. Vista includes a Windows Media Center (**Start, All Programs, Windows Media Center**). The Media Center gives you central access to all your photos, audio and video recordings, recorded TV shows, and movies and enables you to watch DVDs on your computer (assuming your computer is equipped with a DVD player). To watch TV on your computer (and record your favorite shows), it must be equipped with a TV tuner; you can install an expansion card that adds this capacity to your computer.

Creating Playlists with Windows Media Player

Using Windows Media Player, you can record your favorite CD tracks to your computer's hard drive and create a custom playlist. The following steps are for Media Player 11. If you have a different version of Media Player, run Media Player and press **F1** to get some help:

1. Establish a connection to the Internet, if possible. If your computer is connected to the Internet, Media Player can automatically download the title of the album, the name of the artist, and track titles for most CDs so you don't have to enter this information manually.

2. Run the Windows Media Player by selecting **Start, All Programs, Windows Media Player.** Depending on your version of Media Player, it may appear on the **Start, All Programs, Accessories, Entertainment** menu.

3. Insert a CD that has one or more tracks you want to record into your computer's CD player. (Your computer might have a program other than Media Player that runs when you insert an audio CD. At this point, you can either use the player that appears or close the player and proceed with these steps.)

4. Click the **Rip** tab. Media Player displays a list of the tracks stored on the CD, as shown in Figure 27.1, with all tracks on the CD selected. (Media Player may begin ripping the tracks automatically, in which case, you can click **Stop Rip** and proceed to step 5 or just skip to step 7 to let Media Player rip all tracks on the CD.)

Click the Rip tab

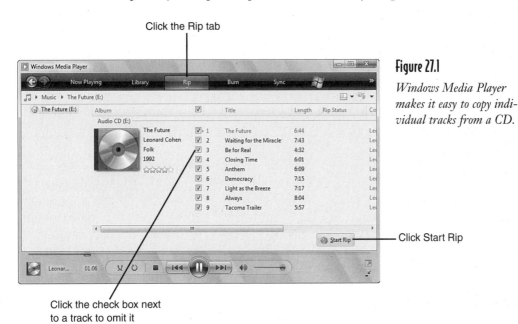

Figure 27.1

Windows Media Player makes it easy to copy individual tracks from a CD.

Click Start Rip

Click the check box next
to a track to omit it

5. Click the check box next to each track you do *not* want to record to remove the check mark from the box.

6. Click **Start Rip.** Media Player begins ripping the selected tracks from the CD and displays its progress.

7. When Media Player is done ripping the selected tracks, eject the CD.

8. Repeat steps 3 to 7 for each CD that has one or more tracks you want to record.

Computer Cheat

If the track names don't appear automatically, you can add them later or edit the existing names. The process is identical to renaming files and folders: click once on a track name to select it, click again to highlight the name, and type the new name.

9. Click the arrow below the **Library** tab and click **Create Playlist.** Media Player displays New Playlist in the right pane.

10. Type a brief, descriptive name for your new playlist.

11. In the list pane (on the left), select a folder or subfolder that has the tracks you want to add to your playlist. (Click the plus sign next to a folder to view its subfolders and then click a folder or subfolder to display its contents.)

12. Select the tracks you want to add to your playlist, as shown in Figure 27.2. (To select multiple tracks, click one track and then **Ctrl+click** the other tracks.)

Figure 27.2

Drag and drop the audio tracks you recorded to your playlist.

Select tracks

Drag selected tracks here

13. Drag and drop one of the selected tracks into the New Playlist pane (on the right). Media player adds the tracks to your playlist.

14. Repeat steps 10 to 12 to add tracks to your playlist. You can add tracks from different CDs to create your own custom list.

15. Drag and drop items up or down in the list to rearrange the tracks in the desired order.

16. Click **Save Playlist.**

To play your clips, click the clip you want to start playing and then click Media Player's **Play** button (near the bottom of the window). Media Player plays the selected song and then the remaining songs in your playlist.

Changing Media Player's Skin

Many cell phones, handheld computers, and other trendy electronic devices now come with thin, detachable covers called *skins.* Likewise, most on-screen MP3 players come with their own virtual skins. You simply pick the desired skin from a list to personalize the appearance of your player.

To change skins in Media Player, open the **View** menu and click **Skin Chooser.** (If you don't see the View menu, press **Ctrl+M** to turn on Classic menus.) The skin chooser appears, as shown in Figure 27.3. Click the name of a skin to preview it. When you find a skin you like, click its name and click **Apply Skin** (above the list of skins). You can switch back to Full Mode by pressing **Ctrl+1;** to switch from Full Mode to Skin Mode, press **Ctrl+2.**

Click Apply Skin

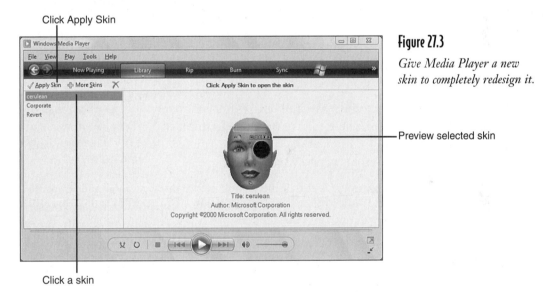

Figure 27.3

Give Media Player a new skin to completely redesign it.

Preview selected skin

Click a skin

If you don't like the selection of skins, click the **More Skins** button (just to the right of Apply Skin). This connects you to Microsoft's website, where you can download additional skins.

Downloading Music from the Web

The web is buzzing with companies that sell downloadable music, audio books, and other digital audio. You can go to iTunes, Napster, Sam Goody's, and a host of other music sites and pack your shopping cart with tracks for under a buck each. You might

Panic Attack

Although downloadable audio files are smaller than their CD counterparts, they're still fairly large. A 4-minute music clip can be more than 4 megabytes, which can take nearly ½ hour to download over a 28.8Kbps modem connection. If you plan to download audio clips on a regular basis, you should have a 56Kbps modem or faster connection.

even be able to legally pick up a few tracks for free. You can then burn the tracks to CDs, copy them to your iPod or MP3 player, and add them to your computer's growing audio library.

The following sections take you on a brief tour of music sites and show you how to download and play audio clips using Internet Explorer and Windows Media Player. You also learn how to copy your clips to a portable music player to take them with you wherever you go.

Before you get started, however, keep in mind that downloading and "sharing" music without paying for it (unless you're downloading a free promotional track) is against the law.

Finding and Downloading Music

Downloading any file is pretty easy. You click a link and follow the on-screen instructions to tell your browser where to save the file. However, before you can download audio clips, you have to find some tunes that are worth downloading. The following sites are popular online stores where you can purchase individual tracks:

iTunes (www.apple.com/itunes) is the home of one of the most popular music stores on the Internet. Here you can download and install a free copy of iTunes, so you can listen to your favorite tunes, preview recent releases, and purchase and download quality clips online for less than $1 per tune.

Rhapsody (www.real.com) is where the creators of RealPlayer host their own online music store. Here, you can purchase and download individual tracks to play on your RealPlayer, transfer to portable players, or burn to CDs.

MusicMatch (www.musicmatch.com) is one of the most popular online music sites, featuring Internet radio stations. If the MusicMatch station is playing a song you like, you can jump to the online store, order it, download it, add it to your playlist, and transfer it over to your portable music player or burn it to a CD.

AOL Music Now (music.aol.com), like MusicMatch, features on-demand Internet radio and customizable, commercial-free listening and enables you to order individual tracks online for less than a buck.

> **Whoa!** _____
>
> Before you start purchasing audio recordings online, be sure you can play them in Windows Media Player or whatever player you use and on your portable music player. Recordings from iTunes play only on an iPod, and the iPod can't play tunes that you download from Rhapsody. Most sites have a link you can click to learn which portable players and programs are compatible with the service.

As soon as you find a clip you want to download, simply click its link to play it. After your computer is finished downloading the clip, it should run your MP3 player, which typically starts playing the clip. If the clip doesn't start, click the **Play** button.

Copying Music to a Portable Music Player

Building a huge music library on your computer is cool, but a computer is a bit too bulky to carry around with you. How do you take your music collection, or at least a portion of it, on the road? The easiest and lightest way is to purchase a portable music player, often called an MP3 player. Portable music players come equipped with enough storage to hold gobs of music. Typically, you can rip tracks from CDs or download them from various sources on the Internet and then transfer (copy) them to your player.

Portable music players are usually equipped with the software you need to transfer clips from your computer to your player. Many of the music stores discussed earlier in this chapter also offer free software that can handle the file transfers. However, this software may not enable you to rip music from the CDs you already own. An alternative is to use Windows Media Player or Apple iTunes to perform both jobs. This assumes, of course, that you have a portable music player one of these programs supports. If you don't, you may need to purchase additional software.

The process of transferring clips to your player is fairly straightforward. The following steps show you how to copy files from your computer to your portable music player using Windows Media Player. If you're using other software, the steps should be similar:

1. Connect your portable music player to your computer as instructed in the player's documentation and turn it on. If you connect the device using a USB cable, you don't have to turn off your computer to make the connection.

2. Run the Windows Media Player as explained earlier in this chapter.

3. Click the **Sync** tab. A pane appears on the right, instructing you to drag tracks into the pane to add them to the Sync list. (If your portable music player or a drive letter for it does not appear, your player may not be supported by Windows Media Player.)

4. From the Library on the left, change to the folder that contains the tracks you want to copy to your portable music player.

5. Drag and drop one of the selected tracks into the Sync pane (on the right).

6. Repeat steps 4 and 5 to copy any remaining tracks to the Sync pane.

7. Click the **Start Sync** button (near the bottom of the Sync pane).

8. Exit Media Player and disconnect your portable music player as instructed in its documentation.

Burning Audio CDs

Ever since companies placed the power of recording technology in the hands of the people, users have copied albums, CDs, audiotapes, TV shows, movies, and anything else they can get their hands on. CDs are no exception. As soon as audio CD burners hit the market, people started their own bootleg operations, churning out free CDs for themselves, their friends, and their family.

Some of this copying is acceptable. For instance, if you purchased the entire collection of Beatles CDs and you want to create your own "favorites" CD to play in your car, you won't be prosecuted for copying songs you paid for to another disc for your own use. However, if you copy your entire collection to give as Christmas gifts, that's crossing the line.

Be that as it may, the technology is available for copying CDs and for transferring your collection of MP3s (however you obtained it) to CDs, and I show you how to do it. I'll leave the legal and ethical decisions up to you, the courts, and the music industry.

Duplicating CDs

If your computer is equipped with a CD-R or CD-RW drive and a program for copying CDs, you can duplicate your audio CDs. Most computers that come with CD-R or CD-RW drives have a program for copying CDs. If you don't have a CD copy program, check out Roxio's Easy Media Creator (www.roxio.com). At about $100, it's a little pricey, but Easy Media Creator can help you make the most of your recordable disc drive. It includes features for backing up your computer's hard drive to CDs or DVDs, copying audio or video clips to CDs or DVDs, transferring MP3 clips to CDs, and much more.

With Roxio's Easy Media Creator, you simply insert the disc you want to copy, run Easy Media Creator, and click the **Copy** button. Easy Media Creator copies everything on the disc and then displays a dialog box telling you to insert a blank recordable disc. After you insert the disc, Easy Media Creator transfers everything it copied from the original disc to the blank disc.

> **Computer Cheat**
>
> Although Windows Media Player features no command for copying directly from an audio CD to a blank CD-R or CD-RW, you can copy all the songs from the CD, save them in a separate playlist, and copy the playlist to a CD. See the next section for details.

Recording a Custom Mix to a CD

Besides the Counting Crows's *August and Everything After* and Tom Waits's *Swordfish Trombones*, I haven't encountered a CD that contains more than three songs I like. Fortunately, with a CD-R or CD-RW drive and the right program, you can pull one or more of your favorite songs off each CD to create and record your own custom mix to a blank CD. You can even add MP3 clips you downloaded from the Internet to the mix.

Again, several programs on the market enable you copy tracks from one CD to another and burn MP3 clips to CDs, but because you already have Windows Media Player, you'll probably want to use it for creating your custom CDs. Here's how it works:

1. Record the desired tracks and copy them to a separate playlist, as explained earlier in this chapter. Click **Burn.**

2. The Burn pane appears on the right, as shown in Figure 27.4. Drag and drop the tracks or playlists you want to burn to the CD into the Burn pane.

3. Insert a recordable CD into your computer's recordable CD drive, open the list above the right pane, and click the icon for your recordable CD drive.

4. To start copying the playlist to the CD, click the **Start Burn** button (near the bottom of the Burn pane).

Figure 27.4

Windows Media Player can write the tracks in a playlist to a disc.

Click Burn

Drag playlists or individual
tracks into the Burn pane

Click Start Burn

Playing DVDs on Your Computer

Can you watch movies on your computer? The short answer is yes; if your PC has a DVD drive, you can watch DVD videos on your PC. However, you probably won't want to watch DVD videos on your PC. I once watched *Apocalypse Now* on my 17-inch monitor and had a headache for 2 days. The picture was sharp and the sound was incredible—my computer has a better sound system than my TV—but the picture was so dinky I had to press my face to the screen to see anything.

If your computer has a DVD drive, it probably came equipped with its own DVD video player. If it didn't, Windows Media Player can handle the job.

The Least You Need to Know

◆ To play an audio CD, insert it into your computer's CD-ROM drive. When a dialog box pops up asking what you want to do, click **Play Audio CD** and click **OK.**

◆ To copy tracks from the CD to the Windows Media Library, click **Copy from CD,** be sure a check mark appears next to only the tracks you want recorded, and click the **Copy Music** button.

◆ To create a new playlist in Media Player, click the **Media Library** button and click the **New playlist** button or open the **Playlists** menu and click **New Playlist.**

◆ To take your tunes on the road, copy them to a portable MP3 player.

◆ You can use a CD burner program, such as Roxio's Easy CD Creator, to duplicate audio CDs or to copy MP3 clips to a blank CD to create your own mix.

Snapping, Enhancing, and Sharing Digital Photos

In This Chapter

- ◆ Snapping shots with a digital camera
- ◆ Computerizing your photos
- ◆ Taking your photos online
- ◆ Sending digital photos via e-mail
- ◆ Making your own photo album

In a few short years, digital cameras have managed to replace the standard 35mm models. You no longer have to fumble with rolls of film, drop them off at the local pharmacy for developing, wait an hour or a day or a week for your prints, or store shoeboxes packed with prints in your closet.

With a digital camera, you get instant gratification. Right after you take a picture, you can check out the results on the LCD display and delete the photo and retake it if it didn't turn out. You can plug your camera into a TV set and view the picture or connect your camera to your computer and print the photo. You don't even have to wait for 1-hour service. In addition, digital photography enables you to e-mail photos to your friends and relatives, post them on your website or blog or an online photo album, and pack them away on CDs or DVDs.

In this chapter, you learn the basics of digital photography, including how to take photographs, enhance your photographs with digital imaging software, print and e-mail photos, and even order prints online.

Learning the Lingo

When you're shopping for a digital camera and first learning to use it, prepare yourself to be pummeled by a barrage of new technical terminology. The following list of terms and their definitions can bring you up to speed in a hurry.

pixel   Short for *picture element*, a pixel is one of the tiny colored dots that makes up a digital image or photograph. Generally, the more dots you have, the bigger and better the picture.

megapixel   A million pixels. Photo size and quality are often measured in megapixels; generally, the more megapixels, the larger the photo and the higher the quality. A 3.1 megapixel camera is considered standard for producing high-quality prints.

> **Inside Tip** _____
>
> When shopping for a camera, don't focus exclusively on megapixel ratings. A camera with a lower megapixel rating but a superior lens can often take a better photograph than a camera with a higher megapixel rating and a lower-quality lens. Also opt for a higher optical zoom—3x at the very least, 4x to 6x for landscapes, or 7x to 12x for long-distance shots, sports photos, or wildlife images.

resolution   *Resolution* is another term for describing the quality of an image. The higher the resolution, the larger the photo and the higher the quality.

optical zoom   The ability of a camera to zoom in on a subject with its lens. Optical zoom is like focusing in with a telescope; it provides you with a clear, up-close view of the subject.

digital zoom   The ability of a camera to zoom in closer than what its lens is capable of. With digital zoom, the camera uses a program to magnify the image, which usually results in making the image a little blurry.

optical viewfinder   The little window you look through when taking a photograph that you use to frame your subject. An optical viewfinder can be somewhat deceptive—it doesn't always show exactly what will appear in the photograph.

LCD   Short for *Liquid Crystal Display*, this is the preview screen on the back of most digital cameras. Unlike an optical viewfinder, the LCD displays the subject just as it will appear in the photograph.

autofocus   A feature on many digital cameras that automatically adjusts the lens to bring the subject into focus. To autofocus on most cameras, you hold down the button halfway for a brief moment. When the camera is focused, you press down the button all the way to snap the photo.

memory card   The equivalent of a roll of film. Instead of storing images on film, a digital camera stores them on a memory card. Most digital cameras use removable memory cards or sticks that range in storage capacity from 16MB up to 1 gigabyte (GB). The number of photos you can store per card varies depending on the capacity of the memory card and the size of the photos.

Taking Digital Snapshots

Digital cameras are modeled off standard 35mm cameras, so snapping a picture is easy. You just point and shoot. If the camera has an autofocus feature, you may need to hold down the button halfway to focus the camera and then press down all the way to snap the shot.

Before you snap too many pictures, check the following camera settings:

Resolution, image size, or megapixels. Most cameras enable you to adjust the size and quality of the image. If you plan on printing the photos, choose a higher setting. If you're only going to e-mail the photos or place them on a web page, a setting of 640×480 pixels is usually sufficient. Larger images are higher quality, but they're also larger files, taking up more space on the memory card.

Mode or environment. Many cameras feature an assortment of modes or environments that automatically adjust the camera settings for different types of photos—for example, parties, landscapes, sporting events, daytime or nighttime portraits, and so on.

Flash. In most cases, leave the flash setting on Auto. If you're taking all your pictures outside, turn off the flash. For backlit scenes, turn on the flash, if this option is available on your camera.

Exposure. Many cameras enable you to bump the exposure up or down for very dark, very light, or high-contrast subjects. (When you're first starting out, you may want to leave this setting alone.)

Date imprint. Some cameras can add a date imprint to your photos so you can tell later the date you snapped them. If you find the date imprint more annoying than helpful, turn it off.

The procedure for checking the camera settings varies from one digital camera to another. Some cameras have two buttons: one for changing to a feature (such as flash, image quality, timer, and audio) and another for changing the settings. You change to the desired feature (for instance, flash) and then press the other button to change the setting (for instance, Autoflash or Flash On).

Digital cameras that have LCDs typically use a menu system for changing settings. In addition, many cameras come with preprogrammed settings for specific environments; you simply flip a switch or turn a dial to pick the environment (beach, indoor party, night scene, museum, etc.) and start snapping pictures—the camera adjusts all the settings for you. You can concentrate on centering your subject in the frame rather than worrying about aperture settings and shutter speeds.

Copying Photographs to Your PC

Digital cameras typically come with their own software that transfers the image files from the camera to your PC. In addition, the camera should include a cable for connecting to one of the ports on your PC, typically the USB port. Some digital cameras require a PC card reader. Other cameras come with their own docking stations; you simply insert the base of the camera into the docking station to connect it to the computer.

To transfer the images, connect the cable to your camera and to the specified port. Run the photo transfer utility and enter the command to retrieve the images. The program retrieves the images from the camera and displays them on screen, as shown in Figure 28.1. You can then delete the images from the PC card or other storage medium.

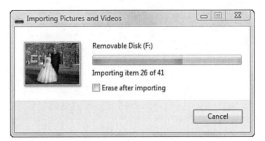

Figure 28.1

The photo transfer utility grabs the photos from the camera and copies them to your computer.

After you transfer the photos to your computer's hard drive, consider copying them to a CD for safekeeping, just in case anything bad were to happen to your hard drive. Be sure to label the CD with a title and date, so you can tell what's on it.

Most photo transfer utilities double as photo-editing tools. After you retrieve the images from your camera, you can adjust the brightness, color, and contrast of an image, crop it, flip it, resize it, and perform other digital imaging gymnastics. Figure 28.2 shows a sample photo displayed in Windows Photo Gallery, included in Windows Vista. If you purchased a special printer for printing photos, it may include its own digital image enhancing software, too.

Inside Tip

Many new printers are equipped with memory card readers. You simply remove the memory card from your camera and plug it into your printer. The memory card reader typically appears as another storage drive on your computer.

Figure 28.2

With digital image editing software, you can enhance your photos.

Adding Digital Photos to E-Mail and Web Pages

One of the best features of digital cameras is that they create graphic files you can immediately use on web pages and in e-mail messages. You don't have to scan the picture after taking it, because it's already in a digital format.

To place a picture on your web page, insert it as you would insert any graphic. In addition, if your e-mail program supports HTML, you can insert images right inside the message area when composing an e-mail message. To insert an image into a message you are composing in Outlook Express, for example, you click in the message area, click the **Insert Picture** button, and use the resulting dialog box to select the image, as shown in Figure 28.3.

The image management software included with many digital cameras features an option that can automatically prepare images for e-mail by reducing the image's resolution and file size. This makes the image travel across the Internet much faster and take up less space on the recipient's computer. If you have software that offers this feature, use it instead of inserting high-resolution photos. The people on the receiving end sure will appreciate it.

Add the file as an attachment ...

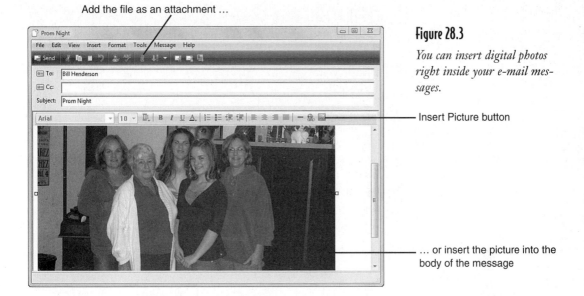

Figure 28.3

You can insert digital photos right inside your e-mail messages.

Insert Picture button

... or insert the picture into the body of the message

Ordering Photo Prints Online

Many new inkjet printers can generate high-quality photo prints on special photo paper. In addition, manufacturers have developed fairly inexpensive printers designed specifically for printing photos. Hewlett Packard's Photosmart, for example, is designed to print exclusively 4×7-inch prints. It even has a slot into which you can plug the memory card from your camera, so you can copy pictures directly to the printer without having to connect the camera to your computer.

If you prefer to leave the photo printing up to the professionals, you can order prints online at any of several online film developers, such as Shutterfly (www.shutterfly.com), Snapfish (www.snapfish.com), or Wal-Mart (www.walmart.com), which can mail prints to your local Wal-Mart for pickup. (This is typically a little cheaper than mailing them to your residence.)

The process is pretty simple. You can either e-mail your photo files to the online photo shop or use the online photo shop's software to upload your photo files to the service. For example, at Shutterfly, you simply click **Choose Pictures** and select the pictures you want to order, as shown in Figure 28.4. You then complete an order form, specifying the size and number of prints you want and your billing and delivery information. Shutterfly processes your pictures and mails them to you.

Figure 28.4

At Shutterfly, you drop off your "film" by selecting the photos you want developed and uploading them.

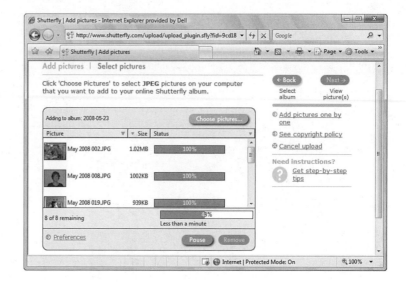

If you're in a big hurry and need 1-hour processing (or faster), take your digital camera to a professional photo shop. Most photo shops have special printers that can transfer your digital photos into high-quality prints in a matter of minutes.

Inside Tip _____

Many stores that traditionally processed film now allow customers to upload their images online and pick up their prints at the store or have them shipped to their homes. Check out the website for your favorite local pharmacy to determine whether it offers this service.

More Ways to Display and Share Photos

Companies are constantly developing new ways to share photos. One item I encourage you to check out is a digital frame. Digital frames are like small, flat-screen TVs (without the TV tuner electronics) designed specifically for displaying digital images. You can store many images on the frame and even have the frame randomly cycle through the images.

Use the Windows My Pictures Slideshow screen saver to display a slideshow on your computer screen of all the photos in a particular folder when you're not using your computer. For more about turning on and selecting a screen saver, see Chapter 9.

Online photo albums are handy, too. With an online photo album, you upload (copy) your photos from your computer to a website, where your friends and relatives can view the photos online and even copy them to their computers (or their own digital frames!). Many companies offer free online photo (and video) sharing. Check out Photobucket (www.photobucket.com), Flickr (www.flickr.com), and Picasa (picasa. google.com).

Inside Tip

To include a photo on a website, the photo must already be stored somewhere online. Many people who have their own websites use online photo albums to store the photos and other digital images displayed on their websites.

The Least You Need to Know

- ◆ Buy a digital camera with a good lens and a rating of 3.1 megapixels or higher.

- ◆ Optical zoom uses the camera's lens to zoom in on a subject, resulting in a sharp image. Digital zoom uses computer tricks to blow up an image, commonly making it fuzzy.

- ◆ Most digital cameras have an LCD screen on the back that can help you frame your picture and preview it to determine if you want to save or delete it.

- ◆ Before you take a snapshot with a digital camera, check your camera's settings.

- ◆ Digital imaging software enables you to crop images, zoom in, adjust the color and brightness, add special effects, remove red eyes, and enhance your photos in other ways.

- ◆ You can order prints online at any of several processing stores, including Shutterfly and Snapfish.

Chapter 29

Editing Digital Video

In This Chapter

- ◆ Working with digital camcorders
- ◆ Editing your videos
- ◆ Adding professional transitions between video clips
- ◆ Recording video clips to CDs or VHS tapes

Back in the 1960s and 1970s, 8mm film was the medium of choice for amateur movie makers. I know people who still have boxes of 8mm film cans in their attics and basements. In the 1980s and 1990s, people traded in their 8mm cameras and projectors for VHS and 8mm camcorders. These relatively compact devices made it easy to record video and play it back on a television set, but the tapes were still bulky and you had to fast-forward through several minutes of tape to find your favorite clips. The new millennium has introduced a new video technology, digital video, allowing us to transfer, edit, and catalog video clips using a computer.

In this chapter, you learn how to take advantage of digital video.

Getting Started with Digital Video

You can approach digital video from two different directions, depending on how much you have invested in an older camcorder, how many old tapes you have, and how much money you're willing to spend. If you don't have a camcorder or old tapes and you have some cash on hand, purchase a digital camcorder and start filming. Digital camcorders record video in a much higher resolution than analog VHS or 8mm camcorders, and the digital clips won't lose quality when copied to your computer. (The quality of video clips recorded with analog camcorders suffers a little when they're converted from an analog to a digital format.)

When shopping for a digital camcorder, think about how you'll connect the camcorder to your computer. Most digital camcorders have an *IEEE-1394* (*FireWire*) or USB connector. If your computer does not have an IEEE-1394 or USB port, you need to install an expansion board to add the required port.

def•i•ni•tion

IEEE-1394 is a standard for transferring data between devices very quickly—at a rate of 400Mbps (megabits per second) or 800Mbps, depending on the version. Compare that to the USB standard of 12Mbps and 480Mbps (in USB 2.0), and you can see why IEEE-1394 is the preferred method of transferring video to a computer. IEEE-1394 goes by many names, the most common of which is Apple's **FireWire**. You might also see IEEE-1394 labeled i.link or Lynx.

If you already have an analog camcorder and plenty of old tapes, or if your computer budget is already strained, consider adding a video capture device to your computer. You have several options here. The most convenient way is to purchase an external unit that connects to your computer's parallel, USB, or IEEE-1394 port, or into a circuit board that comes with the unit. Figure 29.1 shows a device from Pinnacle Systems, which can capture from digital and analog camcorders and standard VHS tapes. Note that you plug the cables from the camcorder or VCR into the jacks on the front of the unit. To save space on your desk, you can opt for a video capture board, which plugs into an expansion slot inside your computer, but having the jacks right in front of you will make your job much easier.

Video capture boards and external units have special ports that let you connect your camcorder to your computer. They typically capture video at a rate of 15 or more frames per second, and they do a fairly good job of converting your analog clips into a digital format. If you're looking for a way to convert your collection of old camcorder or VHS tapes into a digital format and store them on CDs, this is the way to go.

Figure 29.1

An analog-to-digital converter lets you connect a camcorder or VCR to your computer.

(Courtesy of Pinnacle Systems, Inc.)

Setting Up Your A/V Equipment

If you're preparing to record and edit video from a digital camcorder, there's not much to setting up your equipment. You simply connect the USB or IEEE-1394 cable to the USB or IEEE-1394 ports on the camera and your computer, and you're ready to roll.

If you're recording from a VCR or analog camcorder, on the other hand, the setup is a bit more time-consuming, because you have an analog-to-digital converter between your player and your computer. On an external unit, such as Pinnacle System's Video Transfer device, the jacks are color-coded and match up with the standard A/V (Audio/Video) jacks found on most camcorders and VCRs.

Composite video combines the color and brightness data in a single signal, resulting in a lower-quality display. (Your camera is probably going to have *either* a composite-video jack or an S-video jack, not both. Composite video is more common.)

S-video divides the video into two signals—one for color and one for brightness—generating a high-quality image.

Most analog-to-digital converters have *audio jacks:* a left-audio and right-audio input jack. However, most cameras have only a single audio output jack. You can connect the audio output jack on the camera to either the left or right audio-input jack on the converter.

Figure 29.2 shows a schematic drawing of the connections for its Video Transfer converter. Note that the camera or other analog device provides the input (at the top of the diagram). The bottom of the diagram shows a single connection from the USB port on the Video Transfer converter to the computer or other device to which you'll be recording the video.

Figure 29.2

An analog-to-digital converter receives input from the analog device and converts it into a digital stream that can be recorded on a computer.

(Courtesy of Pinnacle Systems, Inc.)

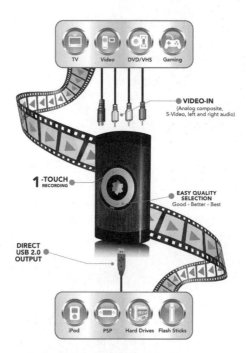

Capturing and Saving Video Clips

Your digital camcorder or video capture device probably came with its own program for recording and editing your video footage. Most of these programs are similar and follow the same overall procedure for recording and editing video. Here's a quick overview of the process:

1. Connect your camcorder or VCR to your computer, as instructed in the previous section. (You may need to connect through an analog-to-digital converter.)

2. Run your video recording program and enter the command to start recording.

3. Use your camcorder or VCR controls to play the video you want to record.

4. When you're ready to stop recording, enter the command to stop recording and press the **Stop** button on the camcorder or VCR. The video recording program chops the recording into *clips* to make them more manageable. It displays a thumbnail view of each clip.

5. Arrange the clips in the order you want them played.

6. Trim the clips. You can trim sections of any clip.

7. Add background music.

8. Add transitions between clips. For example, you can have a clip fade out at the end and fade into the next clip.

9. Save your movie to your hard drive.

10. Record your movie to a CD or tape or e-mail the movie clip.

Windows Vista and XP include their own video recording and editing software, Windows Movie Maker. To run Movie Maker, choose **Start, All Programs, Windows Movie Maker.** (In your version of Windows, Windows Movie Maker may be on the **Start, All Programs, Accessories, Entertainment** menu. In Windows Vista, you can access Movie Maker from the Windows Media Center, too.) Windows Movie Maker appears, as shown in Figure 29.3.

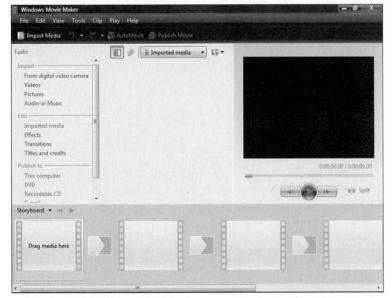

Figure 29.3

Windows Movie Maker enables you to edit digital video like the pros.

To start recording clips in Movie Maker from a VCR or analog camcorder, follow these steps:

1. Connect your VCR or camcorder to the video capture device.

2. In Movie Maker, click **Capture from Video Device.** The Video Capture Wizard appears, prompting you to select the video capture device that's connected to your computer.

3. Select the video capture device you plan on using (if more than one such device is connected to your computer), and specify the audio device, video input source, and audio input source. Click **Next.** Video Capture Wizard prompts you to enter a name for the video.

4. Type a descriptive name for the video you're about to record and click **Next.** Video Capture Wizard prompts you to specify the desired video quality.

> **Whoa!** _____
>
> Before you go adjusting the video quality settings, remember: higher-quality settings result in larger files.

5. Click the option for the desired video quality. By default, Movie Maker is set to record video for optimal playback on a computer. Click **Next.** Video Capture Wizard displays the controls you need to record the video.

6. To have Movie Maker chop your video footage into manageable clips when you're done recording, be sure **Create Clips When Wizard Finishes** is checked.

7. Use the controls on your VCR or camcorder to locate the beginning of the clip you want to record and then rewind it slightly. Video Capture Wizard displays a small preview area where you can watch the video, so you can see what you're doing.

8. Press the **Play** button on your VCR or camcorder, and when the video reaches the point where you want to begin recording, click Video Capture Wizard's **Start Capture** button.

9. When you've reached the end of the clip, click the **Stop Capture** button to stop recording, and press the **Stop** button on your VCR or camcorder.

10. If desired, repeat steps 7 through 9 to capture additional footage from this tape or from another tape.

11. When you're finished capturing video clips for your movie, click Video Capture Wizard's **Finish** button. If you turned on **Create Clips When Wizard Finishes** in step 6, Movie Maker automatically chops the footage you recorded into smaller clips to make them more manageable and displays a thumbnail view of each clip, as shown in Figure 29.4.

movie clips   preview area

Figure 29.4

Windows Movie Maker chops your film footage into smaller clips.

The procedure for recording from a tape in a digital video (DV) camcorder is a little different, because you can control the camera from Movie Maker.

1. Connect the DV camcorder to your computer and set the camcorder mode to play your video.

2. In Movie Maker, click **Capture from Video Device.** The Video Capture Wizard appears, prompting you to select the video capture device that's connected to your computer.

3. Select the DV camcorder from the Available Devices list and click **Next.**

4. Type a filename for the recording and click **Next.**

5. Choose the desired video quality and click **Next.**

6. When prompted to choose a capture method, choose **Capture the Entire Tape Automatically** (to have Movie Maker rewind the tape and record it in its entirety) or choose **Capture Parts of the Tape Manually** (to capture selected portions of the tape).

When recording from a DV camcorder, you can use the camcorder's controls or the controls in Video Capture Wizard to control the camcorder during the capture.

Splicing Your Clips into a Full-Length Movie

As soon as you have a few clips to work with, you're ready to start your new career as a professional film editor, cutting undesirable footage, trimming clips, and rearranging clips to create your own feature film. The editing procedure is surprisingly easy. You simply drag and drop thumbnails of your clips onto the storyboard at the bottom of the Movie Maker window, as shown in Figure 29.5.

Figure 29.5

Drag and drop your clips onto the storyboard.

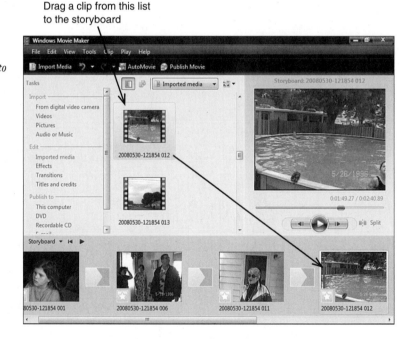

Drag a clip from this list to the storyboard

If a portion of a particular clip is out of focus or contains material you don't want to include in your video, you can trim the clip. This process consists of designating a start and end trim point. Movie Maker then cuts the beginning and end of the clip, leaving the portion between the two trim points intact. Here's what you do:

1. In the bar above the storyboard, click the **Storyboard** button and click **Show Timeline** to view a timeline that shows how the clips are stitched together.

2. Click the clip you want to trim. The play indicator appears at the beginning of the clip as a blue box in the timeline with a vertical line that illustrates where the clip would start playing if you were to click the Play button.

> **Panic Attack**
>
> You cannot trim clips in Storyboard view.

3. Drag the play indicator to the position where you want the beginning of the clip chopped off.

4. Open the **Clip** menu and click **Trim Beginning.** Movie Maker trims the portion of the clip to the left of the play indicator.

5. Drag the play indicator to the position where you want the end of the clip chopped off.

6. Open the **Clip** menu and click **Trim End.** Movie Maker trims the portion of the clip to the right of the play indicator.

7. Repeat steps 2 through 6 to trim any additional clips in the timeline.

To add a title frame at the beginning of your move or before a particular clip or credits at the end, click **Tools**, **Titles and Credits,** and follow the on-screen cues to complete the operation.

Adding an Audio Background

To give your video another dimension, consider recording some background music or narration. Here's how to record narration:

1. Click **Storyboard** or **Timeline** (above the storyboard or timeline) and click **Narrate Timeline.** Narration controls appear in the upper-left quadrant of Movie Maker.

2. Click the **Start Narration** button, and start talking into your microphone.

3. When you're finished, click **Stop Narration** and then name and save your narration.

The easiest way to add background music, assuming you have a CD-ROM drive, is to record tracks from your audio CDs or download some music clips, as explained in Chapter 25. You can then use Movie Maker's **File, Import** command to import the audio clips into Movie Maker.

Inside Tip

To add background music and narration, overlap the narration with the background music. You cannot completely overlap the two audio clips, but you can get pretty close.

After you've imported audio clips into Movie Maker, adding them to your video is a snap:

1. Be sure the timeline is displayed. If the storyboard is displayed instead, click **Storyboard, Show Timeline** (in the bar above the storyboard).

2. Next, drag and drop the desired audio clip over the audio bar, as shown in Figure 29.6.

Drag an audio clip from this list to the storyboard

Figure 29.6

Drag and drop your audio clips onto the audio bar.

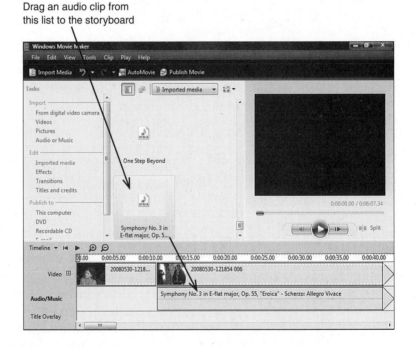

Movie Maker might have trouble importing audio clips recorded with Windows Media Player. If you receive error messages when trying to import these clips, try recording your audio clips with a different CD ripper.

Smoothing Out Your Transitions

When you splice clips and trim sections of clips, some of the transitions might seem a little abrupt and surreal. To reduce the shock, add smooth transitions between clips. With Movie Maker, you can create a transition that makes the end of one clip fade out and the beginning of the next clip fade in.

Here's how to create a transition:

1. Switch to Timeline view, as explained earlier in this chapter.

2. Open the **Tools** menu and click **Transitions.**

3. A list of video transition effects appears above the timeline. Scroll down the list to bring the desired transition into view, drag the transition from the list, and drop it between the two clips where you want the transition to play.

4. To preview the transition, drag the play indicator to a position just before the transition and click **Play.**

When Movie Maker reaches the point in the movie clip where you placed the transition, it displays the effect in the preview area.

Saving Your Project

As you work on your movie and when it's complete, you can save it to your computer's hard drive as a "project." Click **File, Save Project** or press **Ctrl+S,** type a filename for the project, and click **Save.** This saves the file in the Microsoft Windows Movie Maker Format, giving it a filename extension of .MSWMM. Only Movie Make can open the file.

When your movie is complete, you can "publish" it to your computer's hard drive, to a recordable DVD or CD (if your computer has a recordable disc drive), e-mail it to a friend or family member, save it to the web, or record it back to your DV camcorder. When you publish your project, Movie Maker transforms your collection of clips into a single Windows Media Video file, giving it the filename extension WMV. You can then view the movie in Windows Media Player. (If you publish to a DVD, you can then play the movie on most TV-DVD players as well as on your computer.)

To publish your movie, follow these steps:

1. Click **Publish Movie** (in the toolbar near the top of the window). Movie Maker prompts you to choose what you want to do with the movie file, as shown in Figure 29.7. Save it to your computer's hard drive (using My Computer), transfer it to a recordable CD, e-mail it, save it to a web server, or record it to a tape in a DV camcorder.

Figure 29.7

Specify where you want your movie saved.

2. If you plan on saving your movie clip to a recordable CD, insert a blank CD into your computer's recordable CD drive. To record to a DV camcorder tape, be sure a blank tape is loaded into the camcorder and that the camcorder is connected to the video capture device's video out port.

Inside Tip _____

Low-quality settings are excellent for playing the video on a computer. If you plan on playing the video on a TV set, choose a higher setting.

3. Choose the desired option to specify where you want the file saved and click **Next**. Movie Maker prompts you to enter a name for the file.

4. Type a file name for your movie and select the desired location where you want it saved. Click Next. Movie Maker prompts you to specify the desired video quality for the movie.

5. Choose the desired quality setting and click **Next.** Movie Maker processes the movie, creates a file, and saves it to the specified destination. (This can take quite some time, even on a fairly powerful computer.)

Copying Your Movie to a VHS Tape

If you want to copy your movie to a VHS tape to share it with people who don't have computers, good luck. Most video recording devices and programs are much better at pulling video off tapes than recording edited video back to tapes. If your video capture device has an A/V output port, you can connect the device to a VCR to record to tape or a TV set that has RCA jacks. To make the connections, you need an adapter that plugs into the A/V output port on the video capture board and that has the proper connectors for the S-video-in or composite-in jacks on your VCR or TV set (see Figure 29.8).

Now that you've made the physical connection between the computer and the VCR or TV, how do you play the video? Movie Maker has no command for sending the video to a VCR or TV. However, if your video card has an option for using a TV as a display device, here's a little trick you can do to record your movie on a tape using your VCR:

1. Connect your VCR to the A/V-out port on your video card, as shown in Figure 29.8.

2. Right-click a blank area of the Windows desktop and click **Properties.**

3. Click the **Settings** tab and then click the **Advanced** button. This displays advanced options for your particular video card.

4. If you see a Television option, turn it on. If no Television option is available, this feature might not be available for your video card. Check the card's documentation to be sure.

Panic Attack
Some video cards have a very odd configuration. Some have a video-out connector that hooks up to the video-in port on a VCR, but the audio-out jack plugs into the sound card on a computer. So you play the video into the VCR and the audio into the computer, making it impossible to record both the audio and video portions to a tape!

5. Run Windows Media Player, as explained in Chapter 27.

6. Use the **File, Open** command to open the movie file you created.

Figure 29.8

Some video capture cards enable you to output recorded clips to a TV set or VCR.

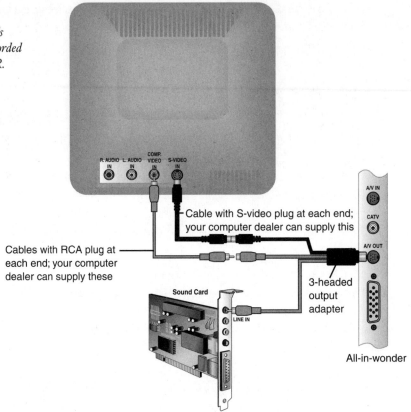

7. Press the **Record** button on your VCR and then perform the next two steps as quickly as possible, so you don't end up with a lot of dead space at the beginning of the tape.

8. Click Media Player's **Play** button.

9. Press **Alt+Enter** to change to full-screen mode.

The Least You Need to Know

◆ You can connect a digital camcorder directly to your computer via an IEEE-1394 port.

◆ To connect an analog camcorder or VCR to your computer, you must install an internal video capture card or an external video capture device.

◆ To run Windows Movie Maker, choose **Start, All Programs, Accessories, Entertainment, Windows Movie Maker.**

◆ To start recording video in Movie Maker, use your camcorder to start playing the video and click the **Start Capture** button.

◆ To create transitions between video clips, display Timeline view, open the **Tools** menu, click **Transitions,** and drag the desired transition between the two video clips where you want the transition to play.

◆ To publish your movie, click **Publish Movie,** and follow the on-screen instructions.

Part 6

Maintaining and Troubleshooting Your Computer

You don't need to be a mechanic to use a computer, but you should perform some basic maintenance tasks on a regular basis to keep your computer in tip-top condition and running at peak performance.

Part 6 acts as your computer maintenance and upgrade manual. Here you learn how to clean your monitor, keyboard, mouse, printer, and system unit; give your computer a regular tune-up to keep it running at top speed; troubleshoot common computer problems; and find valuable technical support.

"Please, honey, no. Remember the car, the shower? The mower? Can we please just call someone? Won't that be nice? Let's just put that screwdriver down and call someone? Whatever you want…"

Chapter 30

Keeping Your Computer Clean

In This Chapter

- Dusting your computer
- Squeegeeing your monitor
- Scrubbing your mouse
- Keeping your printer shiny and new
- Spin-cleaning your disk drives

One of the best clean-air machines on the market is a computer. The cooling fan constantly sucks in the dusty air and filters out the dust. A monitor acts like a dust magnet, pulling in any airborne particles unfortunate enough to get close to it. And the keyboard and mouse act like vacuum cleaners, sucking crumbs and other debris from your desk.

Unfortunately, the dust and smoke that your computer filters out eventually build up on the mechanical and electrical components inside it. When enough dust and debris collect on your computer and accessories, it's time for a thorough cleaning.

Tools of the Computer-Cleaning Trade

Before you start cleaning, turn off your computer and any attached devices, and gather the following cleaning equipment:

- *Screwdriver or wrench.* This is for taking the cover off your system unit. (If you don't feel comfortable going inside the system unit, take your computer to a qualified technician for a thorough annual cleaning. It really does get dusty in there.)

- *Computer vacuum.* Yes, there are vacuum cleaners designed especially for computers.

- *Can of compressed air.* You can get this at a computer or electronics store. Compressed air is great for blowing the dust out of tight spots, such as between keyboard keys.

- *Soft brush.* A clean paintbrush with soft bristles will do. Use this to dislodge any stubborn dust the vacuum won't pick up.

- *Toothpicks.* The only tool you need to clean your mouse.

- *Cotton swabs.* This another good tool for cleaning your mouse, and it's great for swabbing down your keyboard, too.

- *Paper towels.* Use these for wiping dust off your equipment and for cleaning the monitor.

- *Alcohol.* This is not the drinking kind; save that for when you're done.

- *Distilled water.* You can get special wipes for your monitor, but paper towels and distilled water do the trick.

- *Radio or CD player.* When you're cleaning, you need music ....

> **Inside Tip** _____
>
> You've probably seen floppy disk or CD-ROM cleaning kits, but most likely you don't need one. If your drive is having trouble reading disks, buy a cleaning kit and clean it. If it's running smoothly, let it be.

Vacuuming and Dusting Your Computer

Work from the top down and from the outside in—with the power off and the pieces unplugged.

Start with the monitor. You can use your regular vacuum cleaner for this part; if you have a brush attachment, use it. Run your vacuum hose up and down all the slots at the top and sides of the monitor. This is where most of the dust settles. Work down to the tilt-swivel base and vacuum that, too. You might need a narrow hose extension to reach in there.

Next, vacuum your printer, speakers, and any other devices. If dust is stuck to a device, wipe it off with a damp (not soaking wet) paper towel.

The system unit comes next. When vacuuming, be sure you vacuum all the ventilation holes, including the floppy disk drive, power button, CD-ROM drive, open drive bays, and so on. If you have a CD-ROM drive, open it and gently vacuum the tray.

Now for the tough part—inside the system unit. You can't just poke your vacuum hose in there. Use only a vacuum designed for computers. Don't use a DustBuster, your regular vacuum cleaner, or your ShopVac. These can suck components off your circuit boards and can emit enough static electricity to fry a component. A computer vacuum is gentle and grounded. Also be careful not to suck up any loose screws.

You can use a can of compressed air to blow dust off external peripheral devices, such as your keyboard and speakers, but be careful spraying the air against internal components. Compressed air can be very cold and can cause condensation to form on sensitive electrical components.

Touch a metal part of the case to discharge any static electricity from your body, and keep your fingers away from the circuit boards.

Now, take the cover off the system unit and vacuum any dusty areas. Dust likes to collect around the fan, ventilation holes, and disk drives. Try to vacuum the fan blades, too. If you can't get the tip of the vacuum between the blades, gently wipe them off with a cotton swab. Some fans have a filter where the fan is mounted. If you're really ambitious, remove the fan (be careful with the wires) and clean the filter.

Cleaning Your Monitor

If you can write "Wash Me" on your monitor with your fingertip, the monitor needs cleaning. Check the documentation that came with your computer or monitor to see if it's okay to use window cleaner on it. The monitor might have an antiglare coating that can be damaged by alcohol- or ammonia-based cleaning solutions. If it's not okay or if you're not sure, use water.

With your monitor turned off and unplugged, spray the window cleaner (or water) on a paper towel, just enough to make it damp, wipe the screen, and wipe with a dry paper towel to remove excess moisture. *Don't* spray window cleaner or any other liquid directly on the monitor; you don't want moisture to seep in.

You can also purchase special antistatic wipes for your monitor. These not only clean your monitor safely, they also discharge the static electricity to prevent future dust buildup.

If you don't want to spend money on antistatic wipes, wipe your monitor with a *used* dryer sheet. A new dryer sheet might smudge the screen with fabric softener.

Shaking the Crumbs Out of Your Keyboard

Your keyboard is like a big placemat, catching all the cookie crumbs and other debris that fall off your fingers while you're working. Unlike a placemat, however, the keyboard isn't flat; it's full of crannies that are perfect hiding spots for crumbs and debris and are nearly impossible to reach to clean. And the suction from a typical vacuum cleaner just isn't strong enough to pull up the dust (although you can try it).

The easiest way I've found to clean a keyboard is to turn it upside down and shake it gently. Repeat two or three times to get out any particles that fall behind the backs of the keys when you flip it over. If you don't like that idea, get your handy-dandy can of compressed air and blow between the keys.

> **Inside Tip**
>
> Rubbing alcohol is an excellent cleaning solution for most electronic devices, because it cleans well and dries quickly. Use it for your keyboard, plastics, and most glass surfaces (except for some monitors). Avoid using it on rubber (for example, your mouse ball), because it tends to dry out the rubber and make it brittle.

For a more thorough cleaning, shut down your computer and disconnect the keyboard. Dampen a cotton swab with rubbing alcohol and gently scrub the keys. Wait for the alcohol to evaporate completely before reconnecting the keyboard and turning on the power.

If you spill a drink on your keyboard, try to save your work and shut down the computer fast but properly. Flip over the keyboard and turn off your computer. If you spilled water, let the keyboard dry out thoroughly. If you spilled something sticky, give your keyboard a bath or shower with lukewarm water. Take the back off the keyboard, but do not flip over the keyboard with the back off, or parts will scurry across your desktop. Let it dry for a couple days (don't use a blow dryer), and put it back together. If some of the keys are still sticky, clean around them with a cotton swab dipped in rubbing alcohol. If you still have problems, you may have to buy a new keyboard.

Making Your Mouse Cough Up Hairballs

If you can't get your mouse pointer to move where you want it to, you can usually fix the problem by cleaning the mouse. Most new mice are optical or laser mice and use light to detect motion, so they have no moving parts to clean. I've never had a problem with an optical mouse getting gunked up. The only part you may need to clean are the little raised areas on the bottom of the mouse that come in contact with your desk or mouse pad because these can get sticky. Simply dab a lint-free cloth in alcohol and gently wipe the pads.

If you have a mouse with a ball in it (a mechanical mouse), remove the mouse ball cover. (Typically, you press down on the cover and turn counterclockwise.) Wipe the ball thoroughly with a moistened paper towel. Look inside the mouse (where the ball was). You should see three rollers, each with a tiny ring around its middle. The ring is not supposed to be there. The easiest way

Whoa!

Whatever you do, don't allow any cleaning solution or your cleaning cloth to come in contact with your mouse's light sensor, as this could negatively affect its operation.

I've found to remove these rings is to gently scrape them off with a toothpick. You have to spin the rollers to remove the entire ring. Use a pair of tweezers to extract any dust mats you can't pull out with a toothpick. You can also try rubbing off the rings with a cotton swab dipped in rubbing alcohol, but these rings are pretty stubborn. When you're done, turn the mouse back over and shake it to remove the loose crumbs. Reassemble the mouse.

And don't forget to clean your mouse pad or the area of your desk where your mouse scurries about. If the mouse was dirty, there's a very good chance it picked up the dirt from your desk or mouse pad.

When Your Printer Needs Cleaning

Printer maintenance varies so widely from one printer to another that I recommend referring to the manual. In some cases, for example, cleaning the print heads means wiping them off with a damp, lint-free cloth, whereas other printers may have a control panel option for cleaning the print heads, and if you touch the print head, you void the warranty.

If you don't have the printer manual, you can usually visit the manufacturer's website and obtain an electronic version of the manual, as explained in Chapter 33. If no manual is available, search the website for general instructions on printer cleaning and maintenance or try to find a manual for a similar make and model.

Whoa!

Toner used in laser printers can be hazardous to your health. Using compressed air to blow toner out of the printer or a standard vacuum cleaner to suck it out can launch a lot of toner dust into the air. You can buy a special toner vacuum, but they're fairly expensive. You're better off hiring out the job to someone who has the right equipment and experience.

Even with these variables, there are a few things the average user can do to keep the printer in peak condition and ensure high-quality output.

When turning off the printer, always use the power button on the printer (don't use the power button on your power strip) or press the **Online** button to take the printer offline. This ensures that the print head is moved to its rest position. On inkjet printers, this prevents the print head from drying out.

Avoid touching the print heads unless the manufacturer or a tech support person tells you specifically to do so.

If the ink starts to streak on your printouts (or you have frequent paper jams in a laser printer), see if your printer has an option for cleaning the print heads. If it doesn't, get special printer-cleaner paper from an office supply store and follow the instructions to run the sheet through your printer a few times.

Using a damp cotton cloth, wipe paper dust and any ink off the paper feed rollers. Do not use alcohol. Do not use a paper towel; fibers from the paper towel could stick to the wheels.

What About the Disk Drives?

Don't bother cleaning your floppy, CD-ROM, or DVD-ROM drives unless they're giving you trouble. If your CD-ROM or DVD-ROM drive is having trouble reading a disc, the disc is usually the cause of the problem. Clean the disc and check the bottom of the disc for scratches. If the drive has problems reading every disc you insert, try cleaning the drive using a special drive-cleaning kit. The kit usually consists of a disc with some cleaning solution. You squirt the cleaning solution on the disc, insert it, remove it, and your job is done.

If you have a floppy disk drive that has trouble reading any disk you insert, you can purchase a special cleaning kit that works like the CD-ROM drive-cleaning kit. Although cleaning the disk drive might solve the problem, the problem can also be caused by a poorly aligned read/write head inside the drive, which no cleaning kit can correct.

The Least You Need to Know

- ◆ Vacuum your system, especially around its ventilation holes.
- ◆ Wipe the dust off your screen using a paper towel and the cleaning solution recommended by the manufacturer.
- ◆ Blow the crumbs out of your keyboard with compressed air.
- ◆ If you have a mouse with a ball inside it, remove those nasty mouse rings around the rollers with a toothpick.
- ◆ To clean your printer, follow your manufacturer's instructions.
- ◆ Clean your floppy or CD-ROM drive only if it's having trouble reading disks.

Chapter 31

Giving Your Computer a Tune-Up

In This Chapter

- Cleaning up your hard disk
- Repairing hard disk problems
- Doubling your disk space (without installing a new drive)
- Increasing your memory (without installing more RAM)

Over time, you'll notice that your computer has slowed down. Windows takes a little longer to start up, programs that used to snap into action now seem to crawl, scrolling becomes choppy, and your computer locks up more frequently. You might begin to think that you need a new processor, more RAM, a larger hard disk drive, or even a whole new computer.

Before you take such drastic action, work through this chapter to give your computer a tune-up. By clearing useless files from your disk drive, reorganizing files, and reclaiming some of your computer's memory, you can boost your computer's performance and save a lot of money at the same time.

Eliminating Useless Files

Your hard disk probably contains *temporary files* and backup files that your programs create without telling you. These files can quickly clutter your hard drive, consuming space you need for new programs or new data files you create. You can easily delete most of these files yourself.

The easiest way to clear useless files from your hard drive in Windows is to let the Windows Disk Cleanup utility manage the details:

1. Click **Start, All Programs, Accessories, System Tools, Disk Cleanup.** In Windows Vista, if your computer has more than one user account, you have to specify whether you want to clean up files for only the user currently logged on or for all users. If your computer has more than one hard drive, Windows prompts you to select the drive you want to clean.

2. If prompted to select a drive, click the arrow to the right of the Drives box, click the desired drive, and click **OK.** The utility scans your computer's hard drive for useless files and displays a list of file types you probably won't ever need, as shown in Figure 31.1.

def•i•ni•tion

Temporary files, those files that end in *.TMP*, are files that your programs create but often forget to delete. You can safely delete them to make more room on your computer.

Figure 31.1

Disk Cleanup can remove useless files from your hard drive.

Remove the check mark next to any items you want to keep

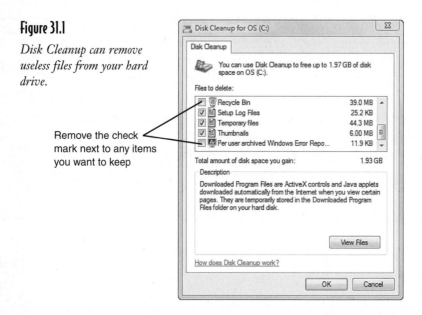

3. Check the box next to each file type you want Disk Cleanup to sweep off your computer's hard drive.

4. For a more aggressive cleanup, click the **More Options** tab (if available) to remove additional items: Windows components, Installed programs, and System Restore points. If you choose to remove System Restore points, Disk Cleanup removes all but the most recent restore point; so unless you're having serious problems with your computer, this is a safe option.

5. Click the **Clean up** button next to any of the additional items you want to remove, and use the resulting dialog box or window to enter your preferences. Windows removes any of the selected items immediately, but you still need to run Disk Cleanup to remove the files you selected in step 3.

6. Click **OK** to commence the proceedings. The Cleanup utility removes the files you selected in step 3.

Computer Cheat

You can clear temporary Internet files off your hard drive without having to perform a full disk cleanup. In Internet Explorer, click **Tools, Internet Options**. Under **Browsing History**, click **Delete**, and use the resulting options to choose the items you want to delete or click the **Delete All** button to delete everything.

Disk Cleanup does not remove copies of old digital photos you never look at, video clips you never watch, or music clips you never listen to. These are the items that really gobble up hard drive space in a hurry. Track down the folders where these files are stored and delete them or move them to CDs or DVDs. For more about managing files and folders, skip back to Chapter 7.

While you're at it, open your e-mail program and delete any e-mail messages you no longer need, including copies of messages you sent. When you delete e-mail messages, some e-mail programs, including Windows Mail and Outlook Express, stick the deleted messages in a separate folder (usually called Deleted Items). Be sure to delete the messages from that folder, too.

Inside Tip _____

Disk Cleanup can dump your Recycle Bin and open up a lot of disk space. If you already did this, that's fine, but know you can dump the Recycle Bin at any time. Just be sure it doesn't contain something you might need. Open the **Recycle Bin** by double-clicking its icon on the desktop and scroll down the list of deleted files to be sure you don't need anything in the Bin. If you find a file you might need, drag it onto the Windows desktop for safekeeping, or right-click the file and select **Restore** to restore the file to its original location. Now, click the Empty Recycle Bin button (in Windows Vista) or open the **File** menu and click **Empty Recycle Bin** (Windows XP).

Checking for and Repairing Damaged Files

Windows comes with a utility called ScanDisk that can test a disk (hard or floppy), repair most problems on a disk, and refresh the disk if needed. What kind of problems? ScanDisk can find defective storage areas on a disk and block them to prevent your computer from using them. ScanDisk can also find and delete misplaced (usually useless) file fragments that might be causing your computer to crash.

Whoa! _____

If you recover files from a damaged floppy disk, don't keep the disk. Transfer the files to another floppy disk or your computer's hard drive for safekeeping. When a floppy disk proves itself unreliable, it goes completely bad in a hurry.

Run ScanDisk regularly, at least once every month, and whenever your computer seems to be acting up and crashing for no apparent reason. Also, if you have a floppy disk that your computer can't read, ScanDisk might be able to repair it and recover any data from it.

To run ScanDisk, follow these steps:

1. Click **Start, Computer** or **My Computer.**

2. Right-click the icon for the drive you want to scan and click **Properties.**

3. Click the **Tools** tab, and (under Error-Checking) click the **Check Now** button. The Check Disk Local Disk dialog box appears, as shown in Figure 31.2.

4. Click the check box next to **Automatically fix file system errors** to place a check in the box.

5. To check for bad areas on the disk, click the check box next to **Scan for and attempt recovery of bad sectors** to place a check in the box. Checking this option tells ScanDisk to do a thorough job, which might take several hours; turn on this option only if you don't plan on using your computer for a while.

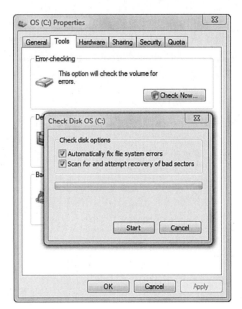

Figure 31.2

ScanDisk can repair most disk problems.

6. When you're ready to begin the scan, click **Start.** ScanDisk either automatically starts to scan the drive or displays a message indicating it will scan the drive the next time you restart Windows.

Panic Attack

If Windows shuts down improperly (if you press the power button on your system unit before Windows is ready, if the power goes out, or if Windows locks up), Windows might run ScanDisk automatically when you restart your computer. It reminds you to shut down properly next time, even though this probably wasn't your fault.

Defragmenting Files

Whenever you delete a file from your hard disk, you leave a space where another file can be stored. When you save a file, your computer stores as much of the file as possible in that empty space and stores the rest of the file in other empty spaces. The file is then said to be *fragmented*, because its parts are stored in different locations on the disk. This slows down your disk drive and makes it more likely that your computer will lose track of a portion of the file or the entire file. Every month or so, run Windows Disk Defragmenter to determine the fragmentation percent and defragment your files if necessary.

Before you start Disk Defragmenter, it's a good idea to disable any power-management utilities that might interfere with Defragmenter and any antivirus programs you're using. It's also a good idea to run Disk Cleanup before defragmenting your drive, as discussed in "Eliminating Useless Files," earlier in this chapter.

Save and close all open documents and exit any programs you currently have running. To disable an antivirus program, right-click its icon in the system tray, at the right end of the taskbar, and click the option to disable the security features or exit the program. (See Chapter 3 for details on how to configure the Windows power management settings.)

When you're ready to have Disk Defragmenter defragment your files, follow these steps:

1. Click **Start, All Programs, Accessories, System Tools, Disk Defragmenter.** Disk Defragmenter appears, as shown in Figure 31.3. (In Windows XP, Disk Defragmenter displays options for analyzing the disk or defragmenting it now.) You can also run Disk Defragmenter from My Computer by right-clicking the drive and then selecting **Properties, Tools, Defragment Now.**

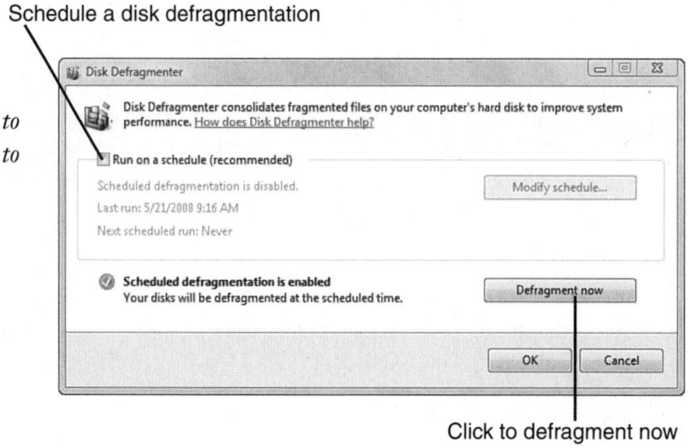

Schedule a disk defragmentation

Figure 31.3

Defragmenter prompts you to select the drive(s) you want to defragment.

Click to defragment now

2. If your computer has more than one hard drive, click the icon for the drive you want to defragment.

3. In Windows XP, you can click **Analyze** to display both the percentage of file fragmentation on the disk and whether you need to defragment the disk.

4. When you're ready for Defragmenter to start working, click the **Defragment now** (Windows Vista) or **Defragment** (Windows XP) button. Defragmenter starts defragmenting the files on the disk.

Wait until the defragmentation is complete. It's best to leave your computer alone during the process. Otherwise, you might change a file and cause Defragmenter to start over. Don't run any programs or play any computer games. When defragmentation is complete, Defragmenter displays a message telling you so.

Performing a Diagnostic Start-Up

When you install programs, many of them take the initiative to configure Windows to run them whenever Windows starts. These programs then run in the background, whether you use them or not. Sometimes, as in the case of antivirus programs, you want these programs running on start-up. In other cases, however, the programs bog down performance.

To determine which programs are running on start-up and to pick and choose which programs you want to run, perform a diagnostic start-up:

1. Perform one of the following steps, depending on which version of Windows you have to run the System Configuration utility:

    ◆ In Windows Vista, click **Start,** type **msconfig** in the Start Search box, click **msconfig,** and click the option to continue.

    ◆ In earlier versions of Windows, including XP, open the **Start** menu, click **Run,** type **msconfig,** and press **Enter** or click **OK.**

2. Click the **Services** tab and click **Hide all Microsoft services** to place a check in its box, as shown in Figure 31.4. By hiding Microsoft services, you avoid accidentally disabling a service that's critical for the operation of Windows.

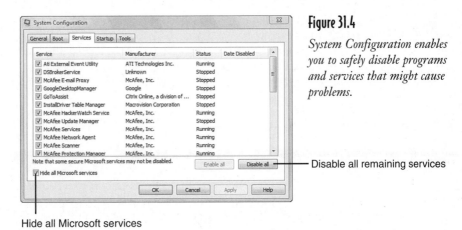

Hide all Microsoft services

Disable all remaining services

Figure 31.4

System Configuration enables you to safely disable programs and services that might cause problems.

3. Click the checkbox next to each service you don't want Windows to run on start-up, being careful not to disable services that are crucial for securing your computer, such as antivirus services. (You can click the **Disable all** button and enable the items you do want Windows to run on start-up.)

4. Click the **Startup** tab. A list of all the background programs that run on start-up appears.

5. Click the checkbox next to each program you don't want Windows to run on start-up, being careful not to disable programs that are crucial for securing your computer, such as antivirus services. (You can click the **Disable All** button and enable the programs you do want Windows to run on start-up.)

6. Click **OK.** The System Configuration dialog box appears, prompting you to restart your computer.

7. Exit any currently running programs and click the **Restart** button. Windows restarts. In Vista, a message appears in the lower-right corner of the screen reminding you that you blocked some programs. In earlier versions of Windows, a dialog box appears displaying the warning; click **OK** and then **Cancel** to continue working.

Chances are pretty good that your computer will run faster now. However, if you encounter problems trying to use a program later, remember that you disabled some programs and services. You may have to run the System Configuration utility again to re-enable one or more of the disabled programs or services.

Inside Tip

In addition to helping your computer run faster, the System Configuration utility is indispensable in troubleshooting problems. If Windows keeps crashing, for example, you could disable everything except Microsoft Services to determine whether a program that's running in the background is causing the problem. You can then re-enable programs and services until the problem recurs to identify the cause. See Chapter 32 for more about troubleshooting.

Scanning for Performance Glitches

If you tuned up Windows yourself and your computer's performance is still woefully inadequate, consider seeking help from a third party. PC Pitstop (www.pcpitstop.com)

offers free diagnostic scans to check your computer's performance, reliability, and security. For more about PC Pitstop, check out Chapter 33.

FinallyFast.com also features free diagnostic scans to check Internet connection speed and identify any problems with adware, spyware, or disk clutter that can be slowing down your computer. If the scan uncovers problems, the site encourages you to purchase its optimization utilities.

The Least You Need to Know

♦ Clear temporary files; unused photos, videos, and music files; old e-mail messages; and temporary Internet files from your hard disk, and don't forget to dump the Recycle Bin.

♦ To avoid system crashes and lost files, run ScanDisk at least once a month and whenever your computer is frequently locking up.

♦ To increase performance and prevent data loss, run Disk Defragmenter at least once a month.

♦ You can use the System Configuration utility (msconfig) to disable programs and services that are set up to run in the background.

♦ Scan your computer for performance issues at PC Pitstop and learn about possible tweaks you can do to improve performance.

Chapter

32

Troubleshooting Common Computer Problems

In This Chapter

- ◆ Figuring out what to do and not do in a crisis
- ◆ Sniffing out the cause of a problem
- ◆ Recovering safely when your computer locks up
- ◆ Getting your speakers to say something
- ◆ Getting your printer to print

Your computer can be quite moody. One day, all the components run properly and all tasks proceed without a glitch. The next day, your mouse pointer won't budge, your printer refuses to print a document, Windows locks up, or cryptic error messages pop up on your screen. Sometimes, simply installing a program or a new component can bring your computer to a grinding halt. In many instances, the computer provides no clue as to what the problem is, leaving you to troubleshoot on your own.

When problems arise, what should you do? Where do you begin to look for help? How do you track down the root cause of the problem? This chapter is your guide to solving a host of common computer problems. Here you learn common troubleshooting tactics and do-it-yourself repairs.

This chapter won't transform you into a professional computer technician, but with a little practice and a lot of patience, by the end of this chapter, you should be able to solve the most common problems and even help your friends with their computer woes.

Troubleshooting Tactics

When you run into a problem that doesn't have an obvious solution, the best course of action is inaction—that is, don't do anything. If you're fidgeting to do something, take a walk or grab a snack. Doing the wrong thing can often make the problem worse. After you've calmed down a little, come back and work through this list:

Are there any on-screen messages? Look at the monitor for any messages that indicate a problem.

Is everything plugged in and turned on? Turn off everything and check the connections. Don't assume that just because something looks connected, it is. Wiggle all the plugs.

When did the problem start? Did you install a new program? Did you enter a command? Did you add a new device? When my speakers went mute, I realized that the problem started after I installed a new hard drive. I had knocked a tiny jumper off the sound card during the hard drive installation.

Is the problem limited to one program? If you have the same problem in every program, the problem is probably caused by your computer or Windows. If the problem occurs in only one program, focus on that program.

> **Whoa!**
>
> Keep a running log of the changes you make to your system. Every time you install a new device or new software, install updates, or change settings, jot down the date and what you did. It takes a little extra time, but it enables you to retrace your steps later.

When did you have the file last? If you lost a file, it probably didn't get sucked into a black hole. It's probably somewhere on your disk, in a separate folder. Chapter 11 reveals several tricks for tracking down lost or misplaced files.

Realize that it's probably not the computer, and it's probably not a virus. The problem is usually in the software—Windows or one of your programs. Of the problems that people blame on computer viruses or the computer itself, 95 percent are actually bugs in the software or problems with specific device drivers (the instructions that tell your computer and Windows how to use the device). Only about 5 percent prove to be caused by viruses.

Thank Goodness for System Restore!

Windows includes a nifty utility called System Restore that can help you return your computer's settings to an earlier time when everything was working properly. System Restore monitors your computer, and when you install a program or a new peripheral device or component, it creates a *restore point* and saves the current settings to your computer's hard drive. System Restore also creates a daily restore point, just in case something goes wrong during the day. If you install a program or change a setting in Windows that causes problems, you can run System Restore and pick the desired restore point.

> ### Inside Tip
> When you return to a restore point, you don't lose any of the work you've done since that restore point. For example, if you made changes to a Word document, those are safe. However, if you installed a device or a program after Windows created the restore point, you'll probably have to reinstall it after you complete the restoration.

To return Windows to a previous state using one of the restore points it created, take the following steps:

1. Click **Start, All Programs, Accessories, System Tools,** and click **System Restore.** What happens next depends on the version of Windows you're running. In Windows XP, the System Restore window appears, asking whether you want to return your system to an earlier time or create a restore point. In Windows Vista, you may be prompted to confirm. Once you give your okay, the System Restore window appears, describing what it does.

2. Take one of the following steps:

    ◆ In Windows Vista, click **Continue** to confirm and click **Next.**

    ◆ In Windows XP, click **Restore My Computer to an Earlier Time** and click **Next.**

System Restore displays available restore points. In Windows Vista, the list appears, as shown in Figure 32.1. In Windows XP, restore points are displayed on a monthly calendar; dates in bold represent days in which a restore point was created.

Figure 32.1

System Restore enables you to return your system to an earlier time.

Select a restore point ——

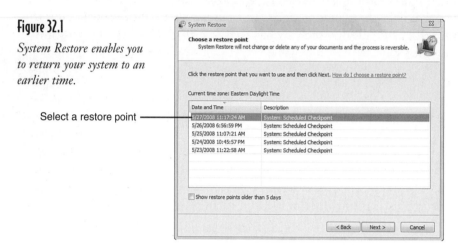

3. Follow the on-screen instructions to complete the restoration.

Inside Tip

If you plan on changing any system settings in Windows, deleting device drivers, or installing applications, run System Restore and create your own restore point before you begin. If something goes wrong, you can immediately return your computer to its previous condition.

System Restore takes a few seconds to collect the information it needs and then restarts Windows and displays the Log On screen. Log on to Windows as you normally do. System Restore runs automatically and displays a window that enables you to undo the restoration. Cancel out of this window and test a few of the applications you normally use to be sure the restoration didn't mess up your system.

If the restoration made things worse instead of better, you can run System Restore again and undo the restoration.

Identifying Troublesome Background Programs

Don't assume that the programs you run are the only programs running on your computer. Many programs you install or that came already installed on your computer run in the background. You won't see buttons for them on the Windows taskbar or even in the system tray, but they're running just the same and can cause conflicts with Windows and your other programs. They can also consume a great deal of your computer's resources.

Fortunately, Windows features a System Configuration utility that enables you to disable these programs when Windows starts. You can disable most of the programs to prevent them from running and then enable each program to identify the program that's causing problems.

Run the System Configuration Utility as instructed in "Performing a Diagnostic Start-Up" section in Chapter 31. Use the utility to disable all services (except Microsoft services) and to disable about one fourth of the programs that run on start-up. Restart your computer. If the problem is no longer present, you know that one of the services or programs you disabled is causing the problem and you can take enable some services and programs to narrow the list of possibilities. If the problem is still present, run the System Configuration utility again, disable more programs, and restart your computer. Using this strategy, you can focus in on the program or service that's causing the problem.

"My Computer Won't Start!"

A computer is a lot like a car; the most frustrating thing that can happen is that you can't even get the engine to turn over. To solve the problem, consider these questions:

Is the computer on? Be sure the power switch on the system unit is turned on. Some computers have a power button that you have to press and hold for a couple seconds.

Is the surge strip on? If your PC is plugged into a surge suppressor or UPC, be sure the power is turned on.

Is the screen completely blank? If you heard the computer beep and saw the drive lights go on and off, the computer probably booted fine. Be sure the monitor is connected and turned on and the brightness controls are turned up. Try moving your mouse or pressing the **Shift** key; your computer may be in sleep mode, and this usually wakes it up. In some cases, you may need to tap (press and release very quickly) the power button to bring the computer out of sleep mode.

Is there a disk in one of the removable disk drives? If you see a message that says "Non-system disk or disk error," you probably left a floppy disk or CD in one of the drives. Remove any disk or CD that's loaded and then press any key to start from the hard disk.

Can you start from a floppy disk or CD? Insert the Windows CD and restart your computer. If you can start from the Windows CD, the problem is on your hard disk. You may need some expert help to get out of this mess.

Booting from the Windows CD can be a little tricky. Most new computers are set up to check the CD-ROM drive on start-up for a bootable CD. When you restart your computer, a message appears asking if you want to start from the CD-ROM drive or the hard drive. Select the option to start from the hard drive. If your computer displays no such message, you may need to enter your computer's setup program and select your CD-ROM drive as the first drive your computer checks for a bootable disc. Watch the screen on start-up for a message telling you which key to press to enter your computer's setup.

> ### Whoa!
>
> Your computer's setup settings are key to its operation, so don't play around with too many settings, and keep a careful record of every setting you change (both the setting before the change and what you changed it to). You won't get into much trouble selecting which drive to use as the start-up drive, but you could cause a lot of problems by changing other settings, such as hard drive settings. As long as you have an accurate record of the original settings, you can always change them back.

"My Computer Locked Up!"

The computer might be too busy to handle your request, so wait a few minutes. If it's still frozen, press **Ctrl+Alt+Del.** The Windows Task Manager appears, showing you the names of the active programs. Next to the program that's causing the problem, you should see "[not responding]." Click that program's name and click **End Task.** Frequently, a second End Task confirmation dialog box appears a few seconds after you click the End Task button; repeat the command to end the task. (You may lose data when you close a program that's not responding.) You should now be able to continue working.

If you close the errant program and Windows is still locked up, press **Ctrl+Alt+Del** again and close any other programs that are causing problems. If you still cannot regain control of your computer, you may have to press **Ctrl+Alt+Del** again or use your computer's reset or power button. Do this only as a last resort. Shutting down your system without exiting programs properly causes you to lose any work you had not saved before shutting down. (Files saved to your hard disk are safe.)

> **Inside Tip**
>
> If your computer is really running slow, press **Ctrl+Alt+Del** to display the Task Manager. Click the Processes tab. In the CPU (Central Processing Unit) column, check the percentage of processing resources each program is using. Don't worry if the number is high for System Idle Process at the end of the list. If you see another process that's consuming a huge percentage of CPU resources, that's probably the process that's bogging down your computer. Try clicking it and then clicking **End Process** to see if that solves the problem.

It Could Be a Program

Many programs, especially web browsers, games, and antivirus programs, typically are buggy. They have programming code that makes the program conflict with Windows, other programs, one of your hardware devices, or even your computer's memory. One common problem is that the program never frees up the memory it uses.

The only permanent solution is to install a patch or bug fix from the manufacturer, assuming a patch is available. (A patch is a set of program instructions designed to fix a programming bug or add capabilities to a program.) Contact the manufacturer's tech support department to determine if a fix for the problem exists, as explained in Chapter 33.

For a temporary solution, use the program in spurts. Use the program for a while, save your work, exit, and restart before your computer locks up. If your computer seems to be getting sluggish, try restarting Windows to free up memory.

Check Your Mouse Driver

Windows might be having a problem with the mouse driver (the instructions that tell Windows how to use your mouse). Check to be sure you don't have two conflicting mouse drivers installed.

1. Click Start, right-click **Computer** or **My Computer,** and click **Properties** to access System Properties.

2. In Windows Vista, click **Device Manager.** In Windows XP, click the **Hardware** tab, and click the **Device Manager** button.

3. Click the plus sign next to **Mouse.**

4. If you have more than one mouse listed, you have more than one mouse driver installed. To disable one of the mouse drivers, double-click the mouse that doesn't match the type of mouse you have, click **Disable in This Hardware Profile,** and click **OK.**

5. Click **OK** again and restart your computer.

> **Whoa!** _____
>
> If you pick the wrong mouse driver, you won't have a mouse pointer in Windows, making it tough to navigate. If you pick the wrong driver, start your computer in Safe mode by tapping the **F8** key during start-up (right after the computer beeps) and choosing the option to start in Safe mode. Then pick a different driver. See "Dealing With Windows in Safe Mode" later in this chapter for details.

If that doesn't fix the problem, go to the computer or mouse manufacturer's tech support web page and check for an updated driver for the mouse (see Chapter 32). In most cases, the updated driver contains the fix for the problem. (See "Updating the Software for Your Hardware" later in this chapter to learn how to install an updated driver.)

If you can't obtain an updated mouse driver, try reinstalling the mouse driver:

1. Click **Start,** right-click **Computer** or **My Computer,** and click **Properties.**

2. In Windows Vista, click **Device Manager.** In Windows XP, click the **Hardware** tab and then click the **Device Manager** button.

3. Click the plus sign next to **Mice and Other Pointing Devices,** right-click the icon for your mouse, and click **Uninstall.**

4. Press **Alt+F4** repeatedly to shut down all programs and display the Windows Shut Down window, and choose the option for restarting Windows.

When Windows starts, it installs the required mouse driver.

Check the Windows Graphics Acceleration Setting

Windows is initially set up to exploit the full potential of your computer. Unfortunately, sometimes Windows is too aggressive, especially when it comes to your system's video acceleration. Windows cranks up the video acceleration rate to the maximum, which can sometimes cause your system to crash without displaying an error message. Try slowing it down:

In Windows Vista: Right-click a blank area of the Windows desktop and select **Personalize.** Click **Display Settings,** and click the **Advanced Settings** button. Click the **Troubleshoot** tab, and click the **Change Settings** button. (Your display driver may not allow you to adjust its hardware acceleration settings, in which case, the Change Settings button appears dim, meaning it is inactive.) Assuming you can change the settings, drag the **Hardware Acceleration** slider to the second or third hash mark, and click **OK.** Click **OK** as needed to back out of the dialog boxes while saving your changes.

In Windows XP: Right-click a blank area of the Windows desktop and select **Properties.** Click the **Settings** tab, and click the **Advanced** button. Click the **Troubleshoot** tab. Drag the **Hardware Acceleration** slider to the second or third hash mark, and click **OK.** Click **OK** as needed to back out of the dialog boxes while saving your changes. If Windows asks whether you want to reboot your system, close any programs that may be running, and click **Yes.**

Get an Updated Video Driver

Hiding behind the scenes of every video card and monitor is a video driver that tells your operating system (Windows) how to use the card and monitor to display pretty pictures. Occasionally, the driver contains a bug that can lock up your system. More frequently, the driver becomes outdated, causing problems with newer programs. In either case, you should obtain an updated driver from the manufacturer of the video card. You can call the manufacturer's tech support line and have the driver sent to you on a floppy disk or obtain the driver from the company's website.

After you obtain the updated driver, follow the manufacturer's instructions to install it. If the manufacturer provided no instructions, refer to "Updating the Software for Your Hardware" later in this chapter for some general instructions.

Inside Tip

Chapter 33 includes website addresses for many of the top computer and computer equipment manufacturers along with the address of a Microsoft web page that contains an index of hundreds of manufacturers.

Dealing With Windows in Safe Mode

Windows typically starts in Safe mode if you install a wrong device driver (especially a wrong video or mouse driver). In Safe mode, "Safe Mode" appears at each corner of the desktop. In most cases, you can simply restart Windows to have it load the previous driver. If on restarting, the Windows desktop is not visible or you cannot use the mouse, restart your computer, wait for it to beep, tap the **F8** key several times, and choose the option for starting Windows in Safe mode. (You have to be quick with the F8 key—press it before you see the Windows screen.)

Windows loads a standard mouse and video driver in Safe mode so you can see what you're doing and use the mouse to point and click. This enables you to install a different or updated driver or change settings back to what they were before you encountered problems.

"I Can't Get the Program to Run!"

If you try to run a program using a shortcut icon, the icon might be pointing to the wrong program. Right-click the shortcut, choose **Properties,** and check the entry in the **Target** text box. This shows the path to the program's folder followed by the name of the program file that launches the program. If the text box is blank or points to the wrong file, click the **Find Target** button and use the resulting dialog box to change to the program's folder and choose the right program file.

If the program starts and immediately closes, your computer might not have sufficient memory or disk space to run the program. To be sure your computer has set aside enough disk space to use as virtual memory, do one of the following:

In Windows Vista: Click **Start,** right-click **Computer,** and click **Properties.** Click **Advanced System Settings** and click **Continue.** Click the **Advanced** tab. Under Performance, click **Settings.** Click the **Advanced** tab. Under Virtual Memory, be sure there's at least 30 megabytes free space. You can click the **Change** button to adjust the amount of free space Windows uses, but Windows can usually manage the free space effectively if it has free space to manage. Problems typically occur if the disk is cluttered, meaning you need to clear files off the disk.

In Windows XP: Click **Start,** right-click **My Computer,** select **Properties,** click the **Advanced** tab, click the **Performance Settings** button, click the **Advanced** tab, and under Virtual Memory, click the **Change** button. Be sure you have at least 30 megabytes free space on the disk that Windows is using for virtual memory. Any less, and you have to clear some files from your hard disk.

If the program still won't run, try reinstalling it. If that doesn't work, contact the program manufacturer's tech support department to determine the problem and the required fix. The program may require special hardware or additional software that's not available on your system.

"I Have a Mouse, but I Can't Find the Pointer!"

After you get your mouse working, you'll probably never need to mess with it again (except for cleaning it, which I talked about in Chapter 30). The hard part is getting the mouse to work in the first place. If you connected a mouse to your computer and you don't see the mouse pointer on-screen, you should investigate:

Is the mouse pointer hidden? Mouse pointers like to hide in the corners or edges of your screen. Roll the mouse on your desktop to see whether you can bring the pointer into view.

When you connected the mouse, did you install a mouse driver? Connecting a mouse to your computer is not enough. You must install a program (called a *mouse driver*) that tells the computer how to use the mouse. Follow the instructions that came with the mouse to figure out how to install the driver.

"I Can't Hear My Speakers!"

Several things can cause your speakers to go mute. Check to be sure your speakers are turned on and that the speaker volume control is turned up.

Then check to see if your speakers (or headphones) are plugged into the correct jacks on your sound card. Some sound cards have several jacks, and it's easy to plug the speakers into the input jacks instead of the output jacks. If you're having trouble recording sounds, be sure your microphone is turned on and plugged into the correct jack.

Does your sound card have a volume control? Crank it all the way up.

How's your system volume? Click **Start, Control Panel, Hardware and Sound** (in Windows Vista) or **Printers and Other Hardware** (in Windows XP). Choose the option for adjusting the system volume, and go through all options in the resulting dialog box to be sure every volume control is set at the desired level and nothing is set to Mute.

If you still can't get your speakers to talk, click **Start,** right-click **Computer** or **My Computer,** and select **Properties.** In Windows Vista, click **Device Manager.** In Windows XP, click the **Hardware** tab, and click the **Device Manager** button. Scroll

> **Inside Tip** _____
>
> To get help troubleshooting problems in Windows Vista, click Start, Help and Support, Troubleshooting. For troubleshooting help in Windows XP, click Start, Help and Support, Fixing a Problem.

down the list and click the plus sign next to the **Sound** option. If your sound card isn't listed, you need to reinstall the sound card driver. If the sound card is listed but has a yellow circle with an exclamation point on it, the sound card is conflicting with another device on your system. Check your sound card's documentation to determine how to resolve hardware conflicts.

"My Printer Won't Print!"

If you run into printer problems, you probably have to do more fiddling than Nero. First, check to see that your printer is plugged in and turned on. Then go through these questions:

Does your printer have paper? Is the paper tray inserted properly?

Is the printer's online light on (not blinking)? If the online light is off or blinking, press the **On Line** button to turn on the light.

Is your program set to print to a file? Many Print dialog boxes have a Print to File option, which sends the document to a file on your disk instead of to the printer. Be sure this option is *not* checked.

Is the print fading? If so, your printer may need a new toner or ink cartridge. If your inkjet cartridge has plenty of ink, check your printer manual to determine how to clean the print head. Inkjet cartridges have some sensitive areas that you should never clean, so be careful.

Is there tape on the print head? If you have an inkjet printer, check the print head and the area next to the print head for tape, and remove the tape. Ink cartridges usually come with two pieces of tape on them. You must remove both pieces before installing the cartridge.

Is your printer marked as the default printer? Open the Control Panel (**Start, Control Panel**) and check to be sure the printer you're trying to print to is set as the default printer. For more about choosing a default printer, see Chapter 18.

Is the printer paused? Double-click the **Printer** icon in the taskbar, open the **Printer** menu, and be sure **Pause Printing** is not checked. If there is a check mark, click **Pause Printing.**

Inside Tip _____

For more about printer ports, see Chapter 18.

Is the correct printer port selected? Right-click the icon for your printer and click **Properties.** Click the **Ports** tab (Windows Vista) or the **Details** tab (Windows XP), and be sure the correct printer port is selected.

Did you get only part of a page? Laser printers are weird; they print an entire page at one time, storing the entire page in memory. If the page has a big complex graphic image or a lot of fonts, the printer may be able to store only a portion of the page. The best fix is to get more memory for your printer. The quickest fix is to use fewer fonts on the page and try using a less-complex graphic image. If you're trying to print a document with a border on a Deskjet or Inkjet printer, the border might not appear due to the printer's limitations.

Is it a printer problem? To determine whether the printer itself isn't working, try to print a test page. Many printers have an option or a button combination you can press to have the printer perform a self-test. Check your printer manual. If the test page prints properly, the problem is with the connection between your computer and the printer, with the program from which you're trying to print, or with your Windows printer setup.

Updating the Software for Your Hardware

Computer hardware and software is in constant transition. Whenever Microsoft updates Windows, manufacturers have to ensure that the hardware they're coming out with works with the new operating system, and Microsoft does its best to be sure the new operating system can handle most hardware devices. In this rush to get their products to market, the computer industry often releases products that contain bugs— imperfections that cause problems.

To help make up for these shortcomings, hardware manufacturers commonly release updated drivers for their devices. The driver works along with the operating system to control the device. You can solve many problems with your display, sound card, printer, joystick, modem, and other devices by installing an updated driver. The best way to get an updated driver is to download it from the Internet, as explained in Chapter 33. If you don't have an Internet connection and you suspect a device driver is causing problems, call the manufacturer's technical support line and ask if they have an updated driver. They may be able to send it to you on a floppy disk or CD.

After you've obtained the required driver, follow the manufacturer's instructions to install it. Sometimes, the manufacturer supplies you with an installation program. You simply run the program and follow the on-screen instructions. In other cases, the manufacturer supplies you with driver files and you use Windows to update the driver, by taking the following steps:

1. If you have the updated driver on a floppy disk or CD, insert the disk.

2. Click **Start,** right-click **Computer** or **My Computer,** and choose **Properties.**

3. In Windows Vista, click **Device Manager.** In Windows XP, click the **Hardware** tab and then click the **Device Manager** `button.`

4. Click the plus sign next to the type of device that requires a new driver.

5. Double-click the name of the device.

6. Click the **Driver** tab and then click the **Update Driver** button.

7. Choose the option for searching for a better driver and click **Next.** If the driver is on a floppy disk, Windows finds it and prompts you to install it. Follow the on-screen instructions and skip the remaining steps.

8. If you downloaded the driver from the Internet, click the **Other Locations** button, choose the disk and folder where the driver file is stored, and click **OK.**

9. Follow the on-screen instructions to complete the installation.

The Least You Need to Know

◆ Use the **Ctrl+Alt+Del** sequence to thaw your computer when it freezes.

◆ Use System Restore to return your computer to an earlier time when it was working properly.

◆ Use the System Configuration utility to troubleshoot problems caused by programs that run in the background.

◆ Don't go into shock when Windows starts in Safe mode. Shutting down and restarting your PC usually corrects the problem.

◆ If your printer won't print, check the cables and the online indicator. You can avoid most printer problems by making sure your printer has plenty of paper and is online before you start printing.

◆ Check regularly for Windows and device driver updates, and install any updated drivers.

33

Help! Finding Technical Support

In This Chapter

- ◆ Calling for tech support
- ◆ Finding answers and updates on the web
- ◆ More troubleshooting help

In Chapter 32, you learned how to troubleshoot and correct most common computer problems. Unfortunately, not all glitches are so obvious or easy to fix. A wrong setting in the Windows Registry can crash your system whenever you run a certain application. A single typo in your Internet setup can prevent your computer from establishing a connection. A buggy device driver can lock up your system. To make matters worse, you might not be able to identify the cause of the problem at all. When a particularly frustrating problem arises, it's tempting to heave your computer out the window or take a sledge hammer to your monitor.

Before you do that, try one other solution: contact the technical support (tech support) department for the program or device that's giving you problems.

In this chapter, you learn the ins and outs of tech support—what they can and cannot help you with, what to ask, what information you should have ready, and how to find answers to common questions on the Internet.

Phone Support (Are You Feeling Lucky?)

If you're very lucky, the documentation that came with your program or hardware device contains a phone number in the back for contacting technical support. It's usually displayed in tiny print to discourage people from calling. Flip through your manuals to find the number you need.

Before you call, be aware that the quality of technical support over the telephone varies widely from one company to another. Most places have a computerized system that asks you to answer a series of questions, usually leading to a dead end. Other places keep you on hold until you eventually give up and call a relative or friend for help. However, some tech support departments provide excellent, toll-free service, enabling you to talk with a qualified technician who can walk you through the steps required to solve your problem.

Whoa!

Don't call when you're angry! If you start screaming at the technical support person, he or she is going to be less likely to offer quality help.

Even if you get to speak with a great tech support person, you need to be prepared. No tech support person can read your mind. You must be able to describe the problem in some detail. Before you call, write down a detailed description of the problem, explaining what went wrong and what you were doing at the time. If possible, write down the steps required to cause the problem again.

Also write down the name, version number, and license (or registration) number of the program you are having trouble with. You can usually get this information by opening the **Help** menu in the problem program and choosing the **About** command. Of course, this assumes you can run the program.

Write down any information about your computer, including the computer brand, chip type (CPU) and speed, monitor type, amount of RAM, and the amount of free disk space. To find this info, in Windows, open the **Start** menu, point to **All Programs, Accessories, System Tools,** and click **System Information.** The System Information utility gives you most of the details you need.

Be sure your computer is turned on. A good tech support person can talk you through most problems if you're sitting at the keyboard. Some may even be able to take control of your computer remotely to fix the problem for you.

Be sure you're calling the right company. If you're having trouble with your printer, don't call Microsoft. Even if you get through to a Microsoft Windows tech support person, the person will tell you to call the printer manufacturer first.

Finding Tech Support Online

Nearly every computer hardware and software company has its own website where you can purchase products directly and find technical support for products you own. If your printer is not feeding paper properly, you're having trouble installing your sound card, you keep receiving cryptic error messages in your favorite program, or you have some other computer-related problem, you can usually find the solution on the Internet.

In addition, computer and software companies often upgrade their software and post both updates and fixes (called *patches*) on their websites for downloading. If you're having problems with a device such as a printer or modem, check the manufacturer's website for updated drivers. If you run into problems with a program, check the software company's website for an update or a patch.

def•i•ni•tion

A **patch** is a program file you install to correct a problem.

The following table provides web page addresses of popular software and hardware manufacturers to help you in your search. Most of the home pages listed have a link for connecting to the support page. If a page doesn't have a link to the support page, use its search tool to locate the page. You might also see a link labeled FAQs (frequently asked questions), Common Questions, or Top Issues. This link can take you to a page that lists the most common problems other users are having and answers from the company, as shown in Figure 33.1.

Computer Hardware and Software Websites

Company	Web Page Address
3COM	www.3com.com
Acer	global.acer.com
Adaptec	www.adaptec.com
Adobe	www.adobe.com

continues

Computer Hardware and Software Websites   (continued)

Company	Web Page Address
AMD	www.amd.com
ATI Technologies	ati.amd.com
Brother	www.brother.com
Canon	www.canon.com
Corel	www.corel.com
Creative Labs	us.creative.com
Dell	www.dell.com
Epson	www.epson.com
Fujitsu	www.fujitsu.com
Gateway	www.gateway.com
Hewlett-Packard	www.hp.com
IBM	www.ibm.com/support/us/en
Intel	www.intel.com
Intuit	www.intuit.com
Iomega	www.iomega.com
Maxtor	www.seagate.com/maxtor
Microsoft	www.microsoft.com
Motorola	www.motorola.com
NEC	www.nec.com
NVidia	www.nvidia.com
Packard Bell	www.packardbell.com
Panasonic	www.panasonic.com
Seagate	www.seagate.com
Sony	www.sony.com
Texas Instruments	www.ti.com
Toshiba	www.toshiba.com
Western Digital	www.westerndigital.com

Figure 33.1

Check out the FAQs or Top Issues link for answers to common questions.

If the manufacturer you're looking for isn't listed in this table, don't give up. Connect to your favorite web search page and search for the manufacturer by name or search for the problem you're having. You should also seek help from online computer magazines, such as *Simple Computing* (www.simplecomputing.com).

Here are some additional resources:

Tech Support Forum (www.techsupportforum.com) is a free online technical support discussion group where you can find solutions to many of the more perplexing computer problems, including hardware and software issues, spyware and virus infestations, and networking problems.

TechRepublic (techrepublic.com) is a technical support site for IT professionals, so it tends to include help that may be somewhat beyond the understanding of beginner computer users, but it's still a great resource to consult when you encounter a problem nobody else seems to be able to solve.

Inside Tip

Microsoft offers an alphabetical listing of hundreds of hardware and software vendors complete with contact information at support.microsoft.com/gp/vendors/en-us.

Protonic (www.protonic.com) is a free online technical support service staffed by qualified volunteers who are eager to help other computer users solve their problems. Post your question and then check the site for answers.

Help2Go.com is maintained by a community of computer users and features free tutorials, a Q&A area, and live support for your computer problems.

ComputerChimp.com is my computer blog, where I post tips, tricks, and solutions to common Windows-based PC problems. Unfortunately, due to time constraints, I cannot offer the type of full-featured tech support manufacturers can offer.

Inside Tip _____

One of the best general troubleshooting resources for Microsoft Windows or other Microsoft products is the Knowledgebase. Go to **www.microsoft.com**, click **Support**, and click **Knowledgebase**. You can then search the Knowledgebase for answers to your questions. The Support page offers links to additional resources for updating your products and solving troubleshooting problems.

Troubleshooting with Diagnostic Software

When you purchase a computer, it doesn't come with its own technical support expert, but the manufacturer may include a diagnostic program that can identify common hardware problems. Gateway computers, for example, include a program called PC Doctor that examines the various components and settings, identifies defects, and offers to help you tweak your system to improve performance. Find it at **Start, All Programs, PC Doctor.**

Newer Dell computers include a Support Center. To access it, click **Start, All Programs, Dell Support Center.** Older Dell computers include a Resource CD that features a diagnostics program for testing the various components that comprise the computer: memory, video card, disk drives, monitor, network card, modem, and so on.

Most manufacturers also place an icon on the **Start, All Programs** (or **Programs**) menu for accessing their online help system. Check the Windows menus and desktop for a support icon.

If your computer does not include a diagnostics program, you can purchase such a program or even have your computer examined on the Internet. An industrial-strength program, such as PC Doctor Service Center (www.pc-doctor.com), can be a little pricey (about $400); but if you plan on becoming a service technician or sharing the cost with some friends, it's well worth the investment. For a more affordable solution, check out TuffTest Pro (www.tufftest.com).

To have your computer examined on the Internet, PC Pitstop (www.pcpitstop.com) can run a full series of tests on your computer and provide you with a rundown of problem areas and security issues, as shown in Figure 33.2. Best of all, the test is free. PC Pitstop also provides links to online technical support (for a fee).

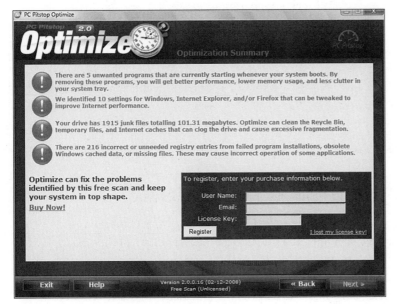

Figure 33.2

Drive your computer to PC Pitstop to have it examined online.

The Least You Need to Know

- Prepare for a productive phone conversation with a tech support person by having as much specific information as you can about your PC and the problem before calling.

- Check out your computer manufacturer's tech support web page.

- Find technical support using computer magazines and support sites on the web.

- Use the diagnostics program that came with your computer, if you're fortunate enough to have such a program.

- Obtain a computer diagnostics program or have your computer tested online at PC Pitstop.

Index

A

abbreviations, e-mail messages, 254-255
access, networks, limiting, 136-137
account icons, customizing, 111-112
accounts (administrator), 108
accounts (checking), reconciling, 203
accounts (e-mail)
  passwords, 247
  setting up, 246-247
accounts (user), 107-108
  account icons, customizing, 111-112
  adding, 108-109
  administrator accounts, 108
  deleting, 112-113
  file sharing, 115-116
  guest user accounts, 113-114
  log-on passwords, establishing, 109-111
  logging on/off, 114-115
AccuPoint pointers, 19
Acer website, 399
Adaptec website, 399
adapters, purchasing, 128
Add/Remove Programs utility, 87-88
Add New Hardware Wizard, 10-11
Add New Printer dialog box, 10-11
Add Printer Wizard, 211

address books, e-mail clients, 249
addresses
  e-mail, 246
  URLs (uniform resource locators), 237-238
addressing outgoing e-mail messages, 248
adjusting audio volume, 98
administrator accounts, 108
Adobe website, 399
AIM (AOL Instant Messenger), 260
  buddy lists, 262-263
  downloading and installing, 260-261
  online chat, 265-266
  text messaging, 262
  videoconferencing, 264-265
  voice-messaging, 263-264
alcohol, computers, cleaning, 366
aligning text, Microsoft Word, 148-149
All Programs button, 11
All Programs command (Start menu), 38
Alt (Alternate) key, 14
AltaVista.com, 238
Amazon.com, 296, 299
AMD website, 400
analog-to-digital converters, 349-350
animated screen savers, activating, 103-104
annual tax returns, preparing, 206-207

anti-virus software, 316-317
  installing, 136
Anywho.com, 239
AOL Music Now, 330
applications, 80
  AIM (AOL Instant Messenger), 260
    buddy lists, 262-263
    downloading and installing, 260-261
    online chat, 265-266
    text messaging, 262
    videoconferencing, 264-265
    voice-messaging, 263-264
  anti-virus applications, 136, 316-317
  background applications, troubleshooting, 386-387
  backup files, deleting, 374-376
  censoring applications, 313-314
  deleting, 87-88
  diagnostic applications, 402-403
  Dreamweaver, 285
  drivers, updating, 395-396
  e-mail clients, 245-246
    account setup, 246-247
    adding graphics, 250-251
    address books, 249
    addressing outgoing messages, 248
    file attachments, 251-252

receiving incoming messages, 249-250
replying to messages, 250
Excel, 159-171
firewalls, 317-319
freezes, troubleshooting, 389
FrontPage, 285
gadgets, 48-49
HotDog, 285
installing, 83-84
media players, 325-326
  burning audio CDs, 332-334
  copying music to portable player, 331-332
  downloading music, 329-331
  playing DVDs, 334
  playlists, 326-328
  skins, 329
Microsoft Word, 141-142
  aligning text, 148-149
  automatic corrections, 145-146
  document creation, 144-145
  editing documents, 153-155
  electronic page, 142-143
  formatting text, 147-148
  grammar checking, 155-157
  inserting today's date, 146
  keyboarding, 143
  line spacing, 149-150
  page views, 144
  paragraph spacing, 150-151
  saving documents, 151-152
  spell checking, 155-157
  templates, 145

minimum system requirements, 80-83
newsreaders, 272-274
Paint, 194-195
patches, 399
personal finance programs
  automatic check-writing process, 202-203
  financial calulators, 206
  online banking, 204
  reconciling accounts, 203
  recurring entries, 204-205
  setting up, 201
  tax return preparations, 206-207
  tracking budgets, 205-206
PowerPoint, 173-183
  workspaces, 174-175
running, 84-87
  single-click, 86-87
  startup, 86
Second Life, 269-270
shortcuts, creating, 85-86
temporary files, deleting, 374-376
troubleshooting, 392
web browsers, 236-242
Web Studio, 285
Yahoo! Messenger, 266-269
arrow keys, 14
arrows, menu commands, 35
Ask.com, 238
assigning sounds, events, 99, 104
ATI Technologies website, 400
attaching files, e-mail messages, 251-252
audio
  CDs, 324-325
  events, assigning, 99, 104

media players, 325-326
  burning audio CDs, 332-334
  copying music to portable player, 331-332
  downloading music, 329-331
  playing DVDs, 334
  playlists, 326-328
  skins, 329
MP3 files, 324-325
speakers, troubleshooting, 393-394
streaming audio, 325
volume, adjusting, 98
audio backgrounds, video clips, adding, 355-356
audio CDs, burning, 332-334
audio equipment, testing, 97-98
audio files
  copying to portable players, 331-332
  downloading, 329-331
audio jacks, 350
August and Everything After, 333
autofocus, digital cameras, 339
automatic corrections, Microsoft Word, 145-146
automating check-writing process, 202-203
autoscrolling, mouse, 18
Avast.com, 317
AVG Anti-Virus software, 136

B

background printing, managing, 217-218
backgrounds, desktops, choosing, 91-92
backup files, deleting, 374-376
backup utility, 49

banking (online), 200-201
    personal finance programs,
        204
Bigfoot.com, 239
BizRate.com, 297
Blogger.com, 290
blogs, publishing, 288-292
Bluehost web hosting services,
    292
Bluetooth, 8
Bluetooth networks, 126
BMP (Bitmapped) graphics,
    191
booking online travel reserva-
    tions, 300
bookmarking webpages, 242
broadband Internet connec-
    tions, 224, 227-229
        security, 136-137
        sharing, 135-136
        testing, 232-233
Brother website, 400
browsers (web), 236-237
    bookmarking, 242
    history lists, 241
    homepage, selecting, 242
    multiple pages, navigating,
        239-240
buddy lists (AIM), 262-263
budgets, tracking, personal
    finance programs, 205-206
burning audio CDs, 332-334
buttons
    All Programs, 11
    Close, 39
    dialog boxes, 37
    Have Disk, 11
    Maximize, 39
    programmable buttons, 15
    Restore, 39
    Show Desktop, 40
    Start, 11, 18
    toolbars, 37-38

C

CA Anti-Virus software, 136
cable connections, 228
calculating formulas and func-
    tions, spreadsheets, 165-166
calculators
    Calculator, 38
    financial calculators, 206
camcorders (analog), PCs,
    connections, 349
camcorders (digital), 348-349
    configuring, 349-350
    filming, 350-354
    FireWire connections, 348
cameras (digital), 338
    autofocus, 339
    configuring, 339-340
    digital zoom, 338
    LCDs (Liquid Crystal
        Displays), 339
    megapixels, 338
    memory cards, 339
    optical viewfinders, 339
    optical zoom, 338
    photographs
        copying to PCs, 340-342
        taking, 339-340
    pixels, 338
    purchasing, 338
    resolution, 338
Canon website, 400
CD-ROM drives, 67, 323
    cleaning, 370-371
    software requirements, 81
CD-RW discs, 325
CD-RW drives, 67, 323
CD burners, 324
CD rippers, 324
CDs (Compact Discs),
    324-325
        burning, 332-334
        loading, 68-69
        mix CDs, recording,
            333-334

Red Book format, 324
    unloading, 68, 69
cell addresses
    spreadsheets, 160
cells (spreadsheets), 160-161
    addresses, 160
    formatting, 167-168
center alignment, text, 148
changes, undoing, 155
charts, spreadsheets, 169
chat rooms, 259
    Yahoo! Chat, 266-268
check-writing process, auto-
    mating, 202-203
check boxes, dialog boxes, 37
checking accounts, reconciling
    statements, 203
check marks, commands, 35
circles, drawing, 193-194
cleaning
    computers, 366-367
    disk drives, 370-371
    keyboards, 368-369
    monitors, 367-368
    mouse, 369
    printers, 369-370
clicking mouse, 17-18
client-server networks,
    124-125
clients
    e-mail, 245-246
        account setup, 246-247
        adding graphics,
            250-251
        address books, 249
        addressing outgoing
            messages, 248
        file attachments,
            251-252
        receiving incoming mes-
            sages, 249-250
        replying to messages,
            250
    networks, 124

clip art
ready-made images, inserting, 187-190
reshaping, 189-190
resizing, 189-190
Clipboard, 15
clips (video)
audio backgrounds, adding, 355-356
saving, 357-359
splicing, 354-355
transitions, 357
VHS tapes, copying to, 359-360
Close button, 39
closing windows, 39
CMS (content management system), 285
CNET Shopper.com, 297
colors, desktop, changing, 102
color schemes, desktops, choosing, 92-93
columns, spreadsheets, 160
labeling, 162-163
command buttons, dialog boxes, 37
commands
See also options
arrows, 35
check marks, 35
ellipses, 35
entering, mouse, 16
grayed commands, 35
selecting, 34-36
Start menu
All Programs, 38
Documents, 120
Programs, 38
rearranging, 94-95, 102
Shut Down, 25
Start, 25
toolbars, 37, 38
Turn Off Computer, 25
compact flash drives, 71

comparison shopping, online shopping, 297-298
Complete Idiots Guide to Microsoft Windows Vista, The, 62
components, 19
AccuPoint pointers, 19
connecting, 7-8
environmental hazards, 23
identifying, 6-7
joysticks, 20
keyboards, 14-16
mouse, 16-19
touchpads, 19
trackballs, 19
unpacking, 5-6
composite video jacks, 349
compressed air, computers, cleaning, 366
ComputerChimp.com, 290, 402
computers
cleaning, 366-367
diagnostic start ups, performing, 379-380
energy consumption, estimating, 22
Energy Star seals, 23
environmental hazards, 23
green PCs, 23-24
power-saving features, 25-26
shared computers
file sharing, 115-116
user accounts, 107-115
shutting down, 25, 55, 62-63
starting, 9-10
troubleshooting
background programs, 386-387
freezes, 388-391
mouse, 393
printers, 394-395
programs, 392

speakers, 393-394
start ups, 387-388
strategies, 384-385
System Restore, 385-386
unpacking, 5-6
configuration
digital camcorders, 349-350
digital cameras, 339-340
firewalls, 317-318
icons, 33-34
printers, 210-212
web browsers, security settings, 314-316
connections
Internet
broadband, 135-137
cable, 228
choosing, 224-225
dial-up connections, 226-227
DSL, 227-228
ISDN, 227
ISPs, 232
satellite, 229
testing, 232-233
Wi-Fi, 229
peripheral devices, 7-8
conserving ink and paper, 27
Content Advisor (Internet Explorer), 310-313
content management system (CMS), 285
context-sensitive help, 54
context menus, 35
contiguous files, 73-74
Control (Ctrl) key, 14
Control Panel, 18, 25
Windows XP, 61
copying
digital photographs to PCs, 340-342
files, 77
folders, 77
music to portable players, 331-332

videos to VHS tapes, 359-360

Corel website, 400

cotton swabs, computers, cleaning, 366

Counting Crows, 333

CPUs (central processing units), software, requirements, 80

Craigslist.com, 305-306

Creative Labs website, 400

Ctrl (Control) key, 14

cumulative kilowatt hours, measuring, Kill-A-Watt meters, 22

cursor-movement keys, 14

cursors, Microsoft Word, 142

customizing
mouse, 18-19
PowerPoint Slide Master, 177
user account icons, 111-112
Windows Vista, 90-100
Windows XP, 100-104

cutting text, 154-155

CyberPatrol, 313

CYBERsitter, 314

D

damaged files, repairing, 376-377

Dashboard (WordPress.com), 291-292

data files, 71-72

date and time, adjusting, 104-105

date imprints, digital cameras, setting, 340

dates, spreadsheets, entering, 163-164

defragmenters, 38

defragmenting files, 377-379

deleting
backup files, 374-376

files, 75-76
folders, 75-76
program files, 75
programs, 75, 87-88
temporary files, 374-376
use accounts, 112-113
web pages, 288

Dell website, 400

deselecting files and folders, 73

designing spreadsheets, 162

desktop, 32-33
backgrounds, choosing, 91-92
colors, changing, 102
color schemes, choosing, 92-93
customizing, Windows Vista, 90-97
icons
adding to, 95
controlling, 103
rearranging, 93, 101
selecting, 32-34
Recycle Bin, 33
space, maximizing, 90-91, 100-101
system tray, 33
taskbar, 32-33
hiding, 94, 101
themes, saving, 99-100
visual effects, controlling, 103
wallpaper, hanging, 102
Windows Vista, 44-45
Windows XP, 58

device drivers, installing, 10-11

devices, 19
AccuPoint pointers, 19
audio equipment, testing, 97-98
connecting, 7-8
disk drives, cleaning, 370-371

environmental hazards, 23
identifying, 6-7
joysticks, 20
keyboards, 14-15
cleaning, 368-369
Logitech Wave keyboard, 14
notebook dual-function keys, 16
Windows key shortcuts, 15-16
modems, 224
installing, 229-230
monitors, cleaning, 367-368
mouse
basic movements, 16-18
cleaning, 369
customizing, 18-19
Logitech MX610 Laser cordless mouse, 17
troubleshooting, 393
printers
cleaning, 369-370
configuring, 210-212
troubleshooting, 218-219, 394-395
speakers, troubleshooting, 393-394
synchronization, Windows Vista, 52
touchpads, 19
trackballs, 19
unpacking, 5-6

diagnostic software, 402-403

diagnostic start ups, performing, 379-380

dial-up connections, 224-227
testing, 232-233

dialog boxes, 34-36
Add New Hardware, 10-11
Add New Printer, 10-11
check boxes, 37
command buttons, 37
drop-down list boxes, 37

File Sharing, 131-132
list boxes, 37
Mouse Properties, 19
option buttons, 37
options, selecting, 34-37
Print, 216-218
Printers and Faxes, 122
Save As, 152
Screen Saver, 96
Search Results, 119
sliders, 37
Sound, 97-99
spin boxes, 37
tabs, 36
text boxes, 37
digital camcorders, 348-349
    configuring, 349-350
    filming, 350-354
    FireWire connections, 348
digital cameras, 337-338
    autofocus, 339
    configuring, 339-340
    digital zoom, 338
    LCDs (Liquid Crystal
        Displays), 339
    megapixels, 338
    memory cards, 339
    optical viewfinders, 339
    optical zoom, 338
    photographs
        copying to PCs, 340-342
        taking, 339-340
    pixels, 338
    purchasing, 338
    resolution, 338
digital photographs, 338
    copying to PCs, 340-342
    e-mail messages, adding to,
        342-343
    managing, 47
    megapixels, 338
    pixels, 338
    prints, ordering online,
        343-344
    resolution, 338

sharing online, 344-345
taking, 339-340
web pages, adding to,
    342-343
digital videos, 347-349
    audio backgrounds, adding
        to, 355-356
    filming, 350-354
    saving, 357-359
    splicing, 354-355
    transitions, 357
    VHS tapes, copying to,
        359-360
digital zoom, digital cameras,
    338
directories (file), 71-72
discs
    CD-RW discs, 325
    recordable discs, 67
    rewritable discs, 67
discussion groups (online),
    278-279
Disk Cleanup utility, 374-376
Disk Defragmenter, 377-379
disk drives
    CD-ROM drives, 67
    CD-RW drives, 67
    cleaning, 370-371, 374-376
    DVD drives, 67
    floppy drives, 66
    hard disk drives, 67
    managing, 66-67
disks
    contents, 71-72
    exploring, 72
    floppy disks, 68
disk space, software, 80
displays. See monitors
distilled water, computers,
    cleaning, 366
documents, 236
    creating, Microsoft Word,
        144-145
    e-mail messages, attaching,
        251-252

editing, Microsoft Word,
    153-155
footers, adding, 214-215
headers, adding, 214-215
laying out, 186-187
margins, setting, 212-214
printing, 209, 215-217
    preprint checklists, 212
ready-made graphics,
    inserting, 187-190
saving, Microsoft Word,
    151-152
sharing, 115
Documents command (Start
menu), 120
double-clicking icons, 18,
33-34
downloading
    AIM, 260-261
    music, 329-331
    program files, 84
Draft view (Word), 144
dragging, mouse, 18
drawing illustrations, 192-195
drawings, scanning, 191-192
Dreamweaver, 285
drive bays, 70
drivers
    installing, 10-11
    mouse drivers, trouble-
        shooting, 389-390
    patches, 399
    updating, 395-396
    video drivers, 391
drives
    compact drives, 71
    disk drives
        CD-ROM drives, 67,
            323
        CD-RW drives, 67, 323
        DVD drives, 67
        floppy drives, 66
        hard disk drives, 67-70
        managing, 66-67

external hard drives, 70
flash drives, 66
Iomega Zip drives, 70
letters, 66
network drives, mapping, 133-134
tape drives, 71
USB flash drives, 70
drop-down list boxes, dialog boxes, 37
DSL connections, 227-228
dual-function keys, notebook PCs, 16
dumping
files and folders, 75-76
programs, 87-88
duplicating audio CDs, 332-333
dusting computers, 366-367
DVD-ROM drives, 67
cleaning, 370-371
software requirements, 81
DVDs (Digital Video Discs)
loading, 68-69
playing, 334
unloading, 68-69

E

e-mail
accounts, setting up, 246-247
addresses, 246
incoming messages, 246
receiving, 249-250
mailing lists, registrations, 279
messages
adding digital photographs, 342-343
adding graphics, 250-251
attaching files, 251-252
emoticons, 254-255
etiquette, 255-256
flames, 256
forwards, 256
inserting links, 251
replying, 250
shorthand, 254-255
spam, 256
outgoing messages, 246
addressing, 248
web based e-mail, 253
Easy Media Creator (Roxio), 332
eBay.com
purchasing Items, 301-304
selling Items, 304-305
editing
documents, 153-155
spreadsheets, 163
electronic pages (Word), 142-143
ellipses, commands, 35
emoticons, e-mail messages, 254-255
End key, 14
energy consumption, computers, estimating, 22
Energy Star seals, computers, 23
entering
dates, spreadsheets, 163-164
values, spreadsheets, 163-164
entries, spreadsheets, editing, 163
environmental hazards, computers, 23
environments, digital cameras, setting, 339
Epson website, 400
Esc (Escape) key, 15
Ethernet cards and hubs, installing, 127
Ethernet networks, 125

etiquette, e-mail messages, 255-256
Eudora e-mail client, 246
events, sounds, assigning, 99, 104
Excel spreadsheets, 159-171
building, 161-162
cell addresses, 160
cells, 160-161
columns, 160
labeling, 162-163
dates, entering, 163-164
designing, 162
entries, editing, 163
formatting, 167-168
formulas, calculating, 165-166
functions, 166
calculating, 165-166
ready-made functions, 166-167
graphs, 169
printing, 169-171
rows, labeling, 162-163
tabs, 160
values, entering, 163-164
Excite.com, 238
Expedia.com, 300
Explorer (Windows), 53, 60-61
disks, exploring, 72
exposures, digital cameras, setting, 340
external hard drives, 70
external modems, 226

F

F1 key, 14
Facebook.com, 292-293
FAQs (frequently asked questions), 401
File menu commands
Open, 118
Save, 120

files, 71-72
  backup files, deleting, 374-376
  contigous files, 73-74
  copying, 77
  damaged files, repairing, 376-377
  data files, 71-72
  defragmenting, 377-379
  deselecting, 73
  dumping, 75-76
  e-mail messages, attaching, 251-252
  finding, 45-46, 118-120
  formats, 191
  media files, 71-72
  moving, 77
  noncontiguous files, 73
  paths, 71
  program files, 71-72
    downloading, 84
  renaming, 76
  saving, 120
    Microsoft Word, 151-152
  selecting, 73-74
  sharing
    disabling, 130-131
    enabling, 130-131
    networked computers, 115-116
  system files, 71-72
  tagged items, 120-121
  temporary files, 374
    deleting, 374-376
File Sharing dialog box, 131-132
filming, digital camcorders, 350-354
FinallyFast.com, 381
finances
  online banking, 200-201
  personal finance programs
    automatic check-writing process, 202-203
    financial calculators, 206

online banking, 204
reconciling accounts, 203
recurring entries, 204-205
setting up, 201
tax return preparations, 206-207
tracking budgets, 205-206
financial calculators, 206
finding
  files and folders, 118-120
  printers, 121-122
firewalls
  configuring, 317-318
  implementing, 317-319
  turning on/off, 318-319
  Windows firewall, activating, 136
FireWire connections, digital camcorders, 348
fixed disks, 65
flames (e-mail messages), 256
flash drives, 66, 70
flashes, digital cameras, setting, 339
Flickr.com, 345
floppy disks, 68
floppy drives, 66
  cleaning, 370-371
folders, 71
  copying, 77
  creating, 74-75
  deselecting, 73
  directory trees, 71-72
  dumping, 75-76
  exploring, 72
  finding, 45-46, 118-120
  moving, 77
  My Documents folder, 71
  renaming, 76
  root directories, 71
  selecting, 73-74
  sharing, 115
fonts, 147

footers, adding, 214-215
formats, files, 191
formatting
  spreadsheets, 167-168
  text
    Microsoft Word, 147-148
    presentations, 179-180
formulas, spreadsheets, calculating, 165-166
forums (online), 278-279
forwards (e-mail messages), 256
free e-mail, 253
free hard disk spaces, software, 80
freezes, troubleshooting, 388-391
FrontPage, 285
Fujitsu website, 400
function keys, 14
functions, spreadsheets, 166
  calculating, 165-166
  ready-made functions, 166-167

G

gadgets, 48-49
games, preloaded games, 38
Gateway website, 400
GIF (Graphics Interchange Format) graphics, 191
Go.com, 238
Google.com, 238
Google Product Search, 297
grammar checking, Microsoft Word, 155-157
graphics, 185
  BMP (Bitmapped) graphics, 191
  drawings, scanning, 191-192
  e-mail messages, adding, 250-251

GIF (Graphics Interchange Format) graphics, 191
illustrations
  drawing and painting, 192-195
  scanning, 191-192
inserting, 191
JPEG (Joint Photographic Experts Group) graphics, 191
overlapped graphics, manipulating, 196-197
photographs, scanning, 191-192
presentations, adding, 180
ready-made graphics, inserting, 187-190
reshaping, 189-190
resizing, 189-190
test boxes, creating, 195-196
TIFF (Tagged Image File Format) graphics, 191
WMF (Windows Metafile) graphics, 191
graphics acceleration settings, adjusting, 390-391
graphics cards, software requirements, 81
graphs, spreadsheets, 169
grayed commands, 35
green PCs, 23-24
groups, selecting, 73
guest user accounts, 113-114

H

hackers, preventing, firewalls, 317-319
hard disk defragmenters, 38
hard disk drives, 67-70
hard disks, 65
  backup files, deleting, 374-376

software, free space, 80
temporary files, deleting, 374-376
hardware
  audio equipment, testing, 97-98
  modems, installing, 229-230
  network hardware, installing, 126-128
  requirements, Windows Vista, 44
  software updates, 395-396
Have Disk button, 11
headers, adding, 214-215
Help, 397
  context-sensitive help, 54
  diagnostic software, 402-403
  online support, 399-402
  telephone support, 398-399
  Windows Vista, 54
  Windows XP, 62
Help2Go.com, 402
Hewlett-Packard website, 400
Hibernate mode, 63
hiding taskbar, 94, 101
history lists, web browsers, 241
Hobo Traveler.com, 300
Home key, 14
home offices, preparing, 4-5
home pages, selecting, 242
Hostels.com, 300
hosting services, web pages, 285
HotDog, 285
hotspots, wireless Internet connectivity, 229
Hotwire.com, 300
HPNA (Home Phoneline Networking Alliance) networks, 126
HTML (Hypertext Markup Language), 284-285

I

IBM website, 400
ICF (Internet Connection Firewall), turning on/off, 318-319
icons, 32
  configuring, 33-34
  controlling, 103
  desktop, adding, 95
  rearranging, 93, 101
  selecting, 33-34
  user account icons, customizing, 111-112
IEEE-1394 connections, digital camcorders, 348
illustrations
  drawing, 192-195
  painting, 192-195
  scanning, 191-192
  text boxes, creating, 195-196
IM (instant messaging), 259
  AIM, 260
    buddy lists, 262-263
    downloading and installing, 260-261
    online chat, 265-266
    test messaging, 262
    videoconferencing, 264-265
    voice-messaging, 263-264
  Second Life, 269-270
  Yahoo! Messenger, 266-269
images, 185
  BMP (Bitmapped) images, 191
  drawings, scanning, 191-192
  e-mail messages, adding, 250-251
  GIF (Graphics Interchange Format) images, 191

illustrations
  drawing and painting, 192-195
  scanning, 191-192
inserting, 191
JPEG (Joint Photographic Experts Group) images, 191
overlapped images, manipulating, 196-197
photographs, scanning, 191-192
presentations, adding, 180
ready-made images, inserting, 187-190
resizing, 189-190
text boxes, creating, 195-196
TIFF (Tagged Image File Format) images, 191
WMF (Windows Metafile) images, 191
image sizes, digital cameras, setting, 339
incoming e-mail messages, 246
  receiving, 249-250
  replying, 250
Infospace.com, 239
ink
  conserving, 27
  recycling, 28
  wasting, 23
inserting
  graphics, 191
  ready-made graphics, 187-190
  slides, presentations, 177-178
insertion points, Microsoft Word, 142
installation
  AIM, 260-261
  antivirus software, 136
  drivers, 10-11

modems, 229-230
networking hardware, 126-128
network printers, 134-135
NICs (network interface cards), 127
program files, 84
software, 83-84
Intel website, 400
internal modems, 226
Internet, 224
  chat rooms, 259
  connections
    cable, 228
    choosing, 224-225
    dial-up connections, 226-227
    DSL, 227-228
    ISDN, 227
    satellite, 229
    testing, 232-233
    Wi-Fi, 229
  e-mail, 245-246
    account setup, 246-247
    adding graphics, 250-251
    address books, 249
    addressing outgoing messages, 248
    file attachments, 251-252
    mailing lists, 279
    receiving incoming messages, 249-250
    replying to messages, 250
  IMs (instant messengers), 259
    AIM, 260-265
    online chat, 265-270
  ISPs (Internet Service Providers), 230-232
  message boards, 278-279
  newsgroups, 272-278
    subscriptions, 274-275

online technical support, 399-402
RSS news feeds, 280
security, 307
  anti-virus software, 316-317
  firewalls, 317-319
  parental controls, 308-316
Internet Connection Wizard, 231
Internet Explorer, 236-237
  Content Advisor, 310-313
  history lists, 241
  home page, selecting, 242
  multiple pages, navigating, 239-240
  new features, 47-48
  security settings, configuring, 314-316
  web pages, bookmarking, 242
Intuit website, 400
Iomega website, 400
Iomega Zip drives, 70
ISDN connections, 227
ISPs (Internet Service Providers)
  choosing, 230-231
  connecting, 232
  mail servers, 246
iTunes, 329-330

J

Joekraynak.com, 290
joysticks, 20
  software requirements, 81
JPEG (Joint Photographic Experts Group) graphics, 191
junj e-mail messages, 256
justifying text, 148

K

KaZipster, 314
keyboarding, Microsoft Word, 143
keyboards, 14-15
  Alt (Alternate) key, 14
  cleaning, 368-369
  Ctrl (Control) key, 14
  cursor-movement keys, 14
  Esc (Escape) key, 15
  function keys, 14
  Logitech Wave keyboard, 14
  notebook dual-function keys, 16
  numeric keypad, 14
  Pause/Break key, 15
  Print Screen/SysRq key, 15
  programmable buttons, 15
  PrtSc key, 15
  Scroll Lock key, 15
  volume controls, 15
  Windows key shortcuts, 15-16
key commands, menus, opening, 35
Kill-A-Watt meters, cumulative kilowatt hours, measuring, 22
Kubrick, Stanley, 34

L

labeling
  spreadsheet columns, 162-163
  spreadsheet rows, 162-163
laptops. *See* notebook PCs
laser printers
  cleaning, 369-370
  conserving energy, 25
  toner, hazards, 370

laying out pages, 186-187, 212-214
LCDs (Liquid Crystal Displays), digital cameras, 339
left alignment, text, 148
letters
  drives, 66
  editing, Microsoft Word, 153-155
lines, drawing, 193-194
line spacing, Microsoft Word, 149-150
LinkedIn.com, 292-293
links, e-mail messages, inserting, 251
Linux, 32
list boxes, dialog boxes, 37
listing printers, 211
LiveJournal.com, 290
loading
  CDs (Compact Discs), 68-69
  DVDs (Digital Video Discs), 68-69
local printers, 211
lock-ups, troubleshooting, 388-391
log-on passwords
  choosing, 110
  user accounts, establishing, 109-111
logging on/off user accounts, 114-115
Logitech MX610 Laser cordless mouse, 17
Logitech Wave keyboard, 14
LPT1 (parallel printer) ports, 210
Lycos.com, 238

M

Mac OS, 32
mailing lists (e-mail), registrations, 279
mail servers, 246
mapping network drives, 133-134
margins, setting, 212-214
maximizing
  desktop space, 90-101
  windows, 39
Maxtor website, 400
McFedries, Paul, 62
media files, 71-72
Media Player (Windows), 38
media players, 325-326
  audio CDs, burning, 332-334
  DVDs, playing, 334
  music
    copying to portable players, 331-332
    downloading, 329-331
  playlists, 326-328
  skins, 329
megapixels
  digital cameras, setting, 339
  digital photographs, 338
memory, software requirements, 81
memory cards, digital cameras, 339
menus
  bypassing, toolbar buttons, 37-38
  commands
    arrows, 35
    check marks, 35
    ellipses, 35
    selecting, 34-36
  context menus, 35
  grayed commands, 35
  opening, key commands, 35

smart menus, 36
Start menu, Windows XP, 58-59
submenus, 35
message boards (online), 278-279
messages (newsgroups)
posting, 277-278
reading and posting, 272-277
subscriptions, 274-275
messages (e-mail)
digital photographs, adding, 342-343
emoticons, 254-255
etiquette, 255-256
files, attaching, 251-252
flames, 256
forwards, 256
graphics, adding, 250-251
incoming messages, 246
receiving, 249-250
inserting links, 251
messages, replying, 250
outgoing messages, 246
addressing, 248
shorthand, 254-255
spam, 256
Microsoft Excel. *See* Excel
Microsoft website, 400
Microsoft Money, setting up, 201
Microsoft Office, smart menus, 36
Microsoft Outlook. *See* Outlook
Microsoft Outlook Express, 246
Microsoft Word. *See* Word
minimizing windows, 39-40
minimum hardware requirements, Windows Vista, 44
minimum system requirements, software, 80-83
mix-and-match networks, 126

mix CDs, recording, 333-334
Mobility Center, 50
modems, 224
external modems, 226
installing, 229-230
internal modems, 226
standard modems, 226-227
modes
digital cameras, setting, 339
Safe mode, 391-392
Money (Microsoft), setting up, 201
Moneydance, setting up, 201
monitors
cleaning, 367-368
software requirements, 80
SVGA (Super Video Graphics Array) monitors, 80
MonsterMarketplace.com, 297
Motorola website, 400
mouse
autoscrolling, 18
basic movements, 16-18
cleaning, 369
clicking, 17-18
commands, entering, 16
customizing, 18-19
double-clicking, 18
dragging, 18
drivers, troubleshooting, 389-390
Logitech MX610 Laser cordless mouse, 17
optical mouse, 17
panning, 18
pointing, 17
right-clicking, 17
rubber balls, 17
scrolling, 18
software requirements, 81
troubleshooting, 393
Mouse Properties dialog box, 19
Movie Maker (Windows), 351-354

moving files and folders, 77
MP3 files, 324-325
copying to portable players, 331-332
downloading, 329-331
MP3 players, 324
multiple webpages, navigating, 239-240
music
downloading, 329-331
portable players, copying to, 331-332
MusicMatch, 330
MX610 Laser cordless mouse (Logitech), 17
My Computer, 60
My Documents folder, 71
mySimon.com, 297
MySpace.com, 292-293

N

Napster, 329
narration, slide shows, adding, 182
NEC website, 400
neighboring files, 73-74
network drives, mapping, 133-134
networked computers, user accounts, 107-109
account icons, 111-112
administrator accounts, 108
deleting, 112-113
file sharing, 115-116
guest user accounts, 113-114
log-on passwords, 109-111
logging on/off, 114-115
networking, Windows Vista, 52
networking hardware, installing, 126-128
Network Neighborhood, 133

network printers, 211
    installing, 134-135
networks, 126
    Bluetooth networks, 126
    broadband Internet con-
        nections, sharing, 135-136
    client-server networks,
        124-125
    clients, 124
    Ethernet networks, 125
    file sharing, disabling and
        enabling, 130-131
    hybrid networks, 126
    network drives, mapping,
        133-134
    networking hardware,
        installing, 126-128
    Network Neighborhood,
        133
    packet collisions, 125
    peer-to-peer networks,
        124-125
    phone-line networks, 126
    printers
        installing, 134-135
        sharing, 130-131
    resource sharing, 131-132
    security, 136-137
    servers, 124
    Wi-Fi (Wireless-Fidelity)
        networks, 125-126
    Windows Network Setup
        Wizard, running, 128-130
Network Setup Wizard,
    128-130
newsgroups
    messages
        posting, 277-278
        reading and posting,
            272-274
    posted messages, reading
        and responding, 276-277
    subscriptions, 274-275
newsreaders, 272-274
    RSS news feeds, 280

news servers, 272
NICs (network interface
    cards), installing, 127
non-neighboring files, 73-74
noncontiguous files, 73
notebook PCs
    dual-function keys, 16
    securing, 137-138
    touchpads, 19
Notepad, 39
numeric keypad, 14
NumLock key, 14
NVidia website, 400

0

Office (Microsoft), smart
    menus, 36
online banking, 200-201
    personal finance programs,
        204
online chat
    AIM, 265-266
    Second Life, 269-270
    Yahoo! Messenger, 266-269
online communities, Yahoo!
    Groups, 268-269
online message boards,
    278-279
online selling, 301-306
    eBay, 304-305
online services, choosing,
    230-231
online shopping, 296-306
    comparison shopping,
        297-298
    eBay, 301-304
    purchases, 298-299
    security, 296-297
    travel reservations, book-
        ing, 300
online social networks,
    292-293
online technical support,
    399-402

Open command (File menu),
    118
opening menus, key com-
    mands, 35
operating systems
    See also Windows Vista and
        Windows XP
    Linux, 32
    Mac OS, 32
    software requirements, 80
optical mouse, 17
optical viewfinders, digital
    cameras, 339
optical zoom, digital cameras,
    338
option buttons (dialog boxes),
    37
options
    See also commands
    dialog boxes, selecting,
        34-37
Orbitz.com, 300
outgoing e-mail messages, 246
    adding graphics, 250-251
    addressing, 248
    files, attaching, 251-252
Outline view (Word), 144
Outlook (Microsoft), 245-246
    accounts, setting up,
        246-247
    address book, 249
    incoming messages, receiv-
        ing, 249-250
    messages
        adding graphics,
            250-251
        attaching files, 251-252
        replying, 250
    outgoing messages,
        addressing, 248
Outlook Express, 246
outputting presentations,
    182-183
overlapped graphics, manipu-
    lating, 196-197

P

Packard Bell website, 400
packet collisions, 125
Page Down key, 14
Page Layout view (Word), 144
pages
    footers, adding, 214-215
    headers, adding, 214-215
    laying out, 186-187,
        212-214
Page Up key, 14
page views, Microsoft Word,
    144
Paint, 39, 194-195
painting illustrations, 192-195
Panasonic website, 400
panning, mouse, 18
paper
    conserving, 27
    recycling, 28
    reusing, 27
    wasting, 23
paper towels, computers,
    cleaning, 366
paragraph spacing, Microsoft
    Word, 150-151
parallel printers, 210
parental controls
    Internet, 308-316
    Windows Vista, 50
partitioning hard disk drives,
    67
passwords
    choosing, 110
    log-on passwords, estab-
        lishing, 109-111
    protecting, 308
    user accounts, 9
pasting
    clip art, 188
    text, 154-155
patches (software), 399
paths, files, 71
Pause/Break key, 15

PayPal, 297
PC Doctor, 402-403
PC Pitstop, 380, 403
peer-to-peer networks,
    124-125
people, locating online, 239
peripherals, 19
    AccuPoint pointers, 19
    audio equipment, testing,
        97-98
    connecting, 7-8
    disk drives, cleaning,
        370-371
    environmental hazards, 23
    identifying, 6-7
    joysticks, 20
    keyboards, 14-15
        cleaning, 368-369
        Logitech Wave key-
            board, 14
        notebook dual-function
            keys, 16
        Windows key shortcuts,
            15-16
    modems, 224
        installing, 229-230
    monitors, cleaning,
        367-368
    mouse
        basic movements, 16-18
        cleaning, 369
        customizing, 18-19
        Logitech MX610 Laser
            cordless mouse, 17
        troubleshooting, 393
    printers
        cleaning, 369-370
        configuring, 210-212
        troubleshooting,
            218-219, 394-395
    speakers, troubleshooting,
        393-394
    touchpads, 19
    trackballs, 19
    unpacking, 5-6

personal finance programs
    accounts reconciling, 203
    budgets, tracking, 205-206
    check-writing process,
        automating, 202-203
    financial calculators, 206
    online banking, 204
    recurring entries, 204-205
    setting up, 201
    tax returns, preparing,
        206-207
personalizing
    Windows Vista, 90-100
    Windows XP, 100-104
phone-line networks, 126
Photobucket.com, 345
photographs (digital), 338
    copying to PCs, 340-342
    e-mail messages, adding,
        342-343
    managing, 47
    prints, ordering online,
        343-344
    scanning, 191-192
    sharing online, 344-345
    taking, 339-340
    web pages, adding, 342-343
Photosmart (Hewlett
    Packard), 343
Picasa.com, 345
pixels, 195
    digital photographs, 338
placeMobility placeCenter, 51
PlaceNameMedia
    PlaceTypeCenter
    (Windows), 46-47
PlaceNameMobility
    PlaceTypeCenter, 51
PlaceNameWindows
    PlaceNameMedia PlaceType
    CenterPlaceName, 46-47
placeNormal view (Word),
    144
placeVista (Windows). *See*
    Windows Vista

playing DVDs, 334

playlists, media players, 326-328

pointers
mouse, troubleshooting, 393
tablet PCs, 19

pointing devices, 19-20

pointing mouse, 17

point size, text, 147

POP (Post Office Protocol) servers, 246

ports
printer ports, 210
serial ports, 210, 226
USB (Universal Serial Bus) ports, 210

posted newsgroup messages, reading and responding, 276-277

posting newsgroups messages, 272-278

power-saving features, Windows, 25-26

power plans (Windows Vista), 25-26

PowerPoint, 173-183
outputting, 182-183
ribbon, 174
selected lists, 174
slide list, 174
Slide Master, customizing, 177
slides
adding text, 178-179
creating, 177
inserting, 177-178
rearranging, 181
slide shows
narrating, 182
previewing, 182
special effects, 181-182
status bar, 174
text, formatting, 179-180
title bar, 174
workspaces, 174-175

predefined templates, Word, 145

preloaded programs, 38-39

preprint checklists, 212

presentations, 173-183
creating, 175-177
graphics, adding, 180
outputting, 182-183
ready-made graphics, inserting, 187-190
Slide Master, customizing, 177
slides
adding text, 178-179
creating, 177
inserting, 177-178
rearranging, 181
slide shows
narrating, 182
previewing, 182
special effects, 181-182
text, formatting, 179-180
themes, selecting, 176-177

previewing slide shows, 182

PriceGrabber.com, 297

Priceline.com, 300

Print dialog box, 216-218

printer ports, 210

printers
background printing, managing, 217-218
cleaning, 369-370
configuring, 210-212
conserving energy, 25
documents, sending, 215-217
finding, 121-122
ink, conserving and recycling, 27-28
listing, 211
local printers, 211
margins, setting, 212-214
network printers, installing, 134-135
paper, conserving and recycling, 27-28

parallel printers, 210
preprint checklists, 212
queues, 217
sharing, 130-131
Windows Vista, 52
toner, hazards, 370
troubleshooting, 218-219, 394-395
wireless printers, 210-211

Printers and Faxes dialog box, 122

printing
documents, 209
spreadsheets, 169-171

prints, digital photographs, ordering online, 343-344

Print Screen/SysRq key, 15

Print view (Word), 144

privacy, screen savers, 95-97

program files, 71-72
deleting, 75
downloading, 84

programmable buttons, 15

programs, 79
AIM, 260-265
anti-virus programs, 316-317
antivirus programs, installing, 136
background programs, troubleshooting, 386-387
backup files, deleting, 374-376
censoring programs, 313-314
deleting, 75, 87-88
diagnostic programs, 402-403
Dreamweaver, 285
drivers, updating, 395-396
e-mail clients, 245-252
Excel, 159-171
finding, 45-46
firewalls, 317-319
freezes, troubleshooting, 389

FrontPage, 285
HotDog, 285
installing, 83-84
media players, 325-329
Microsoft Word, 141-157
minimum system require-
ments, 80-83
newsreaders, 272-274
Paint, 194-195
patches, 399
personal finance programs,
201-207
PowerPoint, 173-183
preloaded programs, 38-39
program shortcuts, creat-
ing, 85-86
running, 84-87
Second Life, 269-270
selecting, Start menu,
84-85
temporary files, deleting,
374-376
toggling, Windows XP,
59-60
troubleshooting, 392
web browsers, 236-242
Web Studio, 285
Yahoo! Messenger, 266-269
Programs command (Start
menu), 38
program shortcuts, creating,
85-86
Protonic.com, 401
PrtSc key, 15
publishing web pages, 283-293
purchasing, online shopping,
298-304

Q-R

queues, print queues, 217
Quicken, setting up, 201

radio buttons (dialog boxes),
37

RAM (random access mem-
ory), 81
reading posted newsgroup
messages, 272-277
ready-made functions,
166-167
ready-made graphics, inserting, 187-190
RealAudio, 325
rearranging
icons, 93, 101
slides, presentations, 181
Start menu commands,
94-95, 102
receiving incoming e-mail
messages, 249-250
recordable discs, 67
recording mix CDs, 333-334
recurring entries, personal
finance programs, setting up,
204-205
Recycle Bin, 33
files, dumping, 75-76
folders, dumping, 75-76
recycling ink and paper, 28
Red Book format, CDs, 324
removable disks, 65
removing
programs, 75, 87-88
user accounts, 112-114
renaming files and folders, 76
repairing damaged files,
376-377
replying, e-mail messages, 250
requirements
software, 80-83
Windows Vista, 44
reservations, travel reservations, booking online, 300
resizing windows, 39-40
resolution, digital cameras,
setting, 338-339
resources, sharing, networks,
131-132
responses, posted newsgroup
messages, 276-277

restoring windows, 39
reusing paper, 27
rewritable discs, 67
Rhapsody, 330
ribbons
PowerPoint, 174
Word, 142
right-clicking mouse, 17
right alignment, text, 148
root directories, 71
routers
firewalls, 317-319
wireless routers, limiting
access, 136-137
rows, spreadsheets, labeling,
162-163
Roxio Easy Media Creator,
332
RSS news feeds, 280
rubber balls, mouse, 17
running programs, 84-87
single-click, 86-87
startup, 86

S

S-video jacks, 349
Safe mode, 391-392
Sam Goodys, 329
satellite connections, 229
Save As dialog box, 152
Save command (File menu),
120
saving
desktop themes, 99-100
documents, Microsoft
Word, 151-152
files, 120
video clips, 357-359
scalability, Windows Vista, 52
ScanDisk, damaged files,
repairing, 376-377
scanning illustrations and
photographs, 191-192

Screen Saver dialog box, 96
screen savers, 26
  animated screen savers,
    activating, 103-104
  privacy, securing, 95-97
screwdrivers, computers,
  disassembling, 366
scrollbars, 40-41
scrolling, mouse, 18
Scroll Lock key, 15
Seagate website, 400
search engines, 238-239
Search Results dialog box, 119
Search utility, 119-120
Second Life, online chat,
  269-270
security
  anti-virus software, 316-317
  firewalls, 317-319
  Internet, 307
  Internet parental controls,
    308-316
  networks, 136-137
  notebook PCs, 137-138
  online shopping, 296-297
  Windows Vista, 47
selected lists, PowerPoint, 174
selecting
  files, 73-74
  folders, 73-74
  groups, 73
  text, 153-154
selling online, 301-306
serial ports, 210, 226
servers
  mail servers, 246
  networks, 124
  news servers, 272
  POP (Post Office Protocol)
    servers, 246
  SMTP (Simple Mail
    Transfer Protocol) serv-
    ers, 246
setting
  margins, 212-214
  tabs, 149

Seurat, Georges, 194
shapes, drawing, 193-194
shared computers, user
  accounts, 107-108
  account icons, 111-112
  adding, 108-109
  administrator accounts, 108
  deleting, 112-113
  file sharing, 115-116
  guest user accounts,
    113-114
  log-on passwords, 109-111
  logging on/off, 114-115
shared printers, Windows
  Vista, 52
sharing
  broadband Internet con-
    nections, 135-136
  digital photographs,
    344-345
  files, networked computers,
    115-116, 130-131
  printers, networks, 52,
    130-131
  resources, networks,
    131-132
shopping online, 296-306
  comparison shopping,
    297-298
  purchases, 298-304
  security, 296-297
  travel reservations, book-
    ing, 300
Shopzilla.com, 297-298
shortcuts (programs), creating,
  85-86
shortcuts (keyboard), 15-16
  menus, opening, 35
shorthand, e-mail messages,
  254-255
Show Desktop button, 40
Shut Down command, 25
Shutterfly.com, 343
shutting down
  computers, 25

Windows Vista, 55
  Windows XP, 62-63
sidebar, 48-49
SideShow (Windows), 50
signal strength, Wi-Fi
  (Wireless-Fidelity) networks,
  126
Simple Computing magazine,
  401
single-clicking icons, 33-34,
  86-87
sizing windows, 39
skins, media players, 329
slide lists, PowerPoint, 174
Slide Master (PowerPoint),
  customizing, 177
sliders, dialog boxes, 37
slides
  creating, 177
  presentations
    inserting, 177-178
    rearranging, 181
  text, adding, 178-179
slide shows
  narrating, 182
  previewing, 182
  special effects, 181-182
smart menus, 36
SMTP (Simple Mail Transfer
  Protocol) servers, 246
Snapfish.com, 343
soft brushes, computers,
  cleaning, 366
software
  anti-virus software, 316-317
  antivirus software, install-
    ing, 136
  applications, 80
  background programs,
    troubleshooting, 386-387
  backup files, deleting,
    374-376
  censoring software,
    313-314
  deleting, 87-88

diagnostic software, 402-403
Dreamweaver, 285
drivers
    installing, 10-11
    updating, 395-396
e-mail clients, 245-252
Excel, 159-171
firewalls, 317-319
freezes, troubleshooting, 389
FrontPage, 285
HotDog, 285
installing, 83-84
media players, 325-332
Microsoft Word, 141-157
minimum system requirements, 80-83
Paint, 194-195
patches, 399
personal finance software, 202-206
PowerPoint, 173-183
running, 84-87
shortcuts, creating, 85-86
system software, 80
temporary files, deleting, 374-376
troubleshooting, 392
voice activation software, 20
web browsers, 236-242
Web Studio, 285
Solitaire, 38
Sony website, 400
sound cards, software requirements, 81
Sound dialog box, 97-99
sounds, events, assigning, 99, 104
space, desktop, maximizing, 90-91, 100-101
spam (e-mail messages), 256
speakers, troubleshooting, 393-394

special effects, slide shows, 181-182
speech-recognition computing, Windows Vista, 49
spell checking, Microsoft Word, 155-157
spin boxes, dialog boxes, 37
splicing video clips, 354-355
spreadsheets, 159-171
    building, 161-162
    cell addresses, 160
    cells, 160-161
    columns, 160
        labeling, 162-163
    dates, entering, 163-164
    designing, 162
    entries, editing, 163
    formatting, 167-168
    formulas, calculating, 165-166
    functions, 166-167
    graphs, 169
    printing, 169-171
    rows, labeling, 162-163
    tabs, 160
    values, entering, 163-164
squares, drawing, 193-194
standard modems, 226-227
Stand By mode, 63
Start button, 11, 18
Start command, 25
starting computers, 9-10
Start menu
    commands
        All Programs, 38
        Documents, 120
        Programs, 38
        rearranging, 94-95, 102
    programs, selecting, 84-85
    Windows XP, 58-59
startup
    diagnostic start ups, 379-380
    programs, running, 86
    troubleshooting, 387-388

user accounts, logging on, 114
statements, checking accounts, reconciling, 203
status bar (PowerPoint), 174
submenus, 35
subscriptions, newsgroups, 274-275
Support Center (Dell), 402-403
surge suppressors, benefits, 5
SVGA (Super Video Graphics Array) monitors, 80
Swordfish Trombones, 333
System Configuration
    background programs, troubleshooting, 386-387
    diagnostic start-ups, performing, 379-380
system files, 71-72
System Information utility, 82
system requirements, Windows Vista, 44
System Restore, 385-386
system software, 80
System Tools, 38
system tray, 33

T

tablet PCs
    pointers, 19
    securing, 137-138
    Windows Vista, 51-52
tabs
    dialog boxes, 36
    setting, 149
    spreadsheets, 160
    web pages, navigating, 239-240
tagged items, Windows Vista, 120-121
tags, web pages, 284
tape drives, 71

taskbar, 32-33
  hiding, 94, 101
tax returns, preparing,
  206-207
technical support, 397
  diagnostic software,
    402-403
  online support, 399-402
  telephone support, 398-399
TechRepublic.com, 401
Tech Support Forum, 401
telephone technical support,
  398-399
templates, Microsoft Word,
  145
temporary files, 374
  deleting, 374-376
testing
  audio equipment, 97-98
  Internet connections,
    232-233
Texas Instruments website,
  400
text
  aligning, 148-149
  cutting, 154-155
  fonts, 147
  formatting, 147-148
  grammar checking,
    155-157
  line spacing, 149-150
  paragraph spacing, 150-151
  pasting, 154-155
  point size, 147
  presentations, formatting,
    179-180
  selecting, 153-154
  slides, adding, 178-179
  spell checking, 155-157
  text boxes, creating,
    195-196
  text wrapping, 189
text boxes
  creating, 195-196
  dialog boxes, 37

text messaging (AIM), 262
text wrapping, 189
themes
  desktop, saving, 99-100
  presentations, selecting,
    176-177
Thunderbird e-mail client,
  246
TIFF (Tagged Image File
  Format) graphics, 191
time and date, adjusting,
  104-105
title bar (PowerPoint), 174
today's date, inserting,
  Microsoft Word, 146
toggling
  programs, Windows XP,
    59-60
  windows, 39-40
toner, hazards, 370
toolbars, 37-38
tools, computers, cleaning,
  366
toothpicks, computers, cleaning, 366
Top Issues links, 401
Toshiba website, 400
touchpads, 19
trackballs, 19
tracking budgets, personal
  finance programs, 205-206
transitions, video clips, adding, 357
Travelocity.com, 300
travel reservations, booking
  online, 300
Trend Micro Antivirus software, 136
troubleshooting
  background programs,
    386-387
  freezes, 388-391
  mouse, 393
  printers, 218-219, 394-395
  programs, 392

speakers, 393-394
start ups, 387-388
strategies, 384-385
System Restore, 385-386
TuffTest Pro, 402
TurboTax, 206-207
turning off computers, 25
Turn Off Computer com-
  mand, 25
Typepad.com, 290

U

undoing changes, 155
uninstalling
  programs, 75
  software, 87-88
uninterruptible power supplies
  (UPSs), benefits, 5
unloading CDs (Compact
  Discs) and DVDs (Digital
  Video Discs), 68-69
unpacking computers, 5-6
updating
  drivers, 395-396
  software patches, 399
  video drivers, 391
UPSs (uninterruptible power
  supplies), benefits, 5
URLs (uniform resource locators), 237-238
USB (Universal Serial Bus)
  ports, 210
USB connections, 226
USB flash drives, 70
user account icons, customizing, 111-112
user accounts, 10, 107-108
  account icons, customizing,
    111-112
  adding, 108-109
  administrator accounts, 108
  deleting, 112-113
  file sharing, 115-116

guest user accounts, 113-114
log-on passwords, establishing, 109-111
logging on/off, 114-115
passwords, 9
utilities
Add/Remove Programs, 87-88
Disk Cleanup, 374-376
Disk Defragmenter, 377-379
PC Doctor, 402-403
ScanDisk, 376-377
Search, 119-120
System Configuration, 379-387
System Restore, 385-386

V

vacuums (computers), 366-367
values, spreadsheets, entering, 163-164
VCRs, PCs, connections, 349
versions, Windows, determining, 33
VHS tapes, video clips, copying to, 359-360
videoconferencing, AIM, 264-265
video drivers, updating, 391
videos (digital), 347-349
audio backgrounds, adding, 355-356
filming, 350-354
saving, 357-359
splicing, 354-355
transitions, 357
VHS tapes, copying to, 359-360
views, Microsoft Word, 144
viruses
anti-virus software, 316-317
hoaxes, 256

visual effects, desktops, controlling, 103
voice-activated computing, Windows Vista, 35
voice-messaging, AIM, 263-264
voice activation software, 20
VoIP (Voice over Internet Protocol), 128
volume, adjusting, 98
volume controls (keyboard), 15

W

Waits, Tom, 333
Wal-Mart.com, 343
wallpaper, desktop, hanging, 102
Wave keyboard (Logitech), 14
web based e-mail, 253
web browsers, 236-237
bookmarking, 242
censoring software, 313-314
history lists, 241
home page, selecting, 242
multiple pages, navigating, 239-240
security settings, configuring, 314-316
Web Layout view (Word), 144
web pages
blogs, 288-292
digital photographs, adding, 342-343
HTML (Hypertext Markup Language), 284-285
links, 251
publishing, 283-293
tags, 284
Web Studio, 285
Welcome Center (Windows Vista), 33

Western Digital website, 400
Whitepages.com, 239
Wi-Fi (Wireless Fidelity) networks, 125
connections, 229
notebook PCs, securing, 137-138
signal strength, 126
wildcard characters, 120
Windows, 31-32
See also Windows Vista and Windows XP
desktop, 32-34
power-saving features, 25-26
printers, configuring, 210-212
user accounts, logging off, 115
versions, determining, 33
Windows Vista, 32
Windows XP, 32
windows
closing, 39
maximizing, 39
minimizing, 39-40
restoring, 39
scrollbars, 40-41
toggling, 39-40
Windows Clipboard, 15
Windows Explorer, 53, 60-61
disks, exploring, 72
Windows firewall, activating, 136
Windows ICF (Internet Connection Firewall), turning on/off, 318-319
Windows key shortcuts, 15-16
Windows Media Player, 38, 325-326
audio CDs, burning, 332-334
DVDs, playing, 334

music
    copying to portable
        players, 331-332
    downloading, 329-331
    playlists, 326-328
    skins, 329
Windows Movie Maker,
    351-354
Windows Network Setup
    Wizard, 128-130
Windows placeVista
    customizing, 90-99
    new features, 45-47, 50-51
    power plans, 26
    tagged items, 121
    Windows Explorer, 53
Windows Search utility,
    119-120
Windows SideShow, 50
Windows Vista, 32, 43
    backup utility, 49
    customizing, 90-100
    date and time, adjusting,
        104-105
    desktop, 44-45
        customizing, 90-97
    determining, 33
    device synchronization, 52
    digital photographs, man-
        aging, 47
    files, finding, 45-46
    folders, finding, 45-46
    gadgets, 48-49
    Help, 54
    icons, selecting, 33-34
    Internet Explorer, 47-48
    minimum hardware
        requirements, 44
    Mobility Center, 50
    networking, 52
    new features, 44-52
    parental controls, 50
    power plans, 25
    programs, finding, 45-46

scalability, 52
security features, 47
shutting down, 55
sidebar, 48-49
speech-recognition capa-
    bilities, 49
tablet PC support, 51-52
tagged items, 120
voice-activated computing,
    35
Welcome Center, 33
Windows Explorer, 53
Windows SideShow, 50
Windows XP, 32, 57
    Control Panel, 61
    customizing, 100-104
    date and time, adjusting,
        104-105
    desktop, 58
    determining, 33
    Help, 62
    icons, selecting, 33-34
    My Computer, 60
    programs, toggling, 59-60
    shutting down, 62-63
    Start menu, 58-59
    Windows Explorer, 60-61
wireless connections, 8
wireless printers, 210
wireless routers
    access, limiting, 136-137
    purchasing, 128
wizards
    Add New Hardware
        Wizard, 10-11
    Add Printer Wizard, 10-11,
        211
    Internet Connection
        Wizard, 231
    Windows Network Setup
        Wizard, 128
        running, 128-130
WMF (Windows Metafile)
    graphics, 191

Word (Microsoft), 141-142
    automatic corrections,
        145-146
    documents
        creating, 144-145
        editing, 153-155
        saving, 151-152
    electronic page, 142-143
    grammar checking,
        155-157
    insertion point, 142
    keyboarding, 143
    line spacing, changing,
        149-150
    pages, laying out, 186-187
    page views, 144
    paragraphs, spacing,
        150-151
    ribbon, 142
    spell checking, 155-157
    templates, 145
    text, formatting, 147-149
    today's date, inserting, 146
WordPad, 39, 143
WordPress.com, 290
    blogs, creating, 289-291
    Dashboard, 291-292
worksheets
    building, 161-162
    cell addresses, 160
    cells, 160-161
    columns, 160
        labeling, 162-163
    dates, entering, 163-164
    designing, 162
    entries, editing, 163
    formatting, 167-168
    formulas, calculating,
        165-166
    functions, 166
        calculating, 165-166
        ready-made functions,
            166-167
    graphs, 169
    printing, 169-171

rows, labeling, 162-163
tabs, 160
values, entering, 163-164
workspaces, preparing, 4-5
World Wide Web, 295
bookmarking, 242
browsing, web browsers, 236-240
history lists, 241
home page, selecting, 242
HTML (Hypertext Markup Language), 284-285
locating people, 239
message boards, 278-279
online selling, 301-306
online shopping, 296-306
booking travel reservations, 300
comparison shopping, 297-298
eBay, 301-304
purchases, 298-299
security, 296-297
search engines, 238-239
security, 307
anti-virus software, 316-317
firewalls, 317-319
parental controls, 308-316
social networks, 292-293
URLs (uniform resource locators), 237-238
web pages, publishing, 283-293
wrapping text, 189
wrenches, computers, disassembling, 366

X-Y-Z

XP (Windows). *See* Windows XP, 32

Yahoo! Chat, 266-268
Yahoo! GeoCities, 285
web pages
deleting, 288
publishing, 285-288
Yahoo! Groups, 268-269
Yahoo! Messenger, 266-269
Yahoo! Travel, 300
Yahoo.com, 238-239

Zip drives (Iomega), 70
zooming, mouse, 18